The
Public Vocation
of Christian Ethics

The
Public Vocation
of Christian Ethics

Edited by
**Beverly W. Harrison
Robert L. Stivers
Ronald H. Stone**

**The Pilgrim Press
New York**

Unless otherwise noted, biblical quotations are from the *Revised Standard Version
of the Bible,* copyright 1946, 1952, and © 1971, 1973 by the Division of Christian
Education, National Council of Churches, and are used by permission. The biblical
quotation marked TEV is from the *Good News Bible,* Today's English Version,
©American Bible Society, 1966, 1971, 1976. The biblical quotation marked KJV is
from the *King James Version.* The biblical quotation marked JB is from *The
Jerusalem Bible,* copyright © 1966 by Darton, Longman & Todd Ltd. and
Doubleday and Company, Inc.

Library of Congress Cataloging-in-Publication Data

The Public vocation of Christian ethics.

  Bibliography: p. 311.
  1. Christian ethics. 2. Social ethics. 3. Shinn, Roger Lincoln. I. Harrison, Beverly
Wildung, 1932-   . II. Stivers, Robert L., 1940-   . III. Stone, Ronald H.
BJ1251.P8 1986   241   86-16951
ISBN 0-8298-0582-6 (pbk.)

The Pilgrim Press, 132 West 31 Street, New York, New York 10001

Contents

Introduction

The essays included here exemplify a variety of Christian ethical work on specific topics and issues that are of special public concern today. In the discourse of Christian ethics, a "public" issue is one that is of interest not only to Christians, but to all morally concerned people in the societies of which Christian communities are a part.[1] These essays, then, are Christian social ethics in the most formal sense of the term.[2]

The book has been written in the expectation that it may be of use as a teaching resource for introducing students to several ways in which Christians engage social issues and moral dilemmas. Most of the essays aim clearly to identify an ethical issue that Christians, along with others, face in the late twentieth century, and do so in a way that isolates specific normative Christian theological-ethical themes relevant to its discussion. Most also seek to clarify some ways in which Christians should affect public policy relating to these dilemmas. The authors were asked to pay attention to some of the methodological questions that anyone doing Christian ethics must consider: What are the appropriate Christian ethical norms relevant to this topic? What are the sources for these norms? How are appeals to "facts" and appeals to moral principles and values related? How are scientific, political, and moral judgments related? Despite relative agreement about methodological starting points, theological, analytic, and ideological differences are apparent, and the essays are diverse enough to enable comparison and contrast of approaches to Christian social ethics. A teacher can use the essays to illustrate some of the more obvious technical considerations that those studying Christian social ethics need to learn and, at the same time, use them to encourage further reflection on the issues themselves.

The essays were gathered and are published in appreciation of the work of one particularly distinguished practitioner of Christian social ethics, Roger Lincoln Shinn. In 1985 he formally retired from Union Theological Seminary in New York, where he had been a professor of Christian ethics since 1959 and Reinhold Niebuhr Professor of Christian Social Ethics since 1970.[3] Many of us who know Roger Shinn anticipate that his formal retirement will enable him to complete several important, long-term projects, including his long-projected work on the role of perception and belief in ethics. Most "festschrifts," or collections of essays honoring distinguished scholars, focus directly on the work of the one whose contribution is the occasion of its publication.[4] The decision to use this occasion to ask his colleagues and former students to engage the work of normative Christian ethics testifies to the sort of scholar Roger Shinn is. He has made his mark by being a *working* ethicist, one who engages concrete issues in a theoretically rich way on behalf of Christian theological-ethical community and tradition, of which he is both a thorough student and a lively interpreter. He does his work in service of the churches' ongoing responsibility for participation in public policy questions. He has done much to shape that participation, especially in the United Church of Christ, and much of his writing is addressed to and from his own community of faith. Because this is so, we have judged that it is altogether consistent with the spirit of the man we honor to focus discussion here on the substance of the discipline he loves. For him, no problem or issue can be addressed without simultaneous attention to its implications, both for the life of Christian communities *and* for wider society. The ethicist must clarify the significance of an issue both within the faith community *and* in the broader society. With this conviction of his in view, the contributors were asked to exemplify this dual focus explicitly by attention to both church strategy and wider public policy.

All the contributors are colleagues of Roger Shinn in one or another professional capacity, and most of us have been his students. Although only the concluding essay and Richard Knox's excellent research bibliography of his extensive writings celebrate his work directly, Roger Shinn's influence here is not only one of personal inspiration, but also one of substance. His work has shaped the planning and execution of this collection of essays in several basic ways.

The editorial decision to make the book a reader for *teaching* ethics was itself inspired by awareness of Roger Shinn's enthusiastic commitment to the vocation of teaching Christian social ethics. Probably no professor of Christian ethics in this or any other nation has surpassed him in the degree of devoted energy poured out in teaching the art he loves. The development of the academic specializations within theological studies that created the somewhat discrete disciplines of theological and social ethics came to fruition dramatically in the years of Roger Shinn's mature career. He has devoted himself unstintingly to teaching students of professional ministry as well as researchers and teachers in Christian ethics. He has been "doctor-father" to nearly half the students who have completed Th.D.s and Ph.D.s at Union Theological Seminary since 1959, and to a sizable proportion of those completing Ph.D. degrees in the Department of Religion at Columbia University, where he has been an adjunct professor since 1962. As any who know him are aware, long hours spent in classroom preparation, in guidance of students, and in meticulous reading of doctoral theses often have slowed his own research and writing projects. Yet the public voice of mainstream Christianity would be much the poorer in this nation and world without his devotion to this work.

Roger Shinn would never acquiesce to viewing his efforts as teacher as a "sacrifice" for the good of others. He approaches teaching as an indispensable source of the intellectual stimulation and challenge a professional Christian ethicist must have to sustain work of genuine distinction. The ideological diversity of these essays attests to another of Roger Shinn's pedagogical graces. Few can better his record in supporting ideological and policy differences between himself and his students or among them.

The methodological convergence of these essays also is shaped by Roger Shinn's impact. He is a proponent of the sort of Christian ethical approach that takes as starting point actual engagement with an ethical issue itself. In his work, Christian theological-ethical tradition and broader social-historical resources for approaching moral issues are conjoined in dialogue with the concrete problem in its present historical setting. Such a methodological focus is sometimes characterized as a "pragmatic" or "contextual" approach to Christian social ethics and is contrasted with methods that arrive at, or ascertain, the appropriate stance of Christians to such issues apart from contemporary involvement. The contributors share Professor Shinn's conviction that an issue-oriented point of departure is the appropriate one precisely because we are historical beings whose theological and moral traditions are also shaped historically by wrestling with questions distinctive to a particular historical context. Like him, many of them also stress the importance of mastering not only the historical, but also the technical aspects of the problems and issues they address. Such competence is critical to responsible engagement with the issues. Roger Shinn repeatedly reminds us that we as Christians and our churches face many dilemmas for which there are few precedents, and failure to master the newer technical aspects of problems renders our moral concern irrelevant.[5]

A further substantive hallmark of Roger Shinn's work shaped the editors' aspirations for this collection. Roger is one of a generation of professional Christian theologians whose career spanned two differing Christian world views: the older Europocentric one and a newer global perspective. The massive shifts that rendered Europocentric and North

American consciousness provincial became apparent early in Roger's career, and he has done far more than most of his contemporaries to respond to this shift and correct the cultural chauvinism of dominant Christianity and broader Western cultural perspectives. Perhaps no North American Christian ethicist of this generation has traveled so widely and engaged so many concrete problems in so richly diverse a cultural context as he has done. Representing his denomination frequently in the work of the World Council of Churches and pursuing global connections at every opportunity have enabled him to do ethical reflection with sustained awareness that non-Western and culturally marginal perceptions and sensibilities must gain a central place in the vocation of Christian ethics today. Furthermore, he has honored the requirements of serious Christian ecumenicity in ways few of his peers have done. Dialogue, for him, has meant engagement not only among the several Christian communions, but between faith communities as well.

We as editors had hoped to do full justice to the dimensions of Roger Shinn's sensibility by including essays written by colleagues and students from other areas of the world and from culturally diverse groups here, and by reflecting his ecumenical concern for the wider interfaith dialogue. Regrettably, we have fallen short on both counts. Editorial time limits, together with the fallibility of communication with scholars in other areas of the world—particularly the heavy engagement of many of his friends and colleagues in their own distinctive social struggles—limited the international contribution and the ecumenical dialogue more than we, or Roger Shinn, would wish. Numerous friends wished to add their voices to these pages but could not because of the press of other commitments. All the contributors are Protestants except two, who are Roman Catholics. In this respect, *The Public Vocation of Christian Ethics* falls short of the ecumenical engagement reflected in Professor Shinn's own work.

Roger Shinn's influence should be apparent in the topics we have chosen. All of them fall broadly within the purview of concerns that he has addressed. The collection begins with a challenge to the discipline of Christian ethics formulated by his longtime colleague John Coleman Bennett, former president and professor of Christian ethics emeritus at Union Seminary. John Bennett's sensibilities regarding the discipline of Christian social ethics resonate with Roger Shinn's and bespeak his own concern for the vocation of Christian ethics. The specific essays on social issues that make up the main portion of the book, taken as a whole, suggest the range of concerns that Christian ethics must engage today. They are grouped to enable their use thematically. Questions of war and peace, population and natural resources, and several dimensions of concern for economic justice at both the global and the domestic level are paired. Concern for racism and urbanization as well as issues raised by new technology are also grouped appropriately. The collection concludes with topics that involve changes in family structure and women's lives. By placing these essays at the end, we do not suggest that such traditionally defined "personal" questions are any less inclusively social than the others treated here. On the contrary, we dissent from any assumption that social reality is *ever* separable from interpersonal dilemmas. What the organization of the essays, taken as a whole, conveys is that there is now an *urgency* for contemporary Christian ethics to place all issues in a global and political-economic setting. *The Public Vocation of Christian Ethics* stands as a tribute to a man whose work has consistently made it more difficult to abstract our thinking as Christians from just these wider contexts.

Although it is surely premature to speak as yet of "the legacy" of one whose life and work continues so vigorously, it is still possible to make the unequivocal assessment that Roger Shinn's contribution has enabled many of us to continue the dual focus of church-based Christian ethical reflection *and* public policy engagement. In a time of increasing specialization, that dual focus has been threatened from many directions. In Roger Shinn's hands, the best legacy of Christian realism has come to fruition.[6] Consistent with Christian realism, he has surmounted the personalistic approach that has stamped too much Christian theological ethics and marked it merely as in-house or sectarian discussion, while at the same time taking Christian theological and moral heritage seriously but not granting it the aura of incontestable sanctity. Political reality *and* ethical insight are both weighed explicitly; neither is sacrificed to theological dogmatism. Addressing public issues both with Christian clarity and appropriate Christian humility has been a leitmotiv of Roger Shinn's work. We will be well pleased if this book, collected in appreciation of him, contributes to these values. Like Roger, we affirm that Christians *must* engage the great public questions not because we have uncontestable light to shed, but because *both* Christian faith *and* our common humanity require it.

The Next Stage
of Christian Ethics
as a Theological Discipline

John C. Bennett

*R*oger Shinn's professional life has coincided with the period in which Christian ethics came of age as a major discipline in Protestant theological study. Catholics have had moral theology that has been closely related to the training of priests for the confessional. Christian ethics has been incidental to the teaching of systematic theology among Protestants, and until recent decades, few teachers have devoted their full time to it. Social ethics as a strong Protestant interest in the United States was much stimulated by the Social Gospel; after the Social Gospel, as a distinct movement, lost most of its influence, the social imperative expressed through it became even more influential in churches and theological schools. Christian realism associated with Reinhold Niebuhr and Roger Shinn, while it began by criticizing views of humanity and history made popular by the Social Gospel, has the same concern for the Christian responsibility for justice and peace in more difficult times.

Historical events have had a major influence on the development of Christian social ethics. In this respect, I am a product of the Great Depression. At that time it was inevitable that one turned one's attention to the issues of economic justice. The decade of the 1930s was probably the most radical period in the development of Christian ethics in this country with the possible exception of today's revolutionary theologies and social movements in the Third World. In the 1930s, there was great doubt concerning the survival of capitalism, and the people who had the most influence on social ethics in liberal theological schools were Chris-

John C. Bennett, President Emeritus of Union Theological Seminary and Reinhold Niebuhr Professor of Social Ethics Emeritus, Union Theological Seminary in New York City.

1

tian socialists: That was true of Reinhold Niebuhr, Paul Tillich, William Temple, and Karl Barth. One of the most powerful books on Christian ethics in that decade was Emil Brunner's *The Divine Imperative.*[1] In that book, he was a strong anticapitalist.

Other events in that decade did a great deal to mold the teaching of Christian ethics: the rise of Hitlerism; the Moscow trials and the disillusionment about Stalinist communism among those who had hope in it; the approach of World War II and the new debate about pacifism and the ethics of war; the new stage in ecumenical social thinking that made the Oxford Conference of Church, Community and State, of 1937, a milestone in the development of social ethics. A different kind of event was the publication in 1932 of Reinhold Niebuhr's *Moral Man and Immoral Society.*[2] Niebuhr had been the chief representative of the liberal Social Gospel since Walter Rauschenbusch, and in that book, he became the severest critic of its optimistic expectations for history and its neglect of the roots of sin in human life. That book is, in some respects, dated, and yet it may still be the best, certainly the most vivid, introduction to central assumptions underlying Christian realism.

Before the 1930s, there were few specialists in Christian ethics, but today, there are hundreds of them in theological schools and in departments of religious studies in colleges and universities. The latter often prefer to identify themselves with "religious ethics." Since the 1930s, hundreds of doctoral dissertations in this field have been written. The American Society of Christian Ethics, with its nearly seven hundred members and its well-attended meetings, dramatizes the importance of Christian ethics as a discipline. Since Vatican II, the Christian ethics community has come to include Roman Catholics as much as Protestants. Catholic moral theologians have moved away from their traditional legalistic manuals and have brought to the study of Christian ethics more precise training than has been characteristic of Protestants in many areas from the ethics of war to medical ethics. Today, in their outlook on most ethical issues, it is no longer possible to distinguish between Catholics and Protestants. In regard to the use of nuclear weapons and to the American economy, Catholics are giving the most courageous ethical leadership on issues of peace and justice. Academic Christian ethics will recognize the pastoral letters of the Catholic bishops on peace and on the economy as landmark events.

Some believe that Christian ethics should be a branch of systematic theology. This is one matter on which Karl Barth and Paul Tillich were agreed. After his experience at Union Seminary, Tillich said that "reasons of expediency may, nevertheless, justify the preservation of departments of Christian Ethics."[3] He may have been only accepting the reality of colleagues! But he may have realized that without departments of Christian ethics, there would be neglect of the concrete materials that are essential for ethical decisions in many areas of application. Also, the concern about ethical methodology, which, to a degree, is common ground between Christian ethics and philosophical ethics, would receive little attention. Advanced studies of Christian ethics require scholars who have become specialists in various fields that involve ethical decisions.

It is desirable to have interdisciplinary studies in the theological curriculum relating Christian ethics to systematic theology, biblical studies, church history and the history of Christian thought, pastoral theology, and such new disciplines as the sociology of religion. The book by Bruce C. Birch and Larry L. Rasmussen, *Bible and Ethics in the Christian Life,*[4] is an example of the kind of writings that are needed. It would be good for someone in Christian ethics and someone in New Testament studies to cooperate in a course based on Elisabeth Schüssler Fiorenza's mind-changing book, *In Memory of Her,*[5] which gives a new view of the place of women in the New Testament. The near-classic by H. Richard Niebuhr, *Christ and Culture,*[6] is an example of the writing that is needed to relate Christian ethics to the history of Christian life and thought. Roland Bainton's *Christian Attitudes Toward War and Peace*[7] and *The Travail of Religious Liberty*[8] illustrate the kind of contribution that church historians make to Christian ethics.

There should be those who are permanent specialists in such fields as economic ethics and medical ethics, but the more common pattern should be for generalists who have been well exposed to the history of Christian ethics and to Christian ethics as a contemporary discipline to set aside blocks of time to gain competence in one or more areas such as business, law, medicine, or international relations. Paul Ramsey has given a good example. He is well grounded in theological ethics and in a number of chapters in its history, and he has gone out of his way to gain competence in regard to weaponry, in regard to aspects of law and medicine that are related to his ethical interests. He has taught in a medical school. Roger Shinn has given special emphasis to achieving competence in the areas of study in scientific ethics that formed the background for the Massachusetts Institute of Technology conference in 1979, under the auspices of the World Council of Churches, and for his book *Forced Options,*[9] which is the best broad introduction to the global ethical problems of the next decades and, as he says in the book's subtitle, of the "21st Century."

Sources of Christian Ethics

Christian ethics stresses its unique sources in the biblical revelation, and in theological reflection on it, and in the experience of the church. I have lived through three periods in regard to the role of the teachings and example of Jesus in Christian ethics. In the early liberal period, the synoptic teachings of Jesus were the surest norm for Christian ethics. In the period associated with neoorthodoxy, a combination of historical skepticism and the shift of emphasis to the *kerygma* led to the neglect of the teachings and example of Jesus. On many sides today, there is a recovery of the centrality of the teachings and example of Jesus as providing the vision of the norm, although these are not seen as isolated from many glimpses of that same vision in the New Testament as a whole. The cross becomes for Christians the ultimate revelation of the character of Jesus and the nature of God. It also represents the example and inspiration for human suffering love and gives meaning to the tragic aspects of history. We can all be thankful that the people of the New Testament did not have responsibility for economic and political structures and policies in the first century. If they had had such responsibilities, we would today have only a blurred vision from them, blurred by the kind of ambiguities and the lesser evils that dominate our own lives. We might have been stuck with their lesser evils as having authority for us in the minds of many. Each generation of Christians can respond to that central vision and make its own adjustments and discover its own lesser evils but always under the judgment of that vision itself. Some Christians have had the role either in monastic communities or in perfectionist sects to keep reminding their Christian neighbors of that vision, but in order to do this, they have had to avoid some institutional responsibilities that others must assume if most people are to be able to live in societies in which there are protections of order and justice.

Some thinkers who have sectarian tendencies, who seek absolutist approaches to political issues, are so placed that they have considerable influence in the mainline churches. John Howard Yoder and Stanley Hauerwas[10] are good examples, as both have taught in a Catholic university and have wide influence in the Christian ethics community. The influence of the journal *Sojourners* is similar.

The experience of the church as a source for Christian ethics has two sides. There have been many inspiring realizations of Christian character and of the beloved and loving community. Repentance and confession of sin and the receiving of forgiveness have themselves been sources of moral renewal and have done much to counteract the corruptions of pride and self-love. The heritage of recognized and unknown saints is an essential part of the life of the church. Spelling out the practical meaning of love for the neighbor—for all kinds of neighbors, including enemies—has always been part of Christian teaching and Christian learning.

There are also some clues in the traditions of the great churches concerning the moral struggles of political life from which we still draw new implications in the light of new experiences. The teachings of Augustine about the criteria for a just war have yielded their ultimate political implications in our time when we face the possibility of a nuclear war that we know could never result in the kind of peace Augustine saw as the goal of all use of military force. Another example of a clue about which we are still learning the meaning is the teaching of Calvin that "the vice or imperfection of men renders it safer and more tolerable for the government to be in the hands of many, that they may afford each other mutual assistance and admonition, and that if anyone arrogates to himself more than is right, the many may act as censors and masters to restrain his ambition."[11] Those words have been embodied in some quite successful structures of government, and most of humanity today is struggling to develop structures of government that have those characteristics, government strong enough to deal with problems of order and economic viability without being oppressive. How straight is the line in idea, if not in influence, from those words of Calvin to Reinhold Niebuhr's defense of democracy in *The Children of Light and the Children of Darkness.*[12]

Transformations in Our Time

Today I am impressed by the extent to which, within recent centuries, confronting a rapidly changing world, the church has learned lessons of enormous importance for Christian ethics about the implications of its ancient teachings. Before mentioning some examples, I will answer in advance those who may say that these new learnings are merely cases of keeping up with contemporary trends. In the case of each example, what has been learned is more consistent with the ethic of radical love for all neighbors than are the earlier positions that have dominated the life of the church. More is involved: large groups of neglected and oppressed neighbors have at last been heard from. They are now able to tell those who have dominated the church how the world is experienced by them, and they have gained the power to push those who have held the power, white Western males.

The first example is on a deeper level than the others and is a case that has led to religious and moral success. It is the abandonment of the assumption that Christians should deny liberty to, and even persecute, neighbors who were regarded as heretical or as being outside the Christian circle. Religious liberty for those whom the church believes are in religious error is now on all sides accepted in the church as a civil right. If it is still believed that error has no rights, to that must be added that consciences in error have rights. This is an about-face for the church, both Protestant and Catholic. The final event that gave clear acceptance of this change was the Declaration of Religious Freedom by Vatican Council II. But this was the result of many centuries of struggle for religious liberty, with churches and states in league to suppress it. This proves that the church is capable of a radical turnaround.

Today we are in the early stages of another turnaround: a movement away from the traditional patriarchalism of both theology and church practice toward the recognition of the equality of women and men in the church. In some churches, this movement has, in principle, gone quite far, although the equality of women and men in the ministry of local churches is far from being realized. In churches that, in principle, insist on the subordination of women and refuse them ordination, fundamental change seems far off, and yet, in the Roman Catholic Church, there are so many able and well-trained women in orders of nuns that the unofficial voice of women is loud and clear. The best that can be said is that today in most churches, the patriarchal principles and prejudices are more on the defensive than ever before. Many theological schools are training almost as many women as men to work for change in their denominations and local churches, change in theological assumptions, symbols, and language, change in the decision-making bodies of churches, changes in church practice.

Also, Christians are in the midst of radical change in the teachings of churches about war and the use of military force. Absolute pacifism is a minority presence in most denominations, but it has more influence on the attitudes of majorities than in the past. The fact that so many churches opposed the Vietnam war while it was being fought as an unjust war marks a new stage in Christian thinking about war. It is seen by many today as part of a regrettable "Vietnam syndrome" that reduces the willingness of Americans to intervene in Central America and wherever leaders in power seek to coerce other nations and especially to prevent revolutionary change in them. The united front against government policy in Central America presented by the mainline churches, both Catholic and Protestant, is a fortunate expression of the "Vietnam syndrome." It is much more than that because it arises from the conviction that some of these countries need revolutionary change.

The Pastoral Letter of the American Roman Catholic bishops, "The Challenge of Peace: God's Promise and Our Response," has been an extraordinary event. It has had strong influence on other churches and is leading them to see that the *use* of nuclear weapons is in absolute conflict with their faith and moral commitment. It does not solve all problems involved in the possession of nuclear weapons or point to the best political means of reversing the arms race, but it helps not only Christians, but all persons of good will to find parameters within which such means should be sought. No other issue should have a more important place on the agenda of teachers of Christian ethics and of the ethical thinking in the churches. This opens up another area in which new thinking is necessary: the relations between our country and the Soviet Union, the only two countries that can destroy each other and their helpless neighbors.

6

A fourth area of change that our generation has witnessed has been the renunciation by churches of the anti-Judaism that had been part of Christian faith. The most decisive event in this process of change was the statement in the report of Vatican II about the Jews.[13] It is amazing that it had to be said that the death of Christ "cannot be blamed upon all the Jews then living, without distinction, nor upon the Jews of today," and that "the Jews should not be presented as repudiated and cursed by God." Liberal Christians against the background of the Enlightenment had moved away from these ideas, but many Protestant denominations have preserved remnants of them in their teaching. Most denominations now repudiate them and try to correct elements in religious education that still unintentionally reflect them. The religious anti-Judaism which has been active in the collective unconscious of the nations that belonged to what was Christendom has been an important source of secular anti-Semitism. For the churches to become defenders of the civil and human rights of the Jews and of the Jewish religion to which their own faith is so deeply indebted, both for its origin and for its present substance, is a new reality for which we can thank the God of Jews and Christians. The Holocaust revealed the unbelievable horrors resulting from anti-Semitism, supported in some circles by religious anti-Judaism, and for all time it will be a negative moral landmark warning against what can happen when a nation becomes obsessed by unrelenting prejudice against any racial, ethnic, or religious group.

One more example of transformation in our own time is the repudiation of white racism in predominantly white churches. In quite recent times, many such churches refused to permit blacks to attend or become members. I have been struck by the statement of Benjamin Mays, a black leader who was not a militant: "I believe that throughout my lifetime, the local white church has been society's most conservative and hypocritical institution in the area of White-Negro relations."[14] All this is not in the past; the effects of white racism are still present in our churches. Catholic and Protestant churches no longer support it, and churches belatedly did throw themselves into the political and social struggles for civil rights. Laws were changed and a new generation learned from new legally supported situations. Yet economic injustice among the races remains a moral and social disaster. Christian ethics needs to deal with the residual sources of racism and the many practical issues of justice and equal respect that remain. Schools of theology, in many cases, have an influential black presence among students and in faculties.

I have mentioned these five examples of learning in the experience of the churches in our own time partly to encourage those who teach in Christian ethics: it is not static! There are many others; to show their diversity, I shall only mention the rejection of capital punishment in most churches and the abandonment of the unconscionably cruel attitudes of churches to suicides and their families. All these examples of changes in positions held by churches have humanized the ethics of Christians and given greater consistency to the teaching of Christian ethics.

New Phases of Old Problems

A new phase of a long-standing struggle for economic justice has taken various forms in Christian history. Ever since the Social Gospel and the sufferings of the 1930s, this has been a major theme in Christian ethics. Today, in the United States, fresh work is needed, since our country is now being led by people who show no interest in justice for the deprived in society except under immediate political pressure. Battles that we thought had been won have to be fought again for the victims of our economic institutions. One central issue is the degree to which economic institutions should be under the pull of equality as a regulative principle. The issue is best raised when we ask how far equal opportunity to which lip service is usually given is made impossible by the extreme inequalities of conditions under which children begin their lives. The severity of the situation is generally neglected in this rich country. The issues of economic justice need to be seen as global issues. In this, the teaching of Christian ethics is greatly helped by the experience of the worldwide church. Current American nationalism and the insistence of our leaders that all problems can be solved by the exporting of the free-market system make it difficult to see the world as it is experienced by the deprived majority of humanity.[15]

Is there any subject about which the churches have been surer that they had the final wisdom than sexual ethics? But today there are few subjects on which the traditional teaching of the churches has less influence. The most extreme example is the double crusade of Pope John Paul II against both contraceptives and abortion. This teaching leaves people, in their personal lives, entrapped, especially women, and it takes no account of the global threat in the growth of population. Fortunately, in this country, both Catholic theologians and lay people are most opposed to the first prohibition and divided on the second, especially when it is made the subject of restrictive law. Protestants have been more helpful on those two issues and have differed from the official Catholic position in recognizing that in some situations, divorce is a morally preferred choice.

A younger generation has not asked permission of churches or ethicists when so many of its members have come to accept living together by men and women without marriage. This is not new in itself, but its acceptance is new in circles that a generation ago would have been shocked by it. There is much more debate about homosexual relations; however, in the community of Christian ethicists, there is a growing body of opinion that—on the basis of the assumption that for an indeterminate number of people, a homosexual orientation is not a matter of choice, but of destiny—accepts the homosexual style of life as right for some people. Ecclesiastical assemblies, while supporting the civil rights of avowed homosexuals, usually oppose their ordination as a total group and have no agreed-on way of giving public sanction to a homosexual union. I believe that ordination should depend on the competence, commitment, and character of each person, and that it is unjust to single out this group as unfit. As in other situations, thought on this subject has been moving away from traditional judgmental attitudes because a minority has gained a voice and keeps reminding the majority of its existence and its claims. Those who have been responsible for the traditional Christian teaching that has given no room for homosexuals, from Paul until the recent past, have never heard the testimony of sensitive Christian homosexuals.

The deepest question about sexual ethics is whether or not the emphasis should be shifted away from specific rules, even taboos, to the application of broader ethical criteria, such as responsibility for the results of one's actions; respect as well as love for other persons affected by what one does; avoidance of the exploitation of others for one's own satisfaction; personal integrity and trustworthiness; no use of one's professional or economic power to take advantage of others; conscientious concern about the effects of what one does in specific cases and about the effects of the generalizing of what one does on the equal dignity of women and men, on the health of families, and, especially, on the development of children. Because in this area, people are swept away by momentary temptations, those who are reflecting on Christian ethics should consider ways in which particular rules may still be important as guides to conduct. Is there any area in which self-deception is more rabid and in greater need of being counteracted? The old legalism no longer convinces and yet study of aspects of truth that it has embodied is needed in Christian ethics.

New Problems

The field of Christian ethics will require a new kind of courage in the next period. There will be room enough for the older kind of courage, when one deals with familiar controversial issues and feels bound to go against popular positions in the church and society and is labeled as ʹradical or subversive. There will continue to be much of this. The new kind of courage involves dealing with questions before the alternatives have been thoroughly canvassed. An extreme example of this would be decisions in triage situations. What should be decided about the allocation of scarce medical resources when the need for them is great?

Positions taken about abortion have been well canvassed, and yet even in this case, Beverly Harrison's *Our Right to Choose*[16] provides a new emphasis in putting in the central place the necessity of "procreative choice" for the dignity and opportunities of all women. How are we to relate justice to half the human race as full persons to their unique capacities and responsibilities as bearers and nurturers of children and to the claims of the unborn? Old questions are involved, but there is a new emphasis.

Ethical issues that surround the "right to die" involve cases in which not only the withdrawing of life support, but also the more active hastening of death seem to many to be right. Medical ethics, in general, has added greatly to the complexity of Christian ethics, to the dilemmas for which there is not the kind of preparation that history has provided for the dilemmas of social justice. The success of medicine in prolonging life has increased some of the dilemmas. The genetic effects of biological experiments open up another world of unexplored dilemmas. What will come next? For the present, we must deal with the more reliable predictions concerning the consequences of nuclear war. I hope that no other issues will crowd out the issue of the use of nuclear weapons, since the escalation of their use would probably destroy the chance for humane solutions of other ethical problems.

Most of the work in Christian ethics with which I have been associated has put major emphasis on objectives, criteria, and methods in decision-making. Many of us have been rightly criticized for neglecting the formation of character and the significance of virtues. We have stressed the theological background and the resources in Christian faith for both character-making and decision-making. Christian character is formed in response to the love of God, to God's grace and forgiveness, and there is much guidance for both character-making and decision-making in the sense of sin and repentance, in awareness of the judgment of God above all human causes, groups, and achievements. Often the ultimate guide for Christian ethics is the theological warning against idolatries. Awareness of the limits arising from the prevalence of sin and from our finiteness is part of Christian ethical guidance. We have taken for granted virtues as the expression of character and as, in themselves, aspects of the highest good for persons and communities.

Also, when we hear as much as we do about moral relativism and skepticism, the surest way of getting one's bearings is to consider the qualities of character that are most admired and those most despised. Most of those claiming to be moral relativists, who are in the circles to which readers of these words belong, know that they despise cruel tyrants and military adventurers and racists. They admire people of integrity, of compassion, people who are free from arrogance, people who show courage in their loyalty to their cause, people who have a sense of responsibility.

Paul's list of the fruits of the Spirit reflects more specifically Christian virtues than those I have named, but it overlaps with them: "love, joy, peace, patience, kindness, goodness, faithfulness, ... self-control [Gal. 5:22-23]."

There can be arguments as to how these virtues are to be related to some of the toughness necessary under difficult situations in either struggling for a great social good against fierce and sometimes violent opposition, or in the everyday tasks of maintaining order. Some vocational virtues have an element of aggressiveness, and even harshness, in them, but unless on deeper levels of character the fruits of the Spirit are active such aggressiveness and harshness become ugly, destructive, and antisocial. Whatever happens in our thinking and teaching about Christian ethics, we must not pit approaches that stress the virtues reflective of character over against the ethics of decision-making. Character in persons is an aim that the good society should achieve while we make decisions. Character is essential for dependability in decision-making.

The Teacher as Activist

One final consideration: how far should the scholar and teacher in the field of Christian ethics be an activist and an advocate? Obviously, there are differences of disposition, style, and vocation, as between individuals. An interesting comparison in this respect is between the two great ethicists: Reinhold and H. Richard Niebuhr. (A description of them would require another essay, and most readers have some knowledge of the differences between them.) They differed very much in the extent to which political activism was a part of their lives. Christian ethics must lead to action, although the area of action depends on personal vocations. Some ethicists act chiefly in their own local situations, and some are political activists on a national, or even global scale. All have responsibility to aid their churches in their policies and actions, and these will have far-reaching implications for the larger society.

The ethics classroom should not be a place for propaganda or efforts to impose one's own views on students. Students should feel free to differ from their teachers. Fairness to other views is an aspect of love and justice. But at some stage in a discussion of a difficult controversial issue, it is often best to say where one stands and to indicate what one believes is mistaken about other positions. Strong advocacy may belong outside the classroom, but there can be no such separation when one has, for months or years, taken strong positions about civil rights, or justice for the disadvantaged, or military interventions in Indo-China or Central America. What one has advocated outside the classroom is known to one's students.

11

Advocacy grows out of one's ethical commitments as a Christian, and in some situations it is morally impossible to remain neutral or silent, for to do so is to support by default the position backed by those with most power. Advocacy is also a stimulus for thought and for research, even though it should not determine the outcome of research. Recognition that others, starting with some of the same Christian assumptions as one's own and with similar Christian character, come to opposite positions is essential for fairness and requires both sides to clarify issues. Differences in perceptions of realities, in methods, and in political strategies are inevitable and can easily be understood. Some differences are more troublesome because they involve positions that seem to one side to be outside the parameters within which ethical commitments have a defensible Christian basis. Perceptions of the facts, of what is real, are usually mixed up with deeper differences of moral choice. The latter have to do with the degree of concern that people have for the dignity and opportunities of neglected and disadvantaged people, of racial minorities and women. They also have to do with the responsibility to prevent nuclear war and with the use of American power to dominate other countries in our interest and to support the ideological goals that we prefer. They often have to do with the division of the world between good and evil nations, with the tendency to see American virtues in absolute terms.

When we become advocates, we should be strong critics of opposing positions, but remember the warning that self-righteous criticism distorts and even corrupts commitment to the best causes. The never-ending responsibility of theological ethics is to keep such warnings alive in our minds and hearts without undermining courage or obscuring the positive ethical vision that draws us.

PART I.

The Nuclear Age

ONE

The Nuclear Dilemma

Larry L. Rasmussen

*T*he nuclear dilemma leaves one dumb with wonder. A terrain of admitted madness, riddled with irony, paradox, and Strangelovian rationality, it is nonetheless the creation of our most sophisticated intelligence. One can be forgiven, then, for hesitating to enter this world, especially if armed with little more than troubled moral concern and the same tool, fragile human reason, that serves the madness. Better to take leave of reality altogether and live as if the nuclear world did not exist. But entering is not a choice. This is home. And for the time being there isn't another.

The dilemma posed by these weapons is the worst imaginable instance of "you can't live with 'em and you can't live without 'em." (Perhaps such familiar phrasing should not be used; it frivolously hides the gravity of the subject.)

As of the mid-1980s, this is nuclear reality: there are at least 43,900 warheads, and perhaps as many as 59,600, with the approximate destructive equivalence of 6,000 World War IIs; the time required for those weapons to reach their targets is shrinking while their accuracy grows; the time permitted to decide about their use, in instances of real or expected conflict, is also shrinking. All this is happening on a fragile planet experiencing the failure of arms control, the slow "success" of proliferation, and the apparently incurable fallibility of its most dangerous species—us. The conclusion is also reality: we cannot survive indefinitely with nuclear arse-

Larry L. Rasmussen, Reinhold Niebuhr Professor of Social Ethics, Union Theological Seminary in New York City.

nals. We cannot live eternally poised an inch from obliteration. The scale of threat and risk is too great, the odds too unfavorable.

One Horn of the Dilemma

There was a time when the best and the brightest thought that we could live with nuclear arms, although it required the strained logic of deterrence: threatening to do in certain circumstances what one must never do in any circumstances—in order to prevent it. Churchill contended in 1955 that by a "process of sublime irony, safety will be the sturdy child of terror, and survival the twin brother of annihilation."[1] In the same period the star-studded cast of the Federal Council of Churches' commission to advise the churches on weapons of mass destruction—Angus Dun, Reinhold Niebuhr, Paul Tillich, Robert Calhoun, Georgia Harkness, and John Bennett among them—gave full support to deterrence strategy and in fact voted 8 to 2 to refuse to oppose a "first-use" policy. Declaring no first use of nuclear weapons would weaken the deterrent effect, the majority argued.[2]

Times have changed, arms and strategy have evolved. If it was plausible to "live with 'em" in the 1950s, it is no longer so in the 1980s. What follows is not the full complement of reasons. They suffice in frightening degree, however.

1. Deterrence has not led to arms control, but rather has fueled the arms race. Deterrence rests on a capacity for retaliation sufficiently strong to keep the enemy from contemplating an initial use of nuclear arms. Everyone is dissuaded from launching a nuclear attack because everyone knows that the damage at home will be of holocaust proportions. If not a logical necessity, in practice this has meant that technological developments in weapons by one side (more destructive, accurate, evasive, and mobile) must be matched with comparable developments by the other side. Otherwise, the ability to retaliate might be overwhelmed by the enemy's superiority. Without assured retaliation, deterrence simply unravels. At bottom the logic is simple and familiar: if the enemy builds a better weapon, the world will be safer only if we do too. But history is deeply unkind to such logic. The actual outcome has been an open-ended arms race (50,000 warheads and counting) and greatly increased insecurity.

The dynamics are not only those of technical "advance." The politics of nation-state sovereignty also marry deterrence to an arms race. Part of it is the personnel. When arms control is pursued, it is not staffed by people whose perspective is global, third party, or neutral. Rather, the nation-state representatives who bring us the arms race meet under the same auspices for arms control efforts. When they do so, they work in every way possible to maintain advantage for their government.[3] Given the logic of deterrence and nation-state actors, arms control under these circumstances has little to do "with the principles of war and their negation." Instead, it concerns "the details of war and their modification."[4]

2. The new weapons systems of the 1970s and 1980s—SS18s, 19s, and 20s, MX, Trident II (D-5), Pershing II, and cruise missiles—represent first-strike capacity. They are, after all, offensive systems.[5] Overt conflict or no, they contribute massively to an atmosphere of anxiety and suspicion, heightening insecurity and jeopardizing careful decision-making during the most dangerous moment in the history of the world.

3. The confidence that nuclear war could be "contained" is, by and large, gone. Even the U.S. Department of Defense and the Reagan Administration acknowledge that use of strategic nuclear weapons by one superpower against the other can be expected to escalate into all-out war.[6] Given the megatonage housed in underground silos, circling in the air, and cruising beneath the sea, the scenario of such destruction escapes every category human imagination possesses.

4. The scientific community has grown totally sober and utterly grim about the effects of any major use of nuclear weapons. Beyond the initial incineration lies the slower wasting of the ecosystem. The findings cannot be detailed here, but there is no substitute for facing them. Most of these studies speculate about the probable consequences of a 5,000- to 10,000-megaton holocaust. Approximately 18,000 megatons sit in deadly silence at present.[7]

5. Relations have deteriorated between the powers that possess the most massive arsenals. Although the United States and the Soviet Union share a responsibility for global security that mightily transcends their differences, there is hardly a thread intact of the ties that bind. About all they share currently are weapons of mass destruction, suspicions that are genuinely mutual, and joint "collaboration" in building the doomsday machine. The elements of real security, such as cultural ties, positive economic bonds, deep knowledge of each other, government-to-government and diplomat-to-diplomat meetings, these and other strands are frazzled, strained to the breaking point, or cut altogether. When President Reagan said in 1984, even jokingly, even off the record in a microphone check, "My fellow Americans, I am pleased to tell you I have signed legislation to outlaw Russia forever. We begin the bombing in five minutes,"[8] he only gave evidence in a different way to relations that are perilously low.

6. Although nuclear arms have knocked the sword of war from our hands as a rational instrument of national purpose, the use of the military for diplomatic ends has grown, and with it the arms race and its dangers. George Kennan, veteran diplomat and premier diplomatic historian, comes to a startling conclusion after reviewing several decades of East-West relations:

I am now bound to say that while the earliest possible elimination of nuclear weaponry is of no less vital importance in my eyes than it ever was, this would not be enough ... to give Western civilization even an adequate chance of survival. *War itself, as a means of settling differences at least between the great industrial powers, will have to be in some way ruled out.*[9]

War as "the extension of politics by other means" (Clausewitz's famed definition) has no rational meaning in the case of *nuclear* war. National values and goals cannot be preserved at acceptable cost by such a war. Yet reliance on the military for diplomatic ends has escalated. In the absence of other powers of persuasion, military force is an obvious one. But it intensifies the arms race. Weapons are built and brandished to create "perception" and bring about an "atmosphere" for serious negotiations. They become "bargaining chips" (the vaunted vocation of the Peacekeeper [MX] missile). And when the purpose of military spending is to create "perception" and weapons are procured primarily as symbols, there are never enough.[10]

Kennan is no pacifist. He is an ardent political realist who knows that good policy is made with a keen sense for the human abuse of power and kept close to the hard facts of historical reality and political possibility. He isn't sure how nuclear weaponry and war might be ruled out, but he has some ideas. What he does know is that utter ruin would trail in the wake of nuclear conflict. For the reasons given thus far, he, like so many others, is fully convinced of one thing: we cannot live with nuclear weapons.

The Dilemma's Other Horn

The conclusion—that we cannot live with nuclear weapons—is evidently not a matter of consensus. NATO and U.S. government policy preserves the option of first use; indeed, NATO strategy is based on the threat of first use and includes a plan for graduated resort to nuclear weapons in the event of a massive Soviet attack using "conventional" weapons. The reason is the same given since the 1950s: publicly holding first-use option strengthens deterrence.

Beyond government policy, many citizens remain convinced that further arms buildup and the deployment of new systems enhance security.[11] And probably a majority, believing the elimination of armed conflict to be impossible, conclude that the known risks of an armed world are preferable to the unknowns of disarming. Better then to lodge one's present and future bets with nuclear arms than with risky disarmament. Differently said, we cannot live *without* nuclear weapons.

For some, the nature of international power relationships no longer admits of nonnuclear possibilities. Richard Rubenstein's conclusion is as clear and blunt as any:

> In the confrontations between nations, radical conflicts of interest can only be resolved on the basis of power relationships. No other basis is credible. This does not mean that every conflict must be resolved by the use of all available power. It does mean that, short of an actual conflict, a nation's power ... will largely be determined by the estimate her adversaries have of that power. All we have left to serve some measure of peace is a balance of mutual nuclear terror. At the very least the great powers are condemned to an inextricable cycle of ever-widening arms races, especially as weapons systems achieve ever greater sophistication. It is my belief that there is no way out of this bind.[12]

Even those whose assessments are different from Rubenstein's, and who have started down the long road to outlaw nuclear weapons and war, find themselves caught up short. Kennan, for example, makes proposals that are bold compared with current policy: unilateral initiatives to destroy 10 percent, even up to 50 percent, of the U.S. nuclear arsenal. But he would retain possession of sufficient nuclear arms to be a deterrent, that is, enough to destroy the adversary's society in a retaliatory strike. Kennan shrinks from sanctioning that level of destruction. He finds it morally unacceptable. Yet, for the time being, there appears no way around "minimal" deterrence.

Like Kennan, the U.S. Roman Catholic bishops find themselves snared on the other horn of the dilemma and do not see how we can live without nuclear arms. They, too, judge that a fresh reappraisal of war is necessary, that nuclear weapons ought not be used, that we "must find means of defending people that do not depend upon the threat of annihilation."[13] Moreover, deterrence has strained "our moral conception." ("May a nation threaten what it may never do? May it possess what it may never use?"[14]) Having choked on deterrence morality and having rejected nuclear weapons, the bishops nonetheless find possession of these arms permissible if deterrence moves into mutual arms reduction and if the weapons are never used first, under any circumstances.[15]

The nuclear freeze movement has come to a similar point on the journey. Deterrence premises are rejected: the threat of annihilation is not a tolerable risk for national defense and international stability. Yet the actual proposals of the freeze movement fall within the framework of deterrence and probably have their appeal because of that.

Alan Geyer rejects deterrence as prime security doctrine and persuasively presses the case for disarmament as the alternative. But faced with stubborn political reality, he ends up advocating an alliance with "deterrence minimalists."[16]

All these folks are "diagnostic radicals" but "prescriptive moderates."[17] Why? Why call for a "moral-about-face" and a "conversion of the heart"[18] and then queue up with modified deterrence and its reliance on the threat of massive destruction? Why reject nuclear arms and then embrace them, albeit with considerable revulsion?

The answer is not that these parties, neck muscles taut and straining toward a nonnuclear world, find deterrence morally acceptable. They abhor deterrence and utterly reject the missiles of death. But they find no alternative that is both morally acceptable and politically viable. This is where the nuclear dilemma has landed us.

But why is a politically viable, morally acceptable course so elusive? The workings of the collective psyches of whole nations and peoples are notoriously mysterious but an educated guess is the inexhaustible springs of fear. Something worse than the multiple presence of nuclear arms can be imagined—possession by one side only. Shared, deterring terror is vastly preferable to a monopoly of terror if you are not the monopoly. So, in Michael Walzer's words, we "threaten evil in order not to do it, and the doing of it would be so terrible that the threat seems in comparison to be morally defensible."[19]

This is the nuclear dilemma, as perceived by so many. The threat and risk are too great, the odds too unfavorable, to live with nuclear weapons indefinitely. They are effective deterrents, but deterrence policy is not infallible. And the price of fallibility may be obliteration. Yet so long as we suspect that anybody has any weapons at all, we will not risk a monopoly of terror. The clincher is that we cannot be absolutely sure that someone won't have some of the damn things somewhere. In any case, knowledge for building them is now unlosable. Surely the capacity to build will remain as well. Thus the jarring conclusion from the prestigious Harvard team: "Living *with* nuclear weapons is our only hope."[20] This repugnancy pushes its way aboard just as we are more certain than ever that we cannot live with nuclear weapons, with hope or anything else.

A Normative Perspective

Any credible ethical stand must include a believable account of the facts for the issue at hand. The first portion of this essay has tried to be unflinchingly honest about the nuclear world.

But an ethical stand is never determined by facts alone, hard as they may kick. It always entails moral norms: the standards for judging human character and conduct, the guides for measuring right and wrong, good and evil. Moral norms interact with factual judgments and general assessments of human nature to yield a normative perspective on the issue under consideration. The next pages undertake a normative Christian perspective for approaching nuclear reality. Clarity about norms and the recommendation of a normative perspective are part of the enterprise of ethics.

The wording is important—*a* normative Christian perspective, not *the* normative view. The reason for the qualification is that moral norms, behavioral norms of human nature, and factual judgments are all subject to change. This means that past Christian thinking may or may not provide adequate guidance for the world of nuclear realities. The prudential judgments that were part of past policy, grounded in judgments about then-prevailing facts, may no longer prove prudent. Nor may the norms of other generations hold as they once did. Nonetheless, there are strong continuities both in human behavior over time and across the many renditions of the Christian story. The enduring themes make the following statement of a normative Christian perspective at least recognizable, even if not a matter of settled consensus, much less an unarguable position.

Nonviolence and its subtraditions. The Christian norm for the use of force is nonviolence. When that is forgotten—and it is often—Christians are pulled back to it by the normative story itself. There the Christian claim is that the fullest expression of God possible in human form happened in Jesus of Nazareth; and the way of Jesus, displaying the very character of God, rejects arms as the manner of God's reign. Rather, peace and justice are made through a cross of dehostilizing love. The crucified God, choosing to suffer evil rather than inflict it, gathers enemies into covenantal intimacy by forgiving them.

From the norm of nonviolence two subtraditions developed. Both acknowledge that force is socially necessary in a world of stiff-necked peoples whose interests can never be made fully harmonious and who miss few chances to organize their own lives at the expense of neighbors near and far. Both subtraditions contend that there should be guards against unchecked power and minimal opportunities for the selfish use of power. Such requires incentives, persuasion, and coercion in varying forms. But in all instances, the subtraditions agree, the use of force should be held to the lowest required levels, be held accountable for the consequences, and respect the humanity of the recipients.

The pacifist subtradition says that although coercion is socially required, among its many forms is one that ought never be used—killing violence. Nonviolence is unexceptionable at this point. Pacifist arguments are really two: one theological-ethical, the other ethical-prudential. The first has rich and varied theological expression.[21] But it might be summarized by saying that we do not take on ourselves killing any whom God regards as unqualifiedly precious and for whom God suffers in patient love; and

21

there is no one for whom this is not the case. Said differently, God is never glorified by human violence nor our humanity ever honored. The ethical-prudential argument is that lethal violence is self-defeating for human society in the long haul, and most of the time in the short run as well. It breeds relationships that generate estrangement, harbor hostility, dehumanize both parties, and issue in further violence. It tends to move in spiral fashion so that each "gain" achieved by violence risks being wiped out by the greater violence it unleashes.

Pacifists read this from history, often gathering the evidence from warriors themselves.

> I made a mistake. Without doubt, an oppressed multitude had to be liberated. But our method only provoked further oppression and atrocious massacres. My living nightmare is to find myself lost in an ocean of red with the blood of innumerable victims. It is too late now to alter the past, but what was needed to save Russia were ten Francis of Assisi's.[22]

Such is the testimony of Vladimir Ilyich Lenin. The pacifist argument continues that recourse to deadly violence is taken for lack of imagined, discerned, or prepared-for alternatives. But such alternatives, nondeadly alternatives, can be created, and in fact have a lively history paralleling the history of violence, as Lenin belatedly acknowledged.[23]

The other subtradition, the "just-war tradition," is poorly named. It is not really about "just wars." Like an "armed peace," it is something of an oxymoron, even by its own norms. It is not about the justification of war as a recurring human event. It is about the morally permissible use of exceptional, deadly violence in stringently limited ways, in war or elsewhere. It begins from and retains nonviolence as the moral norm. But it accepts that some tragic settings may justify an exception to the norm. The exception must safeguard, in an admittedly ironic way, what the norm itself seeks—the protection and promotion of life. Augustine, key theologian in this subtradition, puts it succinctly: "War and conquest are a sad necessity in the eyes of [people] of principle, yet it would be still more unfortunate if the unjust should dominate the just."[24] Participation in the use of violence is thus always an agonized participation, one that tries first to prevent killing altogether (usually with the deterring effect of military or police force) and then to limit the deadly violence used, proportionately and discriminately, if it *is* necessary. Moral courage for such action is required, but it is never a matter of moral heroism. It is a matter of "a burdened conscience and a sense of tragic necessity deliberately chosen."[25] The bearer of death, even when acting in self-defense and defense of others, feels the painful deviation from a strict *imitatio Christi* ethic. Wearing a crucifix while bearing arms is a haunting incongruity. The just warrior knows it, cannot shake it, and lives with it as a matter of real, although regrettable, responsibility.[26]

The arguments for limited, exceptional violence are also two: theological-ethical and ethical-prudential. Theologically, there is a human vocation to care for creation and realize basic human values—justice, freedom, security, peace. Among other places, this calling is expressed in the moral command to love God, and neighbor as self.[27] The welfare of others, including the enemy, is placed in the same framework as one's own and guided by the same standards. But in the fractured society of fallible, contentious, and often brutal human beings, the love command may point in directions that are at odds with one another. It certainly means "do the neighbor no harm," including the enemy neighbor. It also means "protect the neighbor from harm," the enemy included. But what should be done when some neighbors clearly intend the harm of their neighbors? Just-war adherents make a moral case for the lesser evil of limited killing, done to protect neighbors in those settings where violence is already the cruel reality. Like the pacifist, the just-war advocate sees protecting the innocent and securing basic values as echoes of God's own hopes for creation. The just warrior differs from the pacifist only in that the strong presumption against the use of deadly force is temporarily overridden. (The conspiracy against Hitler comes to mind, as does the present struggle of Namibian guerrillas against South African occupation forces. A permanent implementation of just-war views is the well-trained police force, at least in those societies where the police are not simply the private army of the dominant class.)

Just war's prudential argument shares the pacifist abhorrence of violence and even agrees that violence tends to breed violence. But precisely to check escalating violence, the just warrior argues that controlled violence in the short run can be effective for establishing conditions preferable in the long run. (Had it not been met with counterviolence, Nazism would have meant a ghastly future for even more millions.)

The emphasis here, that both subtraditions hold to the same norm and share "a searching distrust of violence,"[28] is intentional. The familial roots of these moral siblings are accented because there has been considerable historical slippage in the case of just war. The clear presumption against even exceptional violence has slid or been pushed under a presumption that warfare or other state-sponsored violence (such as capital punishment or police actions) is morally obligatory for Christian citizens when conducted by a legitimate authority (a prince, king, or queen; a President or Congress). Then the presumptive force of the original question is lost: "May a Christian ever take part in lethal violence against another of God's children?" Or, in the form of Aquinas' *quaestio*: "Is fighting in war always a sin?"[29]

The original just-/unjust-war position, within touching distance of the pacifist's, can be called "selective conscientious participation." (The Christian can, in some cases, under stringent conditions, using justifiable means, with right intention, kill.) This contrasts with the pacifist's "conscientious objection" to all killing. It also contrasts with the nonpacifist, who initially presumes in favor of state-sponsored violence but then finds the morality of a particular war or police action too repugnant to sustain the presumption. For many, Vietnam was such a case, a case of "selective conscientious objection."

Conclusions. Three historical notes follow from the foregoing.

1. Neither subtradition has been the majority view by which most Christians have been living, at least since Constantine.

2. The majority view has been participation in "national-interest wars" and crusades[30]—wars and other actions in which security or some other cause was regarded as too central to be qualified by moral categories. Here the moral universe is reduced to just cause plus utility: "Are we right?" and "What do we need to do to win?" By contrast, just war requires justification of cause and means in each strategic and tactical phase.[31] Negatively stated: if you have to commit a war crime to win the war, morally your side should lose the war and you should not obey those orders. Precisely that principle was upheld in the Nuremberg trials, although it bears recalling that it was upheld by the winners for the losers! (No trial was held for the Allied bombing of Dresden.)[32]

3. Nuclear weapons have forged an alliance of pacifists and just-/unjust-war adherents. Many, probably most, of the latter are now nuclear pacifists. They still hold the just-war premise that some uses of deadly force may be legitimate in some cases, but their conclusion is the pacifist one, that nuclear weapons may never be justifiably used. The salient criteria are still the just-war criteria, proportionality and immunity or discrimination. These and other just-war criteria post a "No" to nuclear arms that moves in next to the pacifist's blanket rejection.

We must be clear and precise. It is not that just warriors have suddenly been converted to the pacifist version of the jointly held norm (unexceptional nonviolence as a way of life). Nor that the theological orientations no longer matter, or differ. Rather, the prudential judgments of just warriors have converged with the judgments of pacifists in those cases where lethal violence could take the feared shape of the mushroom firecloud. This convergence, together with the adherence to their common norm, means a shared perspective. The shared normative perspective in turn presses Christians to devote foremost attention to security systems that are essentially nonviolent, yet forceful. The focus would not be on weapons and their potential. If they are used at all, they would be used only as a final, tragic, temporary recourse. Even then, missiles from the nuclear quiver, and any other weapons of mass destruction, would be ineligible and unavailable. The moral norm and the awesome peril of modern weapons push, not so much for an alternative to deterrence as such, but for an alternative to nuclear deterrence. That is, they push for the development of nonviolent, or minimally violent, nonnuclear security systems.

Strategic Considerations and the Churches

My effort thus far has included a description of the nuclear dilemma and the formulation of a normative perspective from which to respond. Now the subject is thinking as best I can about strategy and its components. Detailed strategy itself is beyond the possibilities here, but brief consideration of the key elements and the role of the churches is not.

An eschatological faith. Like other dimensions of policy issues, strategy for Christians has both theological and prudential ingredients. The former is more decisive for the basic orientation. I begin with that.

There is an eschatological "itch" that issues from Christian faith. God's future (the "eschaton") has power to shape the present and bring the yearnings of the past to fulfillment. The past is not only not dead; it and the present are not yet finished. We are among the actors in that drama, part of the straining forward that is hope, sharing the hunch that nuclear reality and the overwhelming condemnation of its facts are not the final facts. *Reality for Christians is New Creation*, the Peaceable Kingdom, a consummate harmony in which the well-being of each creature is part of the security of all. Christian moral norms themselves arise from this envisioned reality already caught sight of in Jesus.

It is immediately obvious that present reality, by contrast, is a jarring shortfall, perhaps only a lively rumor of New Creation. The present world is nonetheless infinitely cherished by God, a God who struggles to realize all its possibilities for life and fend off its potential for death, including the terminal death of the Bomb. Every hint of new creation amid the old, and all the redeemable possibilities of a fractured world, thus become matters of Christian response and responsibility, tastes of shalom to be shared and savored.

Living with the realities of both "new" and "old" creation means much tension for the Christian life, for it means that a restless, eschatological faith is set in a world that admits only limited possibilities at any given moment. That in turn is reason for a *spectrum* of Christian responses to virtually any public issue. At least for any complex issue, such as transnational security, no *one* action or position can give expression to all that a transcendent norm asks. Some contemplated actions will be severely qualified by the conditions of the present age. They will be taken with an eye to political feasibility and effectiveness. In Christian perspective, such actions should be considered, just as the bishops considered conditioned nuclear deterrence. Yet the same restless faith will also call for other actions, some of them *not* viable for policy formation *under current conditions*, even though they may add a gram to a scale that will register a very different result in the future. For the moment, these latter actions are pure witness to the Peaceable Kingdom, and have their integrity as that. The salient point, however, is that the character of Christian faith itself, as an eschatological faith, means a wide range of appropriate peacemaking actions, a spectrum of responses to nuclear reality. In general, how might that appear, as Christian strategy?

Elements of strategy: plural voices. The intractability of the nuclear dilemma has all the marks of a literal dead end, given present perspectives and institutions. Any breakthrough probably requires both creative incremental *and* radical actions and a plurality of voices. That accords with Christian strategy.

The reasons are theological as well as prudential. Some actions will be the kind of measures that conserve the relative good still present in "old" creation as common grace and blessing (like fragile, but real, protection and security). Other actions will be more dramatic measures that uncompromisingly display the powerful lure of peace as pure, heedless, self-sacrificing nonviolence.[33] For the issue at hand, the former measures mean looking around in nuclear reality to spy out what possibilities might be found or created for wiggling to somewhere else. They are gradual changes, many hardly noticed, that, after a period of time, might "suddenly" present a new constellation, like the slow turning of a kaleidoscope. The more radical measures are the dramatic moves that ignite human imagination, fire human hearts, illumine a new set of possibilities, and show the way for striking out on different paths and enlarging the circle of the politically viable. Both express dimensions of peacemaking. Both are utterly necessary. A comprehensive strategy fosters both.

There is, no doubt, much tension here. Some Christians will be moved by eschatological faith to a resounding, unequivocal, incontrovertible "No!" to the creation and possession of nuclear arms, not to mention any contemplated use of them. Those arms reveal a shocking evil in the human soul that must be exposed and named.

> If my moral sensitivity were not as dulled as my imagination, there would be for me something more staggering than the prospect of nuclear holocaust: the actuality of our total collective preparedness to inflict that annihilation on others. ... With megakill ... an unspeakable ghastliness of intent for a hundred-million fold murder is there.[34]

Nuclear arms also represent idolatry. Weapons of mass destruction mirror what has been the master image of North Atlantic humanity since at least the Enlightenment, the image of mastery itself.[35] They reflect an aberrant quest for identity through domination,[36] a quest for control that will use even threatened annihilation as justifiable means. Mastery, control, domination, and its flip side, the haunting fear of weakness and vulnerability—this is a disposition that by another name is idolatry. The currency may read "In God We Trust." The weapons give that the lie. We trust in our powers to control and intimidate.

Or, to recognize the reality from a different angle: when a nation's cause is so worthy that the nation will sanction plans to sacrifice the lives of tens of thousands, even millions, of both foes and friends, that is idolatry in the guise of patriotism.[37]

When "inactive" nuclear weapons ironically irradiate the presence of mind- and soul-boggling evil and illumine an idolatrous trust, those discoveries need to be vigorously announced in the public square. So does the corollary—the rejection, utter rejection, of the weapons. They are a blasphemy and an indignity of monstrous proportions. By comparison, golden calves hardly qualify as dangerous idols! Christian voices need to, and will, say that.

At the same time, the same eschatological faith loves this present world and seeks its healing. This will mean some acceptance of its current limits and acknowledgment that the possibilities at hand do not yet include those of our most ardent hopes. And even when evil and idolatry *are* named, it remains to respond in more ways than the (necessary) yelling. For strategy on nuclear issues, this means finding ways that have a political chance among openly distrusting parties. It means inevitable risk, but also caution, in arms control and disarmament. It probably means that alliance of apostles of nonviolence with deterrence minimalists, since *some* form of deterrence is likely until a commanding alternative can be fashioned. Such gradualism, caution, and calculation are registered by some Christians in the same moment as others cry out the unconditioned "No!" to nuclear arms. That is real tension! Yet the plurality of voices and the spectrum of response are theological necessities for a faith that knows both "new" and "old" creation, the Peaceable Kingdom and "peace of a sort."

The same plurality and spectrum can be argued on prudential grounds. It is prudentially stupid to ignore, marginalize, or extinguish a utopian witness. The moment when most are entrenching behind walls of fear and clutching at diminishing hopes is precisely the moment that some need to dream more grand dreams and nurture greater hopes. By doing so, voice is given more future chances than the hope-dashing nuclear dilemma would otherwise admit. By anticipating possibilities, the possibilities themselves are brought onto the horizon, distant horizon though it be.

The utopian witness actually enlarges the prudential quest. The quest is the calculation of reasonably expected and hoped-for results, given the best survey that one can make of present and foreseen possibilities. But the quest is invariably cast on the narrower calculation: What way out of the nuclear dilemma might be found, given the present, plainly competitive, deeply suspicious parties? A broader measure asks, What needs to be done to alter the parties themselves and change the range of political possibilities? Both questions are prudential. The latter is stimulated by a more encompassing, even utopian, vision.

Elements of strategy: timelines and conversio morum. "The end of political action is, after all, to affect [people's] deeper convictions."[38] Statecraft is, in part, "soulcraft."[39] What elements of strategy are about "people's deeper convictions"?

Any breakthrough on the nuclear dilemma probably requires a *conversio morum*, a gradual transformation of life, especially moral perspective and habit. Its more dramatic form is *metanoia*, a new mentality and orientation that rather suddenly issues in different actions. Neither happens just because it is necessary, however. They may not happen at all. Yet, over the span of human history, moral transformation on great issues has happened with some frequency to cultures, peoples, individuals. Even long-entrenched arrangements have waned (like slavery) and others have taken form. The new arrangements in turn have affected peoples' convictions by channeling their behavior. We shape institutions and they shape us.

In the case of altering nuclear reality, I will illustrate one social requisite and one matter of moral character.

The nation-state's identity is not quite as Max Weber wrote in *Politics as a Vocation*—the state is defined by its relation to violence, as the sole entity arrogating to itself the power to use violence *legitimately*.[40] It gets to determine which violent acts are crimes and which aren't! There are other elements of identity (as Weber also knew); in any case, the state's cornering of authority for using violence was to secure its *minimal* use. The state sought to prevent and control violence in the realm.

But it is precisely nation-states that fail to minimize and control *international* violence.[41] On the contrary, they are its chief perpetrators. At the same time, nuclear reality, like the Flood, leaves all borders awash. The modern nation-state cannot, because of the nature of its and its foe's weapons, guarantee its own security. It cannot effectively defend itself against destruction by these weapons. (This knowledge is the heart of deterrence, incidentally.)

This means that conceiving security on the nation-state scheme is now more an impediment than a contribution to genuine security. The nation-state will hardly dissolve, of course. It may be almost as unlosable as nuclear knowledge! But that is poor reason not to move toward both local and transnational ways of addressing what is genuinely a planetary issue.

Needed, among other things, is the delegitimating of state-sponsored violence. This requires cultural and behavioral transformation on a vast scale. The identity of citizens of the modern world has been tightly bound to a nation-state identity and to a willingness to let nation-state sovereignty reign. State-sponsored violence operates on a moral leash that is far longer than any the citizenry would accept under other auspices. At the "vigorous ringing of the chauvinist bell,"[42] masses clamor to do what in other settings they find repulsive—kill when someone tells them to kill.

To move away from easy legitimation of state-sponsored violence requires, among other strategies, the long, slow cultivation of moral character. In this instance, it should include the inculcation of a sense of planetary citizenship, of "neighbor" as a genuinely universal term. The character and loyalties of the citizenry are as critical to security as any of the hardware itself. *Conversio morum* is a necessary element *of* strategy.

We must not be naive. It is silly to look to "hearts and minds" change alone, or to any strategy resting primarily in educational and evangelical appeals. More push than that is needed. It is just as silly to think that great behavioral changes are chiefly the results of insight and planning. Social reality is far too complex to sustain that notion. It is also foolish not to recognize that even success in shifting citizen identity from nation to world does not remove the question of how to minimize use of violence, but only relocates it at a transnational level. (In the case of nuclear arms, probably a better location, to be sure.)

Possible pitfalls of naiveté acknowledged, I must go on to say that strategy wanders into ineffectiveness if people's deepest convictions do not support it. The state of moral character matters immensely for effective strategy. This means that strategy should self-consciously work for the gradual transformation of character so that the patterns of mind and habits of life that brought us the nuclear dilemma might cease to hold the day. To draw one more time on Kennan's reflections: "It is [people's] ingrained habits and assumptions ... , and above all [people] in government, which alone can guarantee any enduring state of peaceful relations among nations."[43]

Transformation of character and institutions takes time. Sound strategy on so major an issue as nuclear reality gathers in the near term and the far. It is prudentially unwise and theologically errant to pose peacemaking choices as if they were either short-term, moderate steps within the grasp of immediate realization, or long-term, grand goals whose achievement would mean a different way of life. Those are not mutually exclusive choices; they are mutually related complementary ones.

Elements of strategy: the people's participation. A comprehensive strategy needs everybody. It is obviously the work of policymakers, scientists, and politicians. It is every bit as much the work of educators, artists, liturgists, media personnel, parents, and all the tenders of society's institutions of moral formation and habit.

Perhaps this is the place to underscore the difference between peace-thinking and war-thinking, even war-thinking directed to peacekeeping. Peace-thinking derives from peacemaking as a participatory enterprise that needs and accepts the widest range of gifts. It includes children, the elderly, and the generations between. It happens in homes and schools and at the workplace, recreation place, and worship place. There are no places where it is inappropriate in one or another of its many forms, no boundaries that it should not cross. Moreover, the forms are so diverse that no one is without some contribution and responsibility. This holds without respect to race, creed, class, sex, nationality, occupation, age, or ideological persuasion. Peacemaking is the most universal of human undertakings.

War-thinking, even directed to its proper vocation of peacekeeping, is a sharp contrast. When peace is conceived with a military focus, it becomes an activity essentially tied to one major means—weapons and the threat of violence. It channels those who undertake peacekeeping into physical, mental, and organizational conformities of all kinds, for the sake of the mission itself. It can only include some of the populace, not all, and then in tightly controlled ways. And it can only use some of the gifts of those who are the peacekeepers.

The point is not to pan the place of the military for peacekeeping. It is to say that peace-thinking, for peacemaking, needs and can include everybody. The place of the military is one subset among many. A comprehensive strategy works with the wider possibilities opened up by peace-thinking.[44]

In summary, the total economy of a strategy that might crack the nuclear dilemma includes:

- The presence of voices often at odds with one another and a spectrum of diverse, sometimes conflicting actions; what counts is not the conflict, but that the voices and actions have moral and theological integrity as well as prudential soundness.
- A transformation of persons, institutions, and policies, on a timeline that has both short- and long-term segments.
- Participation in peacemaking that makes room in myriad ways for everybody.

Role of the churches. Much has already been said, since the subject has been strategy in Christian perspective. But is there a particular role or emphasis, a certain posture and line of action, the churches should pursue on the long journey to outlaw nuclear weaponry?

In 1956, President Eisenhower wrote to a friend that one day the United States and the Soviet Union would have to "meet at the conference table with the understanding that the era of armaments has ended, and the human race must conform its action to this or die."[45] But armaments—and violence—will reign if there is no social alternative. A world of crippling fear and deranging danger will continue unless concrete arrangements of a different sort stand in for nuclear reality. The churches can have a part, albeit modest, in the quest.

Again there are theological and prudential dimensions. An eschatological faith requires eschatological communities.[46] The church is called to live in "old" creation *on the terms of* new creation. This means displaying the character of the Peaceable Kingdom in the church's own life, by following the way of Jesus. What is the nature of that in a nuclear world?

The basepoint for the church's participation is its norm, nonviolence,[47] drawn from Jesus' embodiment of God's Way. *The public policy vocation is to seek the most* direct *expressions of that norm.* Nonpacifist churches have too long made the *exception* to nonviolence the point of participation in the public arena. That is, their "peace" ethic has focused on deadly force and its threat, on such issues as the prevention and limitation of war and Christian participation in it. This makes the *exception to the norm* (controlled violence as the exception to nonviolence) *the agenda itself.* "Peace of a sort," armed peace, then, sets the terms for the churches' public participation, rather than the eschatological call to give direct social expression to the Peaceable Kingdom.

What *direct* expressions of the churches' normative perspective would also be prudentially wise in a nuclear world?

1. The churches should and can display the varied dimensions of peacemaking and communicate both its nearly intractable difficulties and its irrepressible lure. The churches have, deep in the faith, a notion of peace (*shalom*)[48] far richer and more fulfilling than peace as the absence of social conflict. Thus they are in a position to lift up what I have discussed earlier as peace-thinking, rather than war-thinking. The education has begun. It must be pursued. Christian faith is also aware of the tragic and the sinful and can train people in the realism necessary for effective peacemaking, an ability to face squarely both the beauty and the terror of life in a nuclear age. At the same time, the faith clings tenaciously to a vision that generates hope and keeps history open to possibilities heretofore unrealized.

Perhaps the way to picture this peacemaking is with an image suggested by John Paul II, that of cathedral-building. Peacemaking, like a cathedral, requires a grand vision, careful planning, thousands of efforts with single stones of many shapes, myriad forms arranged in myriad ways, transgenerational patience, some "gargoyle humor" to exorcize the demons of violence, occasional new starts (cathedrals fall into disrepair—or are bombed!), a steady faith, and a thirst for beauty and truth that experiences moments of ecstasy and satisfaction but remains unquenchable until the task is finished in some future generation's celebration. The nuclear world needs this kind of faith, patience, vision, and tenacity.

2. The churches should and can nurture the kinds of persons who, in a genuinely local *and* transnational institution, live freed from the assumptions of war. The nuclear world yearns in stupored silence for visible social zones of nonviolent relationships and habits, institutions with identities other than nation-state identities, and communities, international and inclusive, that know there is a "truer" human history than the history of violence, that show life can be lived by the habits of peace, and that have as their vocation the forming of peaceful human character. Communities, in short, that are agents of the necessary, but not assured, *conversio morum.* The existence of such communities and institutions, the churches among them, is good news in a nuclear age. They are, concretely, outposts of hope.

3. The churches should and can make the public case for nonviolence as viable public policy. To be sure, apologetics are necessary. It seems that violence and nonviolence are invariably measured by a double standard. Nonviolence is dismissed by many because, in their judgment, it "won't work," meaning that it cannot be shown in advance not to fail. But violence, they assume, does "work." And its many failures don't count against it as much as the imagined failures of untested nonviolence. The churches should make clear that the cost, risks, and failures of nonviolence are frequently measured by stricter standards than the cost, risks, and failures of violence; this despite the apt remark of the Catholic bishops that before a nonviolent security system be dismissed as impractical and unrealistic, "we urge that it be measured against the almost certain effects of a major war."[49]

More than apologetics are in order, however. Now the chief challenge for the churches and other institutions holding to the norm of nonviolence is to show, in an expansion on the tradition of Gandhi and King, that nonviolence has a strong element of social coercion as well as moral persuasion, is a historical and public force as well as an "interior" and attitudinal reality, is assertive rather than capitulative, and is practical and flexible, with varied tactics, rather than otherworldly and rigid. The churches can show that this is not as absent, either in history or in current imagination and planning, as most people believe.[50]

The churches do have a particular role in the wider economy of a strategy to break the nuclear dilemma. In a nuclear world the future of both pacifism and just-war understanding, the future of the social form of the eschatological itch, and, not least, the future of Christian realism is active, creative, forceful nonviolence.

TWO

Christian Realism and the Russians

Ronald H. Stone

*"H*ow ought American Christians relate to the Russians?" The question is a major one for American Christian social ethics. It involves the question of what church policy should be toward the Russian empire and toward Christians in that empire. It also involves what individual Christians should do in their roles as citizens, as members of voluntary associations, as economic agents, and as leaders of the American empire. It is a fateful question, since the future of many peoples of the world is involved in the answer that American Christians give. It is an awesome question, for inappropriate answers by nuclear-armed American Christians could end most of human life in the Northern Hemisphere and probably in the world. The answers that contemporary American Christians give will determine, to some extent, the options that their children are given for wrestling with the question. If we can answer the question wisely, our children may have resources not only to live, but also to improve on our answers. If the question is answered poorly, our children may not have an option of wrestling with the question, or alternatively, the legacy of hatred and animosity mixed with technology and fear may overwhelm them.

Parents and teachers have known for some time that the fears of nuclear war haunt our children. Studies by American psychiatrists have shown that the fears of Russian children are similar to the fears of American children.[1] The Cold War itself has consequences for the lives of our

Ronald H. Stone, Professor of Social Ethics, Pittsburgh Theological Seminary, Pittsburgh, Pennsylvania.

children. For some, these fears are translated into sleepless nights and a pervasive distrust of the future.

On a visit to a Pioneer children's camp outside Moscow, I danced folk dances with the Russian children. Rain had turned their festive paper decorations into sodden, colorful, shapeless masses and their playground into mud. We Americans enjoyed their cookies and fruit-flavored drink in their cabins and danced as best we could in the aisles between their bunks. Instant community was formed, and they presented their American guests with small gifts. As we left the pleasant camp, the macabre sense of my friends in Pittsburgh designing weapons to threaten these children overwhelmed me. I realized, too, that the parents of some of these Russian children were working on weapons that reduced my children to nuclear hostages for American foreign policy.

Realism about the Russians begins with a sense that our children are hostages. The terror and the unacceptability of this threatened nuclear holocaust are primary. We also know that all our churches and all their churches are at risk in this confrontation. The meanings of our civilizations in our libraries, our universities, our theaters, our museums, even our collective human memory, and the genetic pool of human life are all at stake in this fearsome race into nuclear competition on land, in the sea, in the atmosphere, and in space.

Christian Realism

This essay explores how the tradition of Christian realism can shed light on the problem confronting humanity in the USA-USSR nuclear competition. The choice of exploring the problem within one ethical tradition reflects the sense that applied Christian ethics works within different traditions. There is no escape from utilizing a tradition. As individuals, we are morally conditioned by the moral ethos of our families and our communities. As members of the church, we are shaped by the part of the tradition of the church that our denomination takes most seriously. As Christian ethicists, we stand, even though critically, within particular traditions relative to our inheritance and choices we have made.

The tradition of Christian realism in ethics is broad, including immense influence in many denominations, seminaries, universities, and public life. Three major Christian ethicists who have self-consciously and publicly identified with this tradition are Reinhold Niebuhr, John C. Bennett, and Roger L. Shinn. The tradition, as it focuses on the Soviet Union, is enriched by Hans J. Morgenthau, a philosopher of international politics, and George Kennan, a historian of Soviet-American diplomacy. The writings of these five Christian realists form the tradition for these ethical reflections.

The tradition is characterized by (a) the tendency to avoid moral absolutes in international politics; (b) a sharp rejection of the neglect of elements of national power competition that has characterized some writers on international relations; (c) skepticism about claims for human perfection or moral progress in human affairs; (d) a passion for the study and interpretation of the history of political affairs; and (e) the conviction that an explicit conception of humanity in theological perspective is helpful to political thought.[2]

The viewpoint of Christian realism about the Soviet-American competition is rather somber. The competition between these two empires for the advancement of their respective understandings of their interests is assumed to be a constant. The definitions of their interests may change, but the promotion of their own interests is rooted in the ambitions, egoism, and fears of human nature. Nationalism is seen as a strong force in the modern world, as a force that tends to override ideology or the solidarity of either workers or coreligionists in times of crisis. The realm of international relations is seen as being rather chaotic. There are mutual and multilateral agreements that reduce the anarchy. But there is not an international authority that can regulate the behavior of the superpowers. Although nuclear war would be an unmitigated world disaster and immoral by all decent moral standards, it is a possibility. If relations between the Soviet Union and the United States continue to deteriorate, while the militarization of the world continues to escalate, nuclear war moves closer toward a probability.

Given the lack of a world community, the anarchy of world affairs, the immaturity of national governments, and the insecurities of human nature, the prospects for transcending the competition of the Cold War are dim. The reduction of the tensions of the Cold War will need to be achieved by the slow process of working on the historical factors that have given rise to the state of belligerency. The realist philosophy of international relations perceives the major USA-USSR common interest as being the avoidance of wars of mass destruction. There are common interests in working jointly to prevent ecological collapse. There are some common interests in economic relations. There are common interests in cultural, educational, and scientific exchanges. The two would prefer different social structures in the developing nations. Their ideologies clash in world competition. They have contrasting goals in the future unification and orientation of Western Europe and in the orientation of China. Interests diverge in the Middle Eastern crises. The Central Asian instabilities of Afghanistan, Iran, Pakistan, and India are all subject to the competing interests of the superpowers. The forces of democratic institutions and multinational corporations are in tension with Soviet institutional and financial interests.

Christian realism cannot surrender either the moral mandate for peace-making or the grim reality of international competition. The competition, however, in a technological age reduces our children and everything else to nuclear hostages.

The Empire

The Russian empire stretches across Eurasia. An American citizen can experience it in a limited way on the Trans-Siberian Railroad. At the nineteenth-century station in Moscow, he takes on the role of observer-participant as he purchases some bread for the trip from the aged woman who has lived through the Stalin era into modern Soviet life. Also purchasing bread is a young wounded veteran carrying his hand-carved cane from Afghanistan. The American reflects on his own friend who never returned from Vietnam and he feels the tragedy of European colonization of the Asian populations.

The train at first travels north, parallel to the Yaroslav Road. Once past industrial Moscow the homes become low, wooden houses—many with ornate carvings decorating their weather-beaten window frames and low-peaked roofs. The train parallels the road that for centuries the czars and their retinues would travel on their pilgrimage to Zagorsk, the spiritual center of ancient Muscovy. Along the way, certain towns are graced by large churches, which mark the overnight stopping places of the royal pilgrimages. Zagorsk itself (the monastery and seminary) provides a setting that the American, a seminary professor, finds architecturally and spiritually moving. The seminarians from Zagorsk that the American professor has been able to have discussion with in Moscow, East Berlin, and Pittsburgh have impressed him with their brightness, their dedication, and their ready wit. The American, a Calvinist, has found their sense of the church as the arena in which Christ is realized in incarnation to be moving but limited. Of course, they are limited both by their Orthodox heritage, which has, since Constantine, been directed by Caesar, and by the current reality of the power of an officially atheist party dominating not only the state, but also, through the state, every social institution. In contrast, his Calvinism seems worldly to them; they suspect that his democratic worldliness has lost much of its spiritual vitality.

As the train rolls through the Ural Mountains and the hours stretch into days and nights, the American becomes aware of entering Asia. The Urals remind him of his native Allegheny Mountains, which were also a significant barrier to the European population until the nineteenth century. The Soviet Union, governed now from Moscow and not the European-leaning St. Petersburg, is a huge empire. It stretches over 8.5 million square miles; it is 5,500 miles long—the ride from Moscow to the East coast would take ten days. It is 2,700 miles wide from the Arctic to the Central Asian deserts. It encompasses one-sixth of the land mass of the world and 260 million persons. The official Soviet publications report the existence of 130 nationalities living in the USSR.

Passengers on the train reflect the diversity of the empire. They invite the American and the young German who shares his compartment to join them in toasting *mir* (peace) with their cognac and vodka. A fisherman and his wife from Kamchatka Peninsula in the far east share their smoked salmon with them, and the conversation about customs, travels, and peace extends into the long evenings of spring daylight. The American recalls that nowhere in his travels around the world has he met people who are more generous with their food and drink than the Russians. Often they have spontaneously invited him to their tables in restaurants and occasionally strangers have invited him to their homes. The metal statue dominating the hill overlooking Tbilisi, the capital of Georgia, is a female figure holding a bowl in one hand and a sword in the other. On a previous trip, years ago, an old Georgian soldier explained that the statue symbolized wine for guests and death to invaders. Tourists are regarded as guests.

The Russians on the train, of whom many are technocrats, are intoxicated with technology, which is associated with the power of the state and with the modernization wrought by the Communists. They also respect American technology. In the dining car, the bill is calculated with an abacus, but the pride of the manager is a solar-powered Texas Instruments calculator. But like the American, they, too, know of the ambiguity of the calculating, transforming technological culture. Leaning against the train window, a mathematics instructor from Central Asia says softly, as he watches the trainloads of timber and coal pass, "Development means exploitation."

The train does not pass through Gorky and the site of Sakharov's banishment. Gorky himself, after whom the city is named, had been unable to restrain Stalin's murderous ways, and his pen name, Gorky, means bitter. Whether this giant of Russian-approved literature under Stalin fell to Stalin's madness or, as officially proclaimed, was a victim of an anti-Stalin plot, his name reflects the bitter fight of the intellectuals who have striven under the czars and the commissars to defend human rights in the Soviet Union. One hundred fifty miles north of Gorky a toast is raised by a German and an American to Gorky and to Sakharov. The German cautions the American not to speak much about Sakharov and human rights or of peace dissidents while in the train compartment because some of the compartments, probably those assigned to Westerners, are bugged. The other American on the train is less cautious, and one of his traveling companions, a Russian soldier, is lectured to by a man in a trench coat at a railroad stop. When the soldier returns to the compartment, he will only discuss the weather and his children for the next two days; no more politics are discussed with the other American traveling in second class.

The train stops in Omsk, and the American reflects on the bitter fighting here between the Czech divisions who, in 1918, controlled the Trans-Siberian Railroad, allied with the White forces against the Red Army. The anomaly of a British battalion from Middlesex wintering in Omsk, supporting the regime of Admiral Kolchak as he alienated the sympathetic Russian peasantry, is typical of this confused period in American-Soviet relations. American forces were in Siberia for a year and a half, thousands of miles away from the scene of significant fighting around Omsk and in the Urals. The British had hoped to overthrow the Reds; the Japanese had their eye on territorial gains in the East; the French saw possible success for White forces under French leadership. The Americans thought that they were intervening to assist the Czechs, who were supposed to be moving across Siberia to embark on transport to the western front. The supposed American enemy was German-Austrian escaped prisoners. American intelligence was bad as to the facts of the case, but orders were clear that the Americans were not to fight the Russians, but to aid the Czechs and protect military stores at Vladivostok. The allied intervention in the North at Murmansk and Archangel was similarly confused, and the Americans, under British command, were put to purposes for which they were ill equipped. However much one may bewail American naiveté in these incursions, the fact remains that for a year and a half, when the Reds were struggling to solidify their revolution, American troops—although not many—were in the Soviet Union. George Kennan, who regards the intervention as folly, quotes from the *Literary Digest* on the intervention: "Some ... might have liked us more if we had intervened less ... some might have disliked us less if we had intervened more, but ... having concluded that we intended to intervene no more and no less than we actually did, nobody had any use for us at all."[3]

This confused period from 1918 to 1920, in which the Communists secured control of much of the old Russian empire, must be regarded as the low point in Soviet-American relations. The Russians had not threatened the American revolution. Potential conflicts over territory on the western coast of North America were resolved by the czar, abandoning West Coast claims and the selling of Alaska to the United States in 1867. The United States expanded in the nineteenth century and the Russian empire expanded, the former to the West and the latter to the South and East until halted by the Japanese-Russian War negotiated in Portsmouth in 1905. The United States replaced Japan as the military force in part of Korea after World War II, but China, not Russia, was the primary challenge to American strength in that region. On their own common frontier of the Bering Strait, relations have been relatively calm.

Although the migration of native peoples between Siberia and Alaska has been rendered impossible by the Cold War, neither nation can regard the border through the Bering Strait as particularly troublesome. Fishing rights and different ecological standards occasionally are troublesome, but the border is practically as troublefree as the disarmed U.S.-Canadian border.

The two nations were allied in World War II, and both opposed the German empire in World War I, although at different times. The Hitler-Stalin short-lived pact was before U.S. entry into the war, and although it decimated claims of U.S. Communists to superior foreign policy, it has not left a great residue of ill will in the United States. The U.S. recognition of the *de jure* nature of the Communist rule of the Soviet Union was late, but in 1933 it came.

U.S. aid to the Soviet Union to defend itself and then to defeat Hitler was not determinative in the war effort but it helped. The pictures and memories of Russians and Americans meeting victoriously at the River Elbe cast a fond glow over the long-term portrait of adequate relations between the two empires. Russian cemeteries and ceremonies remind Americans that they bore the primary cost of defeating Hitler.

Military alliances depend on the threat of a common enemy. The defeat of Hitler and the Japanese empire left power vacuums all over the world. Both of the now victorious superpowers filled these vacuums as their plans and capacities permitted. Russian forces at the end of the war retained the traditional Russian empire, with the exception of Finland. In the East, they regained what they had lost to the Japanese at Portsmouth, plus Russian power solidified around eastern Germany and moved its borders westward, compensating a dependent Poland at the expense of Germany. Czechoslovakia was denied its independent role, but Austria was allowed to be neutral. Russian power, thwarted in Iran, registered gains over Rumania and Bulgaria but was stopped in Turkey, Greece, and Yugoslavia.

American domination and defense of western Europe was secured by American financial and military power, as were Japan and South Korea. Russian goals and policies for eastern Europe gradually became clear. The American inability to challenge significantly the power of the Red Army was confirmed as movements for change in Hungary, Czechoslovakia, and Poland were suppressed. The 1980s saw two empires—the American and the Russian—astride Europe under the NATO and Warsaw alliances.

World War II had exhausted the other empires of Europe—Britain, France, Belgium, Netherlands, and Portugal. They gradually let go of their colonial possessions, sometimes with grace and moderately smooth transitions, sometimes with costly wars. Both the United States and the Soviet Union abetted the decolonization process and sought influence in the former colonies. The competition of the two semicontinental empires became worldwide.

A Russian professor of political science and the American theologian chatted as the train picked up speed on the Omsk-to-Novosibirsk run. They both feared the terror of nuclear war as they showed each other pictures of their respective children in the dim light of the train's corridors. On the outcome of the world competition to date, they agreed that the United States had gotten the better of it. The Russian spoke of a northern country in which the Europeans were not reproducing themselves as rapidly as their Asiatic citizens. This northern empire was faced with a hostile China on the southeast, which still had territorial claims against the Soviet Union. In Europe, NATO was a formidable military and economic force. Although resolute in regarding the Soviet Union as the motherland of communism, other countries, by claiming to represent communism, blurred the image of a worldwide communism. The theologian argued that religion and nationalism, although essentially antagonistic to each other, often proved to be more attractive than communism. Capitalism, through the transnational corporations, was very much alive and often more active in transforming the world than was communism. The idealistic Marxist critique of capitalists' injustices leveled by the Russian could be agreed to by the theologian, but he expressed no sympathy for the idea that an international communism, led by Moscow, would be interesting to the world. Both were sympathetic to the revolution in Nicaragua that overthrew the Somoza regime; the American hoped for a U.S. policy that would accept it and prevent it from drawing too close to the Soviets.

Before the Russian professor detrained in Novosibirsk, they returned to the theme that between them personally there would be peace. They realized that little was accomplished by Russian critique of American racism or American critique of Russian failures in democratic virtues. They hoped for wisdom on both sides to let ideological critique recede, competition decline, and conflicts of real substance remain without being dangerously exploited. The Russian still expected the triumph of socialism; the American expected and hoped for various economic experiments and argued that mixed economies were preferable in developed countries.

Throughout south central Siberia, the train rolls slowly through the steppes. The simple, rural log cabins remind the American of his ancestral log cabin on the great plains of the American Midwest. Unfortunately, the climate and rainfall here are not equivalent to the lower latitudes of the American great plains. If only 15 percent of this great land mass is suitable for agriculture, the Russians have a geographic problem of great magnitude. The abundance of U.S. agriculture and the paucity of Russian agriculture provide one of the great opportunities for mutual benefit. Of course, trade is political, particularly with the centralized bureaucracy of the Soviet Union, and the arrangements will reflect and affect the political realities.

Novosibirsk, one of the major cities of Siberia, is burgeoning and industrial. Here the twentieth century has arrived with an explosion of development. The Novosibirsk Theatre of Opera and Ballet confronts the contemporary with the traditional. Here on the river Ob, in an industrial city of more than a million persons, up from a population of 5,000 in this century, the former Russian culture speaks to contemporary Siberia in terms that it loves. Roger Shinn commented on this clash after observing the Novosibirsk Ballet in Moscow:

> Prokofiev's "War and Peace," based on Tolstoy's novel, brought 125 singers on stage, with the French army in the wings. The audience exulted in the patriotism, pageantry, fire and thunder, and tender love story. I marveled that central Siberia could mount a show that only one or two American cities could rival. I marveled equally that an avowedly revolutionary society should stage an opera in so old-fashioned a style. As Harold C. Schonberg says of the comparable Bolshoi production, it "breathes a vanished age of opera."
>
> Even more surprising is the Novosibirsk ballet production of Tchaikovsky's "Sleeping Beauty." About 6,000 people—with others outside offering premium prices for a ticket—watched this ethereal fairy tale, performed with grace and wit in an utterly traditional manner. The production had nothing to do with Siberia, Moscow or the world of socialism and production figures. The audience was enthralled.[4]

In Irkutsk, on the shores of Lake Baikal, the deepest freshwater lake in the world, travelers from Asia meet. The city, except for its new dam and the arrival of technological development, is still nineteenth century. Log houses and nineteenth-century stucco buildings dominate the relaxed city center. Here at the station and in the international hotel on the banks of the beautiful river Angara, one meets travelers headed for Vladivostok, Ulan Bator, Sinkiang Uighur, Tashkent, as well as the cities back up the line—Perm, Omsk, and Novosibirsk. The names are as exotic to the American as Chicago's O'Hare Airport must be to a Russian, with planes bound for Indianapolis, Denver, Santa Fe, and St. Louis. There is a whole world out there in eastern Asia of which Americans know little and in which they can have only marginal influence. Looked on from Irkutsk, Russian policies are not enigmatic. They dominate Mongolia as they did not under the czars; their influence in China is less than it was in the early twentieth century, when they controlled the railroad through Manchuria— now they must go around China, not through it. They want to maintain their World War II gains over Japan and to challenge U.S. suzerainty over the Pacific Ocean but not at too great a risk. The tragedy of flight 007 remains shrouded in mystery. The command of Far Eastern air defenses has been shaken up, and the commander regarded as most responsible for the destruction of the civilian flight has himself been killed in a military-related "accident." The Russian determination to hold the line in Asia is clear. China promises to become the great Asian power. Its development, aided by American technology, is a clear threat to Russian Far Eastern interests.

The price of Russian hegemony in Afghanistan is seen in a military hospital compound in Nakhodka, where an American wandering in the streets sees hundreds of wounded Russian soldiers basking in the spring sun. Russian determination to secure its suzerainty in this bordering country cannot be doubted. The confusion in Iran made it easier for the Soviet Union to pursue its interests. The history of Russian nineteenth-century expansion in south central Asia under the czars was one of willingness to expand at the expense of the indigenous populations through sustained campaigns.

If reflections on a train ride represent the mode of observer-participant in Christian social ethical work, we must still return to the tradition we are exploring—Christian realism—to mine it for insights in preventing nuclear war between the two empires. George Kennan has, in speaking of realism, called Reinhold Niebuhr "the father of us all." So I want to consider here Niebuhr's insights into the relationship between the empires and their ideologies.

Christian Realism and the Cold War

Reinhold Niebuhr often wrote on the Soviet Union after his visit there in 1930. His writing stressed the traditional Russian aims of the new state. Its fascination with technology and its attacks on traditional religion threatened the spiritual character of the Russian people. His sharpest critiques of communism were written during the Stalin period. He saw the evil tyranny of Stalin linked both to the traditions in the Russian experience and to weaknesses in Communist political thought.

Like Morgenthau, Niebuhr saw no reasons to hope for a resolution of the Cold War. The Soviet Union and the United States were driven by disparate rivalries for domination to oppose each other. The conflict could last for a generation or more. He hoped that the stubborn facts of history would help both rivals to be less belligerent in their ideology. Neither Russian-type socialism nor American-type individualism would meet the real needs of the world.

His critiques of Marxist thought were usually couched in terms that made them instruments of ideological debate. He welcomed debate and creative competition between the two systems. His hopes were that, given time, the pretensions of both Russian communism and American individualism would wither and that Third World countries would find their own answers.

The authority of Russian communism was weakened by the pluralism within the Communist world. Gradually, the danger of the Soviet Union was seen not to be in its attractiveness as a model. The model was irrelevant to much of the world, and it was terribly flawed. The danger was that miscalculation would lead one of the superpowers to violate the partnership of managing the nuclear umbrella. The great dangers resided in a deterioration of the political relationship with the Soviet Union. The mitigation of the Cold War would be through the processes of diplomacy, negotiating what was negotiable and leaving the rest alone.

Although the danger rested in nuclear-armed competition in an anarchic world, the immediate solutions were neither disarmament nor world government. Nor could great shifts in the ideological debate be projected or planned. Niebuhr relied on reality to overcome the utopianism associated with Marxism. He hoped for the overcoming of the mixture of individualism and utopian nationalism that made the United States so dangerous. But even with a reduction of their respective utopian models, the competition between the two systems would continue for the foreseeable future.

He distrusted the American tendency to overrely on technology and the military. The Russian opponent was an ally in managing the nuclear terror and containing it. Diplomacy, and resistance where necessary and possible, could subtly move the United States into the future, where the problems, given the changes of history, might be reduced and handled.

On questions of disarmament, then, Niebuhr was not a dreamer. His own history had witnessed the difficulty of disarmament plans in the early twentieth century. The ban on nuclear testing in the atmosphere he regarded as a great achievement, as he thought the negotiations to stop the antiballistic missile race were a gain. The nonproliferation treaty seemed, to him, of dubious worth, as it represented the satiation of the "haves" and the repression of the "have-nots."[5] Community had to precede disarmament, or at least accompany it in its formation. The formation of that community was significantly begun in the work of UNESCO (United Nations Educational, Scientific, and Cultural Organization), in which he served as a U.S. delegate, but it finally required the moderation of the revolutionary ardor of communism, the development of the Third World, and wise statecraft on the part of the Atlantic Alliance. So there was no guarantee of peace.

The building of community, as seen in the work of UNESCO, was flawed. The flaws revealed the spiritual nature of contemporary humanity. Modern humanity had to find ways of continuing to build community across international borders and to avoid discouragement when it failed to complete the tasks. Niebuhr's comment on UNESCO stands as his attitude toward the building of world community.

> Here is an organization which seeks to realize the impossible: a world community. It must not regard this end as a simple possibility; but neither can it dismiss the task as an impossibility. It stands, therefore, constantly at the final limit of the human situation where the possible and the impossible are curiously intermingled and where it is difficult to distinguish between God's and our possibilities.[6]

Diplomacy

Like Reinhold Niebuhr, Hans Morgenthau knew that there will be no world peace without a world government. World government is impossible without a lot more world community than is on the horizon. He concluded his philosophy of international politics with the necessity of achieving peace through diplomatic accommodation. World community can be built best through diplomatic accommodation, and it is necessary to have a revitalized diplomacy now to secure what peace is possible and prevent nuclear war.

A revitalized diplomacy would be one divested of crusading spirits so that competing national interests could be compromised. The goals of foreign policy would be defined carefully in terms of the limits of real interests and available power. The perspectives of other nations would always be considered and the needs for compromises protecting those perspectives, recognized.

A revitalized diplomacy recognizing that peace between the superpowers is the sine qua non of diplomacy would not hold to abstract prerogatives of legal right at the sacrifice of political wisdom. It would be careful about claiming positions it cannot hold, and it would avoid strong commitments to weak allies. Diplomacy must subject the armed forces to the procedures of politics and not allow the military to set the political stage. The government of a republic must lead political opinion within the ethos of a country so that its policies are not disrupted by short-sighted passions, particularly those clamoring for conflict. A road to international peace through an accommodating diplomacy is not a romantic road, but the realists tend to regard it as the best opportunity.[7]

Church Policy

Peace has been discussed as peacemaking, the hard struggle to avoid armed conflict in the arena of international relations. The focus has been

45

on the two superpowers. Church statements may sometimes rest their pursuit of peace in the concept of *shalom*. The Hebrew term has a variety of meanings, but in church documents it usually means the wholeness and health of the human community. Christian realists are motivated by *shalom*, but their daily work involves them in seeking less and rejoicing in the partial victories of peacemaking that avoid war in an anarchic, nuclear-armed world.

So how ought the churches help American Christians relate to the Russians? First, in the most fundamental sense, the churches must preach the gospel, administer the sacraments, organize church life, and witness to the world so that the love of humanity for God is increased and the love of Christians for the neighbors is practiced. The church's healing ministry of reducing human pride and insecurity through faith is the most important contribution of the church. The spiritual health of the American people is central to securing the peace.

Second, the following six policies of the church can be highlighted for their importance in moving toward peace.

1. The church can teach its members to avoid a crusading spirit against the social-ideological systems of other nations. God is absolute and tolerates various human experiments; Christians are not called to execute righteous zeal against others. To this end, education about communism, exchanges with the Soviet Union, church publications that realistically analyze the need for cooperation, compromise, and competition with the Soviet Union are important.

2. The militarization of the U.S. economy and society must be reversed. To this end, the development of peace centers, programs, and thought is the work of the church. Particular policies that promote U.S. initiatives toward diplomatic reduction of armaments must be supported with tenacity. The movement for a negotiated mutual freeze on nuclear armaments is a good example of policies that need church support.

3. The development of American society through improved education, improved health, and improved welfare is the concern of the church. The stronger the social fabric of American society, the less attractive are Communist blandishments of improvement through totalitarian socialism. The social ills need to be corrected in their own right without reference to the Cold War, but the strengthening of American society obviously draws funds away from the frightfully expensive nightmare technology desired by the military-industrial-research complex.

4. The essential immorality of most wars, especially nuclear war, and reliance on nuclear deterrence must be a theme of church teaching and preaching.

5. The revitalization of a Christian commitment to democratic politics of participation, debate, and thought can help the peace movement within the church to become more political and produce a national consensus

and leadership that would make a policy of diplomatic accommodation for peace possible.

6. The church, because of its international character, is particularly well placed to help its members and some of the broader public understand social revolution and liberation theology. Domestic revolutions do not have to become fuel for the conflicts of the Cold War. An understanding of social revolution by American Christians can deny right-wing Americans national consensus for counterrevolutionary policies. The teachings of the churches about Central America, the sanctuary program, and the border watch in Nicaragua are all appropriate tools for this ministry.

The peace of God is a gift of grace known both in the United States and in the Soviet Union. The peace between the superpowers is precarious, but there are no vital issues threatening peace that cannot be accommodated now or in the future.

PART II.
The Third World

THREE

Making the World Safe for Transnational Capitalism?

Marvin Mahan Ellison

*T*he strengthening and celebrating of relationships are the quintessential religious activities. Critical questions must be asked, however, about the nature and moral quality of the relationships promulgated by particular religious perspectives and communities. Who and what are being strengthened and celebrated? There is, for example, a theology and ethic of apartheid, as well as a theology and ethic of resistance to apartheid. Christianity is not neutral about matters of life and death. Even when theological language speaks in general terms, at least implicitly there is a naming of *whose* life and *whose* death are of consequence.

This naming and the struggle to provide the conditions to support human life with dignity and meaning are matters of normative ethical significance that require both "true speech" and effective action. In giving credence to specific interests, moral convictions, and loyalties, religion functions either in an oppressive way by legitimating unjust social relations or in an emancipatory way by challenging dehumanizing dynamics.[1] A controversial claim by theologians of liberation is that the truthfulness of all theological statements is to be judged by whether the concrete well-being of persons and groups, most especially the powerless and marginalized, is promoted or thwarted. Christian theology is life-giving "good news" only insofar as it names and critiques the forces that diminish our common humanity and empowers right relationships within and among communities.[2]

Marvin Mahan Ellison, Professor of Christian Ethics, Bangor Theological Seminary, Bangor, Maine.

What structurally frustrates efforts to create genuine community across this planet is unrestrained economic power, which is becoming increasingly concentrated in fewer and fewer hands and remains staunchly resistant to public accountability. In *The Radical Imperative*, John Bennett argues that "a new debate is needed about economic institutions, and on a much more fundamental level" than his own generation had managed to sustain. Such a debate is called for precisely in recognition that capitalist economics consistently neglects social needs in pursuit of profits and generates "vast private economic empires whose power is only slightly tamed by community." The radicality of Bennett's call for a "return to economic ethics" becomes clear, however, only when his recommended test for judging the adequacy of addressing issues of economic justice is taken seriously. That test is whether "a new generation of persons concerned about Christian ethics" is willing and able "to press the socialistic questions even though they do not accept ready-made socialistic answers."[3]

To press the socialist option is to advocate economic democracy and the socialization of ownership and control of economic goods as a necessary condition for creating a just social order at home and abroad.[4] Such advocacy is an urgent moral and political task, but one that Bennett rightly recognizes is quick to run up against "ideological inhibitions that prevent the community at all levels from adventurously investing new agencies responsible to itself for meeting its own neglected needs."[5] Such ideological resistance and conflict are especially apparent around the debates over global economic development. The socialist questions are found in a "great economic debate" about the relative justice of the global capitalist political economy and about alternative paths for economic development. This debate emerged after World War II and is traceable not only among social scientists, economists, and policymakers, but also in parallel fashion within the ecumenical church movement, Protestant and Roman Catholic.[6]

Parties to this debate share a rather commonplace recognition that humanity inhabits a "global village" linked together by a single world economy and that this is the proper context to assess our social responsibilities. Not only is the world a complex web of economic, political, and cultural interrelationships, but also a world in crisis, filled with intense ideological conflict. Agreement is readily forthcoming that this global crisis may be fairly characterized in terms of lack of genuine community and concrete bonds of human connectedness. Controversy immediately arises, however, as soon as interpretive analysis is offered to locate the causes of the crisis, to propose concrete strategies for change, and to weigh the normatively human and religious significance of alternative approaches to our lived-world situation.

That social conflict in our deeply divided and violence-filled world is pervasive and unmistakably ideological is understandable, given the fact that "there is present deep and basic disagreement regarding the historical direction in which we ought to move." What is equally important to recognize is that such ideological conflicts "will ineluctably leave their mark on every theological and ethical position, *without exception*."[7] In this essay, I want to outline and judge the normative socio-ethical significance of the ideological debate over global economic development between developmentalists who advocate capitalist solutions to economic underdevelopment and liberationists who press for socialist alternatives.

The most frequent target of developmentalists is Latin American liberation theology. Michael Novak, for example, has praised this movement for its legitimate moral concern for the "poorest of the poor" and for its intention to link faith and social action. He excoriates it, however, for its "flawed vision of political economy" and use of neo-Marxian economic theory to analyze the present economic crisis. As Novak states his case, "it is precisely here, in its economic theories, that liberation theology comes dangerously close to Marxist analysis—and where most of the confusion arises."[8]

Contrary to Novak, I agree with the Latin American liberationists that only social theory which begins with the class structure of the global economy and seeks to propose effective strategies to transcend these class divisions does justice to our present situation. I also concur with Michael Harrington that social ethicists will continue to *mislocate* the problem of underdevelopment and fail to envision significant alternatives unless they recognize that "the creation of the world with a North Pole of affluence and a South Pole of wretchedness is the outcome of a systemic process. If that theoretical point is not understood, it is literally impossible to come up with practical solutions for immediate and outrageous problems."[9] Because every ethical perspective on these "immediate and outrageous problems" uses a description and evaluation of present social relations, it is of utmost significance in *which* direction we turn within the economic development debate because our lines of vision either help or hinder our capacities for effective agency for justice.

The Occasion for the Development Debate

The current debate over global economic justice is not primarily a controversy about appropriate moral norms. A moral consensus, exhibited in ecumenical church debates, United Nations documents, and elsewhere, continues to hold rather firmly that a just political economy is one in which (a) the basic life-sustenance needs of all people are satisfied ("sufficiency for all"), (b) conditions for the participation of persons and groups are guaranteed to allow for fair decision-making about matters that directly affect their lives ("participatory"), and (c) environmental limits to growth are respected and the natural order protected from irreversible exploitation ("sustainable").[10] Although the capitalist world economy may continue to be profitable for some, by these standards it is unfair—and increasingly unacceptable—to those who Michael Harrington reminds us are the "vast majority" of humankind.

The foundational conflict comes into view only as there is "scratching below the surface" of this value consensus. There is no consensus on proposed strategies for moving toward a more equitable world situation or on the correct interpretation of why present economic patterns of production, distribution, and consumption generate social wealth and power for the few and material deprivation and powerlessness for the many.

The occasion for this debate is the collapse of any political consensus on what would make a global "economy of justice" possible. The conventional wisdom, almost taken for granted by capitalist economists, is that the steady expansion of the capitalist market system and integration of newly independent nations of the South into the international network of trade and finance will manage to develop these former colonies into centers of modern agricultural and industrial growth. The progressive development of these modern economies will, moreover, guarantee the transcendence of a colonial division of labor that has structurally limited the role of colonized peoples to that of "hewers of wood and drawers of water." Although this perspective recognizes that economic progress can be advanced only at some human cost, the trade-off between growth and social needs is either downplayed as a "non-economic" concern or disregarded as merely a transitory problem. There is a prevailing optimism that poor nations can indeed "follow in the footsteps" of the industrialized nations and imitate their course of economic and political modernization, although, granted, at a necessarily accelerated pace. Such thinking shaped, for example, John Kennedy's Alliance for Progress programs, the United Nations' Decade of Development, and numerous church proclamations and service projects.[11]

By the mid-1970s, mainstream economists and neo-Marxian theorists concurred that the standard cures for economic underdevelopment, "more growth, more aid, more trade," had failed to produce a single independent, viable economy in the Third World. In addition, they agreed that nations following capitalist patterns of economic development had experienced "an absolute as well as a relative decline in the average income of the very poor," and a significant decline in political participation on the part of the majority of the population.[12] Liberal economists Irma Adelman and Cynthia Taft Morris drew this conclusion from their 1973 cross-sectional survey of underdeveloped nations and then added this sobering prognosis:

The frightening implication of [our] present work is that hundreds of millions of desperately poor people throughout the world have been *hurt rather than helped* by economic development. Unless their destinies become a major and explicit focus of development policy in the 1970's and 1980's, economic development may serve merely to promote social injustice.[13]

The dominant faith that economic growth is the primary engine for producing social justice and that inequalities within and among nations are only temporary phenomena was shattered by the realization that "in the world as in nations, economic forces left entirely to themselves tend to produce growing inequality."[14] Because economic priorities are also moral priorities, it follows that if the dominant consensus about the "justice-yield" of present economic arrangements and policies has broken down, the moral thesis accompanying it also no longer holds up. What cannot be sustained with any ease these days is the belief that inequality in the world economy functions, in the short or long run, to produce equality.

At present, a global economic justice debate is being waged between a "liberal center" and a "liberation left," each of which advocates a distinct historical project. This debate has gained intensity with the appearance of transnational corporations and national security states. Among liberationists the present global situation is recognized as one of crisis. The problem is the capitalist "mode of production which has not been able to resolve the injustices of the world and overcome the different forms of oppression"[15] and which is presently extending and rigidifying its "global reach."[16]

Before characterizing the parties to the debate and judging the "justice potential" of the differing positions, I need first to suggest why the present debate is properly viewed as a liberal-liberation confrontation. It is quite tempting to proceed *as if* the fundamental socioethical controversy arises as a matter of course between radical and conservative parties and to presume that a liberal or reformist position emerges to offer a compromise or, at least, a more moderate standpoint from which to mediate the claims on either side. This temptation or "recourse to the middle" is misleading and unwarranted. In response to the global economic crisis, we need to move steadily on a liberationist course.[17]

The Parties to the Socioethical Debate

Because the division between rich and poor is the fundamental reality of the contemporary world, only perspectives which take that split as their starting point can begin to do justice to what is going on. Without that starting point, both social science and theology "cannot begin to relate meaningfully to the real situation" and their "questions will lack reality and not relate to real men and women."[18]

When we ask the question, "Who is pressing the economic development debate?" the first thing to become apparent is that conservative social scientists are not interested in drawing attention to the collapse of the dominant consensus about the adequacy of capitalist theory or institutional arrangements. Herman Kahn's *World Economic Development* illustrates the refusal to acknowledge or assess the meaning of the *counterproductive* "capitalist revolution" in the Third World. He reasserted the now specious claim that inequality makes for progress toward global equality and actually benefits the poor. Using a narrow understanding of development as economic growth and gross national product as the standard of judgment for human well-being, Kahn himself was reassured that "the world is doing a lot better than most people realize."[19]

Because Kahn isolated economic activity as an autonomous sphere of life subject to its own fixed, invariant "laws of motion," he suppressed questions of equity and moral responsibility. In particular, he found fault with "the modern liberal view [which] holds that an international system which perpetuates inequalities among nations is morally unacceptable." Kahn did not focus on the injustice of global inequities, much less the human and social costs of maldistribution of economic resources and social power. Rather, he wanted "to help the [North] American people understand the moral basis of our national wealth" and to ascribe the so-called good fortune of the well-off to merit, unrelated to the misfortune of others.[20] From this perspective, poverty is not an issue of social justice, but a "technical problem" located in the realm of nature for which there are technical solutions.

A development strategy that deals with economic reality as inside the realm of nature and outside the political context of power relations and ignores the connections between economic ownership and political control leaves the fate of the poor to economic determination. Such a strategy "must assume either escalating mass misery . . . or the mysterious disappearance of the world's poor."[21] Kahn himself opted for the "mysterious disappearance" of the poor by projecting that in the "next 200 years," those who are presently economically marginalized and disempowered will everywhere be "rich and in control of the forces of nature" if "bad luck or bad management" can be avoided.[22]

In contrast, the liberal center and liberation left understand that poverty is not a matter to be left to "nature" as an inevitable fate. Rather, it is socially conditioned, and thus susceptible to perpetuation or reduction through historical human agency. Such agency should be guided by moral choices, as well as by economic theory, and aimed at political efficacy. So, too, there is a shared conviction that present inequities are morally unacceptable and ought to be redressed for the sake of the common good. This consensus of liberals and liberationists is not total, however. Significant differences, in perspective and strategy, emerge from differing judgments about the difficulty of attaining greater economic justice within the confines of present global political and economic arrangements, as well as about overcoming the vulnerabilities of the dependent nations in the South.

Liberationists have reached the conclusion that established patterns of exploitation and oppression are intrinsic to capitalism and produced by a class structure of unequal relationships within the world economy. Only a political break from capitalist "business as usual" and social reconstruction along the lines of democratic socialist reorganization within and among nations will allow for authentic economic development for the poorest of the poor.[23]

Liberals are inclined toward much more generous estimates of the relative justice, or "rightness," of present socioeconomic arrangements. They minimize the difficulties of transforming distorted, entrenched power dynamics among groups and classes. So, too, they tend to see a "harmony of interests" between the beneficiaries of injustice and its victims and to hold to a "lingering belief" that "somewhere there is an objective truth about a situation which can be discovered and accepted by all."[24] Therefore, fundamental social conflict is often miscast as originating primarily from miscommunication, intellectual misunderstanding, or lack of information rather than from different social commitments and interests. Moves to restore unity and peace may then come at the cost of maintaining the injustice at the source of the conflict. To "be at peace," or make one's peace prematurely with an unjust social order signals complicity in moral evil—the creation of "non-persons" lacking minimal conditions for material well-being and dignity.

The center and left do, however, agree that the capitalist economic order is the "conditioning situation" that determines possibilities for social change toward maximizing economic justice. Two options are available to those who confront this order: "they may either choose among the various alternatives internal to [it] or they may seek to change the conditioning situation itself."[25] Upon that choice much depends, in particular the community relationships of our common humanity. As John Bennett argues, two matters of fundamental moral and, therefore, religious import are simultaneously at stake in this choice: "the survival of a large part of humanity, and the humanity of those who survive because they live in privileged and protected countries."[26]

The choice is between a developmentalist paradigm, which offers modernization on the model of liberal democratic capitalist societies, and a liberation paradigm, which projects a socialist alternative and has been articulated most powerfully by Latin American neo-Marxian dependency theorists and theologians of liberation. Not only is there an irreconcilable conflict between these two paradigms, but it is also morally significant on *which* social scientific theory we depend to figure out what is going on— and what is going wrong—in our contemporary sociohistorical situation. The choice between social theories is not arbitrary and never a matter of indifference. After a brief sketch of the two theories of economic development, the adequacy of each will be judged in terms of the problems brought into view for analysis, proposed solutions and options for action, and their concordance with a normative Christian ethic that identifies justice as the fundamental theological mandate.

The Liberal Developmentalist Paradigm

The developmentalist paradigm, the dominant model of socioeconomic development, continues to be influential, particularly in the United States and Western Europe. Within this perspective, as Michael Harrington has observed, "there has been a good deal of euphemism, much of it politically motivated, with regard to how one speaks about the poor countries."[27] Shifts in parlance have designated these nations as "developing" or, more recently, as "less developed" countries. Such terms are relative and imprecise at best. Underdeveloped nations are defined negatively in relation to those countries considered "developed" or "modern" in terms of advanced industrialization and the appearance of mass-consumption society. The development terminology is politically significant precisely because inequalities of power have allowed North Atlantic countries to name global realities for others and determine the terms of North-South relationships.

This model, in which the historical experiences of select Western nations are taken for granted as models of general applicability, conceptualizes a global process of social change that is equally valid for both rich and poor nations. It projects an evolutionary movement toward acquisition of "modern" characteristics and modalities. With their assumption of "different routes, but only one destination" for all nation-states, modernization theorists account for the failure of some countries to develop either by locating "deficiencies" within those countries or by concluding that "they force the tempo of Western development" and "disorder the sequence" of proper modernization.[28] Deviation from the "attested" path is named as the source of instability and continued economic vulnerability in the Third World.

For developmentalists, underdevelopment is viewed as a state of backwardness and stagnation, measurable by the absence of characteristics associated with industrialized and urbanized modern societies. Traditional societies are said to lag behind their modern counterparts and to be in need of exerted effort to catch up. Several foundational assumptions undergird this lag theory of development.

First, development is understood as the steady, or sometimes not so steady, advance toward a certain designated goal, "modernity." The historical perspective at work has clear affinity with the Western understanding of progress, that is, the confident expectation of a continuous, cumulative, and linear progression toward improved material conditions of individual and collective welfare. Second, the advancement of nations now considered developed is attributed to their own efforts to maximize capacities and "talents" for growth and integrated development. Correspondingly, the underdevelopment of other countries results from an internal failure to use national resources or an incapacity or unwillingness to make the necessary effort. Therefore, developmentalists seek to identify those internal social, political, economic, and cultural factors that may either impede or accelerate social change toward modernization. They go on to suggest appropriate strategies to eliminate the obstacles to development, usually anachronistic social structures and cultural resistance to change.

Third, the addition of "modernizing" influences heretofore absent or underused will make mobilization of resources possible for development planning. These missing ingredients may be generated from within a society, but more often than not, they need to be injected from outside by means of, among other things, foreign aid, technical assistance, and communications systems. Finally, political forces within a society must rally together to support a development policy and sustain the momentum of change in the transition. The role of modernizing elites, those with the proper "will to be modern," is emphasized, along with an "ideology of development" to support the project of nation-building.

Two implications of this social theory are especially noteworthy. The development of some countries is not causally related to the underdevelopment of others. Some recognition is given to the possibility of a conditional relationship between the two, especially in terms of a "demonstration effect," the powerful imaging and lure of the developed on the underdeveloped. Wealth and power are not, however, implicated structurally in poverty and powerlessness. A second and related implication concerns the so-called advantages of being latecomers to the modern world. Lagging behind may enable nations to avoid some of the mistakes, excesses, and social costs incurred by the industrialized nations. Similarly, these nations may well benefit from the availability of financial resources and advanced technology. The appeal to underdeveloped nations is to "steady the course" and follow the lead of the powerful nations.

The project, or "service," approach to problems of underdevelopment was clearly evident in both World Council of Churches documents and papal encyclicals throughout the 1960s and beyond. For example, at the

1961 World Council Assembly at New Delhi, delegates acknowledged the prospect of continuing "rapid technological and social change" throughout the world. They were confident about an underlying harmony of interests between developed and underdeveloped nations and about mutual benefits to be gained from the technological advances in the North and the push toward modernization in the South. What elicited particular enthusiasm was the call for a world strategy of development by which the transfer of capital and technology from the rich nations would enable the poor nations to enter on equal footing the network of modern nations in an increasingly interdependent global community. The task for the churches was primarily educational, exercising moral leadership in promoting the cause of "making the riches of developed countries available to those poor in resources."[29]

In identifying governments and international agencies as the primary agents of change, the New Delhi report called for increased foreign aid to developing countries and efforts to promote their progressive integration in the world market. "In the long run," the report concluded, "trade, not aid, is the most effective instrument in furthering development."[30] In keeping with a developmentalist paradigm, with its technocratic view of change, New Delhi not only offered a prognosis of peaceful and orderly change, rationally controlled "from above," but also a social theory that fit neatly with the dominant "ecumenical ethos" of the time. Arend van Leeuwen describes that liberal ethos as "the long and deeply ingrained Anglo-Saxon tradition of thinking in terms of harmony, equilibrium, balance, integration and cooperation, responsible rationality, and evolutionary change."[31]

For the ecumenical church movement, the developmentalist model offered social change without significant disruption, dislocation, or violence, a kind of "development without tears." That comfortable liberal ideology would be challenged directly by those within and outside the ranks of the churches who shifted to a dependency, or liberationist, paradigm to understand the global economic order and alter patterns of social powerlessness. If "developmentalism ... proposes a sort of change that will 'allow things to continue the way they are,'" with only modifications and slight adjustments,[32] liberationists argue that the fundamental challenge is to engage in a global struggle to promote "change *of* the system, [which] demands political options and not merely technical recommendations. The latter are of course necessary, but their implementation depends on the exercise of power."[33]

The Liberation Dependency Paradigm

Liberationists "start with a rejection of the existing situation, considered as fundamentally unjust and dehumanizing."[34] This difference may not be overemphasized. In an exercise of cultural freedom, they reinterpret the global order from their perspective as citizens of poor and dominated countries within an international network of dependent capitalism. They find that they need to speak, first and foremost, not of integration, but of the need for emancipation from structures of oppression. Emancipation will be achieved only when it is possible to construct a new socioeconomic order that bars the ownership of wealth from being the primary determiner of social well-being.

The dependency theory of economic development emerges from the "underside of history." It is a critique of, and an alternative perspective to, the dominant liberal theory of modernization. The ethnocentric bias of developmentalism is identified whenever modernization is equated with Westernization or, more explicitly, (North) Americanization. Liberationists also detect a prevailing "time-centric illusion" and question the assumption that underdeveloped nations are closed, stagnant, and traditional societies that are just now undergoing social change. They argue that the countries of the Third World have changed considerably under the impact of colonialism and formal political independence. Underdevelopment, they suggest, is adequately comprehended not as an original state of being, or even a "stage" before economic growth, but as a historical process. They observe that the underdevelopment of some nations did not precede, but *follows on* and accompanies the development of others. The history and situation of the underdeveloped, therefore, become explicable only in connection with the history and situation of the developed nations within a single global economic system. From this perspective, underdevelopment is generated by capitalism and the formation of an inclusive international structure of economic, political, and cultural relationships.

As a corrective to the ahistorical view of social change in the developmentalist paradigm, dependency theorists have adopted a historical method that allows the history of the underdeveloped nations, and particularly the history of colonialism, to inform their analysis of the contemporary world. Accordingly, their starting point is not modernization as such, but the meaning of the "modern world" and the historical processes that formed it.[35]

The present division of the globe into an affluent North and an impoverished South is seen as the outcome of a historical process that began in the sixteenth century. The modern world "was not, and is not, the result of the inexorable workings of some inhuman necessity—geographic, geological, genetic, or what have you—but of economic and social structures."[36] The colonial imposition of a capitalist market economy altered the internal life of the now underdeveloped nations. These nations remain dependent parties on the periphery of a global political economy, with the wealthy developed nations at the center. What dependency theorists seek to explain is how economic growth results in the accumulation of wealth for the center and "the development of underdevelopment" on the periphery. Of particular importance is the different historical experiences of first-comers and latecomers.

Although the emergence of a market economy in North Atlantic countries was accompanied by severe dislocations, their development was self-generated and internally coherent. The expansion of one sector of the economy had a multiplier effect on other parts, and internal changes produced integrated growth. In contrast, the internationalization of the capitalist economic system in the process of colonialism had a *disintegrative* effect in the periphery countries by placing their development under alien imperatives. Because economic growth on the periphery is not determined by internal needs, but by foreign interests and capital, the economic structures of these nations lack "the reciprocal interactions that are necessary if there is to be self-sustained growth."[37] The vulnerability of their export-based, usually monoculture economies to unfavorable terms of trade and control by foreign capital has ensured their status as dependent and unequal partners. Even when economic growth does occur, "the mass of profit it generates does not become integrated into the local economy," and therefore, "despite an improvement in living standards, there [is] no structural modification in the economic system" to allow for what might be called "development towards the interior."[38]

In addition, developed countries have been able to perpetuate their ascendancy by exploiting opportunities and sustaining their "initiatory power," above all, the power to modify the "rules of the game" to suit their own interests. This power maintains a neocolonial system in which underdeveloped nations may attempt to catch up, but in so doing they must remain dependent and subordinate.

The operative assumptions of this model, advanced through historical investigations, especially in Latin America, contrast significantly with those of the liberal theory of modernization. First, development and underdevelopment are understood to be interdependent processes. Second, only by positing a "concept of the whole" can a theory of economic development adequately account for the structural dynamics of the world economy as they work out both nationally and internationally. Third, the reality of dependence can be understood only if the conflicting interests of social classes are also examined. The broad classification of "underdeveloped" fails to disclose the small affluent group that usually "controls the means of production and the levers of economic and political power."[39] It also fails to disclose that "external domination" is impracticable without the support of internal elites, who share in the profits of neocolonialism.

Contrary to the theorists of modernization, who look on elites as the carriers of progress, liberationists see them as defending the status quo and the interests of foreign capital. For this reason, the theorists provide not only a historical and holistic model, but also a class analysis of economic injustice that does not "dissociate the common concern with poverty, illiteracy, and unemployment from the structural analysis of power and exploitation in their various forms."[40]

In using this analysis of problems of economic vulnerability and social powerlessness, Latin American liberation theologians argue that the adoption of the basic categories of domination and dependence is the "crux of the matter."[41] Their search is for a theological perspective that articulates the meaning of "living and thinking our faith *within and in opposition to oppression.*"[42] Authentic development, judged in terms of the economic well-being of the poorest members of society and the empowerment of the marginalized, *becomes* historically possible only when patterns of dependence and domination are successfully dismantled. This necessitates a political confrontation with those who resist change and a struggle to construct a new kind of society that minimizes economic exploitation and political control "from above." In Latin America and elsewhere, this struggle has taken form as a social and ecclesial movement toward establishing a socialist alternative to the present order.

The struggle is necessitated by the recognition that the dominant system is not likely to provide the means to end its own abuses. In fact, quite the opposite holds, as massive resistance mounts against grassroots efforts to establish more just and egalitarian social relations. Such resistance includes denunciations of liberation theology, but the fundamental conflict is not over theology per se. At issue is rather the "basic option for liberation as a historical project, the building of a non-exploitative social order, and especially 'taking sides' in real struggle with all its risks."[43] What is especially disconcerting on the current scene is that those in the liberal center, who have been willing to join together issues of economic development and social justice, are now gravitating toward the political right and proposing strategies that will only maintain the privileges and power of the "already arrived" in an unjust world order.

Recent Shifts in the Global Economic Justice Debate

The collapse of the developmentalist center within the development debate has coincided with recent structural shifts in the world economic order and the concomitant emergence of ideologies of a "new globalism." These ideologies present a set of claims about the role of governments, corporations, and churches deemed essential to authentic development. The major feature of capitalism in the post-World War II period is the internationalization of productive and finance capital by global corporations. Large transnational corporations are consolidating economic and political power beyond the control of nation-states and restructuring the rules of supply and demand in the world market. They seek monopolistic power to maintain profits and minimize competition among themselves. Spokespersons for transnational corporations speak of the need to transcend national governments in order to secure "world peace through world trade" and replace the "irrationalities" of international politics.

Critics argue that transnational corporations are designed "for worldwide profit maximization, not the development needs of poor countries." Class divisions are being reproduced at a global level; wealth is spreading geographically, but its ownership and control are being concentrated in the hands of a few.[44] Because these economic enterprises consolidate wealth, power, and technology and are not politically accountable to any nation-state, they are altering customary patterns of production and distribution, as well as the balance of political power within and among nations.

The role assigned to national governments by transnational corporations is the provision of a safe and stable climate for economic expansion. The emergence of national security states in Latin America has been rationalized as a necessary move to make progress possible toward both economic development and political democracy. Military elites, under the ideology of national security, are heralded as the "transition" agents of social change whose leadership is necessary because of the repeated failure of civilian leaders to promote economic development and because of the need to protect the nation-state from communism. The security interests of Latin American states are identified with the national security of the United States, and the presence of transnational corporations is welcomed to enable modernization. All power is concentrated in the state and its executives, who argue that liberation movements only weaken internal security and must, therefore, be eliminated.

Under this political arrangement the churches are to play the role of cultural defenders of "traditional values" and the prevailing social order of the West. As Jose Comblin explains, the national security state offers the churches a new "Constantinianism with a view to a new Christendom," a pact between church and state to promote each other's privileges and power. The churches are to educate the masses into the modern world and promote those values of "good citizenship" that will make the nation-state safe from its enemies.[45] In soliciting the support of the churches, the military regimes contend that communism is the only threat to freedom and that internal cultural resistance to modernization is the only block to prosperity.

Liberal economists in the development center now argue that "the price of development is apt to be political and economic authoritarianism" and that military dictatorships "may be unavoidable, even necessary" for the resolution of internal social conflict and economic crisis.[46] Repressive political governments are "acceptable" in the short run in order to provide the conditions needed for economic development. They claim that there is little chance of escaping the humanly painful trade-off between economic growth and the promotion of human well-being for the vast majority of persons within these societies.

The shift within the development debate is well illustrated by Sylvia Ann Hewlett's *The Cruel Dilemmas of Development: Twentieth-Century Brazil*. Hewlett proposes that social injustice, in the form of chronic poverty and political repression, is unpleasant but an ordinary consequence of "normal" development. As she explains, "the former is a direct result of the capital accumulation process; the latter is the apparatus of control necessary to prevent the effective revolt on the part of the oppressed."[47] She acknowledges that a major goal of the Brazilian government has been the suppression of internal dissent and that the reason for the recent relaxation of repressive measures is the elimination of opposition. What she cannot show, however, is any improvement through economic development in the life situations of poor Brazilians. Rather, she focuses on the rich, claiming that "the need for the more excessive types of political repression has proved to be rather temporary" and that "*elite groups* have regained at least some of their civilian and political freedoms."[48]

Those on the ideological left in Latin America who are still alive have quite a different reading of what is going on in the name of "economic development." Brazilian economist Helio Jaguaribe, for example, argues that repression is used in his country for no other reason than to extend the privileges of the wealthy. Repression is not used to change the status quo or begin a process of sharing, but to block organized resistance to the rapprochement between domestic elites and transnational economic interests. His term to describe Brazil's governmental policies is colonial fascism. Its model for development avoids altering existing power dynamics of ownership and control, and his country remains dependent, particularly on the United States, for economic assistance and foreign markets.[49] Even with a turn toward democratic reforms, the extension of formal political rights or "limited democracy" does not challenge existing patterns of economic power and privilege, but only allows an easing of internal repression to create a stabler climate for economic investors without need for direct coercion.

If progressive developmentalists are lending ideological support to authoritarian military regimes, they do so in part because their own economic assumptions lead them to speak, as Hewlett does, of an unavoidable "cruel choice" between efficiency and justice. Liberationists counter by saying that the fundamental issue is not the costs of economic development, but who is asked to pay them. Moreover, the most significant variables in economic transformation are not technological innovation, increased rates of growth, or forced savings and capital accumulation, but social and political change in the direction of greater egalitarianism. In rejecting the artificial distinction that divides economic from "non-economic" factors, liberationists seek to connect the generation of wealth and power for the few with the impoverishment and disempowerment of the many. According to Samuel Parmar:

> Once the relation between power and poverty is seen, the whole strategy of change from above falls apart. Pressure from below is the only way to galvanize decision-makers into responding to demands for justice. That means that education for radical change must motivate and mobilize people at the grassroots for development action.[50]

Moral and Political Choices

The appearance of grassroots movements for social justice, especially in Latin America but also in Africa and Asia, has been dramatic. So, too, has been the resistance. As Jose Miguez Bonino notes, "the capitalist transnational project, as experience clearly shows, will not spare any effort—however costly in human terms—to block all attempts at effecting qualitative change."[51] This transnational project presents itself as the "natural" successor to the liberal democratic society and is characterized by two features. Economically, it espouses further control of the world economy by transnational capital that relocates production where profits may be maximized and government cooperation is offered to support corporate expansion. Politically, it projects limited democracies under bureaucratic management with formally guaranteed civil liberties for the middle and upper strata but with no alteration of economic inequality. Miguez Bonino observes that this capitalist transnational project is transforming "the whole world into one massive security state" whose purpose is to provide a tranquil labor force and a steady reallocation of national resources in the direction of corporate subsidies and military expenditures.[52]

Although the development of a corporate right-military alliance is most pronounced in Latin America, the United States, under the Reagan "counter-revolution," is experiencing a similar transformation. The movement is to abandon the liberal welfare state philosophy and policies of the New Deal and adopt national security state policies that seek a right-of-center political base to support unregulated corporate "free enterprise" and escalating militarization of the U.S. economy and foreign policy. With a decline in productivity, the domestic failure to provide full employment, and increased economic competition with other "core states" for capitalist production and investment, the United States still retains hegemonic military power but has lost its political and economic "superiority." Under these conditions the United States is relying on its military strength to compensate for its loss, attempting to keep in place a global system that it is no longer able to control unilaterally.[53]

United States' opposition to socialist revolutionary movements in Latin America and its support of authoritarian regimes are defended as necessary both to protect U.S. security interests and promote the "flowering of freedom and democracy." As Penny Lernoux points out, however, the most promising source of democratic possibilities in Latin America is found in the myriad grassroots rural and urban community organizations. These include thousands of Christian base communities, which offer genuine political participation and mobilization for social reconstruction. Present U.S. foreign policy does not have a progressive effect on such popular efforts, but "perpetuates an *anti-democratic* political system in which the indigenous military serves as an occupying army, and the people are treated as the enemy."[54]

U.S. resistance is especially directed at successful independent nationalistic revolutions, such as in Nicaragua, that are seeking to socialize ownership and control of economic resources and chart an independent political course. Such resistance is grounded in the fear that the Nicaraguan "contagion" may spread and have a devastating "demonstration effort" not only in neighboring countries of the region, but potentially at home in the United States as well. Revolution might be imported! From a liberationist perspective, current U.S. policy is not the promotion of democracy, but the struggle "from above" to make the world safe for the capitalist transnational project.

At this historical juncture, Christians face a pressing choice. The choice is between joining with those who no longer believe in the moral authority of the dominant global order and are seeking to organize resistance against its entrenchment, and joining with those who have decided to "make their peace" with dominating power and provide ideological justification for withdrawing from the conflict. At the same time that some liberal social scientists are shifting toward the right and claiming that right-wing military dictatorships are the best hope for freedom and democracy, some church leaders are arguing within the ecumenical movement for a distinctively "spiritual" mission of the church in the world. This includes backing off from any partnership with liberation movements.

The ecclesiastical battle against socialist alternatives, as Latin American liberation theologians conjecture, has most often been motivated not by doctrinal or even pastoral considerations, but by churchly geopolitical self-interests. As Jose Comblin argues, "the church exists in the West; the West seeks security in fighting the East (communism); so the church seeks its geopolitical security in doing the same."[55] The churches' avoidance of socialist alternatives only serves to prolong the vested interests and political control of those who do not wish to see the churches involved in *liberation* politics. Their fear of the transformative power of emancipatory faith is clearly evidenced by the reactionary rejection of theologies of liberation in their various modes and locales. Michael Novak's warning to churches not to "be mortgaged to ideologies foreign to the faith"[56] should tip us off to the fact that not all ideological options are the same; nor are all understandings of Christian faithfulness.

FOUR

Democracy in Argentina

John R. Stumme

*C*hristians in the United States of North America concerned for justice in Latin America frequently encounter the argument that the only option to repressive, antipopular military regimes is armed revolution leading to socialism. The choice, it is claimed, has to be between this option and fascism, between socialism and barbarism, between the path followed by Cuba after 1959 and that followed by Brazil after 1964.[1] In this political polarization both sides tend to consign constitutional democracy to the past. It is argued, or simply assumed, that such democracy is not viable in Latin America. The policy of the United States of North America (USNA) has often forgotten its professed democratic ideals and actively supported antirevolutionary and antidemocratic regimes, and persons critical of this policy have sometimes concluded that they should support armed revolution as the only genuine alternative in an oppressed continent. In this context, hopes for democratic change are considered, at best, naive and unrealistic and, at worst, dangerous. For some, constitutional democracy legitimates capitalist exploitation, and for others, it permits Communist infiltration. Caught in the cross fire of revolutionary and counterrevolutionary movements, those who favor change through constitutional processes are seen as holdovers from a bygone age.

John R. Stumme, Professor of Systematic Theology, Instituto Superior Evangélico du Estudios Teológicos, Buenos Aires, Argentina.

Political Options in Latin America

The assumption that political democracy in Latin America has failed and belongs to the past is found, for example, in José Míguez Bonino's recent book, *Toward a Christian Political Ethics*. He sketches his understanding of the current historical context in two chapters entitled "Latin America: From Authoritarianism to Democracy" and "Latin America: From Democracy to National Security State."[2] He links political democracy with the liberal modernization that began in the past century.[3] "The news coming out of Latin America the last few years," writes Míguez, ". . . news of social unrest, guerilla activity escalating in some cases to civil war, military coups, repressive governments, systematic violations of human rights, economic crisis—cannot but prompt the question: whatever happened to the project for democratic modernization? . . . We sowed modern democracy and reaped the national security state. What went wrong?"[4] As he gives his answer, one based largely on the crisis of international capitalism, Míguez makes clear his belief that liberal democracy has had its day in Latin America. He describes "the demise of the democratic liberal project" and proposes a socialist project of liberation to replace it.[5]

Certainly one can find much evidence to support the view that modern democracy in Latin America is a relic of the past. I mention one item: in 1961 in South America, Paraguay was " 'a military island' in an ocean of Latin American civilian governments."[6] In 1976, there were military dictatorships in Argentina, Bolivia, Brazil, Chile, Ecuador, Peru, and Uruguay. It is also clear that modernization theory did not anticipate, nor was it able to explain, the origin of these military regimes.[7] Furthermore, the question of revolution has been decisive in some countries: in Nicaragua, for example, where the United States is supporting an unjust counterrevolution.

Yet in a number of nations in Latin America, many reject the conclusion that political democracy has died. The news coming out of Latin America also includes reports of people voting in Venezuela, of constitutional government being reestablished in Argentina and Uruguay, and of popular democratic movements in Brazil and Chile. For those who expect that the future of Latin America will be a struggle between revolution and counterrevolution, these events seem only to be illusory hopes. Yet many political veterans, as well as younger leaders, stake their lives on the premise that the judgment of political democracy's death is either obsolete or premature. Many intellectuals, including critical Marxists, are reevaluating the meaning and role of political democracy. The national security state does not deserve the honor of having killed and buried democracy in Latin America.

Even brief references should make one suspicious of any sweeping prognoses about the whole of Latin America's political future. Generalizations that the entire continent is on the verge of revolution, or that the region will face interminable fascist regimes—all final and universal obituaries to political democracy—are to be as distrusted. More often than not, such global projections only obscure and oversimplify the complexities of particular situations. The numerous nation-states of Latin America have their own history and characteristics. Even a common experience of colonialism and neocolonialism does not override important differences. Nicaragua is not a model for Argentina. Costa Rica's path after 1948 and Brazil's after 1964 cannot be universalized. The diversity of situations present distinct historical options. It is an elementary methodological principle that reflection on political systems and change in Latin America must consider the particularities of each country, including the relation of each to the international context.[8]

A crucial issue of Latin American politics is the USNA because its influence across the continent is great, to say the least. Technologically, culturally, and religiously, one finds the imprint and the pressure of the giant neighbor to the north. Reinhold Niebuhr taught long ago that where there is an unequal distribution of power, there is bound to be injustice.[9] Míguez tells us that while the pressure for change comes from below, the consent or the resistance to change from above is an important factor in deciding what will be its human cost.[10] The public responsibility of Christians and churches in the USNA is to understand this impact and to seek to reduce and modify it, to support change in unjust power relations, and to learn to respond creatively to demands for change in Latin America. Criticism by many of the present Administration's Central American policy is evidence of this sort of responsibility.

Christians and their churches should oppose their government's aid to and alliances with military dictatorships. It is less clear what political alternatives deserve allegiance. There are no clear-cut formulas that tell us when we should side with constitutional democracy and when we should side with revolutionary struggle. There are bogus democracies and illusory calls for revolution. There are situations in which any of the alternatives to military dictatorship, be they revolutionary groups or democratic parties, are ambiguous, and there are situations in which the alternatives represent genuine improvement in people's lives. For concerned Christians in the USNA who wish to respond positively to events in Latin America, there is no substitute for careful study of the complexities of particular nations or for evaluating divergent interpretations of each situation. To help one appreciate the importance of such a methodology, the prospects for democracy in one nation, Argentina, are examined in detail.

Even the treatment of this particular situation is necessarily partial and incomplete here. Nevertheless, considering the prospect for constitutional democracy in one situation allows us both to test the validity of some generalizations made about political change in Latin America and to appreciate why one people, who in recent years have experienced both an attempt at revolution and a military dictatorship, are making a decision for constitutional democracy. Recent events demonstrate that in Argentina, democracy, even with its battered historical record, is alive but fragile and uncertain. My contention is that for those who are committed to seeking justice, current efforts at democracy in Argentina are worthy of strong support. An ethical judgment to support current democratic efforts shares this risk and venture. The issue is not an absolute defense of political democracy as the best structure of government in all historical situations, but to defend this option as ethically optimal in this situation. Given the alternatives, constitutional democracy is the political structure that offers the best hope for embracing and protecting justice in Argentina.

There are various distinguishable methodological elements in any ethical, historical evaluation by Christians. Here I identify three. The first is a theological perspective that provides certain fundamental assumptions. In this essay, my theology remains largely implicit. I stand broadly within Lutheran tradition, and not unexpectedly, I find certain themes from Reinhold Niebuhr's theological ethic congenial. Niebuhr's anthropological argument for democracy is both an expression of hope and a reminder of reality: "The human's capacity for justice makes democracy possible; but the human's inclination to injustice makes democracy necessary."[11]

A second methodological element is a commitment to certain values that political democracy embodies and serves. It is not my intention to develop a theory of democracy here, but it is important to indicate how I use the term. I use the term to refer to a political structure characterized by:

> legal freedom to formulate and advocate political alternatives with the concomitant rights of free association, free speech, and other basic freedoms of persons; free and nonviolent competition among leaders with periodic validation of their claim to rule; inclusion of all effective political offices in democratic process; and provision for the participation of all members of the political community, whatever their preferences.[12]

Such a structure of government is secured by Argentina's Constitution. It creates a framework of law based on the consent of the people that guarantees equal political rights for citizens. It recognizes the right of the majority to govern and the right of others to dissent and to organize to replace those in power in regular elections. The Argentinian Constitution has its unique features, some of them important, but it belongs to the family of political democracy.

The values appealed to here are grounded in the dignity of all people. I assume an understanding of human good or justice that includes freedom *from* political violence and illegitimate coercion and freedom to participate with others in shaping a common future. Justice also involves a commitment to greater equality in the distribution of goods and resources in society, a value that goes beyond a formal definition of constitutional democracy.[13] In what follows, then, I will be giving reasons for by believing that in Argentina, constitutional democracy is the way of politically ordering society that best serves freedom, participation, and equality.

A third methodological element in any social ethical analysis is an evaluative interpretation of the possibilities and limits of a particular situation. Social analysis is a blend of factual and evaluative claims. What is said to have happened is crucial in deciding what ought to be done. Observations from the disciplines of sociology and political science must be used to supplement a historical perspective. One can distinguish between such information and the commitment informing historical ethical judgment, but their intrinsic relationship needs to be recognized as well.[14] My perception of the situation is influenced by my theology and my commitment to democracy.

Here my assumption is that a democratic decision opposes both the alternatives of armed revolution and military dictatorship. By armed revolution I mean political action outside of constitutional norms, such as when efforts in the name of the proletariat to establish a socialist society by force are attempted. Armed revolution embraces violence as a method of change, as it did when tried in Argentina. By military dictatorship I refer to a regime that suspends the Constitution in the name of some supposedly higher good (e.g., order, national security, or Christian civilization) and in which the armed forces control the governmental apparatus. Historical experience shows that such regimes are violent and usually connected with elements of the upper class. In speaking of armed revolution and military dictatorship, I have in mind the forms of each taken in Argentina in the past fifteen years.

My thesis is that given the alternatives, change through constitutional democracy is the best hope for embracing and protecting justice. I speak in terms of "hope" because it captures well the historical character of our question. Hope refers to a human attitude assumed in the present, deepened by the memory of suffering in the past and oriented toward newness and goodness in the future. Hopeful people recognize that the not-yet of history exhibits openness while aware that openness is both limited and constantly threatened. Hope's content emerges from the possibilities of the historical situation for which hopeful people assume responsibility for directing; hope unites what can and what ought to be. Hope expresses the attitude of many in Argentina at this critical moment when democracy replaces the terror of military dictatorship.

Here my analysis aims to engage aspects of the political thinking of Latin American liberation theologians. For more than fifteen years their commitment to the poor and their creative theology have shed new light on how Christians should be involved in opposing injustice and oppression. Appropriately, their writings occupy a special place for USNA Christians who wish to understand Latin America and find ways to act faithfully and effectively in relation to changes there.[15] As should be clear, many Latin American liberation theologians have not advocated the political position I propose here.[16] Although I share their criticism of the national security state, I find their traditional attitude toward constitutional democracy ambiguous, inadequate, or mistaken, at least with respect to the Argentine context. It is difficult to find a positive word about "liberal democracy" in their writings. Often it represents the political system to be destabilized and, at best, to be manipulated to advance a political project that goes beyond it toward socialism. They define their alternative project as "democratic" (few political systems in the twentieth century do not), but usually the term is so vague and undefined that one does not know what specific political structure is being proposed.[17] Here I will pose my commitment to political constitutional democracy in somewhat polemical fashion, with the hope that the question will be further clarified in liberation theology. My conviction is that democratic praxis requires democratic theory.

In 1983, democracy returned to Argentina. I will place this event in a broader historical framework and ask about the possibilities of maintaining such democracy. Then I will examine the experience, possibility, and potential for justice of the revolutionary alternative in Argentina. I will conclude with some further reflections on democracy and liberation.[18]

The Significance of 1983 for the Return of Constitutional Democracy

In 1983, Argentines voted for the first time in a decade. Even after ten years of military dictatorships and in spite of an extremely serious economic situation—a 400 percent inflation rate, for example—the electoral process was open and orderly, with little overt violence. Political competition and participation were high, and new elected officials at every level of government assumed offices as recognized representatives of the people. For the first time in history, the Radical party candidate in direct competition with the Peronist candidate was elected President of the nation.

These facts, noteworthy as they are, do not, however, indicate the full importance of what happened. Not only a change of government occurred, but also a change in the structure of government took place, change from a military to a democratically elected regime. These events represent a repudiation of military dictatorship and an affirmation of constitutional democracy by Argentines. We need to analyze the significance of this fundamental change in Argentina's political life more closely.

The coup of March 24, 1976, had inaugurated an unconstitutional regime in which total control of the government and the coercive apparatus of the state were invested in the armed forces. The President was removed, Congress abolished, provincial and municipal powers abrogated, and judicial power subjected to the military. The coup "meant military solutions to the problems of Argentina. National institutions were rapidly militarized, and political power was controlled by the Junta, which named the President and the Governors of the provinces."[19] The measures introduced included (a) suppression of public freedoms; (b) the dissolution and suspension of political parties and organizations: (c) the suppression of the General Confederation of Labour, the interdiction of unions, and the total control of the universities; (d) control and manipulation of the means of communication; (e) attacks on professional sectors, such as lawyers, journalists, psychologists, the popular church, educators, writers, and others.[20]

In its effort to suppress leftist subversion the armed forces "created a terrorist state."[21] The assumption of who might be a subversive was broad: "a terrorist," said its first President, "is not simply someone with arms or a bomb, but also someone who spreads ideas contrary to Western Christian civilization."[22] Elementary legal and human rights were denied. Torture and murder in secret detention centers became common. Instead of formal detentions and political jailings, official and unofficial security forces used new methods: people were kidnapped and later simply "disappeared," never to be heard from again.[23] There are at least 10,000 *desaparecidos* whose fate is unknown and whose relatives have suffered the anxiety of not knowing if their loved ones are dead or alive. Thousands fled the country to live in exile. Most who remained lived in fear.

Argentina has known the reality of radical political evil, and its human meaning—the loss of individual life, the agony of the suffering in families and in other intimate relationships, the destruction of basic social ties is the tragic background for Argentina's return to democracy and a key element in an ethical judgment in its favor.

The armed forces "process" in force from 1976 to 1983 is one example of that "national security state" that has appeared in Latin America since 1964. José Comblin, Penny Lernoux, Míguez, and others have analyzed the nature and ideology of such states and their relationship to USNA security interests and to transnational capitalism.[24] The political character of the national security state must be stressed. Míguez quotes a report of the International Commission of Jurists that characterized it as "establishing a new power structure which brings with it the destruction of the traditional democratic system and the elimination of all forms of opposition."[25] The national security state is the antithesis and the enemy of political democracy.

Already by 1979, political scientist Guillermo O'Donnell pointed to "tensions in the Bureaucratic-Authoritarian State and the Question of Democracy."[26] His analysis is complementary to those who use the term national security state. "The Bureaucratic-Authoritarian (BA) State" refers to a new type of authoritarian regime in which the military as an institution, not merely as individual military rulers, dominates and adopts a technocratic-bureaucratic approach to policymaking rather than a political one.

O'Donnell noted that there are basically three "mediations," or linkages, between the "private" life of civil society and the "public" and universal role of the state. One is "the nation," "the collective identities that define a 'we,' " the network of solidarities that allows the recognition of a collectivity distinct from other nations. A second fundamental political mediation is

> citizenship, in the double sense of: 1. Abstract equality which—basically by means of universal suffrage and the corresponding regime of political democracy—is the foundation of the claim that the power exercised through the institutions of the state by the occupants of governmental roles is based on the consent of the citizens; and 2. the right to have recourse to juridically regulated protection against arbitrary acts on the part of state institutions.

The third mediation is *"el pueblo* or *lo popular,"* which "involve a 'we' that is a carrier of demands for substantive justice which forms the basis for the obligations of the state toward the less favored segments of the population." He notes that "in Latin America the formation of the nation was accomplished much more through the mediation of *lo popular* than through that of citizenship."[27]

O'Donnell found that "the principal social base of the BA state [the] upper bourgeosie" was tied to transnational capitalist interests. Institutionally, organizations of "specialists in coercion have decisive weight" in restoring order, and civilian technocrats are important in normalizing the economy. It is a system that deactivates and excludes the popular sector and suppresses citizenship.

> BA appears as if placed before a sick nation . . . whose general interests must be involved; yet, because of the depth of the crisis BA cannot claim to be the representative of that sick nation, which is

seen as contaminated by innumerable internal enemies. Thus, BA is based on the suppression of two fundamental mediations—citizenship and *lo popular*. In an ambiguous way it may evoke the other mediation—the nation—but only as a "project" (and not as an actual reality) which it proposes to carry out through drastic surgical measures.[28]

After lengthy discussion of the inner contradictions of this mediationless system of domination, O'Donnell concluded that for the rulers, "the only thing that remains is the aspiration for the very thing that BA has radically denied: democracy." But a type of democracy that "maintains the exclusion of the popular sector. . . . Furthermore, the rulers know that the question 'How to democratize? . . . can open a Pandora's box of popular political reactivation."[29]

O'Donnell concluded:

> The issue of democracy is important not only because it contains the Achilles heel of this system of domination, but also because it contains a dynamic that can be the unifying element in the long-term effort to establish a society that is more nearly in accord with certain fundamental values. . . . The proposal for a limited form of democracy, without pueblo and ultimately without nation, is not the gracious concession of a triumphant power, but the expression of its intrinsic weakness.[30]

O'Donnell's analysis pointed to what would become the decisive Argentinian political issue during the 1980s: What would replace military dictatorship, qualified or constitutional democracy? National security states "make changes in the constitution. They assign a permanent role to the military in any institutionalized government as a kind of backup insurance. They attempt to create center-right political coalitions that will look favorable in the military's ideas.[31] In those years of military dictatorship, it was very much an open question whether or not the armed forces would succeed in imposing an antipopular limited democracy to ensure their domination.

Surprising events, beginning April 2, 1982, that had unintended consequences played a crucial role in answering this question.[32] The sending of Argentine soldiers to retake the Malvinas Islands and the resulting South Atlantic War were precipitating factors. The decision to do so was an appeal to the "nation" mediation, undertaken to create the possibility of continued military presence in the governing of Argentina. Military defeat, however, ended this government's legitimacy, even as protector of the national interest. The Process had already encountered growing popular resistance because of its economic policies (*lo popular* mediation) and its systematic violation of human rights (citizenship mediation). Military defeat (nation mediation) created a crisis, compelled the military to choose to follow its "doves," who advocated reestablishing full constitutional government.[33]

Even in 1983, however, the armed forces, while sustaining the commitment to hold open elections, sought in a final document of "auto-amnesty" for its human rights violations that would also insert its ideology into the country's institutional life. In a remarkable speech in May 1983, before 50,000 demonstrators, Míguez, as spokesperson for the Permanent Assembly of Human Rights, pinpointed the issue. With the passage of the law, he said,

> the subversion of democracy would remain inserted in the very heart of the state. We cannot enter into a fraud: qualified, guided, strong, limited, controlled, protected democracies do not exist. The only alternative to democracy is totalitarianism. And it is this with which we are dealing. Democracy is not simply completing electoral acts: it is the full functioning of the law, the free and impartial exercise of justice, the control of the people over the management of the state, free information, in summary, the unrestricted enforcement of the Constitution[34]

The first legislative action of the new constitutional authorities was to repeal the military's final document. "Adjectival" democracy did not triumph.

Míguez claimed rightly that the march toward democracy was "guaranteed by the explicit will of the Argentine people."[35] Argentines in all sectors of society have endorsed constitutional democracy. Political parties, unions, business, industry and agriculture, the Roman Catholic Church, Jewish synagogues, human rights organizations, student groups, Indian spokespeople, intellectuals and cultural leaders, soccer stars, the mass media, and people on the streets in Buenos Aires and in the interior of the country have voiced their support. The Protestant churches are also affirming the democratic option.[36] Those who may be opposed do not express their opinion publicly.

The significance of these events is obvious. Argentina moved rapidly from a regime founded largely on coercion to a situation in which the coercive power of the state can be sanctioned and moderated by the consent of the people and by constitutional legal norms. It has gone from a state marked by the absence of mediations to one whose claim to legitimacy is credibly linked to the mediations of nation, citizenship, and *el pueblo*. The return to full constitutional democracy means the end of a system of domination and the beginning of another system whose dynamic may be "the unifying element in the long-term effort to establish a society that is more nearly in accord with certain fundamental values."

The repudiation of a regime principally responsible for Argentina's radical political evil does not mean that the country has arrived at a perfect political arrangement. My thesis is that constitutional democracy is the best—and only—bulwark against another bureaucratic-authoritarian state whose "specialists in coercion" cannot be limited by popular and constitutional restraints. Proposals for Argentina's political future that do not take into account a possible return of the military ignore history. The horrors of the past could conceivably happen again; the moral mandate to prevent them from recurring must have priority. Constitutional democracy is the only viable political option that may serve as an "insurmountable barrier to every form of violence."[37]

The tragic experiences of the recent past are instructive in another way. The three mediations O'Donnell identifies are all important, and they are mutually linked. Political suppression and the reality of the disappeared remind us that respect for the rights of citizenship are vital for all sectors of society. The policies pursued by the civilian technocrats of the dictatorship led to an economic situation in which it was *el pueblo* that most suffered when excluded from political participation. Argentina's loss of prestige in the world because of its repressive policies at home and the consequences of the South Atlantic War makes clear that national and military policy are too important to be left in the hands of the military and their supporting elites. Political democracy is a structure that acknowledges the validity of all three mediations, offering protection from the terrors of the state and enabling participation in public decisions. It provides means of settling conflicts without recourse to political violence. Respect for the rights of citizenship intrinsic to constitutional democracy offers the best assurance that demands for substantive justice and national well-being may be creatively articulated and proximate responses found. The obvious character of the affirmation should not distract from its importance: constitutional democracy holds more promise to serve justice, understood as freedom, participation, and equality, than does its most probable alternative, military dictatorship.

Democracy's Possibility in Light of Argentine History

Argentina is now in the first phases of consolidating democracy and reconstructing its life and institutions in accord with this democratic commitment. There is positive evidence—as well as some setbacks—of growing democratization in political parties, unions, and universities, as well as in the armed forces. Former authorities of the military regime are facing legal charges in military and civilian courts. The government has acted to clarify what happened to the disappeared and dismantle the old repressive apparatus. Not all agree that enough has been done, however. Argentina's powerful unions are once again exercising their right to strike, and some fear a chaotic situation. Radicals, Peronists, and the small parties on both their left and their right are making proposals on human rights, on economic independence, recovery, and distribution; on the role of the armed forces in a Third World democratic society; on national unity and sovereignty; and on the country's role in Latin America and in a world dominated by the two superpowers. Such debates are the testing ground for Argentina's young democracy.

Will all this continue, or are present events just one more swing of the pendulum from civilian-to-military-to-civilian government that has characterized Argentinian political life? One historian has called contemporary Argentine history a "cemetery of failed transitions."[38] Will failure also be the future of this transition? To pose such questions is to acknowledge that the situation is precarious. My own projection is modest: democracy is now a reality in Argentina and there is a possibility that it will continue.

A brief review of the country's political history makes clear how often events contradict the formal structure of constitutional democracy. Argentina did not adopt its Constitution until 1853, nearly half a century after its independence. The years before its adoption were marked by civil war, anarchy, and tyranny. Those who wrote the Constitution and benefited most from it were "the oligarchy," who possessed a large *latifundio* in Argentina's rich plains and who directed the country's economic and intellectual orientation toward Europe. This group dominated the country for more than fifty years, and it was not until 1912 that electoral reform granted universal male suffrage. Women were not enfranchised until 1947. Because of the first electoral reform, the radicals, representing the then lower-class groups of immigrants, gained power by means of the ballot box in 1916. They were ousted in the country's first military coup in 1930[39]; and the old conservative elite inaugurated "the infamous decade" of corruption and electoral fraud that ended in 1943 with a military takeover by a new generation of officers influenced by events in Europe. Col. Juan Perón emerged as the dominant leader, and he forged an alliance with the new urban classes. Perón was elected in 1946 and became the last elected president to have finished his term of office up to the present. Reelected in 1952, he was removed from office by the military in 1955, and the Peronist party was proscribed from participating in elections until 1973. A rotation of civilian and military governments ensued: elections in 1958, a coup in 1962; elections in 1963, a coup in 1966. In 1973, there were two general elections, both won by the Peronists. The first Peronist President resigned so that the seventy-eight-year-old Perón, after eighteen years in exile, could once again become President. He died in 1974, and the Vice-President, his wife, Isabel Perón, replaced him until the coup of March 24, 1976. Raúl Alfonsín assumed the Presidency on December 10, 1983, and the new democratization began.

Obviously, then, there exist deeply rooted antidemocratic forces in Argentina. The armed forces have played a central political role, and five of the six coups they have executed since 1930 have been in alliance with conservative economic groups. It is precisely the strong evidence of this past that leads me to insist that the most probable alternative to democracy in Argentina is an antipopular authoritarian military regime. Even when Perón won the open elections of 1946, his government soon showed authoritarian trends in which *lo popular* tended to undercut certain rights of citizenship. These tendencies were reinforced by the "disloyal opposition" of the old parties.[40] There also emerged a new "constant" that constrained and limited the possibilities of political action: the polarization between Peronists and anti-Peronists that resulted from "the articulation of power and opposition according to rules that were not shared." Argentina was not divided by two parties but became "'two countries': one whose inhabitants could only accept Argentina with Perón, and another that could only accept Argentina without Perón, and in terms of power, without Peronismo."[41] In 1973, democracy reemerged amid great social and political turmoil, a situation made even more difficult by Perón's death in 1974. Argentina's history with democracy should help us to understand that its existence in the present is a threatened one.

The Debate over Constitutional Democracy

Míguez's belief in "the demise of the democratic liberal project" mentioned earlier is grounded in "the thesis that in capitalist social formation the economic factor plays the predominant role."[42] Today, this economic dependence is characterized by "the third colonial pact" between transnational corporations and technical-military elites in dependent countries.[43] Míguez describes what he takes to be a worldwide phenomenon: "The liberal modernization project, as incorporated in the liberal democratic state built on the base of free-enterprise capitalism, seems to have run its course and proven unable to respond to the needs of humanity at the present stage of human development." The "capitalist transnational project," with its controlled development within the framework of the world capitalist system and "limited democracy under the management of technocratic elites," is faced by "two main obstacles" in the Third World. Economically, the capitalist system finds it increasingly difficult to incorporate "peripheral economies" into that system. Politically, it has been "unable to co-opt the popular majorities of the Third World." Thus, popular pressure tends to destabilize the political situation of Third World nations. "Either it generates the kind of unrest and violence that threaten democratic life, or it justifies the centralization of power, tightened state control, and enhanced repression, whether hidden or overt—which also amounts to the demise of the democratic liberal project."[44]

Míguez is correct in saying that the world is in crisis, although he would have to write more to show that it is only "the liberal modernization project" that is unable to respond to the needs of humanity today.[45] He is also right in identifying the pressures on a dependent, peripheral country that result from an unjust economic order in crisis. Although other factors need also to be considered, economic pressures do place a question mark over the democratic process in Argentina. Certainly he identifies the major challenge that confronts existing democracy in Argentina: that of seeking more justice with an order of freedom *and* participation. Will the demands for both equality and freedom enhance or destroy the country's present democratic order? The conclusion that seems to follow from Míguez's premises would doom Argentina's new experiment with constitutional democracy to chaos or tyranny.

There are, however, reasons to believe that Míguez's analysis is not entirely adequate for Argentina. He foresaw, for example, only a "limited democracy" as the political structure that would follow the national security state. Yet, in fact, *el pueblo* defeated this political program of the "capitalist transnational project." One should remember, of course, that Míguez is trying to describe a worldwide, long-term development; nevertheless, with respect to Argentina, his analysis appears to give too much predominance to "the economic factor." His discussion of the national security state does not do justice to the complex tensions within its alliance that O'Donnell outlined or that were apparent in the Malvinas incident. Nor does this help one to understand, for example, why Argentina's security state's political relations were better with the Soviet Union than with the USNA during the Carter Administration because of the latter's human rights policy and grain embargos. Most important, it does not aid one to understand why "liberal democracy," instead of experiencing its "demise," shows signs of vitality. Míguez admits in theory to the relative autonomy of politics,[46] but his generalizations about the liberal democratic state subordinate it to transnational capitalism. The autonomy of politics is thereby obscured. Constitutional democratic politics and private capitalist economics are claimed to be part of one single tightly wrapped historical package: "the liberal democratic project." To understand the events of 1983 and the significance of the difference between limited democracy and constitutional democracy one needs to distinguish more sharply between the political order and the economic and, in this context, to give more weight to the political factor. While today, Argentina remains a dependent capitalist economy, there are conflicts between the political projects that emerge within its democracy and the interests of international capitalism. Democratic constitutional government does have room, I would argue, to act for the benefit of the people in relation to external economic forces and to balance the demands for equality and freedom without eliminating the validity of either aspiration.

In this regard I find helpful Irving Horowitz's endorsement of "C. Wright Mills' belief that there are three large scale factors that have primary importance: the political, the economic and the military; and that these cannot a priori be reduced to each other, is a central element in any serious theory of international stratification." In the Third World, the military is critical, but "the relative strength of the military *vis-a-vis* the political or economic is an empirical question, not a matter of including the military as a part of the social formation. . . . We cannot simply say that any given variable is fundamental and any other is derivative."[47] The return to constitutional democracy in Argentina is a reassertion of the political variable in relation to the other two. The political cannot be separated from these other two factors, but neither should it be seen simply as their extension. My claim for the relative autonomy of politics involves belief in the possibility of its creative use to contain the military as well as to negotiate for the nation's welfare in relation to capitalists' interests.

Horowitz claims that "the transition from inauspicious military beginnings to democratic forms has become the central Third World task in the final decades of the twentieth century."[48] As Argentina pursues this task, it can count on the fact that its democratic tradition persists, despite its past instability and the limited fulfillment of its promise. One reason for its persistence is that democracy is part of Argentina's collective identity as a nation. Most Argentines do not see democracy as a foreign imposition, but as an integral part of their national tradition. Loyalty to the Constitution has helped form the nation, and for a century, it has been the only formula of legitimacy permanently acceptable to the majority. Even the enemies of democracy have acted to destroy democracy in the name of democracy.

A second reason that democratic tradition lives on is that popular sectors have achieved social and economic gains by democratic means. In 1916 and 1946, for example, new social sectors achieved significant political power through elections. Both the middle classes and the working class have become political forces in opposition to established economic elites precisely by participating in democratic institutions. The social, economic, and educational gains of workers through their union resulted from the functioning of this system. There is a historical base for claiming that popularly elected governments offer the best political alternative to counter antipopular and antinational economic interests and to enhance economic and social equality.

The belief that freedom is important and the constitutional democracy will sustain it also thrives in Argentina. This is not surprising in a complex industrialized and pluralistic society with deep roots in the Western cultural tradition. After recent events, few today simply dismiss constitutional freedoms as privileges of a bourgeoisie elite. Human rights' concerns are tied to the future of democracy.

In 1981, Horowitz saw Argentina moving toward a "constitutional dictatorship" and "as an exception to any sort of democratization process in the Third World."[49] His prediction, too, was mistaken, but he was right to question "a particular consensus forming, from both Left and Right sources, that a swing of the Third World to fascism is taking place. He believed that there were also present "politically counter-cyclical" tendencies "toward a broad based democratization." He also contended that "democracy has a compelling force; the drive toward democracy characterizes the entire sweep of the twentieth century." Everywhere major political movements are raising questions about egalitarianism, and questions of liberty have become central. "The linchpin of all these issues is neither communism, capitalism, nor welfarism, but how all would address the question of egalitarianism and libertarian persuasions."[50]

Democracy's future in Argentina will, of course, depend on the wisdom shown in mediating the conflicting claims that emerge between freedom and equality. Knowing the high cost of military rule, Argentina does not seem to be tempted by what Horowitz calls the "fake dialectic" of the Stalinist model, which assumed "that a society had to surrender democracy in order to have development."[51] The possibility exists that democracy will continue in Argentina because "large segments of society, still believe, rightly or wrongly, in the desirability of an open, competitive, democractic political system."[52]

Is this current transition in any way different from earlier ones? This is a complex question that I cannot exhaust here. Some factors not yet mentioned encourage hope that this transition will result in enduring democracy: the election of a President committed to democracy, who is widely considered to be both charismatic and reasonable[53]; the victory of the Radical party that softens the Peronist/anti-Peronist polarization, giving time for the Peronist party to renew itself; a historical point when two parties are strongest, and when ideological convergence on a range of issues prevails; the strength and importance of human rights organizations; a pro-democractic stance from a Roman Catholic hierarchy that in times past was not so clear about democracy, which is now supported by a popular Pope; and the felt need to regain national prestige in the world. In a country where 45 percent of the population have their roots in Spain, the democratic shift there is also helpful, as is European democratic socialism's new interest in Latin America. The two superpowers' consent to democracy in Argentina is also helpful.

From a moral viewpoint, however, the reality now sustaining constitutional democracy that should not be ignored is the collective memory of radical political evil, especially that embodied in the military dictatorship, but also that found in earlier revolutionary violence. The period just past is described frequently in poetic image as "the blind years," "the long night," or, in Juan Luis Segundo's phrase, "the years of desperation."[54] Reminders that the political experience of the past fifteen years must be avoided in the future conveys a sense that a "forced option" exists, that Argentina is "condemned" to constitutional democracy.

Argentina's "decision" for democracy is not analogous to a personal choice. The usage is metaphorical. It signifies political change through complex processes involving millions of people with various degrees of responsibility for such processes. It suggests that human freedom is an ingredient in structuring society. As noted, this freedom is socially located and occurs within the limits and possibilities of an overall situation. Democracy's future will not be determined outside the historical, cultural, political, and economic factors at work in and on Argentina, nor will it be decided independently of the experiences, ideas, hopes, fears, and deeds of its protagonists. We have reason to be suspicious of predictions that ignore *either* freedom or destiny; in history, the two are inseparably linked. The attitudes and actions of those responsible for political processes are key. If democracy is lost, I hope that there will continue to be people who can say, "This was not necessary."[55] And if it does endure, it will be said: "We can be grateful that there were hopeful people who, knowing the limits and the threats of the situation, took advantage of history's possibilities."

The Revolutionary Option

The affirmation that constitutional democracy is the political structure that offers the best hope for embracing and protecting justice in Argentina runs counter to the claim that a revolutionary strategy whose goal is socialism is the only option that can bring justice. There are those who have claimed this in Argentina, and some have thought that the moment was ripe for this sort of revolutionary change. In what follows I will argue that for ethical, political reasons, the revolutionary option should be discarded in a democratic Argentina. Those who seek fundamental change should give their unambiguous consent to constitutional democracy.

Christians believe that all persons are God's creatures, worthy of life and respect. We possess reasons of heart and mind to be morally repelled by political violence, no matter what its origin or its goals. Our attitudes and actions ought to be governed by a strong presumption against strategies for change that require killing others for a cause believed just. Those Christians like myself who do not hold an absolute prohibition on the use of political violence must nevertheless take a basic operational posture of skepticism when faced with calls to armed struggle.

To be sure, we are also to seek justice, and this search does take place in a violent, oppressive world in which people face conflicting claims of value and loyalty. In the pursuit of justice, however, our presumptions should be that nonviolent methods are morally preferable.[56] We are also compelled to consider circumstances when use of violence might be justified morally. I accept Míguez's proposal that in assessing structural change, "the basic criterion is the maximizing of universal human possibilities and the minimizing of human costs."[57] The question thus becomes: "when, if ever, might political violence maximize human possibilities and minimize human costs?" The answer cannot be given a priori but must be discerned in particular situations.

For further guidance in this necessary process of historical calculation, I accept the criteria of the just war as valid in helping to determine the difference between just and unjust political violence in relation to questions of revolution.[58] Just-war criteria suggest that violence is justifiable only when used by legitimate authority, that there be right intention in its use, that it be used only as a last resort, that it be used with proportionality, that its use have reasonable chance of success, and that there be moderation in pressing violent conflict. These criteria offer some direction for decision-making in particular contexts.[59]

On the basis of this ethical perspective, let us assess the revolutionary options that formed in Argentina in the late 1960s and the first part of the 1970s. Although there are dangers in moral evaluation of the past, it is necessary to evaluate the past and learn from it, for the sake of the future.

In 1967, Richard Shaull predicted that the "next stage in Latin America" would be shaped by the "conviction that armed struggle built upon the guerrilla *foco* [center] is the only way to move ahead." He reported that sensitivity to the desperate economic and social situation of the rural and urban masses and despair of constitutional democratic political processes were leading a growing number of committed religious people to concur with Régis Debray "that a total national struggle of liberation centering around the guerrilla *foco* is not only possible in Latin America but is the only solution." Shaull agreed that "what remains is a long-term, total military struggle against the old order and those external forces sustaining it."[60] Shaull reflected the increasing importance of Cuba's revolutionary strategy for Latin America, as spelled out in Debray's book *Revolution in the Revolution*,[61] exemplified in Che Guevara's action in Bolivia and proclaimed and supported by the Organization of Latin American Solidarity conference held in August 1967 in Havana.[62] Here the legal strategy of the traditional Moscow-line Communist parties was rejected in favor of one in which small, clandestine military groups would engage in prolonged armed struggle to break the power of the capitalist state as, it was claimed, had happened in Cuba.

In Argentina, various guerrilla organizations formed, the most important being the Montoneros, who identified themselves with the Peronist movement.[63] Their often highly dramatic violent acts, such as bombing, robbery, extortion, kidnapping, killing, assassination, assault on army garrisons, became a prominent feature of Argentine life. Right-wing groups, some also connected with Peronism, fought these groups. Montoneros held important positions during the first Peronist government of 1973, but after Perón's public criticism of them on May 1, 1974, the Peronist government opposed them. Thousands were either killed, made to disappear, or driven into exile by antisubversive violence.

The guerrilla *foco* in Argentina did not, it is obvious, achieve its goal, but it brought about bloodshed and suffering. Revolutionary violence did not change systemic violence, but it did provoke counterrevolutionary violence that demonstrated its capacity for brutality. "Indeed, their only contribution to history was accelerating the creation of the new rightist totalitarian systems. *Foquismo* is dead, politically dead." The naive notion that "they were able to challenge the power of the state and the armed forces" proved to be humanly costly.[64] The middle-class origins of guerrilla leaders and their elitist antipopular strategy undercut any claim that they were the legitimate representatives of the masses. Although it is true that they began their violent resistance under a military dictatorship after 1966, it is also certain that they continued it under popularly elected governments. Their methods deserve to be condemned. "It is difficult to admit that terrorism, provoking repression, summary 'judgments' and 'executions' protected by a supposed 'revolutionary legality' can be justified ethically or politically."[65] Míguez's words apply to the groups that used the *foco* strategy in Argentina: "Elites can easily be mesmerized by their own rhetoric and engage in adventures that leave behind a tragic residue of death and suffering."[66]

Segundo adds another element to this analysis, what he terms the ecological dimension.[67] In his framework, the causes of this violence are rooted in centuries-old institutional violence, and he recognizes that existing repressive violence was much greater than was the subversive violence that countered it. Nevertheless, he argues, even a situation of institutionalized violence constitutes a "certain social *ecology*." To seek change is a duty, "but to change an ecology is not to change just anything. And the temptation, when it exists, can be to change it in just any way, that is, to *violate* it." The events of these painful years, he argues, reveal "the unsuspected density of a reality which, with the best desires in the world, we had conceived as much simpler than it was." He acknowledges that urgency combined with political pessimism resulted "in a stage of reflexive impoverishment, rationalistic simplism, and enthusiastic activism" in which Marxism was used "in its most simple and simplifying versions." The concept of "social ecology" is introduced to point to "the complex equilibrium" of social systems, to the systematic and intricate relations of people with their context. The fact that these conditions were ignored by the guerrillas "produced chain reactions" that went far beyond and offset their original intentions.[68] Prolonged subversive violence provoked ecological destruction, he insists. In contrast with conventional warfare, in which the boundaries are clear, guerrilla war waged by those who believe that their cause justifies the destruction of persons does not respect limits. Along with those who are to be destroyed, this type of warfare uses the ordinary social relations of family, friendship, and hospitality to carry on the struggle. This, insists Segundo, "violates them in their very root: confidence." In this view, those who wage subversive violence are the internal and incognito enemies consciously equated with those with whom they maintain basic social relations, and those in turn are credited with sympathies they themselves have not chosen, but for which, later and involuntarily, they can be jailed, tortured, and killed. The soldier in the covert war, when she acts like a normal citizen, necessarily makes all knowledgeable persons that protect her the possessors of vital military secrets for the other side. Or the doctor who heals a guerrilla without denouncing him is considered "safe" by the organization and later can be exhorted to lend more decisive aid. In such ways, clandestine war distorts the basic rules of human and social conviviality.[69]

Segundo's analysis deepens our understanding of the high human cost of the sort of revolutionary theory and praxis expressed in Argentina's recent past. When day-to-day living became entangled in the web of political violence, what was undercut was not simply a political regime, but also the basic confidence that holds human life together. His distinction between institutionalized violence and social ecology, together with his penetrating discussion of the importance of the latter, clarifies the complexity of social relations and the inextricably mixed good and evil of history. Social orderings, the constants of human living, are more than injustice, and violence is a poor instrument to use to separate the wheat and the tares in the living field of social relations. When used in Argentina with the promise that it was the only possible solution to injustice, the result was a further violation of the fragile social fabric. More than ever the country needs a political structure that respects its social ecology.

"No community can live in a permanent state of civil war, which would result from a revolutionary socialism unable to press through to its goal. If violence can be justified at all, its terror must have the tempo of a surgeon's skill and healing must follow quickly upon its wounds."[70] What happened in Argentina was neither skillful nor healing; its time prolonged, its methods crass, its human price dear, and its aftereffect unleashed a viciousness whose consequences will be felt for years. Revolutionary socialism's prospects in the present are dim. Although its violence might conceivably serve to destroy constitutional democracy, its possibility of pressing through to its goal is exceedingly slight; it lacks a reasonable chance of success. Even a mass-based revolutionary movement would need to show that it is doing more than contributing to "a permanent state of civil war." A convincing case cannot be made in the present that such political violence maximizes human possibilities and minimizes human costs. It cannot satisfy the criteria of the just revolution. On the contrary, the historical mandate to seek to eliminate violence as a method of political change in Argentina is both timely and morally compelling. The cry "no more violence" has ethical validity and priority, and constitutional democracy is the only available alternative to reduce and control, if not eliminate, political violence, whether in its revolutionary or counterrevolutionary form. Where "no single political force ... can break through and completely reorganize the present unstable equilibrium of forces in modern society," then "a non-violent type of political coercion is clearly preferable to a violent one. Parliamentary socialism would, in that case, be justified, even if it were robbed of the hope of a final and complete triumph."[71] Revolutionary socialists, he suggests, are also condemned to democratic process.

If a democratic order is morally and politically imperative, the antidemocratic attitude connected with the revolutionary option needs to be exposed and challenged. It is inappropriate for the Argentine context. In 1974, Míguez outlined the attitude to be criticized under the rubric "the new Latin American consciousness." The fundamental element of this consciousness is the discovery of Latin American economic dependence, and "a second is the exposure of the 'hoax of democracy.'" In his earlier book, Míguez described the continent's democratic experience in unrelentingly negative terms. Its forms, he claimed, remained "external to the life of the people," and its promised constitutional freedoms have been "the privilege of the elite." For the masses, "the harvest of one century of 'liberal democracy'" has been undernourishment, slavery, illiteracy, exploitation, and repression.[72] I have already argued that these generalizations do not adequately deal with the Argentine historical evidence, whatever may be the case in other Latin American countries. Here, the political meaning of exposing this "hoax" is to communicate a message that to seek change within constitutional democracy is a deception, and therefore the struggle for liberation is right in subverting, overthrowing, and replacing it. The message functions to de-legitimatize existing democracy and to legitimatize revolutionary efforts to destroy it, to destabilize one political order as an essential part of creating a new one. This exposure, however, assumes two things. One is that there exists a better, viable alternative to "liberal democracy" because to expose a fraud presupposes that we know what is genuine. The other is that nothing worse could possibly replace this "hoax." Neither assumption is confirmed by Argentine history. To continue to conceive democracy as a fraud is a luxury that no one in Argentina can afford.

The legitimacy question will continue to be crucial for Argentina's constitutional democracy. Although the vast majority believe in its legitimacy, the depth and intensity of this loyalty, especially among sectors that in the past have attacked it, must be tested. Argentina's past has been plagued by a conditioned, politically strategic allegiance by groups on both the right and the left. O'Donnell noted that one of the constants in Argentina's political climate has been that "the democratic 'rules of the game' were to be given only limited and conditioned adherence by the ruling sectors; the application of these rules was subject to the proviso that it produce the 'correct' government."[73] The failure of the last de facto government reduced this sector's room to maneuver, and the successful functioning of a strong, orderly democracy would further reduce it. Whether this occurs or not depends in part on the attitude of leftist elites. Fidel Castro's counsel to the priests of the Christians for Socialism movement states the basic principle: "In a revolutionary process, one can utilize bourgeois legality, but one cannot make a revolution if this legality is legitimized, and the people are submitted to it ideologically."[74] If such a manipulative attitude again becomes prominent in Argentina, the result would probably be to destroy the current democratic government's legitimacy, with a loss in its capacity to survive or to enhance justice. A more fundamental commitment to sustain constitutional democracy is required from both right and left rather than one that views it simply as a strategic instrument to advance a particular program.

The political scientist Juan Linz describes the role that revolutionaries may play in the breakdown of democracy:

> The radical critic of the existing social order . . . might maintain that if in the short run democracy cannot serve as an instrument for decisive social change, it does not deserve his loyalty. What he might not realize is that the alternative is not revolutionary change, imposed in authoritarian fashion, but the reversal of slow processes of change under conditions of freedom and compromise, by counterrevolutionary authoritarian rule.[75]

The violent revolutionary option, then, is not a viable ethical or political alternative in democratic Argentina. Legitimate nonviolent methods of political persuasion and coercion must replace political violence. Those who seek justice should do it with a clear and firm consent to constitutional democracy. Míguez was correct in his recent human rights' speech as he was not in his earlier assessment: "The only alternative to democracy is totalitarianism."

Democracy and Liberation

Míguez speaks of liberation, O'Donnell of *el pueblo,* Horowitz of equality. All are referring to the persuasive demand for substantive justice for the poorest sectors of society. Argentina's democratic society must move to meet the needs of its people, especially those of the popular classes, for adequate work, food, shelter, health, and education. It must work for a more just distribution of goods and power, and it must seek to change its relationship of dependence on international capitalism. These "musts" express valid moral imperatives as well as political necessities, insofar as the continuing legitimacy of constitutional democracy depends on its capacity to respond effectively to expectations for more justice.

The cry for liberation forcefully articulated in Argentina should surprise no one. In a country that for years has been "a rare example of economic devolution rather than evolution,"[76] and in which popular sectors have had to carry the principal burden of the worsening situation, economic justice is a central issue. The country has a foreign debt of more than $40 billion, and few doubt the reality of economic dependence. In a nation with long historical claims to the Malvinas Islands, there is little need to argue about the existence of neocolonialism. It is certainly a misconception to believe that because Argentina is now democratic that relations with the USNA are bound to be cozy. People rightly perceive injustice and conflicts of interest in the unequal power relationship with the superpower in their hemisphere. Neither dependence nor the validity of the call for liberation are disputed among most Argentinians, nor should they be.

A peripheral country in a system of economic dependence faces what Leonardo Boff calls a "bitter dilemma." It is posed by the often conflicting requirements of breaking the bonds of dependence and of developing. "Liberation certainly leads to independence but not necessarily to development. Latin American countries have not been able to develop their own technology and no one can develop it alone." He quotes Comblin's view of the dilemma: " 'To liberate oneself and not develop or to choose development and submit oneself. The third term is no more than a compromise: limit development to maintain a certain autonomy; limit independence while choosing sectors that ought to be developed. But this leads us beyond the simple theory of dependence.' "[77] Viable social economic projects must somehow address this dilemma. To face this dilemma and to forge an Argentine project of liberation requires constitutional democracy. The democratic ethos and institutions are formed by the belief that the *el pueblo* are responsible for determining their future. Even given existing inequalities in the access to power, such democracy allows for more popular participation in deciding what projects best serve the people's interest than do systems in which such decisions are left in the hands of elites. The mutual interdependence of constitutional democracy and liberation rests in the capacity of democracy to stimulate alternative proposals for liberation. A diversity of proposed projects is needed to be tested, corrected, and refined through public debate. The give-and-take of democratic processes encourages this. A social change project that does not incorporate democracy as both means and end can hardly be considered liberating. The existence of a democratic structure of government in Argentina does not assure liberation, but it is an essential condition for pursuing this goal.

If this be accepted, the important question becomes "What project of liberation will best serve Argentina?" Surely such a project will include commitment to national independence, social justice, and human rights, as it does in most existing political platforms. Yet differences remain in what these mean and how the bitter dilemma of liberation and economic development should be met. Here I can only mention some elements in the Argentine debate.

Míguez proposes a socialist project of liberation. He accepts Gustavo Gutiérrez's fourfold formula to describe this project: the societal appropriation of the means of production, of political power, and of freedom, and the creation of a new social consciousness. This "fourfold formula," writes Míguez, "points to concrete historical features in the emerging new society. It points to a society which can be described as socialist in the organization of its economy, democratic in terms of the political participation of the people, and open in the sense of ensuring the conditions for personal realization, cultural freedom and opportunity, and the mechanisms for self-correction."[78]

Socialist proposals for Argentina predate liberation theology. Míguez himself, owing in part perhaps to a social gospel tradition in his Methodist Church, was a socialist years before he wrote explicit liberation theology.[79] This socialist tradition goes back to the 1890s, and over the years there has developed a variety of proposals for the sort of socialism required. There is a spectrum of political proposals on the reform-revolutionary spectrum already referred to, as well as on a nationalist-internationalist spectrum as to how specifically economic development should occur.

None of these spectra of socialisms in Argentina has captured the loyalty of the majority of workers. Since the 1940s most workers have identified themselves as Peronists, not socialists. Perón defined his nationalist, multiclass movement not only as anti-Yankee, but also as anti-Marxist. In the crucial 1946 election, some socialist parties and the Communist party sided with the anti-Peronist, conservative coalition that was also supported openly by the USNA embassy. Since then, the historical antagonism between the socialists and the Peronists has continued. Socialists point to Peronist failures vis-à-vis the working classes and what their own ideology could do, and Peronists point to what they have done for the workers and what the socialist ideology has been unable to accomplish.

Socialists view Peronism as a reformist movement within capitalism that, because its ideology does not accept class struggle as the basic social contradiction, is unable to overcome the central contradictions of capitalism. Enrique Dussel formulates a common socialist criticism of Peronist populism as "the alliance of the industrial bourgeoisie, who inevitably always favor transnational companies. Populism, another possible form of dependent capitalism, reveals its limits, however, and in the end betrays the popular cause."[80] Some socialists (such as the Montoneros or the Priests for the Third World[81]) work within Peronism to give it a socialist ideology, whereas others seek to develop alternative parties.

Peronism, which also represents a wide variety of political positions, counters with a negative evaluation of Marxist forms of socialism. For them, Marxism is a foreign, non-Christian ideology that emphasizes class struggle at the expense of real national liberation. Marxist explanations that interpret workers' support for Peronism as a result of the deception, manipulation, or immaturity of the workers are held to be condescending. Marxism in Argentina is considered to be a middle-class ideology, and Peronists point to voting patterns to document workers' support of Peronism since the 1940s. "No one can believe in Argentina that so-called 'leftist' parties and movements represent the workers."[82] This claim was confirmed in the last elections. While the Radicals received 52 percent of the vote for President and the Peronists 40 percent, the socialist parties received less than 1 percent. In a lengthy analysis of the elections, a Marxist magazine spoke of "the eclipse or rather the evaporation of the left."[83]

Whether an Argentine project of liberation grows out of one of the major traditional parties or out of a socialist party is a question that *el pueblo* will decide. For now, the people have entrusted the Radicals with the principal responsibility of governing the nation. A modest yet bold hope for this government is that it may consolidate democracy, achieve a rough justice in relation to the past radical political evil of the military government, that it can begin to undo the damage caused by earlier economic policies and lay the bases for more profound change. The movement of Argentina's newest democratic turn from infancy to maturity is bound to be difficult, uneven, and precarious, yet it is an essential movement for those committed to Argentina's liberation. Hope for liberation includes hope that democracy is the best political structure for the country.

A Concluding Postscript

The USNA reader must not imagine Argentina's future remote from his or her concerns. Such an attitude must be challenged. There are no shortcuts or substitutes for understanding the complexity of nations like Argentina for Christians in USNA who seek to support genuine liberation. Those who want to support Latin American peoples face an immense and difficult task of discernment. We must understand situations in some depth. Churches must stimulate and coordinate serious study of other nations' historical and cultural context. The responsibility of the churches in USNA for Latin American well-being includes a far more profound knowledge of this continent.

A democratic Argentina is an option that deserves a deep, affirmative response from USNA Christians and also from the USNA government. Christians have reason to scrutinize carefully what USNA interests do in relation to Argentina. We must face the fact that USNA credibility as a friend of democracy in Latin America is severely strained. Its policy is perceived as supportive of democracy only when it is within its economic and military interests to do so. Its aid to fraudulent democracies and to military regimes, and its willingness to help to overthrow "unacceptable" democratic governments such as Chile in 1973 have persuaded many Latin-Americans that its commitment to democracy is conditioned by a narrow perception of its own interests. USNA policy seems aimed at having weak, partial democracies in Latin America rather than strong, independent ones. Argentina's democratic decision of 1983 can only deepen to serve the people, if it becomes strong and independent. What USNA governmental and business interests do in relation to the democratic prospect in Argentina will be an important element in determining whether democracy thrives. Christians and churches must play a role in ensuring that USNA influence in Argentina genuinely serves justice for Argentines themselves.

FIVE

Third World Theology
—A New Context
for Ecumenical Ethics

J.R. Chandran

*T*his essay is a narrative reflection on the significance of Third World theology in the work of the Ecumenical Association of Third World Theologians (EATWOT) and its relation to earlier forms of ecumenism. The emergence of this group challenges all Christians to take seriously the intrinsic priority of justice to Christian ecumenical dialogue, whether in theology or ethics. The association was formed at a conference of Christian theologians from Africa, Asia, and Latin America belonging to different churches—Roman Catholic, Protestant, and Orthodox—held at the University of Dar es Salaam, Tanzania, in August 1976. The following statement in the Preamble of the Constitution of EATWOT suggests what the founders of the association meant by the expression Third World theology, or Third World theologians:

> The growing concern among Christians of the Third World about the structures of domination and injustices keeping a wide gap between the rich and the poor among the nations and within the nations was followed by an equally important concern about the continuing dependence of Third World theologies on models inherited from the affluent West. These models have been incapable of challenging and overcoming the injustices and of developing new models of theology which would interpret the Gospel in a more meaningful way to the peoples of the Third World and promote their struggles for liberation. In particular, these new models would promote a deeper rooting of

J.R. Chandran, formerly Principal of United Theological College, Bangalore, India, and currently Visiting Professor of Theology and Ethics at Pacific Theological College, Suva, Fiji.

the Christian message within the cultures of the people, in respectful dialogue with the persons and their traditional or popular religions.

The desire for a meeting of theologians from the Third World was first expressed by Roman Catholic theologians from Africa doing advanced studies in Europe, particularly at Louvain, who had become aware of the limitations of traditional Catholic theology for dealing with African realities. Their request received a positive response from the authorities in Rome, and a small group of Roman Catholic theologians from the Third World, including Fr. Njindu Mushete of Zaire, Fr. D.S. Amalorpavadas of India, and Fr. Sergio Torres of Chile, were asked to explore possibilities for this conference. Their recommendation was that insofar as the issue raised was not peculiar to Roman Catholics, such a conference should have a more inclusive ecumenical basis. Accordingly, they called together a small but representative group of theologians from African, Asian, and Latin American countries, both Catholic and Protestant, at Nairobi in December 1975, correlating with the meeting of the Fifth Assembly of the World Council of Churches, where many Third World theologians were in attendance. Proposals from this group led to an ad hoc conference held at Dar es Salaam, entitled "Ecumenical Dialogue of Third World Theologians," with equal numbers of participants from Africa, Asia, and Latin America. Half the participants were Roman Catholic and the other half were from various Protestant and Orthodox churches. A full report of the conference, including the papers presented there and the final statement issued, was published as *The Emergent Gospel—Theology from the Underside of History.*[1]

The program of the conference had three main parts: (1) a critical analysis of the political, social, economic, cultural, racial, and religious history of the Third World; (2) a review of the nature of the presence and the role played by the Christian churches in the Third World countries; (3) an effort at formulating new directions for Christian theology in the Third World. Even though nothing approaching a consensus about the shape of Third World theology emerged from the conference, there was agreement that new models of theology were needed to articulate the power of the gospel within Third World nations.

The final statement issued by the conference observed:

> The Churches are still burdened by the traditions, theologies, and institutions of a colonial past, while the countries want to move rapidly into the modern world and peoples clamour for radical changes in favour of justice and freedom, all round inculturation, and increased inter-religious dialogue and collaboration.[2]

With respect to the dependence of Third World churches on theologies borrowed from the West, it declared:

> The theologies from Europe and North America are dominant today in our churches and represent one form of cultural domination. They must be understood to have arisen out of situations related to those countries, and therefore must not be uncritically adopted without our raising the question of their relevance in the context of our countries. Indeed, we must, in order to be faithful to the Gospel and to our peoples, reflect on realities of our own situations and interpret the Word of God in relation to these realities. We reject as irrelevant an academic type of theology that is divorced from action. We are prepared for a radical break in epistemology which makes commitment the first act in theology and engages in critical reflection on the praxis of the reality of the Third World.[3]

What is implied here is that Christian theology in the Third World cannot simply mimic the traditional deductive approach, accepting uncritically the formulations of Christian faith that were developed in a different time, culture, and place. What is affirmed is that the proper starting point for doing theology rests in discerning the new forms of obedience that the gospel of Jesus Christ demands in our concrete situations. The needed theological formulations develop from the concrete process of reflection as to how the gospel transforms us within our own historicocultural situations. Instead of an uncritical application of the "classical" theological formulations of the past, we must make a critical sociocultural analysis of these formulations, asking whether and to what degree these give some guidance for our present theological task. Third World theologians insist that every theological formulation is socially, culturally, and philosophically conditioned and that no theology has perennial validity.

At the Dar es Salaam meeting, the participants agreed to plan annual conferences over a four-year period: a Pan-African Conference, an Asian Conference, a Latin American Conference, and a Global Third World Theologians Conference. It was also envisaged that after this series of conferences, another was needed for dialogue and interaction between the theologians of the First and the Third Worlds. These events have taken place more or less according to this original plan, thanks to the generous financial support from churches and organizations of the First World, both Protestant and Roman Catholic.

The theme of the Pan-African Conference, held in Accra, Ghana, in December 1977, was "The Christian Commitment in Africa Today—Concerns of Emerging Christian Theologies." The final statement issued by the conference affirmed:

The African situation requires a new theological methodology that is different from the dominant theologies of the West. African Theology must reject, therefore, the prefabricated ideas of North Atlantic Theology by defining itself according to the struggles of the people in their resistance against the structures of domination. Our task as theologians is to create a theology that arises out of and is accountable to the African people.[4]

The theologians assembled identified three characteristics required for the African theology that arises from this commitment to the freedom struggles of African people:

1. Contextual theology—accountable to the context in which the people live.
2. Liberation theology—because oppression is found not only in culture, but also in political and economic structures.
3. Involvement of theology in the struggle against sexism and the recognition that women are an integral part of the liberation struggle.[5]

The substance of the Accra affirmation was that African theology should articulate a discernment of the good news of God in Christ in solidarity with struggling African peoples.

The Asian Theological Conference was held at Wennapuwa, near Colombo, Sri Lanka, in January 1979. Its theme was "Asia's Struggle for Full Humanity—Towards a Relevant Theology."[6] Here, too, participants made a conscious effort to relate theological reflection to the experiences of people in the diverse situations of the Asian continent. They shared case studies of the struggles going on in different countries as well as a "live-in" experience that exposed them to the actual life situations of various depressed and marginated sectors of Sri Lankan society. In summarizing the reports from the "live-in" experience, Fr. Samuel Rayan said:

One of the convictions the "live-in" deepens is that truth is not words and books. Truth is people, their lives, their minds, their self-understanding. If the Gospel is directly addressed to the poor, they are the ones likely to have the best grasp of its intent and meaning. It is in their praxis that the Gospel becomes an historical force for transformation, and thus acquires historical truth. We do well in going to them to encounter the revelation that is being made in their midst.[7]

At the Asian conference, a demand was made to find fresh answers to the questions "What is theology?" and "Who is a theologian?" It was again affirmed that in order to be relevant to Asian life, Christian theology must undergo a radical transformation. It was recognized that Asian theological thought must grapple not only with the sociopolitical reality, but also that the religiocultural reality of Asia requires engagement with the traditions of the great non-Christian religions that have shaped life on our continent. The insights gained from these engagements must be taken seriously in doing Asian Christian theology. On the question of the methodology of doing Christian theology, the conference opposed any sharp either/or choice or dichotomy between exposition of Christian tradition and political and cultural analysis. The group opted for maintaining a dialectical relationship between both. The final statement of the conference affirmed:

> The first act of theology, its very heart, is commitment. This commitment is response to the challenge of the poor in their struggle for full humanity. We affirm that the poor and the oppressed of Asia are called by God to be the architects and builders of their own destiny.[8]

On the subject of theology, the statement said:

> To be truly liberating, this theology must arise from the Asian poor with a liberated consciousness. It is articulated and expressed by the oppressed community using the technical skills of Biblical scholars, Social Scientists, Psychologists, Anthropologists and others. ... This does not exclude the so-called specialists in Theology. ... But their theologizing becomes authentic only when rooted in the history and struggle of the poor and the oppressed.[9]

Affirming the biblical perspective, the statement went on to say:

> The God encountered in the history of the people is none other than the God who revealed himself in the events of Jesus' life, death and resurrection. We believe that God and Christ continue to be present in the struggles of the people to achieve full humanity as we look forward in hope to the consummation of all things when God will be all in all.[10]

The Latin American Conference was held at São Paulo, Brazil, in February-March 1980. Its theme was "The Ecclesiology of Popular Christian Communities."[11] Along with the final document, this conference issued a "Letter to Christians in Popular Christian Communities in the Poor Countries and Regions of the World." The witness of many Christians, individuals and groups in situations of oppression and violence in different Latin American countries, and particularly the witness of the many Basic Christian Communities—groups of Christians who work, pray, and study scripture together within a local community where they join together to provide food, shelter, and mutual support for survival—that exist across Latin America formed an important background for this discussion. The pronouncements of the Roman Catholic bishops made at Medellín in 1968 and at Puebla in 1979 shaped much of this discussion at São Paulo. One of the important theses of the São Paulo document is that genuine evangelization is inextricably linked with the church's option for the poor:

> To evangelize is to announce the true God, the God revealed in Christ, the God who makes a covenant with the oppressed and defends their cause, the God who liberates this people from injustice, from oppression and from sin.
>
> The liberation of the poor is a journey full of grief, marked by both the passion of Christ and by the signs of resurrection. The liberation of the poor is a vast history that embraces all of human history and gives it true meaning. The Gospel proclaims the history of total liberation as it is present in today's events. It shows how, here and now, among the poor masses of Latin America and all marginated peoples, God is freeing his people.[12]

The document affirms an integral relationship between the discipleship of Jesus and participation in the struggles against oppression and injustice.

> In the following of Jesus, the spiritual experience is never separated from the liberating struggle. In the heart of this process God is experienced as a Father to whom every effort and every struggle is offered.
> . . .
> Jesus' journey, that of the basic ecclesial communities, is a journey of faith in a God whom we do not see and of a love of our brothers and sisters whom we do see. Those who say they believe, but do not love, or who say that they love but in practice do not, are not on Jesus' path. Thus the martyrs of justice, who give their lives for the freedom of their oppressed brothers and sisters are also martyrs of faith, for they learn from the Gospel the commandment of fraternal love as a sign of the Lord's disciples.[13]

The path to Christian ecumenism, including the unity of the churches, is also discerned to be grounded in solidarity with the cause of the poor. The document affirms:

> We affirm with joy that through solidarity with the cause of the poor, through participation in their struggles, in their sufferings and in their persecution, the first great barrier that for so long had divided our churches is being broken down. Many Christians are rediscovering the gift of unity as they encounter the one Christ in the poor of the Third World (Matt. 25). . . .

In this option for the poor and in the practice of justice we have deepened the roots of our faith in the one Lord, the one Church, the one God and Father. In the following of Jesus we confess Christ as the Son of God and brother of all people. In the struggle for a just life for the poor we confess the one God, Father of all. In our ecclesial commitment we confess the one God, Father of all. In our ecclesial commitment we confess the Church of Jesus Christ as his body in history and as sacrament of liberation.[14]

The final conference brought together Third World theologians from all over the globe. It was held at New Delhi, India, in August 1981. The theme was "The Irruption of the Third World—a Challenge to Theology."[15] One of the objectives of this conference was to review the work of EATWOT during the previous five-year period and to plan for supporting the further development of these emergent Third World theologies. The final report from the New Delhi conference was, in many respects, a sharpening of the insights of the earlier conferences, this time from a global perspective. The irruption of the Third World was described as follows:

> Over against this dramatic picture of poverty, oppression, and the threat of total destruction, a new consciousness has arisen among the downtrodden. This growing consciousness of the tragic reality of the Third World has caused an irruption of exploited classes, marginalized cultures, and humiliated races. They are bursting from the underside of history into the world long dominated by the West. It is an irruption expressed in revolutionary struggles, political uprisings, and liberation movements. It is an irruption of religious and ethnic groups looking for affirmation of their authentic identity, of women demanding recognition and equality, of youth protesting dominant systems and values. It is an irruption of all those who struggle for full humanity and for their rightful place in history.[16]

The conference reaffirmed its judgment of the inadequacies of traditional Western theologies:

> The tools and categories of traditional theology are inadequate for doing theology in context. They are still too wedded to Western culture and the capitalist system. Traditional theology has not involved itself in the real drama of the people's lives or spoken in the religious and cultural idioms and expressions of the masses in a meaningful way. It has remained highly academic, speculative and individualistic without regard for the societal and structural aspects of sin.
>
> The Bible itself has not always been used to convey the liberating message of Jesus. Oftentimes it has been used to legitimize Christian participation in oppression, and to benefit the dominant race, class and sex.[17]

As in earlier conferences of EATWOT, the Delhi conference highlighted a new, emerging methodology for doing theology in which theological reflection is recognized to be rooted in commitment and action. At the same time, the role of contemplation was highlighted.

> Action in service of the people is necessary for genuine theological reflection, but equally necessary is silent contemplation. To be committed to the people's struggle for social justice and to contemplate God within this involvement—both form the essential matrix of theology. Without this prayerful contemplation, God's face is only partially seen and God's Word only partially heard within our participation in God's liberating and fulfilling action in history.[18]

The next EATWOT event was held at Geneva in January 1983. This was the conference proposed to further dialogue between Third World and First World theologians. Accordingly, the participants were about equally divided between the First World of Europe and North America and the Third World. The dialogue, however, was not focused between Third World theologians and mainline theologians from the First World because those from the First World who participated, even when they had critical questions to raise about the earlier EATWOT conferences, were, on the whole, sympathetic to and appreciative of the main affirmations enunciated from the Third World meetings. Many shared with EATWOT participants similar convictions about the appropriate methodology for doing Christian theology. Many embraced the concerns expressed in the two conferences held in Detroit in 1975 and 1980 on "Theology in the Americas," which had called for a new way of doing theology in North America. The Geneva conference focused on "Doing Theology in a Divided World." The outcome of the conference was a mutual recognition of the role of Christian theology in discerning the presence of God in Christ in the struggles of peoples everywhere for justice and fullness of humanity against social, economic, and political structures of domination and oppression, including racism, sexism, economic exploitation, and cultural imperialism.

It is in the light of the affirmations of all these meetings that Christians must understand the significance of Third World theology. The expression Third World in this context is not to be understood in terms of geographic regions, even though the expression is often used to refer to the regions of Africa, Asia, and Latin America, more than two-thirds of the territory of the world. The constitution of EATWOT, however, defines Third World to include in its membership all peoples belonging to the diaspora from these continents who now live in other parts of the world, such as those in the Caribbean from Africa and Afro-Americans in North America. Third World theology is related to a *condition* of Third World-ness, and in the reflection of Third World theologians, as well as social and political scientists, the term is descriptive of the concrete consequences of oppression and exploitation created by divergent but related forms of domination, including colonialism and imperialism. In the so-called First World, many peoples are subjected to conditions of Third World-ness, such as the blacks, Hispanics, indigenous people in both the United States and Canada, and migrant workers in both Europe and America. In the so-called Third World, there are also elites and groups who perpetuate structures of domination and oppression and enjoy life-styles that are similar to many in the affluent First World. This Third World theology, then, means doing theology with the explicit objective of shaping theological reflection on the meaning of the gospel of Jesus Christ in its intrinsic relation to the specific struggles against the conditions that produce Third World-ness. Third World-ness is a consequence of sin and has to be removed or overcome. The gospel, as the power of God for salvation, is intrinsically related to overcoming Third World-ness. The ultimate or eschatological goal and hope of Third World theology is in the vision of One/New/Humanity, in which all forms of separation, hostility, exploitation, and oppression have been overcome through the good news of the gospel of Jesus Christ, his solidarity with those who concretely suffer, and his ministry of reconciliation.

It is my thesis that serious concern for Christian unity be manifested globally as well as locally. This requires that we learn from the work of Third World theologians. There are two expressions of the movement of Christian unity today—the ecumenical movement and the church union movement—and we may ask how the development of this emergent movement of Third World theologies relates to these established movements.

If one takes the World Council of Churches as an expression of the ecumenical movement, two important characteristics of the church appear to be the dominant guidelines in shaping the established ecumenical movement. The first is a central commitment to Christocentric theology. A symbolic expression of this is voiced in the main themes for the various assemblies of the World Council: "Jesus Christ the Hope of the World" at Evanston, Illinois; "Jesus Christ the Light of the World" at New Delhi, India; "Behold I Make All Things New" at Uppsala, Sweden; "Jesus Christ Frees and Unites" at Nairobi, Kenya; and "Jesus Christ the Life of the World" at Vancouver, Canada. A second characteristic is the related commitment to keep the integral relationship between the unity of the church and its total mission. During recent processes of reorganization of the World Council, a proposal was made that the Faith and Order Commission be regarded as the organ for the concern for unity within Christianity and that the rest of the World Council structure be responsible for the concern of relating Christianity to the broader world, as mission and evangelism, service, justice, and peace. This suggestion was rightly rejected on the grounds that all activities of the World Council are rooted in Christ and that all attest to the unity of the church. While the Faith and Order Commission is vital as an instrument for helping the churches understand and overcome historic divisions based on different perceptions of matters relating to the theology and organization of Christian communities, the other units of the World Council have also reflected a remarkable convergence of these sorts of concerns.

The meetings of the Faith and Order Commission also reflect this inseparability. After the World Conference on Faith and Order at Lund, Sweden, in 1952, there was an attempt to arrive at a common mind about the nature of the unity we are called to seek, based on insights about the relationship between Christology and ecclesiology. By 1963, after the Faith and Order meeting at Montreal, the unity question was reformulated to clarify the nature of the relationship between the unity of the Christian church *and* the unity of all humanity. This refocusing of the question raised a number of complex issues and has not been brought to any definite conclusion. However, the continuing direction of inquiry was indicated at the meeting of the Faith and Order Commission at Louvain in 1971 by its theme: "Unity of the Church—Unity of Mankind." It was affirmed both that the character of the church is christological and that the church is the "sign of the coming unity of mankind." Significantly at this meeting, it was stressed that the unity of the church is directly related to the human struggle for justice, the struggle against racism, the encounter with other faiths, and the concern for the handicapped in society. The Louvain report explicitly affirmed that "Christ of the Eucharist is the Christ of the Poor," and therefore the church that manifests its unity in the celebration of the eucharist must also, with equal earnestness, manifest its unity and identity with the poor and involve itself in the struggle for justice in society.[19] The more recent Faith and Order document formulated at Lima in 1982 on "Baptism, Eucharist and the Ministry" also, although not so explicitly, affirms the integral relation between ecclesiology, Christology, and justice. The section on baptism calls for a "new ethical orientation" for the baptized. The section on the eucharist draws attention to how our participation in the eucharist places us "under continual judgment by the persistence of unjust relationships of all kinds in our society."

In the work of the other departments of the World Council, particularly the Department of Church and Society and the Commission on World Mission and Evangelism, there has been an even greater and more explicit and systematic move toward understanding ecumenism to involve the relationship between Christian witness and solidarity with the poor and the oppressed. The World Council has initiated a process of sharpening the churches' concern for both justice and peace, using the concept of a

Responsible Society as the basis for a Christian's address to societal issues, and has moved on to affirm the norms of Justice, Participation, and Sustainability as characteristics of such a society. One of the convictions affirmed with increasing urgency has been that witnessing to the gospel of Jesus Christ *necessarily* involves the churches in the transformation of sociopolitical structures. It has been recognized that in order to be true to their calling, the churches must find ways of being in solidarity with the poor and the oppressed in their struggles. Richard D.N. Dickinson, in discussing "Christian Ethics in the World Council Arena," has stressed this point: "Recent ecumenical literature urges Churches to become partisan in favour of the poor, to be in solidarity with the poor—as the ecumenical community by and large believes that Biblical witness shows that God took sides on behalf of the poor."[20] He also interprets ecumenical ethics as implying that in the struggle for justice, the poor have a privileged role to play. Describing churches as "sign communities" in solidarity, Dickinson says that "Christian faith is nurtured and strengthened, even discovered afresh, by participating in the struggles of the poor for justice and liberation. So also real Christian unity."[21] One of the important clues to the meaning of the ecumenical concern for Christian unity is the affirmation of the relation between ecclesiology, Christology, and social justice. As we have seen, this affirmation is basic to Third World theology and signals a genuine convergence between established ecumenical agencies and Third World theological-ethical concerns.

How does the second sort of ecumenical movement—the church union movement—relate to the EATWOT concerns? The church union movement has a record of remarkable achievement during the past few decades. In India, the Church of South India (CSI) and the Church of North India (CNI) have come into existence through mergers of several Christian communities, and a joint council of the CNI, the CSI and the Mar Thoma Church was recently formed. In many other parts of the world, united churches also have come into existence through church union movements. An objective of the church union movement is that visible disunity should be overcome and the One Church of Christ be made manifest. It was this sort of quest for visible unity that led the Faith and Order Commission to produce the Lima document on Baptism, Eucharist, and Ministry (BEM). The assumption here is that a new theological consensus among the churches on issues of faith and order that have kept them divided will facilitate concrete efforts to unite. A challenge is made to the churches to make deliberate efforts to overcome past divisions in faith and liturgical order. It is affirmed that our one baptism in Christ constitutes a call to the churches to overcome divisions and visibly manifest their fellowship.

It needs to be observed, however, that those of us who are engaged in the church union movement have discovered that reaching agreement on doctrinal and sacramental issues does *not* necessarily lead to visible unity. For example, the Methodist Church in India did not join the CNI, even though it had participated in formulating the agreements that brought the CNI together. Furthermore, the CSI-Lutheran plan for the formation of a united church has made little progress since 1967, even though doctrinal and liturgical agreements had been reached and no further questions raised about them by any of the negotiating churches. Several other examples of similar absence of progress after reaching agreements could be cited.

The reasons for failure or unwillingness to move forward toward visible unity must be probed. The question must be raised whether the goal of visible unity can be adequate only with the process of establishing new ecclesiastical structures to replace existing structures apart from the questions raised by Third World theologians. The oneness of disciples for which Christ prayed was of the sort that enables *the world* to believe that Jesus was the Christ sent by God. This certainly implies that the unity for which Christ prayed, the unity that the church is called to manifest, has power and vitality to challenge the broader world to faith. What is this reality that we are to manifest? What is the essential ecclesial reality underlying existing ecclesiastical structures? Is it not the reality of the Risen Lord continuing the ministry that Jesus began in Galilee through the stirrings of people.

How the church union movement discerns where the presence of Christ is manifest in the world today is crucial; how it understands the relation between Christology, ecclesiology, and human struggles for justice is important to its future. In Asia, today, one of the concerns must be to take seriously the role of the so-called action groups involved in justice struggles, many of them inspired by the gospel of Jesus Christ but at the same time unrelated to traditional church structures. In recent Asian discussions, the question of the ecclesial character of such groups has been raised. The Executive Committee of the Joint Council of the CSI-CNI-Mar Thoma has suggested that dialogue is needed with the members of three churches who are involved in such action groups. Although some regard the "action groups" as being outside the scope of the church, and therefore irrelevant to ecclesiology and Christology, others seek to recognize their fellowship with the established church. The question for the church union movement is the manner in which ecclesial reality and the ecumenical witness to the Christ who came as Jesus of Nazareth are to be expressed.

This brief survey indicates that the established ecumenical movement and the church union movement are involved in clarifying issues central to discussions of Third World theologians. Such discussions are by no means simple. The developments cause new tensions and new potential for divisions. At the beginning of the life and work movement, the slogan was "Doctrine divides, Service unites." But later history, particularly our present global situation, has demonstrated that disunity is manifested in both our doctrinal and our ethical perceptions. Third World theology and the ecumenical and church union movements are all rooted in faith in God, who in Christ reconciles the world, and in the recognition of our shared need for God's grace and forgiving love. None deny that we need God's grace and power to discern the reality of Christ among us and to be united through Christian ministry in the world. All affirm that we enter the experience of the power of the resurrection only through the suffering and death of Christ. Yet Third World theology is rooted in and challenges established ecumenical and union movements that pray and work for Christian unity to place greater commitment, meaning, and hope in understanding that reconciliation comes *through* solidarity with the victims of sin, of injustice and oppression.

PART III.
Racism and Urban Life

SIX

Urban Racism and
Afro-American Integrity

Samuel K. Roberts

Mass social upheavals have always provoked human beings to ask fundamental questions about their existence, the meaning of human history, and the unfolding of human destiny. And perhaps the more traumatic and more disturbing the upheaval—even when perceived by viewers in a time much distant from the event itself—the more anguish we encounter in an effort fully to understand the event. Such is the case with slavery and the way the corporate memory of black America has appropriated that gruesome institution yet today.

Even when viewed from the latter years of the twentieth century, the cruel and forced migrations of Africans to the New World during the years of the slave trade have an enduring social and psychological impact on the descendants of those displaced Africans and, for that matter, on others whose sense of justice is outraged by the peculiar form of slavery that these Africans experienced in the Americas. Viewed from the context of place centuries later, the fact that a significant segment of the Afro-American population continues to experience the lingering effects of such slavery in urban poverty tends to underscore the existential bond between the first traumatic introduction of Africans to the New World and the contemporary urban condition.

After setting forth a theoretical framework that will attempt to understand the persistence of racism as an identifiable thread in the fabric of the urban environment, this essay will reflect on the Afro-American response

Samuel K. Roberts, Professor of Ethics and Society, School of Theology, Virginia Union University, Richmond, Virginia.

to such racism and a posture for ethics in addressing the problems that urban racism poses.

Toward a Theoretical Framework

In response to the question "What is a city?" Max Weber produced a straightforward and enduring answer. For Weber, the city was a settlement where people lived in a relatively closed setting "primarily off trade and commerce rather than agriculture."[1] But Weber was quick to point out that not all settlements that engaged in trade could rightly be called cities. Apparently, the complexity of the trading was crucial to an understanding of the true city. Hence "economic versatility" was also posited by Weber as an essential aspect of the city. But, inquired Weber, versatility in what sense and under what conditions? He asserted that there were at least two ways by which economic versatility could be established. The first way was under the aegis of a feudal lord, whose estate would demand a wide variety of work performed or goods bartered—all under his control. The other method was through the "regular rather than an occasional exchange of goods" in a marketplace. But Weber realized that not all marketplaces converted the localities in which they were found into cities. For example, periodic trade fairs could not produce cities; interaction over a more sustained period was necessary. Accordingly, Weber believed that one could only speak of a "city" in cases where "the local inhabitants satisfy an economically substantial part of their daily wants in the local market, and to an essential extent by products which the local population and that of the immediate hinterland produced for sale in the market or acquired in other ways."[2] Thus Max Weber's studies of oriental and occidental human settlements persuaded him that only free market forces could produce what came to be known as the "city."

A fundamental paradox is at the heart of the dynamics of the city as a form of human interaction, especially as this form of interaction has developed in the West. Although the city represented the full flowering of liberation from the constraints of traditional society and village life, it also contained the seeds for human misery. Traditional societies, characterized by ethnic or racial homogeneity, face-to-face relationships, and low density of population, could provide a bulwark against spiritual uncertainty and emotional isolation. To be sure, one paid the price of the stultification of initiative, the discouragement of new ideas, and the tedium of the ever-recurring pattern of the daily round within traditional societies. By contrast, the city offered ethnic and racial heterogeneity, a measure of freedom from the intensity of face-to-face scrutiny, and exposure to the ferment of human creativity. As in the case of traditional societies, there was also a price for urban freedom. Emile Durkheim, for example, identi-

112

fied a resultant sense of anomie, a sterile anonymity that could lead to suicide and a general breakdown of the spiritual order or moral community[3]

A second and related paradox lies at the heart of the dynamics of the city. If the first paradox has to do with the structure of the city, which at once offers freedom *and* bondage, hope *and* despair, the second paradox has to do with the individual's search for self-actualization and fulfillment. It must always be remembered that cities were perhaps the first human settlements in which diversity was tolerated and encouraged. Individual initiative could be played out on the stage of a relatively open society, at least when compared with traditional or folk society, or that society characterized by Robert Redfield as being small, isolated, and homogeneous and having a strong sense of group solidarity.[4] One cannot really speak of individuality or individualism with any serious meaning within the context of traditional society. Identity in traditional society was a function of family or clan membership and social position within the context of a social order governed by custom and tradition. Hence any notion of individual identity was conceived and enacted relative to fixed roles (pater, mater) or social positions (priest, slave) or vocations (stonecutter or weaver). Cities challenged unity of blood, station, and custom and provided the individual with a measure of freedom and a framework to pursue individual identity.

What is paradoxical is that this ethos of the city—allowing for individualism and individual fulfillment—also created the conditions for emergence of a centralized political economy and a mass society, social phenomena that are most antithetical to the autonomy of the individual. Without the power of individual initiative, and the gathering of diverse peoples and the markets they provided, it is doubtful that modern capitalist political economy would ever have emerged in its modern form. Yet the city itself in its present state threatens these characteristics that give rise to it. The city, which was the progenitor of the modern conception of the individual in society, has come to be the context in which the integrity of that individual is compromised by anonymity and undifferentiated mass society.

If Weber is correct, economic activity and expansion is the unabashed aim of the city. This is not to deny the obvious importance of cities as cultural centers or sophisticated centers for learning or enlightenment. But these are consequential to the great economic activity that has already taken place and on whose foundation cultural and educational pursuits can move forward.

Now the question is in what peculiar kind of social context does this economic activity take place? What theory or framework can best explain the aims of economic activity and the peculiar social patterns, including urban racism, that develop in the city? A significant number of theorists, urban planners, and social scientists have been struck by the usefulness of

113

the ecological theory of urban life, and it is to an overview of that theory that I now turn in an attempt to understand the phenomenon of urban racism.

In American sociology, the ecological theory of the city has been most closely associated with the work of Robert Ezra Park, a journalist-turned-sociologist, whose theoretical work at the University of Chicago and field studies of Chicago have become classics in the area of urban studies. Park drew heavily on the theory of evolution as it had been formulated by Charles Darwin. He was fascinated by Darwin's insights into food chains and the interdependence among organisms in a territorially organized setting. Moreover, he was struck by the notion that the active principle in the ordering and regulating of life within the realm of animate nature was, as Darwin described it, "the struggle for existence." Those organisms that survived would be pitted relentlessly among themselves in some form of competition. Competition was viewed by the ecologists as the first phase of nature's effort to reach a state of equilibrium or balance. The inevitable result of competition would lead to the second phase, temporary dominance of one organism over another. The third phase, succession, was designated as that "orderly sequence of changes through which a biotic community passes in the course of its development from a primary and relatively unstable to a relatively permanent or climax stage."[5]

Park saw the obvious implications of ecological theory for the life of the city. He wrote, for example, that "the principle of dominance operates in the human as well as in the plant and animal communities. The so-called natural or functional areas of a metropolitan community—for example, the slum, the rooming-house area, the central shopping section and the banking center—each and all owe their existence directly to the factor of dominance, and indirectly to competition."[6] Further, "the area of dominance in any community is usually the area of highest land values."[7]

Park's appropriation of ecological theory and his graphic language have implications for the role of race, race prejudice, and racism in the dynamics of the city. Although ecological theory cannot explain the origin of urban racism, it can help to explain the persistence of this phenomenon in the urban environment. If competition and the will to dominance are characteristic aspects of urban life, especially given the intentional economic thrust of the city, then it is reasonable to expect any group to use any available advantage to further its interests. From a purely ecological point of view, the act of assigning an inferior status to another race or group can act as a powerful lever to secure such advantages as are needed in a competitive struggle. Within the context of the observations that have been made about the paradoxical nature of the city and the point of view of ecological theory, urban racism may be understood as that web of prejudicial assumptions that cast a determined group of people in prescribed roles and limit their life chances in the competitive environment of the city. Such prescribed roles are an advantage for the dominant group and enable it to further its economic and political aims.

The Afro-American Response

The appearance in 1619 of nineteen captured Africans in Jamestown, Virginia, represented the confluence of several historic forces that are related to the paradoxical nature of the city. Jamestown was the first permanent English-speaking settlement in the New World, the result of the mercantilist impulse inherent in the growing drive of the English urban bourgeoisie for world economic expansion. Thus there was a clear economic import in the founding of the colony, a calculated goal of making a profit for its founders, the London Company. Founded in 1607, the colony survived one disaster after another. It was subjected to raids by the indigenous peoples of the Powhatan nation, but by 1619, the colony finally began to show some signs of stability and hope for prosperity, in large part because of the cultivation of a special type of sweet Spanish tobacco.

However, the full economic potential of the settlement could not be reached without cheap, forced labor. Alien African labor provided the missing link. Carl Degler has shown quite persuasively that a racist attitude toward African cultures and peoples was in the minds of the English settlers before actual encounters with Africans. Such attitudes formed the ground on which actual enslavement of Africans could be justified. Thus, in colonial America, "discrimination was a precondition of . . . slavery and not a consequence."[8] In a very real sense, then, the bringing of slaves to Jamestown is symbolic of the way racism has been propagated and extended in America since 1619. Enslaved Africans provided the cheap labor needed to develop the urban centers after the Revolutionary period until the present time. Racism has helped to drive the engine of economic ascendancy for dominant ethnic groups in urban centers. It has created the advantage for such groups and put blacks at a disadvantage. Thus one paradox of urban racism is that while black Americans have contributed vital labor necessary to the growth of cities, they have been relegated historically to the edges of power and social standing in the cities and segregated within them.

This reality has remained in force even during periods of burgeoning economic growth. In the latter half of the nineteenth century, blacks migrated to cities to take advantage of presumed opportunities. Along with foreign-born immigrants, Afro-Americans came to the cities and, more often than not, competed for the same jobs calling for unskilled labor, but labor nevertheless basic to the economic development of urban America. It is not surprising that racism became a factor in the struggle of competing ethnic groups to secure an economic foothold in the cities. In

1866, one year after the Civil War ended, the federal army was called into Memphis, Tennessee, to put down a riot between Irish immigrants and blacks. In his dispatch to General Ulysses Grant, the commanding officer cited the tension that had been rising between the blacks and the "Irishmen, who consider the negro as his competitor and natural enemy."[9]

Racial hostility continued to plague the attempts of blacks to compete successfully in the urban environment throughout the remainder of the nineteenth century and the early years of the twentieth. Yet blacks did manage to become integrally meshed in the infrastructure of economic life of the cities. Although contained at the lower levels of factory employment and income, the black presence was necessary and critical economically. For example, there is documentation that black involvement in the industrial life of Baltimore during the 1920s was massive. In the fertilizer, brickyard, and tanning industries, the preponderance of labor was black; 75 percent of the laborers in the brickyard industry and 90 percent of the laborers in the tanning industry were black.[10] Most of the longshoremen and stevedores were also black. Doubtless the work was disagreeable and often seasonal, the pay low, and the opportunities for advancement limited because the supervisory positions were reserved for whites. But one wonders how the economy of Baltimore would have fared had it not been for the contributions of these industries to the city. Conversely, the political rule and leadership of the city was a clear reflection of white determination to subject blacks or, from Park's point of view, to achieve dominance.

Machine politics, that curiously American phenomenon which evolved as an instrument to serve the ethnic groups that were in power in the big cities, effectively divided, weakened, or ignored the black presence. In his analysis of Philadelphia politics, W.E.B. DuBois lamented that "the political hold of the 'machine' in Philadelphia has been so great and far-reaching, their majorities so overwhelming, and the white citizens so supine in their bondage, that the 'machine' cares little for the 25,000 Negro votes."[11]

The economic and social marginality that black Americans have experienced has always been relative to other ethnic groups within the context of urban society. Although it has always been the case in the American experience that racial heterogeneity has been an aspect of the urban fabric, racial harmony has, unfortunately, not been a noticeable pattern in that fabric. Various immigrant groups, seized with a passion for realizing their actualization and full potential in their new country, away from the oppression in their native lands, were often pitted against blacks in a deadly struggle for opportunity in the land that was only ostensibly "free" for all. The chronicle of frequent and vicious race riots in America is a grim reminder of this fact.

116

The second paradox also gives shape to the type of racism that has been part of the urban condition. The search for self-actualization for blacks in the city has been fraught with internal contradictions and ambiguities. It has proceeded predictably along a pattern of displacement (voluntary or involuntary) from rural, agrarian settings to settlement in the city, where not limitless opportunity, but segregated housing and facilities awaited them. Yet the search for both self-actualization and Afro-American integrity in the cities has been sustained by the pervasive institutions of black life that bespoke such ideals as community, a sense of place, and familial solidarity. The very values that were so much a part of the rural, face-to-face culture left behind by urbanized blacks have continued to ground the urban struggle to a considerable degree.

The paradox and the quest for black integrity in the face of urban racism can be traced, for example, in the flourishing of black benevolent and mutual aid societies beginning as early as the latter part of the eighteenth century. The mutual aid society, a social invention among Northern free blacks, was designed to mitigate the harshness of economic marginality. Perhaps the first mutual aid society among blacks was the African Union Society, which was evidently begun under the leadership of Newport Gardner in Newport, Rhode Island, in 1780.[12] Through modest and regular contributions from all the members of a society, an individual would be assured of a proper burial for a spouse, relief if fire destroyed a home, or a small pension for surviving orphans. The formation of such groups quickly followed that of the African Union Society. In 1789, after having been denied full equality as participants in the spiritual life of the Methodist Church in Philadelphia, Richard Allen and Absalom Jones withdrew to form the Free African Society, a forerunner of the African Methodist Episcopal Church, which was organized formally in 1816. Soon after 1789, African societies in Boston and New York were formed. Mutual aid societies flourished in the latter years of the eighteenth century and throughout the nineteenth, forming the foundation for many economic ventures, including funeral homes, banks, dry goods stores, and hotels. Thus, in the context of racism experienced by blacks during the early years of the nation and until the twentieth century, mutual aid societies functioned in a dramatic way to provide some measure of economic viability.

E. Franklin Frazier, in his seminal study on the black church, notes how many of the mutual aid societies were connected with churches and ministers. After the Civil War, black churches served as the bases for numerous cooperative ventures and mutual aid societies, especially among tenant farmers. One notable example is the way in which the zeal of a charismatic preacher, Washington Browne, could help to transform an organization into an economic power. Browne was born a slave in Georgia in 1849. During the Civil War, he escaped from slavery and acquired the rudiments of an education in the North. After the war, he returned to the South and joined the Good Templars, an anti-whiskey movement. Soon thereafter he became convinced that blacks should develop a separate organization that could meet their special needs. Thus, in 1876, he succeeded in bringing together several groups to form the Grand Fountain of the True Reformers. The organization sponsored several economic ventures, including a bank and an insurance company located in Richmond, Virginia.[13]

Recent developments in the life of cities suggest that while some aspects of the timeworn posture between the races have improved, the essential structural dynamics of urban racism still prevail. The most obvious changes are those that are political. It is no longer true that blacks are relegated to the edges of political power in the cities. Owing largely to the net in-migration of blacks to cities, which did not abate until the mid-1970s, and the net out-migration of whites, major eastern U.S. cities now have black majorities. With such demographic shifts has come a larger measure of political power at the local, and even state, levels. In 1970, seven major cities had black population majorities. Only four of these had black mayors. By 1980, however, seventeen cities had majority black populations, thirteen of which had elected black mayors.[14] At the same time, however, the whites who have left the central cities have become far more affluent than the blacks who have taken their places. In fact, while in 1970 about 54 percent of blacks living below the poverty level lived in metropolitan areas, by 1980 the number had risen to 72 percent. Thus the political control by blacks of urban centers is sadly skewed by the economic distress of most of the cities' black citizens.

The ecology of the city continues to manifest patterns of a will to dominance in economic terms by whites even while showing some semblance of shared political power with blacks and other minorities. In an attempt to understand the paradoxical nature of the urban experience and the problems that black Americans have confronted in the urban environment, I have suggested that, owing to its origin and continuing function as a place for market exchanges, the dynamics of the city may be illumined by the ecological theory of urban life. Ecological theory presumes that a driving force in human relations is competition. Such a notion would explain the persistence of racism in the urban context to the extent that one race would be able to direct racism against another group in order to secure an advantage in the ecosystem. Yet the city has lured, disappointed, enthralled, and entrapped countless millions who have sought the good life there. While a detailed analysis of policies for urban renewal and the eradication of racism is clearly beyond the scope of this chapter, a few guiding principles and comments may be helpful.

118

The centrality of economic vitality in urban life cannot be ignored or discounted; neither can the propensity among human beings to seek ways and methods of securing advantages over others in the marketplace of the city. A notion of the just city would be one in which the function of the city is allowed to flourish—that is, its economic vitality and expansion—but one in which all people would be allowed to derive the full benefit of urban living. In such a context, no one would be deprived of such benefits because of the arbitrary ascription of disadvantages such as race, residence, or station in life. This chapter simply asserts that left to their own devices, urban dwellers will seek the advantage over others in order to further their own interest. If this is the case, an ethical stance would discourage all policies that in intent, design, or consequence give the advantage to one class or income level over another. Policies that exacerbate the natural propensity to seek the advantage are inherently unjust. Conversely, policies that limit the aspirations and life chances of a designated class of people, based on color, residence, or income level, are also inherently unjust.

Thus public policy must be especially sensitive to the attempts among the victims of urban racism to secure a fuller measure of integrity within a system that has been historically fraught with inequity. Significant challenges need to be made to traditional monopolies of entrepreneurial pursuits that have frozen out effective black and minority participation. A good example of the interface between public policy, racism, and the aspirations of minority groups is the taxi industry in the city of New York. Since the 1940s the industry has attempted successfully to control the number of taximedallions in circulation. A medallion is a metal plate attached to the hood of the taxi that gives the owner the right to operate or "cruise" in downtown areas of Manhattan and the airports. The right to operate legitimately in these areas ensures these taxis a relatively higher occupancy rate and the drivers, a higher level of income. Moreover, tips are more generous in downtown Manhattan, since such passengers tend to be more affluent. Operators who do not own medallions, or "gypsy" drivers, cannot operate legitimately in these areas and are thus deprived of the opportunity to earn incomes on a par with the legitimate drivers. They are consigned to the outer boroughs and a relatively less affluent ridership. Moreover, the average price of a medallion (as much as $61,000 in the mid 1970s) is beyond the reach of most gypsy drivers, who are predominantly black and Hispanic. Thus a policy that reflects the economic interest of a predominantly white interest group and that has been affirmed by the city has produced adverse consequences for blacks and Hispanics. Clearly such a policy needs to be changed if one aspect of economic injustice in the city is to be eradicated. Other examples of problem areas are city housing and real estate codes that give enormous tax advantages to real estate developers, who go on to develop luxury housing and displace poor residents.

The call for justice amid the paradoxes of the urban environment should be as relentless as the suffering such paradoxes engender. But in the travail of living out their faith in an often bewildering world, Christians are accustomed to paradox. A leap of faith will always risk a stumble toward despair. Yet if we are not to flee from where we are in the city, only our hope in one another and openness to what we may become will enable us to hold out a vision for what the truly good city can become.

SEVEN

Racism and Economics: The Perspective of Oliver C. Cox

Katie G. Cannon

*M*y work as a scholar in Christian ethics took a decidedly new turn when I became aware of the white academic community's flourishing publishing monopoly on the writing of black history, black thought, and black world view. Black scholars did not abdicate their roles in these fields to white academicians. Blacks have written monographs, theses, conference papers, proposals, and outlines for books on various aspects of black reality since the 1700s, but white publishers did not give them serious consideration until the 1970s.[1]

For years I had concentrated on mastering the spate of books, articles, and pamphlets written *by* whites *about* blacks. Suddenly, I was reading in rapid-fire the writings of black scholars whose biases favored the victims and the survivors of racism.[2] These black scholars corrected the racist ideologies that assessed a black person as "three-fifths of a white man." They refused to allow the colonization of information and interpretation of the history of black people to continue. Instead, they provided data that heightened my sensitivity to *what has been* in direct relationship to the viable possibilities of *what can be*.[3] This research cleared away much ambiguity, revealing an autonomous development of black cultural traditions, value systems, ideas, and institutional forms.

This turn in my scholarship led me to focus carefully on the varying social theoretical perspectives developed by black scholars on the dynamics of racism. Not all theories of racism agree as to how to act against it. For instance, Carter G. Woodson[4] (1875-1950), a distinguished black his-

Katie Geneva Cannon, a Black Christian Feminist Liberation Ethicist on the faculty of the Episcopal Divinity School Cambridge, Massachusetts.

torian who popularized the field of black studies, had a nineteenth-century faith in education as the major strategy against racism. He believed wholeheartedly that race relations would improve through increased knowledge. Woodson defined racism as the logical result of faulty education. Racism, he argued, is the socialized indoctrination of systematic lies that exploit the imperfections of the black race. It was the inevitable outcome of the tradition of chattel slavery that had become institutionalized through instruction.

For Woodson, racism as mis-education is a conscious and deliberate manipulation of falsehood. Black people are presented as negligible contributors to the substantive interpretation of the world, whereas whites are depicted as the source of all the worthwhile intellectual accomplishments. Such twisted education presumes that blacks are not oppressed, but inferior. Brutality and criminality against blacks are appropriate to their meager talent and limited intellect. For Woodson, racism abounds in assiduous propaganda based on untested opinion and distorted arguments to justify black exploitation.

Woodson argued that people in the United States are taught from cradle to grave that blacks are inferior. The assumptions of racist dogmas forcibly handicap blacks from every walk of life. Whites, as well as blacks, are imbued with the alleged inherent superiority of whites and presumed inherent inferiority of blacks in order to perpetuate white racial power and control. Woodson's numerous writings redress ignorance about blacks, marshal irrefutable evidence concerning black life and culture, and restore the most luminous achievements of blacks as great African people within human civilization. Carter G. Woodson's life and work were dedicated to the affirmation of the black race as one of the great human races, inferior to none in accomplishment and ability.[5]

George D. Kelsey,[6] a Drew University professor of Christian ethics, developed a theological theory depicting racism as an idolatrous religion and an abortive search for meaning. According to Kelsey, racism emerged as an ideological justification during slavery so that powerful entrepreneurs could continue their political and economic control. The idea of the superior race has been heightened and deepened so that now it points beyond the historical structures of slavery to the conviction that race superiority is ordained by God.

Kelsey contends that racism poses the problem of idol worship in a unique way. The faith character of racism within organized religion divides human beings as human beings. The racist glorifies in the *being* of whiteness. What the racist scorns and rejects in black people is precisely their *human beingness.* Millions of men and women gain their sense of power of being from their membership in the so-called superior race. Kelsey pointed out that the fundamental presupposition undergirding racism is that the white race is glorious and pure in its essential being and the black race, defective and depraved in its essential being. Racism teaches the superior race that the place of blacks is fixed in the basic *order* of reality. The so-called inferiority of blacks is not a matter of historical victimization, but is held to be determined in the divine order of creation.

Kelsey argued that racism as idolatrous religion calls into question the nature of divine action itself. God made a creative error in bringing the inferior race into existence. The theological assertion is that God condemned blacks to be "the hewers of wood and drawers of water, now, henceforth and forever under the curse of Ham."[7] A variation of this doctrine is that black people share in the universal condemnation of the human race in Adam but bear the added condemnation of God in a special, racial fall as descendants of Cain, the first criminal. Because no promise of renewal and redemption is ever correlated with this second, special fall, racists maintain that black people are permanent victims of history and ultimately without hope.

The central purpose of this essay is neither to assess Woodson's understanding of racism nor to elaborate Kelsey's thesis of in-group/out-group relations. Rather, I propose to weigh carefully the thesis of another major but little-known theorist, Oliver C. Cox, whose contribution was to relate racism to the economy of U.S. society. Cox maintained that racism must be understood as a historical reality embedded over time specifically in a capitalist mode of political economy, a mode that now has come to control the world. Because he criticized capitalism, Cox has been quickly dismissed and little understood. He was charged with selling out to Karl Marx. Because so many postcapitalistic regimes, such as Cuba and Nicaragua, have not fully transcended racism, many refuse to reconsider his work. Yet Cox did not believe that social ownership of the means of production would, per se, eradicate racism. He did believe, however, that moving beyond capitalism would be a *necessary step* in the eradication of white supremacy. I share Cox's conviction that once chattel slavery and white supremacy have become interstructured through capitalist political economy, only the elimination of a capitalist mode of production can open the way to making racism dysfunctional. The goals of the chapter, then, are to introduce Cox's perspective and demonstrate dimensions of racism as economic reality that would not be identifiable if this historical interweaving were neglected.

Oliver C. Cox as Social Theorist

Oliver Cromwell Cox, born in Port of Spain, Trinidad, on August 25, 1901, was a premier social theorist, the most systematic expositor of the relationship of economics and race of his era. At age eighteen he came to the United States to work and complete his education. After graduating from the YMCA High School in Chicago, he earned a law degree from Northwestern University in 1928 and two advanced degrees from the University of Chicago, a master's degree in economics in 1932 and a Ph.D. in sociology in 1938. Cox taught for several years at Wiley College in Marshall, Texas, and at Tuskegee Institute in Alabama before joining the faculty at Lincoln University in Jefferson City, Missouri. His position at the time of his death (1974) was at Wayne State University in Detroit.[8]

Although Cox was a prolific writer, he received little of the public recognition he deserved. This was due in large measure to his theoretical and ideological approach as a sociologist. Cox's primary orientation was not toward the reigning paradigm of empirical sociology. Rather, he used a historicocomparative research method that he contended could provide opportunities for genuine theoretical advance. Cox engaged only in hands-on structural observation. He rejected a focus on isolated, observable phenomena. For him, using questionnaires and interviews to assemble opinion and statistical data was helpful only insofar as these methods illumined basic structures for social change. Cox regarded the value of social research to rest in clarifying conceptual definitions that aided in identifying the basic social dynamics operating in society. He was influenced by Karl Marx's contention that only a careful critical historical/structural analysis was genuinely "scientific."

Unlike many social theorists, Cox explicitly spelled out the role of ethics within his own methodological process. He affirmed the duty of the sociologist to unmask views of society that render some as victims. The sociologist must aim to burrow through the complexity of factual material, to discover the actual social processes at work, to define these social processes as clearly as possible, and to point to the factors and derive the theory involved in their development. The cogency of his analysis rested on his conclusion that all these responsibilities were aimed at a sociology that was fully historical. The sociologist must remain a maverick historian who gains *critical* historical understanding of how human oppression develops.[9] This is the true goal of social science. Cox summed up his sociological philosophy this way:

> Clearly the social scientist should be accurate and objective but not neutral; he should be passionately partisan in favor of the welfare of the people and against the interest of the few when they seem to submerge that welfare. In a word, the reason for the existence of the social scientist is that his scientific findings contribute to the betterment of the people's well-being.[10]

Cox was ostracized by his colleagues because early in his career he challenged not only the method, but also the conceptual formulation of Gunnar Myrdal, the Swedish economist, and his numerous respected black assistants, such as E. Franklin Frazier, St. Clair Drake, Charles S. Johnson, and Horace Cayton.[11] Cox disagreed with the underlying thesis of *An American Dilemma*. He argued that the crux of racism is not analogous to caste, but to class, that is, to relationships created by how the production of wealth is organized. Racism cannot be reduced merely to prejudice, ancient bigotry, and the strangeness of ethnic differences that the idea of "caste" suggests; rather, racism must be viewed as an inherent part of the basic political economy—the capitalist system.[12] To be sure, racism provided the moral rationale for the subjugation and exploitation of blacks as "inferior" people, but it was their labor power that had made chattel slavery an irreplaceable necessity to whites.

> Slave trade did not develop because Indians and Negroes were red and black, or because their cranial capacity averaged a certain number of cubic centimeters, but simply because they were the best workers to be found for the heavy labor in the mines and plantations across the Atlantic. . . . *Race relations was not an abstract but rather a practical exploitative relationship with its socioattitudinal facilitation.*[13]

Because Cox stressed the concrete material sources of racism, he was treated as an outcast.

According to Gordan D. Morgan, Oliver C. Cox was all but disbarred from the fraternity of "promising" black sociologists of the first generation.[14] He was not only highly critical of the race relations hypothesis of Myrdal, but also disagreed vehemently with the noted sociologist Robert E. Park.[15] Morgan contends that Cox paid a high price for this independence of thought because black peers who worked within the approved theoretical frameworks of white scholars were often given grants. In his earlier years, Cox never received financial support from any foundation for the pursuit of his research. Despite the lack of financial support, Cox continued his work prodigiously and authored four books and numerous articles.[16] With Morgan, I believe that Oliver C. Cox was probably the soundest, most rigorous thinker of the first generation of black sociologists.

Cox's Central Thesis

It was Oliver C. Cox's thesis that the capitalist mode of political economy is the essential structural problem of contemporary society. As the most powerful and dynamic form of social organization ever created, the capitalist political economy generates a political order that is ostensibly democratic but that leaves economic power unchecked. It also generates a suitable religion to nationalize and loosen all social restraints rooted in mysticism and cultural ritual. In other words, Cox argued that capitalism is a form of social organization in which the distinctive economic order slowly shapes government and religious structures into a neutralized network of national and territorial units wherein commercial and exploitative economic relationships can flourish. A body of international law, traditions, and rules develops that is increasingly weighted in favor of the most economically powerful individuals and nations. The "miraculousness" of capital culture, declared Cox, rests in its seeming capacity to create wealth from nothing. In such a culture, existence comes more and more to be based purely on the acquisitive instinct. To fill out the details of this thesis, Cox identified eight historical dynamics of a capitalist society.

1. *The development of the nation-state as sovereign republic.* Cox pointed out that capitalism creates a political economic order in which the totality of relationships among groups and individuals is drawn into interdependence. Such a society comes to have enormous capacity for cultural assimilation because social interrelations are increasingly conditioned and mediated through the national, political, and economic order. The people in the society depend significantly on this unified system to teach them their fundamental behavioral patterns and thought processes. Cox insisted that this learning usually occurs with such facility and speed from infancy onward that members of the society are likely to be unaware of their cultural origins outside the system, and thus come to think of their social relations as natural and instinctive. For instance, "Race prejudice, from its inception became part of the social heritage, and as such both exploiters and exploited for the most part are born heirs to it. It is possible that most of those who propagate and defend race prejudice are not conscious of its fundamental motivation."[17] "Civilization," then, comes to mean one's ability to adjust and integrate oneself consistently into these patterns and processes.

2. *The perpetuation of the dominant ideology of the ruling class.* Cox recognized that power in capitalist civilization tends to be associated with wealth that is acquired by the economic ingenuity of those who best exploit relations with foreign peoples. The tendency here is toward more and more cooperation of the owners of wealth in pursuit of opportunistic foreign transactions. According to Cox, capitalists must trade or perish. Foreign commerce and territorial expansion are indispensable to a capitalist nation, which must expand or collapse.

In Cox's view, cooperative expansion abroad, together with the conflict of interests of economic groups within the domestic economy, calls for "rules" and so-called impartial leadership. The President of the United

States supposedly embodies power as the head of state "of, by and for the people." Yet ultimate power in capitalist political economy actually resides increasingly in a ruling class.[18] Cox contended that this ruling class has openly taken over the national legislature. It has achieved such a degree of consistency between economic power and the law that it has won outright government protection of and assistance to private economic interests. The welfare of the state is now fully identified with the interests of the wealthy class. Everything else is subordinate to the prosperity of the wealthiest business people and to the welfare of the commercial class as a whole. Contrary to ideology, Cox notes, this group has assumed the unquestioned leadership of the nation. Their control of taxation, judiciary, and the armed forces gives them free access to all political processes so that capitalist power grows commensurate with the capitalist control of wealth. Cox contends that the changes made from time to time in government increasingly support the aspirations and power of business-oriented families. The consensus of business executives *becomes* national policy in a capitalist system, with the result that the interest of the ruling class becomes *de facto* the interest of the "public."[19]

In terms of Cox's economic analysis, a capitalist political economy necessitates a relatively elaborate system of civil, criminal, and international law. The laws regulating property and commerce set the direction of all other relationships. The sanctity of property predominates, with the result that severe penalties always are attached to thefts but not always to crimes of violence against persons. Individuals may gain rights but only in relation to the rules of business transactions, e.g., child labor laws, sanitary and food inspection laws. Cox observes the ways in which the judicial system is administered so that there is no appreciable participation of the masses in the administration of justice, to say nothing of revolt or serious objection to laws that disadvantage them.

Nor do all citizens have the same status in a capitalist society. Participation at the top is a valuable privilege controlled by an elite who makes room only for the social mobility of a few. Cox claimed that only those who emerge as active, self-seeking, "responsible" individuals with a direct material interest in the state and a passionate allegiance to the country and its dominant ideology come to be granted access to mobility. Such in-group identification and the privileges that it affords are selectively lavished on a small portion of the population. It is maintained by an invidious controlling attitude that is exclusive, proud, and defiant. Cox argued that the heart of racist privilege is sustained by the reality that the control of wealth and profits (not merely wages) from capital is for white citizens only.[20]

Cox argued that the economic structure of a culture tends to have a prominent role in the attribution of social status. It was his thesis that a salient trait of capitalist culture is the way in which honor is distributed or denied by this system of wealth control. Because wealth acquired through commerce is *the* fundamental status-giving factor, capitalist societies have the persistent tendency of making rich families richer in order to reinforce upper-class status as an exclusive coterie of privileged participants. The appearance that prosperity is widely shared by all the people is one of the features of capitalism that reinforces loyalty to it despite growing control by a few.

Cox argued that there is a close relation between the continual need for news and information and the development of the capitalist system. Thus learning, in all its forms—especially the arts and sciences—is readily available for privileged citizens in capitalist society. The extension of education enables more people to gain access to information about social conditions, changes in various trading areas, war, famine, deaths, births, marriages, and weather conditions, but education and information are shaped by the ideology of the dominant groups.

3. *Integrated diplomacy—the new institution of capitalist society.* Cox identified a third characteristic of the evolution of capitalist political economy: the development of integrated global diplomacy. One of the prime necessities of capitalist commerce is the maintenance of order in international relations so that economic activity is not impeded. Because capitalist nations reap their greatest harvests in stable political environments, a capitalist political economy evolves toward diplomacy as a permanent formal institution. Cox's explanation of integrated diplomacy as a new institution implies that diplomatic bureaucracies—ambassadors and consulates—function chiefly to tie countries of the world into a web of commercial relations, defined by treaties centered in the sovereign republic that they represent. The fine art of diplomacy becomes more and more important to foster the industrial and commercial interests of nation-states. U.S. ambassadors, he noted, deal on the highest level with foreign rulers concerning matters of broad economic scope, but they also take care of practical matters, including the detailed adjustments needed to carry out the terms of treaties.

Cox located the basis of capitalist control of foreign people not in the need to facilitate exchange, but in the need to sell goods abroad. Profit-making, commercial exploitation, business practices not tolerated at home work better abroad, and weak nations are virgin soil for the capitalist, providing a relatively noncompetitive market and lack of experience in resisting the commercial organization that produces goods to be consumed. Because the entire domestic economic structure depends on the success of foreign trade, ambassadors and consuls function to bring other nations under the exploitative hammer of national corporations. A careful observer of the activities of our diplomatic service, Cox concluded that it was regularly overhauled and reorganized to support business more efficiently.

4. *The necessity of religious tolerance.* Cox also emphasized that capitalist society requires a nationally oriented church, one unmastered by foreign power or cultures not americanized. Religion must become virtually inseparable from capitalist philosophical assumptions, science, and economic thinking. In other words, religion must be subordinated to economic interests so that nothing challenges the dictum that "wealth in a capitalist society should be made to produce more wealth."[21] Religious scruples against wealth and worldly activity must cease to interfere with the unconstrained enhancement of material welfare. Cox insisted that under capitalism, the separation of church and state comes to *mean* that the state subjects the church to conditions friendly to our national political economy.

Cox stressed that capitalism must be extremely tolerant in religious matters. There is no problem in permitting divergent sects to worship in relative freedom, and in fact, religious tolerance is helpful in attracting the best laborers from other countries who are fleeing religious persecution. Such tolerance has been a principal means of gaining a nation populous in labor resources. However, whenever the religious practices of a group prove to be inimical to capitalist economic welfare, the system is quick to show displeasure and to discriminate. The "civil utility of tolerance"[22] is rooted in economic need, which also means that, historically, pressure accelerates to assure that religious teachings become consistent with national economic purpose.

In Cox's view, a capitalist nation seeks order for commercial expansion but expects war. Peace is espoused as a primary value, but the ruthless processes of foreign relations shaped by economic penetration inevitably create hostilities that lead to war. Both diplomacy and a willingness and capacity to fight to open up new markets, to keep markets accessible, to eliminate serious competitors, or to quell the resistance of weaker nations must be maintained. "Besides wars for the protection of 'the life line,' all sorts of territories have to be acquired by the capitalist on terms which are seldom if ever fully congenial to the natives. Ultimate settlement ordinarily relied upon force."[23] The perennial obsession of capitalist nations, so Cox maintained, is monopoly of commercial opportunities. Supremacy in military power determines dominion in world markets, and such supremacy becomes a preoccupation.

Thus militarism is a consequence of the system of commodity exchange that must be defended from the sporadic moral attacks on it, attacks that arise principally from the church. In Cox's view, capitalism largely has succeeded in deflating and harnessing the intractable cultural forces of religion that oppose military expenditure and war. It is also of the utmost importance to recognize that in a capitalist culture, welfare institutions emerge in abundance. Many presume that "big business" society deserves credit for providing pure water, a clean city, care for the sick and poor, an organized system of inspectors and police, protection from dishonest merchants, attention to the wounded in time of war and peace, pensioning of retired civil servants, provisions for widows and orphans, free legal aid for the defenseless, and permanent health offices. In Cox's view, these are all pretentious manifestations of humanitarianism, or, at best, concessions to domestic discontent, aimed to adjust conditions to make capitalist political economy appear to provide a respected way of life. Most capitalists believe that decent working conditions and humane treatment of workers are incompatible with optimal profit-making. Business people use the ingenious manipulations available to finance and industry to seduce the church into serving as an indispensable component of the legitimating structure of the dominant political economy. The ideology of capitalism, in which profit often is maintained by force, manipulation, and fraud, is usually couched in some form of Christian teaching, appealing to the Bible as its apparent source of inspiration.[24] The expansion of capitalism is portrayed as virtually assuring the expansion of Christianity and vice versa.

Cox was further convinced that religion increasingly serves as a primary instrument of social control. The church, Cox noted, is where common people are disciplined: there they are taught in the name of God to obey and respect authority and to accept the society as they find it. The church functions to encourage members to transfer faith to greater reliance in the efficacy of science and engineering. Thus capitalists come to consider Christianity a priceless cultural possession.

5. *Capitalist "freedom": the right to choose capitalist values.* Since the Industrial Revolution, Cox argued, there has been an increasing dependence under capitalism on new and improved modes of production. The urge to invent new technology is a strong and persistent dynamic of this mode of economy. Technology also reduces the dependency of the economy on humans, animals, seasons, and geography. Cox insisted that accelerated exploitation of resources on a worldwide scale enhances the unconstrained freedom and power of the dominant capitalist community. Capitalist economy is a congenial milieu for inventive activity and treasures the reservoir of industrial know-how. In short, it aims to carry out the exploitation of both workers and machines as systematically and efficiently as possible. "Freedom" in society is chiefly of the sort that serves the efficiency of production.

Cox recognized that the greater the dependence of a society on its industrial sector, the greater the likelihood of resistance to such exploitation, chiefly through the appearance of determined resistance of labor and its organization. He judged that unionization stemmed from a growing consciousness among workers that their interests differed fundamentally from those of owners and that status as workers would be permanent. The principal goals of trade unions needed to be increasing wages and bettering conditions of work on one hand and gaining governmental power for political leaders supportive of labor on the other. Union "freedom" would be curtailed, he thought, whenever the success of organized workers seriously interfered with maximizing profits.

6. *The inevitable dynamics of Third World imperialism.* Cox was among the first to stress that the emergent structure of the capitalist world market system had its indispensable anchor in Third World countries. Cox conceived imperialism as being grounded in economic subservence. Defined by the degree of their economic value, Third World peoples are considered appendages in reference to labor, raw materials, and the requirements of manufacturing. To this system, the most valuable people of color are those most completely and contentedly exploitable. In Cox's estimate, commerce is not only a less costly means than war to ravish a people, but it is also regarded by capitalists as being far more effective in that it brings the world's peoples within the orbit of the dominant capitalist nations, bringing them "civilization."

Cox long argued that it always would be considered a cardinal offense to capitalist nations for Third World people to withdraw from the system of capitalist political economy. Cox claimed that, in fact, the most ferocious and spectacular capitalist wars have been and would continue to be fought out as a struggle for leadership in African, Asian, and Latin American countries. To bring the argument down to particulars, Cox maintained that when Third World nations tried to extricate themselves, violence was brought to bear and that this attests to the vital importance of their resources and markets within the global system. It is clear that Cox regarded the stakes of war to be the control of the economic life of the world.

Cox argued that the only remedy yet discovered by capitalist democracies for unemployment was *total war.* Only in war and the preparation for war could capitalists secure full employment by socialization of demand without socialization of production.[25] Everything relates, here as elsewhere, to exploitation for profit. Government spending for military purposes, usually referred to as national security, increased consumption but did nothing to distribute wealth. The profits went to private producers. The threat of war, Cox asserted, provided a capitalist rationale for stockpiling. Because no one knows the moment when maximum military danger may occur, the nation must perpetually engage in military buildup and live in a state of military emergency. Many domestic industries come to rely on government protection and military spending, believing that the state should underwrite their success. Aircraft and automobile production, shipbuilding, mining, and even watchmaking and agriculture are secured by government purchases and supports, especially in the interest and name of national defense.

The linkage between capitalist economy and national emergency was characterized by Cox in several ways. First, defense industries are used to stabilize the domestic economy, for example, by shifting spending to economically depressed areas or by purchasing from private enterprise services that traditionally were rendered by military personnel. Globally, the government uses military aid to bolster its economy by selling productive facilities, including war industries, to Third World countries. For Cox, military outlays assume strategic economic significance.

Cox believed that the United States had become the most powerful and incontestable national leader to emerge from centuries of capitalist development. The United States now stands at the center of an international structure, resting on a broad base of economically underdeveloped countries. The U.S. internal economy is inseparably tied into this world system not only through its progressive dependence on military expenditures, but also in its ever-growing exploitation of Third World people.

Linking past and present, Cox traced the way in which the United States emerged as the world leader in technological innovation and mechanical production. He contended that by 1914, the United States had made its superb national resources accessible to intensive exploitation, stimulated foreign trade outlets, established a flexible system of protective tariffs, received financial assistance from older nations, and developed a magnificent network of transportation and communication.[26] Cox documented the way in which American businessmen during World War I moved quickly into areas of weakened competition to sew up postwar control of markets. Latin America was a major target, especially attractive because it would never be a U.S. competitor in iron, steel, and kindred industries; nor would it be able to satisfy its domestic demands for such products.[27] After World War I, Cox insisted, capitalist leaders embarked on a more complete and pervasive integration of U.S. domestic production with production in Third World countries, thereby continually increasing U.S. reliance on foreign economic relations for stability of its own economy. Cox insisted that certain indispensable imports were provided by Africa, Asia, and Latin America: wool, silk, fibers, cotton, rubber, hides, ores (including copper, manganese, tin, and nitrates), sugar, coffee, tea, cocoa, and fruits. He argued that imperialist greed was reflected in U.S. control of these major raw materials in the world market.

Cox also documented the manner in which U.S. control of important markets for manufacturing goods was secured through large investments in the very foreign projects calling for use of those goods.[28] The United States purchased essential raw materials from Third World countries and returned them as semiluxury or nonessential manufactured goods. The more debt Third World countries incurred by borrowing from the United States, the greater was the sale of U.S. products abroad. Cox observed that to enhance the purchasing power of its customers, it was necessary to grant loans, to enable them to make further purchases of U.S. commodities. "If you want our money, you must buy our goods."[29] The "capitalist mind," he claimed, required indoctrination of the public in the principles of international commerce. A convinced public, psychologically invested in commerce, influenced Congress to give more direct aid or loans to enlarge opportunities for foreign investment and commerce.

This pattern of economic dependency was also reinforced by militarism. Military expenditure constituted an essential part of the national budget, and military consignments to Third World countries were seen as a form of economic aid. To receive such aid from the United States, Third World countries had to encourage the flow of production and foreign investment. Governments might use such aid for public services—health, education, sanitation, and agricultural techniques—but could not use them for industrial development. U.S. military programs gave large grants for equipment and training in Third World countries, and our government induced them to make strenuous contributions for "defense" from their limited resources. All such economic aid serves as a brake on social transformation. The thrust of Cox's insight lies in his perception that defense spending is the central thrust and urgent concern of the United States, not of Third World peoples themselves. For Cox, then, the very act of enhancing the war machine of Third World nations was designed to keep capitalist nations technologically and commercially ahead.

7. *Racism as justification for continuing capitalist control.* Cox's elaboration of these dynamics of economic control are of utmost significance, both for understanding the subsequent development of his thought and for grasping his contribution to economic and race analysis. Cox's theses have been sustained again and again since the end of World War II. Since then, American political economic elites have acted as if they believed themselves authorized to arrange, order, and guide the destiny of the global system—a duty that has even included responsibility for the internal stability of the European nations. "Never in modern times has the economic destiny of the peoples of the world so rested within the hands of one nation."[30] Nearly all the world's primary natural resources now serve the needs of the central capitalist economy.

Cox's goal was to demonstrate how the reality of Third World self-development and self-determination would run counter to the notion of development conceived as an auxiliary to expansion of the core capitalist system. Cox focused on the fact that a concentrated attempt must be made by the core system to breed universal contempt for those people exploited by the system.[31] The constant theme in Cox's work was that racist ideology is the ingredient that assures a favorable climate for capitalist development, a pattern of "development" that must be congenial to capitalist interest. The heart of Cox's analysis of racism is that capitalist-imperialist penetration of the world must use racist ideology to assure that "backward peoples" will "allow" themselves to develop gradually under the continued tutelage of private business enterprise.[32] Cox's most penetrating insight is that what this system requires is the belief that capitalists have the right to hold people of color in subjection until they are "civilized." They do not use their power to expedite the process of Third World people's capacity to govern themselves because aspirations for self-determination lead to unrest and demands for further emancipation. Against this background, Cox added that the United States invests money and effort to demonstrate to Third World nations that racism is *not* an intrinsic attitudinal component of capitalism.[33]

Cox recognized and emphasized that a major challenge for the United States was to hold Third World countries within the orbit of the existing political economic system. It was incumbent that they develop according to the processes of private enterprise. The newer form of capitalist development now being encouraged, Cox recognized, is subtler and more poisonous than the old colonialism because it masquerades under the guise of nationalist self-development. In the name of national independence, Third World peoples are persuaded to surrender their desire for freedom to their own emerging national security states and to economic "progress." U.S. policy presumes that the ultimate desire of Third World countries is to become miniatures of the United States and that their people could want or deserve nothing more.

In order to keep the threat of self-government at a minimum, Third World rulers are amply rewarded for their collaboration. In exchange for providing labor and land, the primary production processes are now moved to some Third World countries, which also become markets for finished products. In exchange for what these nations provide, native rulers receive an extraordinary return, which allows them to maintain the services of large retinues of servants and police. This arrangement is reinforced by the vastly superior military might of the United States.

8. *The accelerating exploitation of black people and people of color.* Finally, we must focus on and critically assess Cox's view of the meaning of racism within this structural dynamic. For this social theorist, race relations in a capitalist society must be understood basically as an aspect of labor relations. Cox's unshakable conclusion is that blacks have always occupied and will continue to occupy the lowest rungs of the labor hierarchy. Racism cannot be eliminated *unless* this division of labor is broken. Domestically, employers will work to depress black wages, to restrict

blacks to poor working conditions, and to limit job opportunities. Globally, African populations will remain the poorest of the poor.

The central and basic issue is that under a capitalist political economy, blacks cannot achieve more than second-class citizenship. Capitalists are critical to the spread of racial antagonism. The rich do not overtly suppress the development of the masses of non-white people because the belief that there is room for social mobility must be sustained. Nevertheless, the biological difference of color provides the dominant class with a concrete symbol to which fear of failure and projective hate can be anchored. The dominant group's control of the media enables a subtle, but direct, derogatory and discriminatory propaganda against black people to continue. At the same time, a paternalistic relationship toward the masses of black people has come to be the traditional pattern of dealing with black life and culture. In light of this analysis, it is no mystery why Cox believed that the aristocracy of the capitalist system preserved its interests in cheap, tractable black labor by establishing control over a single, provincial political party dedicated to perpetuating that system.[34] Cox reiterated the point by citing the many ways in which the capitalist political economy abrogated the fundamental citizenship rights of blacks, ways that leave black people brutalized, slanderized, and peonized, virtually helpless both socially and economically.

He insisted that the more that black laborers are used within the capitalist productive system, the greater is the opportunity to "seize" surplus value and maximize profits because black wage labor is easily exploited. Black workers have always been paid lower wages than their white counterparts. The surplus produced by their labor has been appropriated without giving blacks even the limited return that white workers receive. Exploitation results from the demand for harder work, from lowering wages paid to blacks, or by enhancing productivity through technological change that can easily be imposed on vulnerable black workers. The black worker can be subjected to the full force of entrepreneurial exploitation even more ruthlessly than the white worker. The maximum use of black labor as a factor of production enhances the employer's welfare, not the welfare of black people. Black exploitation indeed makes capitalism profitable for owners of the means of production.[35]

The insight at the heart of Cox's social theory is that an ideology of white supremacy bolsters and reinforces America's leadership of the world capitalist system.[36] Racial superiority is fundamental to the wider capitalist ethos wherein white citizens may identify with the system by looking down with ill-disguised contempt on people of other races. Racism, race antagonism, and the illusion of mobility are not only compatible with but also contribute to the successful functioning of capitalist society. Cox's work abounds with statements that capitalist historical development shapes a specific, distinctive, and *virulent* modality of racism.

Racial exploitation and race prejudice developed among Europeans with the rise of capitalism and nationalism and because of the world-wide ramifications of capitalism, all racial antagonists can be traced to the policies and attitudes of the leading capitalist people, the white people of Europe and North America.[37]

Elsewhere he claims:

The stability of color and inertness of culture together with effective control over firearms, subsequently made it possible for whites to achieve a more or less separate and dominant position even in the homeland of colored peoples. ... It is probable that without capitalism, a cultural chance occurrence among whites, the world might never have experienced race prejudice.[38]

Chattel slavery was an extreme institutional expression of capitalist exploitation. The frightful principle of capitalism—private ownership of the means of production, including labor—dictated that the greater the need for black labor, the greater would be black subjugation. Black people not only had to be kept poor, but they had to be themselves *owned* by whites. As slaves, they received no pay. To assure their "happiness" under these meanest of circumstances, blacks had also to be kept ignorant. Laws were passed making it illegal for blacks to read and write. Cox's genius is reflected in his recognition and insistence that racism is always nurtured by economics and cannot be separated from relations of economic dependency.[39]

Cox's interpretation was that after slavery was formally ended, Southern whites gradually regained monopoly power over the constitutionally freed labor supply and relegated black people to non-citizenship. Cox traced the way in which whites controlled blacks chiefly by extralegal mob violence, by intimidation, by distortion of truth, by cheating, by economic boycott, by undermining efforts by and for black education, and by total control of political processes. No room was left for debate.

In 1957, Cox pointed out that not a single piece of civil rights legislation had passed the U.S. Senate for more than eighty years. Southern demagoguery reigned supreme. He reminded his readers that Senator James Eastland had pledged support for white supremacy throughout eternity.

Stressing that racism was a structured dimension of modern capitalist political economy, Cox nevertheless was not at all reluctant to denounce the virulent power of racism as a social force. For Cox, democracy for blacks was always an anti-capitalist movement.[40] The equation of capitalist exploitation and racism offered him a way of making sense of basic sociohistorical facts. He flatly predicted that economic elites and their political allies would invariably identify every attempt to secure citizenship rights for blacks as Communist activity. If Cox's thesis is correct, then seeking human rights for blacks is always to engage in "cold war" activity against the reigning class that controls society.

Conclusions from Cox's Analysis

Oliver C. Cox understood racism to be a dynamic historical structure—an intrinsic economic reality that enabled whites to monopolize economic power through demagoguery and to use military power, laws, and ideology to assure the dependency of the majority of humans. Thus manifest destiny required that the leaders of capitalist nations control and guide the people of color, still too "backward" to be allowed self-determination, for the good of the whole.

The virulence of modern racism gets its distinctive shape from the capitalist structure of labor exploitation. The suppression and mistreatment of black people is maintained despite its malevolence and its moral dubiousness because it serves the needs of this system. Racism rationalizes the enslavement and oppression of people of color. The racial supremacy of whites is a lie that keeps its legitimacy because it has been used, widely and profitably, to justify the subjugation of people of color on grounds that they are inherently inferior.

Oligarchic economic power uses racial inferiority as justification for cruelty, discrimination, even wholesale murder. The U.S. political economy has always denied blacks full access to the democratic process because genuine democracy is incompatible with the best interests and highest profits of business entrepreneurs. Self-aggrandizing social choices, including increased investment of profits in high-yield ventures, always have the result of further entrapping the black community in poverty and disease. Racism supports the belief, conscientiously held, that poverty and ignorance sustained by force and fraud are desirable for people of color and that white power and prestige must remain at any cost.

The form of Christianity shaped by obeisance to economic interests of a capitalist system is a new form of Christianity, one that legitimates exploitation. This type of exploitative religious rationale accommodates to all sorts of social ruthlessness so long as profits increase. Christianity conflated to the dominant system invariably rejects the claim that the essence of the gospel mandate is liberation of the oppressed. Instead, a form of capitalist Christianity combines defense of the sanctity of the economic system with racial and theological conformity. Such Christianity separates the spiritual person from the bodily person and calls on people to be spiritual and avoid politics. The freedom and radical human equality professed in early Christian proclamations are assimilated into the propagation of a capitalist world view. In Cox's formulation, the implicit liberating power of religion is supplanted by the more profitable social

137

principal of fundamental racial difference. Thereby the church sanctions and stabilizes the mundane interests of the ruling class. The dominant churches continue to be the ominous symbol of white dominance.

Oliver C. Cox insisted that racism becomes an unquestioned dictum of history and literature to assure the persistence and expansion of existing economic arrangements and to give continuous reign and recognition to white supremacy. The myth of racial inferiority enables capitalist governments, economic organizations, and financial structures to penetrate the world. The hatred and fear of people of color now has developed into a global system of ideological subjugation, justifying the legitimacy of control of Third World countries through massive debt, monopoly industry, and direct military imperialism.

EIGHT

Emerging Issues in Urban Ethics

Donald W. Shriver Jr.

*E*thical thinking is first a matter of sorting out primary and secondary human loyalties. It is then a matter of relating the two.

The New Testament seems preoccupied more with the first step than with the second. In the Gospel narratives we observe that Christian ethics begins in pain, struggle, and conflict inside persons and between them. Jesus calls his disciples with the simple imperative, "Follow me." Soon after, the new disciples discover, with much distress, the results of a primary loyalty to Jesus. Family? The disciple must be willing to leave it for a journey to Jerusalem. Farm, business, economic livelihood? Abandon them all; humans do not live by bread alone. Wealth? Give it all away if you would enter the kingdom of God. Government? Caesar has his place, but Jesus is Lord. Life itself? Whoever would save his or her own life must lose it for Jesus' sake and the gospel's—repeatedly an invitation to a primary loyalty that may have radical, rearranging effect on all other human loyalties. Without that clear primacy, there is no beginning to the *Christian* way of life. "Why call ye me, 'Lord, Lord,' and do not the things which I say [Luke 6:46, KJV]?"

This New Testament stress on a primary loyalty that defines all specific goods as secondary has led many scholars to conclude that—for all practical purposes—there is no "social ethic" to be found. Apparently, we have there only an ethic for Christians in their church communities, separated from "the world" and urged by the Holy Spirit to "obey God rather

Donald W. Shriver Jr., President of the Faculty and William E. Dodge Professor of Applied Christianity, Union Theological Seminary in New York City.

than Caesar (cf. Acts 4:19)." The Christian life seems to be a matter of "Christ against culture," a life in society but in opposition to it.[1]

Early and late in the history of the Christian movement, however, that call to primary loyalty has proved only the beginning of the ethical thinking and struggles of Christians. What *is* the relationship of a primary loyalty to all the other loyalties that bid for respect in any human society? Meat sacrificed to idols? You may have to decide if the fact that God created it makes it fit for consumption. Neighbors who worship at their own religious shrines? You, Christian, will have to decide how to live next door to them. The commercial prosperity of your city? Your own life may depend on it; you cannot be even a tentmaker without customers. The government's coercive power to maintain law and order? You may find it useful someday, for the protection of your liberty to remain Christian and to preach the gospel to the world.

Such reflections, prompted wholly by passages in the letters of the apostle Paul, reflect the life of the early Christian churches in the *cities* of the Roman Empire. As the names given to the Pauline epistles vividly testify, Christianity, in its infancy, was very much an urban religious movement.[2] Paul, in particular, went from city to city preaching the good news of Jesus; and he yearned, as an apostle, to preach the gospel "also at Rome [Acts 23:11]," urban headquarters of the most powerful, longest lasting empire in the ancient world. One might even speak of an *urban bias* in the early church's sense of mission: a bias rooted in the powerful impulse to open the way of discipleship to *all* humans everywhere. Because more people gathered in cities than in any other equivalent space, and because the varieties of tribal humanity gathered there, the cities were a natural place for promoting Christian witness. An urban bias expressed religious *universalism,* a faith and an ethic open in principle to diverse humans and their varied cultures.

At stake here are two general issues in Christian ethical theory: Is there, then, in spite of superficial appearances, a Christian ethic *for* society? If there is, what does the society itself *contribute* to the content of that ethic? Stated another way: once the primary loyalties of the Christian community are clear, does that very primacy have implications for the behavior of Christians in society? If so, do secondary loyalties also have a role in the ethical reflection of Christians in a way that prompts them to make their residence in cities an agenda for reflection and shapes their "normative" behavior in certain directions? Is the general standard of Christian behavior somewhat different in urban society and in rural society? In an empire and in a democracy?

The answers to these two questions have been various indeed over two thousand years; contemporary debates among Christian ethical scholars resemble the ancient ones. Some, from Diognetus to Kierkegaard, understand the external behavior of the Christian to be similar to that of everyone else, while inwardly, the Christian is to be radically oriented by faith in God. Others, from the monastics to the Pennsylvania Amish, form island communities, small "Christian" societies within secular societies. Others, from John of Patmos to Jacques Ellul, flirt with the dualism that assigns corruption to all human institutional life and salvation to the eschatological City of God. Others, from Francis of Assisi to Mother Teresa, do works of Christian love among the poor of the city, expecting little change in the societal structures that account for poverty. Still others, from John Calvin to Harvey Cox, perceive the new commercial cities of the West as arenas for individual and social innovation that lead to new works of justice realized by Christians and secular partners. Yet others, from Augustine to John Courtney Murray, distinguish the "City of Earth" from the "City of God" but relate the two by the hinge of natural law, manifest in the human capacity to govern the one city and to anticipate the other.

What all these varied Christian perspectives share is an effort both to assert continuity with some themes of New Testament faith and ethics that they regard as authoritative and to propose some themes and structures from their own reflection on Christian social behavior. Understanding and interpretation of biblical norms may change over time among Christians, but they strive to maintain continuity. Choice and priority among contemporary social facts and possibilities there must be, but they must seek some relatedness or "relevance." At all points in history, reflective ethical Christians have to ask one another: Does continuity with our communal past obscure attention to our particular present social context? Or is our problem the reverse? How do we maintain the tension and relation between continuity and particularity in the method and content of our thinking about what we do?

These schools of thought reflect much conflict with one another as to how they perceive and interpret biblical continuity; in their rejection or celebration of certain contemporary forces of their societies; in their relative discomfort with the dangers of dualism and cultural idolatry, respectively; in their relative preference for being "right in principle" on the one hand and "contributors to real solutions to contemporary problems" on the other.

All these variables have entered into one or another of these thinkers' reflection about Christian ethics and the life of Christians in cities. They also impact the debate about whether the church has anything distinctive to say about urban life as such. Is there a Christian "urban ethic"? The question deserves an ambiguous answer, but against the background of the great debates about the possibility of a distinctive Christian ethic for society, there are some compelling reasons, from both the ancient and the modern urban contexts of the Christian movement, for paying intense attention to the city as moral context and moral opportunity for Christian life and thought.

The City as an Indispensable Context for Modern Christian Social Ethics

The Bible, both the Old and the New Testaments, entertains profound ambivalences about human life in cities. A careful reading of postbiblical church history sustains that ambivalence: again and again, the Christian movement experienced some of its great tragedies and triumphs in connection with the rise and fall of urban centers of power and culture.

Ancient Israel had a natural reason to fear the religious and imperial power of cities. In both Egypt and the "promised land" its enemies built shrines, organized empires, and enslaved captive peoples from seats of urban power. Some early Christian readers of the Hebrew Bible were quick to see an anti-urban bias in its pages. (Augustine associated the guilt of Cain with the fact that he was a "builder of cities," over against the herdsman Abel, his murdered brother, "who built none.") Expressive of this bias may be the Tower of Babel—symbol of the human ambition to wrest control of the world from God.[3] A more consistent theme of the prophetic writings, however, centers on the ambiguous virtues of the "City of David"—Jerusalem, headquarters of Hebrew kingdoms. Rare is the prophet from 1000 to 500 B.C.E. who does not take moral aim at the pride, power, oppression, and idolatrous worship to which Jerusalem and its leaders were prone.

This suspicion of Jerusalem, the allegedly holy city, reached new intensity among the early Christians who remembered that Jesus was crucified outside its walls by the combined wills of religious and political leaders. Much of the New Testament was written in the years just before or after the great destruction of Jerusalem by the armies of Rome (70 C.E.). Its pages are filled with a certain sadness about the fate of Jerusalem and a continued mixture of respect and contempt for Rome and all its political works. (Cf. Luke 19:41-44; 13:34-35.)

Ironically, during its first four centuries, the emerging Christian church borrowed strength and influence from its host cities. By the time of Augustine, Christianity had become the official religion of the empire, now in drastic decline. Augustine tried to reassure Christians that barbarian invasions could not destroy the *truly* "Eternal City" (the City of God), whatever might happen to Rome's proud claim to that title. In his quarrels with the rigorist Donatists, Augustine backed off from such a "transcendental" perspective on *church* politics and declared it theologically orthodox that all Christians should obey their bishops, headquartered mostly in the larger cities of the empire. Forever afterward, the political conflicts of the church itself were to be shaped by rival centers of episcopal power, especially Rome and Constantinople. It was no wonder, then, that monks and other protestors of the now established church should seek a rural setting—the mountain, the desert, the village—for their protest. To them, cities were symbolic of the church's corruption by a society it now legitimated.[4]

When we start our reflection on Christian ethics and the city with these memories of the ancient urban context of Hebrew and Christian faiths, we are a long way historically from the cities of the United States. For more than six hundred years after the fall of Rome, the cities of that empire declined in vigor. Their cultural and political power shrank; real power and wealth gravitated to feudal estates in the countryside. The church, coterminously with the feudal system, then structured itself to fit the medieval patchwork of baronies, fiefdoms, and petty kingdoms. The church itself became one of the great landowners in a society that counted land as the only secure form of wealth and power. By the time of Francis of Assisi, in the thirteenth century, one could have spoken of a *rural* bias of the church. When Francis began his ministry to poor people in the early commercial-industrial cities of Italy, he did so in defiance of the official church, for whose leaders the notion of unchecked population growth in cities meant ruptured social stability. In the feudal system, there was not much conceptual room for cities.

The future of twentieth-century American cities was brewing, however, in these new commercial cities of the late medieval era. Enterprising merchants began to prove that land was not the only form of wealth in the human world. Kings saw benefit for themselves in this discovery—money for armies, energy for nation-building and empire-building. And—part product, part producer of all this energy—a new movement in the church, to be called Protestantism, rode the waves of the new urban commercialism in the service of some of its own distinctive commitments.

Of no portion of the new Protestantism was association with the *commercial* city so characteristic as the followers of John Calvin of Geneva. In this tiny city-state, Calvin sought refuge in 1536 from the persecution of Protestants in nearby France. He did not look toward a rural monastic retreat, but to an urban haven, a maneuver made plausible by the relative independence of Geneva's merchants from political and economic control outside the city. Forever after, Calvinism was to demonstrate an affinity with the agenda of the commercial-industrial city. Whatever the cause-and-effect relation of Calvinism and capitalism—the subject of a famous sociological debate begun by Max Weber[5]—it is clear that industriousness, frugality, hatred of poverty, and open eyes for "a just profit" were virtues of the Calvinist character. Such virtues Calvinists brought with them in their pilgrimages to the "New World," where their search for religious freedom assumed the advantages of a new economic freedom to combat poverty and pursue wealth through trade. As John Winthrop put it to his future neighbors in the Massachusetts Bay Colony in 1630, they were to set up a new Christian community, "a City set upon a hill," in this new world.

This cursory glance at changing relations of the Christian movement to the life of its host cities may seem all too simple and hasty. But even in the glance peeps out an important ingredient in the "ethical method" that many modern Christian ethicists—H. Richard Niebuhr, Reinhold Niebuhr, and Roger Shinn among them—feel compelled to recommend. *No Christian social ethic is possible without accurate recollection of ancient biblical norms and equally accurate empirical perception of what a society has been historically and is tending to become in the future.* What Christians should and should not say to their society *will* usually be conditioned by what they perceive that society to be: but further, it *should* be so conditioned. An ethic whose hopes for human behavior are rooted only in a past revelation of God, the teachings of Jesus and the prophets, or the traditions of the church will not connect to contemporary human behavior, however traditional or novel.

Christians in the United States, for example, will not understand their urban environment enough to think with ethical accuracy about it if they do not understand a great formative fact about their cities: they are mostly products of the *new commercialism* of the past four hundred years of Euro-American urban development. Of all the world's cities, North America's were built on commerce. More, our cities are being built right now by the forces of commerce.

The Rise of the American City

To appreciate the centrality of this circumstance, some further retrospective glances at the history of city-building on the North American continent may be useful.

The origins of almost every city north of the Rio Grande River in America consist in combinations of geography and the requirements of a growing commercial civilization controlled ultimately by English settlers. Early and late, Charleston and Norfolk grew as export cities for the products of up-country plantations. From the seventeenth into the twentieth centuries, Philadelphia, New York, and Boston funneled people and products into the westward expansion of colonies and a nation. Pittsburgh, Cincinnati, and St. Louis grew from river docks to nodes of national commerce that anticipated the nation that would be the United States. Buffalo, Cleveland, and Chicago combined water and rail transportation with the invention of steel to become burgeoning nineteenth-century industrial cities. Kansas City, Fort Worth, Denver, and San Francisco joined the national network of cities by combining railroads, cattle trails, and agricultural markets. And the new cities of post-1950 America—Atlanta, Dallas, Los Angeles, Seattle—boast newness chiefly in their distinctive mid-twentieth-century facilities for commerce: airports, interstate highways, and national defense-related industry.

Awesome change separates the settlement of Boston in 1630 and the freeway city of Los Angeles in 1985, but economic themes connect them. Some of the changes are as obvious as they are momentous for the lives of Americans: from small village-like cities to "conurbations" of multiple-city systems; from small-scale to large-scale production and distribution of commercial products; from a time of modest involvements of federal government in urban growth or decline to a time of national political debate over how much involvement; from "provincial" cities in slender commercial exchange relations with one another to national and world cities in ever-denser relations with one another through investment decisions, world raw material sources, and world markets; from the age of the "joint stock company" organized by three or a dozen investors to the age of the multinational corporation with headquarters around the world and thousands of stockholders; from a time when residents of a single city felt themselves part of a stable local community to a time when one American in four moves every year, when city neighborhoods change from white to black to Hispanic majorities in a few years, when the "urban experience" of people in the United States gets translated into a hundred versions of strategies for individual survival.

Religion and Ethics in American Urban Culture

Does the *religious* and *ethical thinking* of the earliest Christian settlers of the United States have anything to do with all this vast development? Urban historian Sam Bass Warner has traced this history, and he discerns in it both continuity and a break between the ideals of the first Puritan city-builders and the ideals that have come to dominate the urban culture of twentieth-century North Americans. These first city-builders, he says, "carried in their heads the specifications for a good life and a decent community, and for a time they were able to realize them" in their small New England towns.[6] Two strong convictions carried over from their "heads" to their planning of these towns: (1) a desire for individual economic freedom, expressed in parcels of land allocated to individuals or families, and (2) a sense of just constraint on the right of any individual to possess or accumulate wealth in large disproportion to the wealth of a neighbor.

True descendants of both the Exodus and the medieval traditions, the Puritans saw "freedom" linked to the possession of land. Not only did they bring with them from Europe a hunger for land, but also in America, that hunger was fed by vast thinly populated tracts to the west. This first element in their "town planning" undid the other element: the religious or political authorities of a small town could hardly enforce an idea of just distribution of land when over the frontier lay huge acreages that the technology of guns could easily wrest from the "natives." Land, they knew, produced the things of commerce: food, minerals, timber, and raw materials with uses yet to be discovered. From the first beginning of white America, land was thus the key to wealth, and attitudes toward land have shaped the lives of people in our cities for great good and evil.

Critically lacking in the Puritans' vision of the free and just human city, says Warner, was the very element that the frontier was to accentuate for all immigrant Americans: social freedom to *change*. Puritanism helped to supply the American political tradition with its deep preference for personal freedom; it contributed less successfully to the fragile sense of economic justice in the United States; and it shaped hardly at all a sense of constraint or discipline for guiding change in group terms. "What is good for me?" is a popular question in the culture of the United States. "What is good for us?" was an equally popular question among the Puritans, but it got lost in the flood of individualism that was to overtake this culture in the eighteenth and nineteenth centuries. Many of the "emerging issues in urban ethics," to be treated later, emerge from this basic conflict in American life. It is the conflict between ethics conceived individualistically and ethics conceived communally.

One must not leave this dimension of historical recollection without remembering at least one more element in the history of American cities over the past one hundred years: An English historian once remarked that "John Calvin was the virtual founder of the United States of America." He was speaking about the Puritan strain in early American culture, and his remark applies chiefly to the first two hundred years of English settlement on this continent. In the mid-nineteenth and throughout the twentieth centuries of U.S. life, the cultural supremacy of white Anglo-Saxon Calvinistic ways of thinking gradually gave way before waves of *other* ways of thinking rooted in a vast array of other world cultures. Beginning with the first great nonwhite immigration to these shores—the forced immigration of more than 2 million Africans—non-English and non-Protestant peoples overwhelmed the Puritan consensus and, especially in the great new industrial cities, drowned it in a flood of unprecedented *cultural pluralism.*[7] These tides of external and internal immigration have been changing the social makeup of U.S. city populations for well over a century. Waves of south European immigrants poured into the northern cities in the late nineteenth century, to be succeeded by waves of black sharecroppers between two world wars in the twentieth. They in turn have been succeeded in the past thirty years by waves of Hispanics and Asians. *If there is anything old in the culture of the American city, it is the search of all its residents for economic "progress" for themselves. If there is anything new, it is the unprecedented variety of cultural definitions of that progress and its meaning for the relation of city dwellers to one another.* Protestant Americans, in particular, have new partners for their exploration of what it means to be Christian and city dwellers in urban America. I turn now to some major issues of that exploration.

Issues Confronting the Christian Churches of the Contemporary United States

In his probing analysis of the modern city, *Ethics and the Urban Ethos,* Christian ethicist Max C. Stackhouse suggested that Christians must bring three resources to bear on their reflection: (1) we need a *vision* of human fulfillment, such as Winthrop's vision of the "City on the Hill," where no one was poor, none excessively rich, all had a certain equality before God, and each had a role or service to the public good; (2) we require a notion of *right social order* for the achievement of the vision that includes some rules governing property ownership, definitions of just and unjust competition, and principles for understanding in what sense all humans are simultaneously "equal" and "unequal"; and (3) we require a scheme of *organization* for society—a "polity"—roughly similar to a constitution.[8]

What resources does the contemporary Christian movement, especially in its Protestant expressions, have for this vision, for order and polity of American urban society? If we are to believe Sam Bass Warner's account of American urban culture, Protestantism has already made a tangible, but fragmentary and ironic, contribution to that culture. In virtual parallel with Stackhouse, Warner believes that Americans have a cultural tradition with three great themes relevant for their behavior as city dwellers. These themes function for Warner as ethical measuring rods: (1) the *freedom* of individuals to seek futures for themselves different from their pasts; (2) an *equality* of persons, expressed in their right of access to fair competition with one another; and (3) a definition of social, political, and economic systems of the city as *inclusive* of all people, whatever their current social, political, and economic status. Personal freedom, interpersonal equality, and social inclusiveness: this is the "good city" as Americans should define it, according to Warner.[9] How should Warner's culturally pluralistic ethical basepoints and Stackhouse's theological contributions be related? This is the agenda of a Christian social ethic.

147

How anyone shapes and explores this agenda will be greatly influenced by his or her answers to questions like "Whose definition of a good city shall we accept? Whose reading of the Bible? Whose church history? Whose history of the American city?" Almost any reader will detect a shifting boundary between what authors *perceive* about the Christian and the American cultural visions and what they *believe* about them. Human beings bring beliefs to their acts of perception, and they sustain or modify their beliefs by what they claim to perceive. That is the inevitable, inter-twined mix of "fact" and "value" in all human thinking, especially ethical thinking.

An eloquent illustration of this mixture can be found in Warner's sum-mation of the ethical and policy issues he detects in the current struggle of Americans to build humane cities. The summation reflects his reading of history and his ethical commitments:

> During the past half century these extensions from the past have mired our society in a series of contradictions and confusions which we must now come to understand if we are to find policies that will enable us to realize humane solutions. Every component of the forces that bear upon the American urban system, as well as the system itself, harbors twin potentials—for mass repression or for the expan-sion of popular freedoms. Science and technology can be directed toward war and manipulation or toward services for everyday living; the multiple ways of modern transportation can be either an escape route for the affluent or a means of expanding everyone's horizons; the service economy can be directed toward world domination or toward everyday human needs; the national network of cities can be linked only to the enrichment of local business and political elites or can become the foundation for broadened employment and equalized living standards; the reach and complexity of urban markets can be instruments for bureaucratic control or levers to release personal and group autonomy; the abundant land of the megalopolis can be restricted to the present unequal contest between the classes and races or can become the site of humane physical environments. Our history shows that the capacity of the American urban system for war production, private profit, and inequality, and for ignoring and inflic-tion of deprivation and suffering is seemingly limitless and certainly enduring. What is new in our time is the enlarged potential of the system to promote the freedom of all groups within it.[10]

This summation is notable for the central focus that Warner gives "freedom" as a social value. In this thought he is characteristically North American. Not so characteristic of all our social thought is his insistence on equality and inclusive community as necessary for the real "expansion of freedom" in this society. Readings of history, ethics, and social policy interweave in his analysis. No "issue" in a society is simply "there" to be recognized. Issues emerge from *relations* between the eyes of beholders and things beheld.

I, too, am such a beholder. I read the past and future goods and evils of modern city life conditioned by particular books like those of Warner and Stackhouse and especially by one book, the Bible. I experience the city in certain ways that both expand and constrict my perceptions of others who live there with me. From this mixture of conditions, I see certain ethical issues facing those of us who are Christians in our calling to be both city dwellers and disciples of the One who wept over Jerusalem on his way to dying there. There are at least three questions, far from exhaustive, that I deem important for the ethics of contemporary urban Christians. They are crucial for us to ask because they are required by our biblical faith and the principles of justice we derive from it.

1. Can white Protestant Americans become chief contributors to a humane urban pluralism, rather than its chief opponents? I live in a city, New York, whose inhabitants, a hundred years ago, numbered a majority of white Protestants. Today the religious demography of New York City tells a story of crisis in the relations of Protestants and the city: the majority of white Christians in the five boroughs of the city are Roman Catholics. The second largest Jewish community in the world lives in these boroughs. And on the island of Manhattan, 80 percent of people who are Protestants are black or Hispanic. Where did so many white Protestants go? They went, of course, to the suburbs.

For historically conscious Christians of all ethnic identities, this growing mixture of cultures, colors, and life-styles in large U.S. cities resonates with the situation of the earliest Christian churches. It reminds us of the Pentecost-birth of the church from a miraculous experience of community among people of many languages. It resonates as well with the memory of pluralism in the churches of the first urban Christians. But the intervening history of the Christian movement, especially for white American Protestants, has introduced a momentous contradiction between this memory and the demography of the contemporary American city. Why did so many Protestants—and now many of their Roman Catholic neighbors—move to the suburbs? Some moved because they were uncomfortable with their new black, Hispanic, and other nonwhite neighbors. Indeed, a dominant image of "economic progress" in the United States in the twentieth century has been a move from the inner city to the suburbs.

Because suburbs are part of *urbs Americana*, they, too, could be understood as places where a pluralistic vision of urban society might come to expression. But everyone knows that city dwellers in the United States often define their social and economic *differences* from others through their places of residence. White Protestant churches have often ratified and strengthened these definitions of who our neighbors are. They have done so particularly by their readiness to move with "the people" to the suburbs, thereby excluding from "the people" those newer residents of the neighborhood who never heard of John Calvin or Martin Luther.

At stake here is not simply the question of institutional strategies that may permit church congregations to survive in the midst of major change in the ethnic constituencies of their neighborhoods. Many mobile urban Christians attend worship many miles from their places of residence. At stake are theologically and ethically shaped questions of loyalty to *the original Christian vision of a humanly inclusive church that sets up precedent and pressure toward a humanly inclusive city.* Theologically, we must learn to define any gathering of Christians as putting their fidelity to the gospel at risk if the persons in that gathering come from only a narrow social segment of the surrounding community. Where cultures are in collision, should there not be a church seeking to forge community out of that collision? The word pluralism does *not* mean merely "a mixture of viewpoints and values among people who happen to live near each other." Pluralism means the possibility that humans can affirm one another *in their differences,* can live together in freedom, justice, and community, not merely in "tolerance."

The answer to the question "Can Protestant churches contribute to the coming of such a pluralism to America's cities?" may have to resemble Dr. Maltby's answer to the question "Can Christians dance?" Some can, some can't. Some churches have the ethical capacity to contribute to urban pluralism, some do not. Some church congregations in our cities gather persons from many segments of ethnically diverse neighborhoods and some fail to do so. At higher levels of organization than the congregation—conferences, dioceses, presbyteries, associations—these diversities may meet and minister to human need across the city as a whole. Further yet, there are ecumenical organizations that enable the suburban white Protestant to join the suburban white Catholic and inner-city black congregation in search for ways to effect a Christian vision, order, and polity for the city's neglected citizens. But such "urban ecumenicity" is uncommon in the cities of America. Churches sometimes are responsible for the frustration of a pluralistic vision in almost every suburban neighborhood in the nation.

2. *One cannot pose the issue of pluralism and polity ethically without also asking, are local, state, and federal government agencies, corporations, and religious bodies capable of the commitment and the priorities necessary for doing justice to the needs of the urban poor.* For a century now, cities have been magnets for the poor people, immigrating to cities from within the United States or from other countries. For thirty centuries, the Hebrew and Christian traditions brought to their host societies a sense of God's priority-preference for the needs of the poorest of those societies.

Modern biblical and theological scholarship has strengthened this sense that there is the divine priority that Christians must honor for the world. With its persistent theme of the struggle against poverty, our broader social history also seems to honor this priority in the form of an expectation that individuals will work hard to overcome their own poverty. Such expectations have strong roots in Puritanism.

The secular tradition of personal and commercial ethics is more ambiguous than is the biblical ethic on the question of whether individuals deserve *help* in their economic struggles. Stripped of the early Puritan insistence on communal support for personal efforts toward economic well-being, the competitive capitalist spirit took over much of our society's thinking on this matter, yielding widespread advice like: "Come to the city you who are poor, get a job, work hard, save your money, and make progress for yourself and your children." But it added: "No one owes you a living. Surely government does not."

It is questionable if, even in the days of free land to the west, economic success in the United States was frequently or usually due to such individualistic striving. Land grants in the West were, after all, an act of the U.S. government. The railroads for going west were creations of governments and corporations supported by government policies. Now, especially in the modern, interconnected cities and neighborhoods of this nation, the economic ambitions of poor people are laced and fenced around with complex political, economic, and social systems that shape the lives of every person in the land. Is this society capable of "liberty and justice for all," including the 15 percent of us whom our government classifies as "poor"?

If we as U.S. Christians are to move with any integrity across the bridge from ordinary biblical tradition to dealing with the plight of poor people, we will have to find the courage to confront and contradict some of the myths of U.S. economic culture and ideology: "God helps those who help themselves" not only does not appear in the Bible, but it is also a motto profoundly antagonistic to the whole Hebrew and Christian tradition of faith and ethics. God helps the helpless and expects the helped to help their neighbors in turn. This is a far more accurate summation of the biblical tradition than the secular, self-help ideology many espouse.

The assistance that the poor need for their own combat against poverty is visible on all the streets of this nation to Christians with eyes to see what is before them. Why, beginning about 1970, did the number of apparently hungry people on those streets begin to decline? Because of a new federal food stamp program, by which the Congress of the United States enacted public policy that acknowledged that the country is rich enough to feed all of its citizens. Why, beginning about 1981, did the number of hungry people on city streets begin to increase again? Because of the cuts in this federal food stamp program and an increase in unemployment spurred partly by the policies of an administration willing to pay that price for decreased inflation while drastically increasing our military budget.

The food stamp program is an illustration of how government policy in modern America can effect some improvement in the lot of the poor throughout the society but especially in inner cities, where these poor are disproportionately concentrated. Less exemplary is what governments—local, state, and federal—have done to meet another basic need of poor people, decent housing. Owning one's own house has been a twentieth-century economic goal of many in this society. Since World War II, the federal government has subsidized home mortgages that brought ownership within the reach of two-thirds of the population. The rest of the population could rent their housing, this policy assumed, and some, the very poorest, could live in housing constructed with public funds. The result of this policy is visible now to any perceptive view of the American city from one of its tallest buildings or an airplane: single-family houses in the suburbs, largely through Federal Housing Administration financing; large inner-city public housing tracts, there because the poor and public housing are not welcome throughout the city; and in between, assortments of rental apartments, some slum and some luxury, which are profitable to owners but not always congenial to renters. Almost invariably, this third, in-betweenish housing of the city was once occupied by middle strata people who gradually shifted to suburban status, abandoning their deteriorating former homes to lower-income folk rich enough to avoid public housing but not rich enough to qualify for home mortgages. During the late 1970s and early 1980s, many young middle-income professional people of our cities began to discover that high interest rates prevented *even* them from contracting for a private home. Indeed, it is estimated that in 1984, no more than 20 percent of young American families could afford such a home, suggesting that the majority of the population now finds the housing component of the "American dream" beyond its reach. Like the very poor, their ambitions are subject to drastic curtailment by economic forces over which they have little control.

In sum, the rhetoric of "equal opportunity" in the American city is empty for numerous of its inhabitants. Furthermore, black families with money to purchase homes in suburbia are seldom free to do so because of racism; and poor families without money are not free in any sense even to try to do so. Popular suburban prejudice decrees that the presence of public housing marks any community as "deteriorating," most particularly in its property values.

Perhaps the most powerful myth at work here in this culture is the sanctity of private property. As Warner makes momentously clear, the early English settlers of the land (to the horror of native Americans) made buying, selling, and owning of property supremely simple—most land could be transferred and owned "in fee simple."[11] Few countries on earth *conceive* property owners as so immune from public discipline and accountability as does the United States. Nor is tax policy in many other societies so encouraging to land speculation, to the manipulation of urban planning according to tax benefits, and to governmental collaboration in the rapid escalation of certain land values. Many downtown city parking lots, for example, occupy land put to temporary low-profit use by owners who expect them to become sites for office buildings which city government officials have already decided that corporations may build. Why should land values, influenced upward by public policies, benefit owners first and the public second or not at all? Why should the use of *any* piece of urban land be determined by the profit it will yield to its owner? To ask such questions is to trespass on the sanctity of some principles basic to a capitalist economy. Neither the Hebrew nor the Christian ethic has ever been constructed as supporting the sanctity of any economic system. Much closer to sanctity is the principle that every society on earth will be judged by God according to its treatment of its poorest people. In this ordering perspective, property values, even in the suburbs, must not be allowed to shut out the poor from decent housing, and city dwellers from park land, not-for-profit institutional land, land for breathing space, and other humane uses of land.

Can the citizens of our cities weigh all the social dynamics of urban change, growth, and decay in the balance of an ethical vision that subordinates economic "forces" to *human fulfillment*? To liberty, justice, and community for all? Only economic determinists—of whatever ideological stripe—will dismiss the question as moralistic.

3. *How will Christians and others contribute to a new political vision for the U.S. city and learn to make political commitments to match it?* This is the complex challenge that confronts the ethically sensitive Christian in any American city. We live in a time when federal government budgets are huge "policy statements" of a nation's priorities; when national defense allocations grow at the expense of medical care, housing, and food stamp programs; when human service systems limp along under crisis municipal budgets; and when tax policies favor private expenditure and depreciate public. At a time when suburban voters get the luxury "needs" met by governments alert to their large turnout of voters, the inner-city poor make it easy for government to ignore them because a culture of poverty is reflected in apathy and low voter turnout. At a time when great corporate investments shift from old industrial cities of the East to new "Sun Belt" cities of the South and West, interregional sympathy and responsibility barely get mentioned in a logrolling Congress and an administration little concerned about human suffering in the workings of

competitive economics. Here are many ethical and policy issues crying out for attention in America's cities.

In the final analysis, the purpose of the Christian movement, and of ethical perspectives related to it, is not to demonstrate authoritative expertise about all the problems of society or to promote some alleged Christian solution to all those problems. The Christian vision of human community subjects our cities and other human ways of living together to standards of freedom, equality, and community under God; to the expectation that humans will order their relations with one another according to justice, compassion, and peace, which Christians glimpse in Jesus their Lord; and to the hope that active, organized systems will be invented for including all human beings in the benefits of such a society. Neither ministers nor priests, professors nor scholars, expert policymakers nor experienced leaders of government or business are capable of saying what we should do together even to approximate such a society.

"What we all do together" is a way of speaking about *politics*. The role of Christians and churches in activating one another and their neighbors to participate in the urban-democratic political process is perhaps the largest practical ethical issue of all. Political activation underlies many of the issues enumerated above, for politics is the process whereby groups of people make decisions about what has to be decided, make those decisions, and make institutional arrangement for carrying those decisions into action.

In the United States, with its constitutional "wall of separation between church and state," do churches have something distinctive to contribute to this society's search for "liberty and justice for all"? The answer is not just a hopeful theoretical "yes." The answer is pragmatic: *only those Christians who actually participate in a political process will ever discover what it is we have to contribute to it.*

Perhaps the most convincing demonstration of this principle that political practice is ethically necessary is the experience of black churches in the civil rights movement of the 1950s and 1960s. Black leaders did not know then how pliable the various levels of government might be to their demands for a new level of justice for black Americans. But they did know that the nearest thing to a political organization in the black community was the church, the only organization in American society over which black people have exercised real control since the Civil War. In the civil rights movement, many black churches moved into the streets in public protest and into the halls of government, demanding changed laws. This collective effort activated some black people politically for the first time in their lives. The strength and interpersonal support for doing so came from the churches.

In the late 1970s, "evangelical" church groups across the country were discovering the same potential of their members for carrying some part of their Christian beliefs into the public arena. They discovered what several recent studies have documented: human relationships in the church give some of its members the security to act together for public purposes. Moreover, the studies show that action together for public purposes has surprising positive effects on the strength of religious faith itself: Personal faith without public political works remains mute, fragile, and frustrating. It also remains closed to truth and insight about society that only participation in the rough and tumble of public political conflict may enable one to grasp.[12]

These claims may be unwelcome assertions for many white Protestant Christians in the United States. They are less so for many black Christians, whose tradition never asserted that "religion and politics don't mix." Religion is not the same as politics. Religion enables its adherents to repent of some of their political actions by informing them of the difference between how deeply they are called to love their neighbors and how inadequately, in fact, they do so. But political experience serves the faith and vigor of religious people by acquainting them with the cost of real justice in society, the complexity of human community, the true breadth of pluralism, and the necessity for people of diverse faith and experience to work together *in spite* of their differences if there is to *be* a human community.

The cities of the United States contain a complex array of possibilities and frustrations for *any* vision for change in the way such cities benefit and harm their citizens. To touch the human problems of those cities is to touch systems as large as multinational corporations, as intimate as neighborhoods, as complex as state and federal government, and as global as the economic interchanges of cities across the whole earth. But no city dweller, and no Christian, can act wisely and courageously in relation to any of these formidable systems without some fortifying combination of faith, companionship, and growing acquaintance with neighbors in the process of relating to them politically. This is the most fundamental challenge facing the churches in urban America today. It is the challenge of equipping their members for faithful participation in the politics of change toward a society that is truly free, just, and inclusive.

PART IV.

Land
and Resources

NINE

Indigenous Peoples, the Land, and Self-government

Terence R. Anderson

A long-time, open wound of North American society, both Canadian and American, has been the situation of indigenous peoples (Indian, Inuit, Eskimo, Aleut, and Metis) and the relationship between them and nonnative peoples. Once again, major policies and political/economic structures in regard to that relationship are being refashioned or newly forged. We are faced with choices that will bequeath to our children and grandchildren institutions they will experience as bitter "fate" or, more hopefully, as a "destiny" with creative possibilities.[1]

With regard to the situation of indigenous peoples in North America, I shall focus on public policy goals, the formulation of hoped-for results, that in turn shape the myriad specific social programs and practices affecting native peoples and our relationship with them. After a brief sketch of the background and present situation of native peoples' struggles, I shall outline some of the main policy goal options before us and assess them ethically from a Christian perspective.

The Struggle of Indigenous Peoples

The situation of North American native peoples, victims of injustice, rapid social change, and neglect, is only part of the wider phenomenon of indigenous peoples who occupied and used certain lands from "time immemorial" in various parts of the globe and who now, as a result of the

Terence R. Anderson, Professor of Christian Social Ethics, Vancouver School of Theology, Vancouver, British Columbia.

imperial expansion of mainly European powers during the past four hundred years, find themselves remnant enclaves or "colonies within"[2] larger political/economic units. They are threatened with extinction as "peoples" through violence or subtler forms of assimilation by alien cultures and systems. This "Fourth World"—a forgotten world of aboriginal peoples locked into independent sovereign states but without an adequate voice or say in the decisions that affect their lives[3]—is found in northern Europe, parts of Asia, some of the Pacific Islands, Central and South America, Australia, and Greenland, as well as in North America.

"The unrelenting demand for resources" of modern industrial societies is one of the root causes of the threat to the survival of aboriginal peoples.[4] In the eighteenth and nineteenth centuries, it was the thirst for agricultural land, timber, gold, silver, and base metals that led to violence, confiscation, land settlement agreements, the treaties, and, subsequently, their violation. More recently, the energy crisis of the 1970s generated an intensive search for and exploitation of oil, gas, coal, uranium deposits, and water resources for hydroelectric power. For indigenous peoples, this created a fresh surge of familiar pressure on their lands and environment. Ironically, the lands "reserved for Indian use" in North America, deemed in the nineteenth century less valuable for nonnatives, now frequently turn out to have scarce energy resources. Once again, native lands are coveted. But the search for new resources has also "opened up a new frontier" in North America, the far north—Alaska, the Yukon, Northwest Territories, and northern parts of Canadian provinces (two thirds of Canada's land mass).

In the meantime, there has been a revitalization of indigenous peoples. In North America, population growth after years of decline, renewed spirituality, interest and confidence in cultural heritage (including language), renewed political vigor are some of the emerging indicators. The new political consciousness found also in Greenland, Australia, northern Europe, and Central and South America is reflected in the formation of international organizations of indigenous peoples.[5]

The many different indigenous tribes and nations in North America representing a great variety of languages, traditions, cultures, and political and economic interests are engaged in a plethora of issues. But broadly speaking, their struggle is taking place in four main areas. One has to do with the ongoing interpretation and honoring of past treaties and agreements, the restoration of lost lands and rights, and the resistance to new encroachments. This has been an area of major activity, especially in the United States, during the 1970s.[6]

Another entails the clarification of aboriginal rights and their entrenchment. In Canada, this centers on the new constitution. Having finally succeeded in getting an aboriginal rights clause (Section 37) in the new constitution, efforts have shifted to the task of working out how this is to be defined in terms of securing existing treaty rights, title to traditional lands, and governmental powers for native tribes.

In the United States, "Indians stand approximately where blacks stood in 1937," says native lawyer Vine Deloria. "They are confronted with one powerful legal-political doctrine which encompasses all efforts toward reform and which places Indians beyond the reach of constitutional protections."[7] This is the Commerce Clause of the Constitution (Article 1, Section 8), which gives Congress plenary powers over Indian affairs. Consequently, policies and programs affecting native people have been subject to changing public moods and political currents reflecting the

> complex dialectic that is quintessentially American, to wit: the unresolved struggle between individualism and collectivism, between personal rights and group rights, between capitalism and communitarianism, between white actions and Indian responses, and between a non-Indian ideology that abhors special favors to groups under the law, and a non-Indian ideology that champions fair play and compassion.[8]

Deloria calls upon churches, theologians, and legal thinkers to join Indian leaders in reassessing basic policies and formulating "the proper theory to accomplish the task of establishing a definite body of rights for Indian tribes."[9]

A third front has to do with self-government. This has taken the form of a struggle between tribes and federal government bureaucracies concerning administrative control of health, social services, and education. But in 1983 in Canada, the Penner Report, *Indian Self-government in Canada,* written by an all-party parliamentary committee after extensive consultation with native groups, came forth with recommendations entailing a fundamental departure from past policies and practices. "Self-government" should include "full legislative and policy-making powers on matters affecting Indian people, and full self-control over the territory and resources within the bounds of Indian lands." These powers would extend over "such areas as social and cultural development, including education and family relations, land and resource use, revenue raising, economic and commercial development, and justice and law enforcement among others."[10] The rights to self-government so understood are to be enshrined in the constitution. As of this writing, the existing federal government of Canada has indicated broad agreement with the report, thereby placing the whole "self-government" struggle on a new level of exciting possibilities.

The fourth area is "comprehensive land claims negotiations," the American and Canadian governments' phrase to describe the attempt to work out agreements with native nations who have not previously entered into a valid treaty with the federal government. In Canada, this includes native peoples across vast tracts of land lying north of the 60th parallel, plus northern Quebec and most of British Columbia. There are six land claims settlements in various stages of negotiation and another four have been accepted for negotiation.[11]

In the United States, the Alaska Native Claims Settlement Act (ANCSA) of 1971, arising out of the 1968 discovery of the large oil field in Prudhoe Bay, is the major focus of the comprehensive land claim issue. This settlement was hailed as a new and just agreement with indigenous people and has been exerting strong influence on comprehensive land claims in Canada, Greenland, Australia, and elsewhere. But from a native perspective, serious problems are emerging. In 1984, the Alaska Native Review Commission, under Thomas Berger, was established, significantly by a native group, the Inuit Circumpolar Conference (ICC).[12] After hearings in native villages and discussions with leaders of indigenous people in the lower forty-eight states and in various other countries, plus additional experts, the commission will report recommended changes to Congress.

Considering the varied cultures and context of the native peoples involved and the little consultation between them until recently, there is remarkable commonality among them regarding the central concern underlying their struggle in these four areas. Their central interest is to continue as distinctive peoples, carrying forward their own rich heritage. In the language of self-determination, they seek "freedom to be left alone for awhile, or a freedom to choose, maybe not as individuals, but *as a group of people,* a course of action."[13] They claim "the right to be different," says Deloria.[14] Of central importance is control of their own land, not only because it provides an economic base, but also because it is central to their cultural identity in a way and to an extent that is frequently difficult for nonnative people to grasp. As distinctive peoples, tribes, or "nations," they seek to enter with nonnative people into a new relationship of mutual respect and partnership. Differences among native people arise not over this central goal, but over what kind and degree of power and authority, what political/economic arrangements are needed for their continuance as distinctive peoples and the best means for achieving this.

The churches have been deeply involved in the history of indigenous peoples since first contact with European culture in all the morally ambivalent ways tragically embedded in the missions and colonization pattern. They had a part in creating and carrying out past public policies that usually sought to protect but ultimately proved so injurious.[15] A more positive side of past missions is that a number of leaders and tribes at the forefront of native renewal are strong Christians.[16] More recently, the churches, especially through ecumenical agencies, including the World Council of Churches, National Council of Churches, and, in Canada, Project North and Citizens for Public Justice, have been supportive of native struggles to refashion public policy and practice.[17]

How, from a Christian perspective, are we now to respond to the plethora of issues regarding native people and to the many proposals and counterproposals before us? One place to begin is to delineate the various broad policy goals that underline divergent practices, views, and proposals with regard to native people. An assessment of the alternative policy goals in terms of Christian convictions might then provide some bearing for guiding our involvement in the four areas outlined earlier.

Policy Goal Options

Subjection/protection. The aim is, first, to make and keep native people subject to and dependent on the existing dominant culture group and, second, to preserve and protect native people and their culture as distinct, although dependent, people. This is a colonial policy. A colony is any territory in which the conditions of life—social, economic, political—are defined for the whole population by a minority different from the local majority in culture, history, beliefs, and often race.[18] Although one usually thinks of the colonizing minority as being from another country, it can also be a group belonging to the same country, creating "colonies within." This policy goal was operative in the early era of French and British emigration to North America. It was carried forward by the United States through most of the treaty-making period, the Indian wars, and "removal and relocation" until the early 1870s.[19] Nobody publicly advocates it today, but some believe that present programs and administration in both countries still function to this end.

Assimilation. The hoped-for result in this option is the amalgamation of native people economically, politically, and culturally into the mainstream of Canadian or American life, resulting finally in their disappearance as distinct peoples. There is a form of assimilation in which "peoples" or cultures of approximately equal size and strength agree to merge to form a distinctively new "people" or nation. But where one cultural group predominates because of numbers or power, assimilation means effectively the absorption of the small group into the dominant one. The latter would clearly be the result of such a policy in North America.

The assimilation goal was the predominant, operational goal of public policy regarding native people in the United States, probably beginning with the 1871 congressional appropriation rider declaring that Indians will no longer be recognized as independent powers with whom treaties can be made. In Canada, it was the operational goal from 1857 to 1973.[20] Occasionally, it was openly declared as such. The means used by both countries to effect this goal have been varied, even seemingly contradictory, but education, religion, economic schemes, enfranchisement have all been used in a so far largely futile effort to accomplish this end.

Integration. In the case of integration, the object is not only full participation of native people as equals in mainstream political and economic structures, but also—and here is where this goal differs from assimilation—maintenance of their distinctive native culture alongside other cultural groups. Native people would have no special legal, economic, or political status, but would be regarded as ethnic minority groups alongside other such minority groups. This goal has been called, most recently by Trudeau, a "cultural mosaic," as distinct from the melting-pot image of assimilation.[21]

Interdependence. Interdependence entails the recognition and enhancement of native "peoples" not only in terms of their ethnic cultural distinctiveness, as in the integration goal, but also in terms of distinctive political structures and control over economic development.

The term nation has been appropriately used by native people to describe their situation. Most native societies are not only ethnic groups, each with its own language, heritage, customs, and standards, but in addition have distinctive political purposes and institutions. Thus they have the distinguishing characteristics of a nation, "sense of shared political destiny with others, a preference for being united with them politically in an independent state, and preparedness to be committed to common political action."[22]

The aim of the interdependence option is recognition of native nations as collectivities with their own order of government and a measure of political and economic power roughly similar to that now held by Canadian provinces and American state governments within the relevant sovereign country: Canada, the United States of America, Australia, and the like. The Penner Report, referred to earlier, advocates this policy and outlines a "third order" of government to distinguish it from provincial and federal orders. In polar contrast to the subjection/protection goal, which also entails the recognition of native nations, the interdependence goal involves enhancement, not subjection, of native nations.

Independence. In this public policy goal option, each native nation or some cluster of nations would become independent sovereign states. This is similar to the Quebec separatist proposal.

Ethical Reflection

Which of these possible goals is most congruent with God's glorious promise of shalom? Sound moral assessment in terms of the promise of shalom will be based in part on scrutinizing the available options in light of two broad but basic principles: love of neighbor and stewardship of creation with regard for the specifics of a given context.

Love of neighbor. Love of neighbor as God loves human beings is a rich and many-faceted calling and command, and a large portion of Christian ethics has been devoted to exploring and disputing its meaning and implications. One aspect of agape clearly is a recognition of the worth of all persons as children of God and a respect for their dignity as moral agents, the same right to their choices and actions as we have to our own.[23] This finds expression in the moral principle of "autonomy," that "autonomous actions and choices should not be constrained by others."[24] There have to be good reasons in unusual circumstances morally to justify one person unilaterally deciding what is best for another (paternalism). This in turn leads to formulations of familiar principles of liberty concerned with political freedoms, including the right of persons to be involved in decisions that significantly affect their well-being. Such notions of liberty are further reinforced by a Christian understanding of human sin, the propensity of all persons and groups, even the "enlightened" and "redeemed" (however defined), to pursue their own self-interest at the expense of others, frequently under the guise of serving the public good. No group or person is good enough, then, to have too much power over others.[25]

We are led, then, to insist on full participation by indigenous peoples in any choice of policy goals concerning them. In North America, they have not been permitted to participate significantly in such matters until quite recently. A related concern now arises. We must seek procedures by which fair and just policy decisions are made (procedural justice) in the sense not only that native peoples participate, but also with an appropriate weight given to their views and interests.

The subjection/protection option obviously violates all these moral principles and concerns arising from love of neighbor, as do the goals of assimilation, integration, and interdependence if chosen without the participation or consent of native peoples. Policies of subjection/protection and coerced assimilation did not succeed in achieving their purpose. But they have led to conditions assessed by all interested parties as negative—paternalistic dominance by government bureaucracies, growing and costly dependence by native people, increasingly shredded cultures, and the colonial syndrome of despair—making many especially vulnerable to the

165

more alien features of modernity, including loss of identity, alcoholism, drug addiction, and self-inflicted violence.

A policy goal that permits native people freely to choose assimilation or integration is not morally controversial nor strongly opposed as a policy goal, although in practice, native people often encounter resistance. Independence is not advocated by any major indigenous group in North America, probably because as enclaves in large societies, full sovereignty as separate states is not a viable alternative for native nations.

The really disputed option, then, is interdependence—placing with native nations a significant degree of government power within the framework of Canadian and American constitutions. A large number of native peoples seek some form of this option. Yet the call for recognition of native nations by granting them important government powers has been, until the Penner report on self-government, simply not heard, misunderstood, deliberately ignored, or firmly rejected by the dominant societies.

I believe, from a Christian perspective, that we should seek a policy goal that makes the interdependence option possible for indigenous peoples without closing the door to integration or assimilation for those who may choose either of them. Why should we open the door to interdependence, with all its accompanying unresolved issues? Why not pursue a goal solely of integration, with its more familiar set of problems, in which indigenous peoples are encouraged to continue as distinctive cultures but not as political/economic entities (ethnic groups but not nations), with access to land but not control over it, participation in the administration of services to their people but not in their own government powers or jurisdiction? In responding to this question, I shall focus on the Canadian context,[26] although I think a similar argument could be made for the United States, Australia, and perhaps elsewhere.

Moral burden of proof. To begin with, I think that the moral burden of proof properly rests on answering the contrary question "Why should the interdependence option not be allowed?" It rests on this question because of a combination of certain conditions that presently prevail, together with the principle of liberty.

The social arrangement by which most native people now live continues to be what has been defined as "nations," albeit sometimes in attenuated forms. R.K. Thomas, a Cherokee anthropologist, categorizes Indian societies in North America according to their way of responding to the incursion of alien forces and the resulting massive changes. Only one of his three categories is marked by a pattern of becoming "the local variant of an Indian ethnic group"—in my terms, integration. The other two categories, containing the large portion of Indian tribes, continue to manifest the characteristics of nations (not sovereign states) either because of relative isolation until recently or because of deliberate strategies.[27]

As previously noted, the colonial powers accepted the reality of indigenous nations. As the native nations became economically and militarily irrelevant to the newcomers, greatly weakened by the ravages of disease and government policies and no longer strong independent states, nonnative peoples have had increasing difficulty even perceiving of them as nations.

Perception of reality, particularly regarding human society, is not a simple empirical matter of determining the "facts." Roger Shinn observes that while we frequently speak of "seeing is believing," the social sciences are now confirming what was long held by some philosophies and theologies, that our perceptions are influenced by beliefs and values. They affect what facts we attend to, how we interpret them, the frame of reference in which we place them, and the like. In many ways, then, "believing is seeing."[28]

An understanding of human nature is a key belief affecting the way indigenous societies are perceived. An assumption common in Western liberal societies is that human beings are first of all individuals and only secondarily members of groups. All groups are eyed suspiciously as likely threats to individual liberty. From this viewpoint, native people are perceived primarily as individuals with rights the same as all other individuals, and their "peoplehood," as merely a past block to personal liberty soon destined, in modern society, to become irrelevant or of minor importance.

This individualistic understanding of humanity is one foundation of human rights. It has engendered a number of important freedoms over against the opposite understanding that human beings are primarily members of collectives and only secondarily individuals. But it blinds us to some important realities, including the whole range of social, relational needs and propensities of people that are so essential to the good life and the good society. As a result, this individualistic viewpoint is, in the phrase of political scientist Christian Bay, "no longer a vision of emancipation" in our society.[29]

A different understanding of human nature is found in much Christian thought. Reinhold Niebuhr claimed that while the relation between individuals and community is complex, we are clearly both individuals and members of collectives at the same time and not primarily one or the other. The community sustains and fulfills the life of the individual, and yet, in some senses, the individual transcends the community. "The community will always remain both the fulfillment and the frustration of the individual."[30] Karl Barth argues that if we base our thinking on Romans 5:12-21, "we can have nothing to do with either collectivism on the one hand or individualism on the other."[31]

The latter viewpoint better enables us to perceive native people in terms of their own self-understanding. Their strong sense of "peoplehood" is regarded not as a passing impediment, but as an enduring form of community integral to identity. Native nations can be seen from this perspective as the historic and most appropriate social arrangement expressing and preserving "peoplehood."

This fact, combined with the principle of liberty previously discussed, is what places the moral burden of proof on those who would seek to prevent these diverse nations from continuing, i.e., who would reject the interdependence option. This principle of liberty receives, from a Christian perspective, special force in its application to native issues by another aspect of love of neighbor derived from God's care for us. John Bennett describes this aspect with more precision than most. "There is an extraordinarily broad agreement among theologians today on the conviction that God's love for all persons implies a strategic concentration on the victims of society, on the weak, the exploited, the neglected persons who are a large majority of the human race."[32]

The moral burden of proof rests, then, on answering why indigenous peoples in North America, as minorities long exploited and victims of injustice, should not be free to continue and enhance their way of life as nations in interdependence with the dominant society in a single sovereign state.

Are there any sound moral reasons this should be resisted? Does such a policy goal offend love of neighbor or stewardship of creation? The theories traditionally used by imperial European powers to justify the acquisition of colonial territories and continued rule over indigenous peoples come to mind. But they are unable to bear much ethical scrutiny, as even a listing quickly reveals.[33] "Discovery" of "new" territories as a rationale is quaintly ethnocentric and discredited in international law as a basis for any territorial claims. Conquest was once deemed an appropriate basis for such claims but only as a result of a just war, and even then not as justification for continued possession. In any case, it is not applicable to the Canadian scene, where indigenous people were, for the most part, not defeated by force of arms and many never entered into any agreement or treaty.

Occupation and settlement of unoccupied lands have been appealed to recently. Again, international law has rejected this justification as legitimate grounds.[34] In addition, the matter of perception arises once more. The vast Canadian North is seen by many to be an empty frontier. But careful studies reveal it to be very much the homeland of indigenous peoples crisscrossed with the "highways" of people busily engaged in a hunting and fishing economy.

The argument for a "civilizing mission" is blatantly ethnocentric.[35] Its assumption of dominant group cultural superiority, which at one stage of history appeared as the evolutionary wave of the future, now manifests major fault lines as Western modernity is called into question. Further, the imposition of modernity runs contrary to agape as respect for our neighbor's dignity.

Justice. An ethically more potent consideration regarding the interdependence pattern is whether it contravenes substantive justice, which is essential, along with liberty and procedural justice, to love of neighbor. Thus the disturbing charge of racism is raised in objection to the interdependence goal. The specter of apartheid in South Africa is called forth—special "homelands," ethnic-defined territorial and political boundaries, "separate but equal," and the like. Behind the charge lies the characteristically liberal, individualistic view of human nature previously discussed, with its conviction that non-chosen group identity is inimical to personal liberty and to equality. From this viewpoint, highlighting visible ethnic differences in policy, let alone embedding them in special rights, law, and political structures, opens the door to favored treatment for some and to negative discrimination for others, of which apartheid is a vivid example. Either assimilation or integration, in which individuals are free to continue ethnic ties and customs but no special legal or political/ economic structures are involved, is therefore preferred.

Great caution *is* required when acknowledging ethnic differences in public policy and law, lest they be used in a racist fashion. But several things need to be said concerning such differences in regard to the interdependence option. First, and crucial, is that the attempts to eliminate ethnic differences (assimilation) or significantly suppress them (integration) are as vulnerable, if not more so, to the charge of reflecting or fostering racism. Be as little "different" from the majority as possible, lest it be used against you is a familiar admonition to victims of racism—Jews, blacks, aboriginal peoples. Many oppressed minorities have been tempted by this solution (most recently women) only to find that not only does it not work, but it also ends in self-hatred.

Racism stems not from differences between human beings and groups, or even recognition of such differences, but from how those differences are regarded and treated. We need to work for public policies and the corresponding political economic structures that foster respect for, and even celebration of, ethnic differences between peoples, while recognizing the human commonalities among us and the equal worth of all.

Second, the policy goal proposed here is one that entails the freedom of native peoples to choose to continue as nations. It does not entail forcing them to do so. The danger of racism looms largest when any of the policy goal options listed, including interdependence, is coerced.

Third, the apartheid specter reminds us that important safeguards against the distorting power of racism need to be built into the pattern of interdependence. One is some assurance that native nations would receive a fair share of benefits and burdens compared with other Canadians. Another has to do with individual rights. There are undoubtedly some incompatibilities between tribal societies and the traditions of liberal individualism, including what constitutes true liberty and well-being. These require more careful examination, not immediate resolution in favor of liberal assumptions, for they touch on some of the ills of modernity and alienation of industrial societies. The incompatibilities should push us instead to assess what is lacking in the liberal tradition and which of its values and assumptions really are essential from a Christian perspective. But suffice it to point out here that the interdependence option, as presented by Canadian native nations, is not incompatible with the basic individual rights of liberalism that Christians have grounded in the principle of neighbor love. An important check against racism and other forms of injustice, then, is that native nations would be subject to the Canadian constitution and charter of rights.

Especially important for the tradition of rights is maintaining the freedom of individuals, both native and nonnative, to move in or out of native nations in the way that freedom now exists in other Canadian territories. Put differently, these political boundaries (a "third order" of government) should not be based strictly on ethnic or "racial" criteria, i.e., according to biological descent, but on nationality—commitment to continue the communal life and cultural identity of the group, a "grand solidarity" that seeks a political/economic expression.[36] The Dene proposal regarding Demendeh (our Land) is exemplary in this regard.[37]

The expectation, however, in the interdependence pattern is that native peoples would continue to be the formative, shaping power of these nations. Does granting only some ethnic groups and not others the privilege to establish governments with certain political and economic powers not contravene the principle of "similar treatment for similar cases," so essential to justice?

The policy option of interdependence does not violate this principle because native ethnic groups are dissimilar from other ethnic groups in important and relevant respects. Not only were they the original inhabitants of Canada and already function to some degree as nations, but they also have a different history and a different kind of relation to confederation. Ethnic immigrant groups came freely to Canada with at least an implicit understanding that while they might continue some of the ways of their culture, they were entering not as political entities with ancestral lands (nations), but joining with others to form a new "people" or nation, however heterogeneous it might turn out to be. Native nations, in contrast, were not given a choice regarding confederation. To assure them a choice of policy options now would help to correct the previous injustice.

A second, ethically significant objection against allowing interdependence as an option is that this policy goal threatens the unity, and thus the security, of Canadian society and its existence as a state. This time the specter of tribalism that makes difficult the achievement of larger, more viable states in Africa may be called forth. Assuming that Canada's existence in some form is important (as I would claim), and that threat to its security is a morally important, although not sufficient, ground for setting aside the freedom of native peoples to continue as nations,[38] would the interdependence option really make impossible or seriously jeopardize Canadian unity? The answer depends in part on what kind of society or country, and therefore what kind of unity, is envisaged.

The interdependence pattern may well threaten a society whose unity depends on common goals and purposes that everyone who claims to be a citizen is expected to adopt. It is likewise disturbing to a unity based on a belief that respects variations among human beings as grounded in "nature," yet deems that what these differences have in common is more important than what distinguishes them. Here we have the underpinnings of the cultural mosaic and the integration policy. Another understanding of social unity, however, perceives the differences among humans as equally important as their commonality. As Hannah Arendt puts it: "We are all the same, that is human, in such a way that nobody is ever the same as anybody else who ever lived, lives or will live."[39] A society arranged to reflect this reality may be likened to an orchestra, suggests, Lionel Rubinoff. "The various instruments are combined or orchestrated in such a way that even though each instrument maintains its separate identity, the outcome is recognizably 'music' rather than simply noise or 'chaos.' Indeed the very coherence and beauty of the music depends upon the preservation and cultivation of differences.[40] A multination country and state such as the interdependence option would entail does not necessarily follow from this view of society, but it is one possible expression of it and certainly not inimical to this kind of unity.

A strong case could be made in terms of Christian conviction for preferring this latter view of a society, but that is not necessary here. The point to be made is that the interdependence option does not undermine the unity or viability per se of Canada, but only certain versions of unity. This is an objection that is morally much weaker.

As in the case of racism, so with unity; a much greater danger to it than interdependence is denying native people the freedom to choose among these policy options. Reinhold Niebuhr reminded us some years ago that "even the wisest statecraft cannot create social tissue. It can cut, sew and redesign social fabric to a limited degree but the social fabric upon which it works must be 'given.' "[41] Unless native people freely choose differently, native nations in some form will continue to be part of the Canadian social fabric. Wise Canadian statecraft will recognize this and attempt to harmonize it with other groups and interests rather than attempt to eliminate or ignore it.

We may conclude that there are not sufficient moral reasons in terms of neighbor love and its principles of liberty and justice to deny native people the freedom of choosing to continue as nations in an interdependence policy. There are, however, also some good reasons, according to those same principles, why this choice is beneficial to Canada as a whole. Space permits only one example. If native nations were strengthened to function in province-like units, this would help to disperse more equitably both political and economic power in Canada and provide an important check against the dangerous concentration of economic power in the hands of small elites. Small political units increase possibilities of direct participation by people in decisions that affect them.

Stewardship of creation. This brings us to a second basic principle that, from a Christian perspective, should be a basis for assessing and ethically justifying public policies: *human beings should be stewards of God's creation after the pattern of Jesus Christ, the master steward.* By God's creation I mean nonhuman life and the environment that is our common home or household. This is to focus on only one, albeit a major, aspect of stewardship, since Ephesians speaks of the "stewardship of God's grace [Eph. 3:2]," and as Douglas Hall points out, it is a many-faceted and inclusive concept.[42] Stewardship of God's creation entails an understanding of the place and relationship of the human species to the rest of nature. This has been the center of much controversy. In claiming stewardship as a basic ethical principle, I subscribe to the view that the recovery of this biblical tradition is needed rather than turning to an alternative view of nature. The ecological problems facing us have their roots not in the biblical understanding of dominion and stewardship, but in distorted versions of it.[43]

Stewardship as used here, then, includes the following notions: God is creator and "owner" of all creation that God designated good and over which God has ultimate dominion. God has a redemptive purpose for the nonhuman part of creation as well as the human; nonhuman creation is not merely instrumental to human good, but is also bound up with it both in the fall and in redemption. Human beings have a special place in that creation. We are created and called to be managers of the rest of creation with a delegated or "qualified dominion," servants of God accountable for the care of creation entrusted to us. The model for that kind of servanthood with delegated dominion is Jesus Christ (Philippians 2:5-11). The management of the household of creation should be in accord with God's purpose. Our use and treatment of nature must be of service to God, to our fellow humans, and to nature.[44] As with the basic principle of love of neighbor, so with stewardship of creation; there are various subprinciples and guidelines that can be derived from it to provide benchmarks, although not precise directives, for our actions. But the question to be raised here is how does the policy goal permitting the option of interdependence stand in the light of the stewardship principle?

Native societies (not necessarily all native persons) in North America are bearers of a tradition that views nature somewhat differently than does the Christian tradition of stewardship but nonetheless resonates more fully with it than prevailing views of technological dominance and in any case undergirds a land ethic congruent with the principle of stewardship. Further, part of the impetus behind native nations continuing is their seeking to fashion economic and political institutions that will enable a way of life in accord with this tradition. The pursuit of such an enterprise has the further effect of enhancing good stewardship in the rest of the country.

View of land and nature. It is not possible here to examine even cursorily the beliefs about nature that are found in the religious traditions of the many indigenous cultures or the fate of these under the influence of European contact in general and Christianity in particular. However, this is not necessary for the argument being made here because I am not proposing, as do Arnold Toynbee and others, a return to either pantheism or animism as the religious solution to our ecological problems. Nor am I claiming that native peoples do or can preserve in purity such beliefs.[45] Rather, I am claiming that the view of the land as expressed with remarkable commonality, consistency, and tenacity by contemporary native peoples and their struggle to carry forward its essence are congruent with the stewardship principle.

Territory that has been occupied and used by a tribe since time immemorial (more than 35,000 years in one case) is seen as a vital economic base essential to survival and as a precious homeland with a history, sacred sites, and the like. But it is much more. The land is regarded as a sacred trust, a gift of the creator, a holy land to be cared for accordingly. As Chief Seattle expressed it so eloquently in 1854, "How can you buy or sell the sky, the warmth of the land? The idea is strange to us. We do not own the freshness of the air or the sparkle of the water. How can you buy them from us? Every part of this earth is sacred to my people. . . . We are part of the earth, and it is part of us."[46] This sacred gift, then, is bound up in myth with the genesis and identity of a particular people or nation.

Central to Indian spirituality, explains Cherokee R.K. Thomas, is that "the land," which in English is called "nature,"

> is alive and is filled with supernatural meaning. It is integrated in your own life. One is an integral part of that world out there. And it is personal and particular. Those items out there, that tree, isn't just a

potential post for the old time Indian. That tree is God's creation, the same as you. It has a right to be growing there and to be treated with respect. Even if you chop it down for wood and take its life you know that it isn't just an object.[47]

It includes, then, the notion of what another writer calls "reciprocal appropriation." People invest themselves in the landscape and at the same time appropriate the landscape into their own most fundamental experience.[48] Lenore Coltheart, describing the place of land in Australia aboriginal cosmology, suggests an analogy in Western thought: "The relationship of people and land is ... like the *polis* in Platonic thought, the land links the Aborigine and the understanding of being—each is seen as the psyche 'writ large.' "[49]

A good portion of this is similar to that found in the Bible; land is seen not only as a gift entrusted to the care of humans by the Creator, "actual earthly turf where people can be safe and secure, where meaning and well-being are enjoyed without pressure or concern" but also as a symbol of wholeness, of joy, prosperity, and freedom.[50] The well-being, and even the very existence, of the people is bound up with the faithful honoring of that trust in terms of use and management.

Land ethic. Such views of the land and nature are different from seeing them primarily as the basis of personal wealth, as in early capitalism, or as merely one of many commodities for exchange, as in more recent capitalism. William Everett, in his discussion of land ethics, provides us with categories for stating these important differences more precisely.[51]

Any land ethic, he says, involves implicitly or explicitly definitions of and relations between parties, rights, and goods. The parties claiming rights to the land are God; "Nature"—embracing "not only the physical condition of the world but the processes and laws which seem to govern this environment"; society—"the total complex of human relations laying claim to the land" and the organizations that represent them; and persons. The latter includes "natural persons"—individuals and families—as well as "corporate persons" both public (state, quasi-public utilities, etc.) and private (corporations, cooperatives, etc.). The rights or claims made by or for these different parties include *use* of the land—occupancy or utilization; *income*—in terms of products from the land or rents; *transfer*—through sale, gift, inheritance, or confiscation; *alteration*—"changing the use possibilities of the land." The goods sought by parties through the exercise of claims or rights are security, expression, enjoyment, and perfection.

Everett outlines several models of land ethics delineated according to moral claims made regarding which parties should be entitled to which rights in pursuit of what goods. Thus, in the "Market Model," the prevailing one in North America, "the primary claimants to the land are persons, whether natural or corporate. Land is distributed among persons and used by them according to their own perceived good." By contrast, the "Ecological Model" is marked by seeing nature as the chief party with primary rights of transfer, alteration, and even use. In other words, "decisions regarding the land are controlled by the needs and limits of the ecosystem," presumably determined by those who know nature best—professional ecologists. The main good sought is achievement of perfect equilibrium among all the factors of nature. Accordingly, careful planning of land use instead of simply leaving it to market forces is judged essential for good management.

The "Covenantal Model," Everett believes, stands at the center of the biblical tradition. It expresses the stewardship principle. God is seen as the party whose claims to all land rights are primary. The other parties are mediators of God's claims, and their own claims to the land are derivative, not absolute. "As a medium of God's covenant nature provides gracious boundaries for our dominating lust as well as projects and wonders to overcome our slothful isolation." Alterations are to be made in accord with the needs and goods of nature. Use and income rights are entrusted to societies and persons but are to be exercised in accord with God's purpose. Therefore, use and income rights must be arranged so that all persons can achieve at least the minimal goods needed for human life. Whatever model precontact native societies manifested, the understanding of the land and its use as articulated and practiced by the less shredded native societies today has affinities with both ecological and covenantal models but finally is closer to the latter.[52] In either case, it is clearly more in harmony with the stewardship principle than the Market Model. Those native groups seeking to continue as nations want the political and economic power necessary to exercise such a land ethic rather than be drawn into the prevailing Market Model. Such efforts obviously accord well with the stewardship principle.

Political/economic institutions. Native nations not only carry a view of nature, a land ethic, and a tradition of social discipline congruent with the stewardship principle, but they are also searching for political/economic arrangements that best enable them to bring forward this heritage as distinctive peoples in ways that are feasible in the modern, economic world. The pattern whereby the federal government holds native lands in trust, i.e., the reserve system of the treaties, has resulted in control by distant bureaucracies and a dependency syndrome that seriously erodes the very values and social discipline deemed essential to native identity, let alone management of the land in terms of those values. The influential ANCSA, referred to earlier, established a different arrangement. Native corporations were set up for the ownership and management of the billion dollars paid as compensation for relinquished aboriginal lands and the 44 million acres retained by native people. Most of the land and money were conveyed to newly formed native regional corporations, who hold it as fee simple property. Every eligible native person born before December 1971 is a shareholder. After twenty years (1991), the lands held by these native corporations will be subject to taxation and the shares may be sold on the open market. ANCSA is clearly fashioned to achieve, intentionally or not, a goal of integration—continuation of native cultural identity as an ethnic group but assimilation into mainstream economic and political structures and life.

The Alaska Native Review Commission, also referred to earlier, is currently examining the adequacy of this corporate model for meeting the aspirations of Alaska natives in general and care of the land in particular and comparing it with other institutional options in the United States and elsewhere. The hearings to date indicate that the corporation system appears to be effective in achieving the native objective of establishing a solid economic base viable in terms of the dominant, modern society that would enable them to move from "a past characterized by poverty, unemployment, disease, poor housing, and second-class citizenship to a future in which the 'invisible reservation' would cease to exist."[53] But other hopes and objectives strongly expressed by Alaskan natives in 1971—continuity in use and occupancy of the land in terms of these traditional values, continuity in cultural integrity, and self-determination as a people—are much less certain of attainment under the present settlement act, especially after 1991.

There is concern over whether native control will continue. Natives born after 1971 cannot participate in control of the land until and if they inherit corporation shares. Further, land may, after 1991, pass from native hands if enough stock in the corporations is sold. As Byron Mollot, from Yakutut and president of Sealaska (one of the native regional corporations), expresses it: "One of the battle cries in the days of land claims was, 'take our land, take our life,' and if you can move that into the future, you might be able to, at that point, say, 'take our stock, take our land, take our life,' "[54]

But especially significant with regard to the stewardship principle is the doubt being raised as to whether the corporate model is ultimately compatible with either grassroots native control or care of the land in terms of native perspectives. Mollott expresses the problem succinctly:

> Corporations demand an incredible sense of discipline and economic focus in order to be competitive on the business side. And the utilization of corporate assets [including land] requires that almost all of these assets be employed in some sort of economic activity, and the demands upon the management and the policy-makers of those insti-

tutions are so much . . . an almost pure focus on economic and business kinds of activities, that, over time, other priorities and other obligations, if you're not careful, begin to fade. And in my judgment also, that is a difficulty we face as a people.[55]

He acknowledges that the native regional corporations have not so far sold any significant portions of land or engaged in destructive forms of development despite "the pressures upon them, for economic success, . . . and they've done it because of the strong sense that they are stewards. But the question becomes, how long can that be maintained with the business and legal imperatives and obligations that corporations, as institutions have upon them?"[56] As Guy Martin (assistant secretary, Department of Interior under the Carter Administration) commented at the Review hearings, the corporate structure entails not only a management form, but also "a kind of mentality."[57] The recommendations by this Review Commission to the U.S. Congress will be important and in the direction of the interdependence goal.

Meanwhile, most of the native nations in Canada engaged in comprehensive land claims have already concluded that the corporate arrangement of ANCSA, or its supposedly improved version in the James Bay Treaty in northern Quebec, is not adequate. There may well be some place for native corporations, but some political/economic arrangement that makes use of indigenous political institutions to manage land in accord with traditional values and yet deals with the demands of modern economic conditions is also required. The Penner Report has responded positively to their recommendations. The interdependence option would allow this experiment in different political/economic arrangements for land management and development to move forward. Given the native nations' land ethic, this seems once again highly compatible with the stewardship principle.

Toward a Postmodern Society

Views of nature, land ethics, political/economic institutions are all points of tension between indigenous societies and the dominant culture of North America. The struggle of indigenous peoples with that culture to secure for theselves a distinctive and contemporary place is much more, then, than the clash of competing powers over political and economic interests. In the perception of most native people, it is a struggle between contrasting spiritualities. In sociological terms, it is a confrontation between modern and traditional societies "over competing ideologies, symbol systems, and life commitments." This is reflected throughout the Third World and the controversies over development.[58]

Rapidly fading is the assumption that modern, Western industrialized society is *the* crest of *the* wave of the future, the measuring rod for "development," the litmus test for assessing whether people are "backward" or "progressive." The human cost is proving too high and the globe cannot sustain it. In any case, new technologies and changing patterns of capital formation are creating traumas in the most "advanced" countries. Thus the question many native and Third World people have long been asking is now becoming ours also: Is there a way of appropriating the great advantages of advanced technology without the more destructive features of "modern life"? A fresh vision and change of direction are required.

The active search by native nations for a new way of bringing together the "best of both worlds," and the resources that they bring to the task, is yet another reason for welcoming a choice of interdependence. This is very different from any appeal to a romantic version of the old protectionist policy that would defend the preservation of native nations as museums of an ancient, static culture. However, native nations, at their best, do bring many badly needed resources from their traditional societies to this task of shaping a postmodern society. Their people experience vividly the dark side of modernity and, as we have seen, challenge it precisely at its weak spots. They are bearers of a living tradition that holds values and exhibits alternatives in the areas of life to which modernity is so destructive—care of the natural environment and communal space, communities of personal familial and neighborhood life and the serious restrictions imposed on the creative capacities of persons by highly routinized and repetitive patterns of work and life, respect for the wisdom of elders, willingness to share, and others.

The adoption of a public policy goal that includes the freedom of native nations to continue in a pattern of interdependence accords, then, with love of neighbor (and its principles of liberty and justice) and the stewardship of creation. It sets the direction of journey toward social justice and the healing of an ancient wound in line with God's promise of shalom. It is hoped that we may cease attempts to remake native societies into our own Western image and come to realize that the presence of strengthened native nations in the very bosom of Western industrial society is a gracious gift that, by one of those delicious ironies of providence, may be instrumental in our redemption.

TEN

Justice, Participation, and Sustainable Sufficiency

Robert L. Stivers

The Issue

*N*o matter what it is called—limits to growth, sustainability, or even scarcity—the logic of the problem is simple enough. Population, food production, the consumption of energy and mineral resources, and some forms of pollution are all growing exponentially. Exponential growth in a finite space spells disaster. Limits of one kind or another will eventually be reached. Our economic system, our present life-style, and our values are in jeopardy. Here the simplicity ends.

One side of the debate over sustainability stresses the importance of this logic and its current relevance.[1] Take food and population, for example. The annual rate of increase in world population currently is about 1.7 percent. Although this rate is down from 2 percent in recent years because of strenuous efforts by the Chinese, it still represents an increase of about 79 million persons each year and a doubling of population about every forty years. Fortunately, total food production has kept pace until now, but limits in the form of decreasing returns to genetic manipulation, the economic costs of bringing new land into production, soil depletion, poverty and injustice, and shortages of fertilizer and water will soon produce a situation in which population will outstrip the capacity to produce. The result will be mass starvation. Similarly, the exponentially growing consumption of finite resources, for example, oil and natural gas, will lead to their near exhaustion as higher prices ration dwindling supplies. In short, we are polluting and consuming at a rate

Robert L. Stivers, Professor of Religion, Pacific Lutheran University, Tacoma, Washington.

that cannot be sustained. Even the so-called technological fix will not avoid the outcome, for it, too, is limited. What is demanded is a whole new way of life based on the concept of long-range sustainability. This will necessitate changed economic and political structures, new values, and new patterns of life.

The other side concedes the logic, and usually its application to the population problem, but disputes its relevance in other areas. Many economists and business leaders minimize the relevance of the logic for the production of food and the consumption of resources.[2] They appeal in their arguments to the counterlogic of new technology taking its cue from rising prices. Rising prices signal scarcity, which, when combined with the profit motive, sets in motion efforts to find new methods and more abundant resources to substitute for scarce ones. With regard to pollution, technologies exist to control it; only the political will is missing. Thus our decendants are not in jeopardy. Our technologies will help us to avoid limits. What is needed is the unleashing of our technological prowess.

In contrast, a view from the Third World sees the logic of limits as naive and those who apply it as innocent visionaries who design utopian fantasies empty of significant content.[3] What the debate represents is the anxiety of a pampered minority about its wasteful way of life. World sustainability is not a real problem. When most of the energy runs out, the poor will survive because they are already living at sustainable levels. The real issue is justice.

What can we conclude from this? Is the debate over sustainability a smokescreen, or is there fire in the smoke? The passion and intensity of the debate suggests that there is something more at stake than an academic discussion. Most of the protagonists agree that the issue is one of physical limits. Their contention must be examined. Likewise, we must examine the debate for assumed values and ideology and the claim of Third World Christians that justice, not sustainability, is the real issue. We may conclude that the debate will be around for a while, if for no other reason than it deals with the future. We may project into the future, but there is an element of unpredictability to it. It is a fertile field for both fools and experts. As the present catches up to the future, the future will yield its secrets to historical analysis, but for now it serves equally well as the soil for fact or fantasy. The problem of sustainability has become one of those permanent issues on the human agenda.

Two Questions

Central to the debate over sustainability are two related questions. The first, a factual question, has to do with the predictability of limits and the need for more sustainable modes. Are there actually physical limits to the expansion of the food supply, to the consumption of energy and resources, to the pollution absorption capacity of the earth, and to the social capacity to devise and manage technological innovation? And beyond these questions there is one related to time. Assuming that there are limits, how soon will they occur? The question is crucial, for if the limits are near, drastic action is demanded; if they are far away, only token change is required.

The second, a value question, is not so easily stated. Probably the best way is to put it in terms of the future. What kind of future do we want? Or slightly different, what sort of society is most consistent with action guides derivable from the need for long-range sustainability and from the Christian tradition? This question calls for a probing of the values in the growth debate and an understanding of relevant aspects of the Christian tradition.

The two questions are not separate, but closely related. The literature in the debate is loaded with ideology parading as factual projection. Both sides confuse values and facts and are selective in their use of evidence. This is nothing new, but the frequency and intensity of it in this debate is remarkable.

The Factual Question

Certain forms of growth, even economic growth, are sustainable indefinitely. For example, an increase in the provision of most human services can continue to the point of satiation and even beyond. The forms of growth that participants in the debate find troublesome are four in number: (1) food and population, (2) energy and natural resources, (3) pollution, and (4) the social capacity to devise and manage technological systems.

1. *Food and population.* By conservative estimate, 700 million persons are malnourished throughout the world, with 35,000 deaths (down from 41,000 in 1977) attributable directly to a lack of food. Sub-Saharan Africa is the most hard pressed. Ethiopia is currently in the spotlight, but the situation in other sub-Saharan countries is also of crisis proportions.

To the popular imagination, the world food problem is a matter of too many people, too little land, and unpredictable climate. This is partly true, but a distinction must be made between short- and long-term problems. In the long term, it is obvious that present rates of population growth cannot be sustained. A 2.3 percent per year growth in the production of food matched against a 1.7 percent growth of population may look comforting. So may the statistics that show there is ample food in the world for every person to have an adequate diet. But to project indefinitely a population growth rate that adds 79 million more persons to feed each year strains the credulity of even the most ingrained optimist.

The limiting factors are many and ways around them are few. Of the 40 percent of the earth's total land capable of production, only about 25 percent, or one-tenth, is cultivatable with existing technologies.[4] Because the major problem is lack of moisture, massive amounts of water provided by giant desalinization projects could alter the situation. But this would require prodigious amounts of energy and produce considerable waste heat. The "green revolution," produced by combining genetically manipulated new strains with ample water, pesticides, herbicides, and large amounts of fertilizer, is yielding striking gains in production. It has altered the situation already; but the economic costs of producing food in this way are substantial, and decreasing returns to genetic manipulation are evident for some stocks. For these and other reasons, population and food production will stabilize either because of human choice or because of natural necessity. Only the time remains in doubt. Best estimates project stabilization in the middle of the next century at a population level of 12 to 20 billion.[5] Some observers think that even this level is too high.

The short-term problem is different and must be considered, for in it are the seeds of conflict. In contrast to the problem in the longer range, too many people, too little land, and unpredictable climate are not the most significant factors causing malnourishment. Nor is it so much a matter of ignorance, lack of will power, or failed contraception. There is even ample food to go around. It is just not available at a cheap price where men and women are hungry. The simple fact is that men and women and their children are malnourished usually because they are poor.

Poverty is also an important cause of high birth rates. Poor men and women have many children because they are an economic necessity. Children do not eliminate poverty, but they do spread the burden of work, earn income at an early age, and provide what old-age security there is, all at low economic cost to their parents. To gain economic security poor parents need only to exercise the prudent choice of having five or six children so that at least one will survive.

The matter of poverty is not as easily analyzed. Many Americans place the blame for continued poverty on corruption, poor administration, cultural factors, and laziness; that is, they blame the poor. In turn the view from the bottom puts the blame on a repressive colonial heritage whose modern form is the collusion of transnational corporations and local elites. It insists that poverty and inequality are not the fault of the poor or a matter of choice. They are a result not of tradition and ignorance, but of the armed might of the United States and the economic power of the industrialized countries whose interests are served by present arrangements. Both could be reduced and the economic plight of the poor significantly bettered with a policy of "food first," which makes agriculture the highest priority and promotes self-sufficiency based on agrarian reform.[6] Agrarian reform is critical, according to this view. It is a combination of land reform, technical modernization, credit and marketing support services, and a dedication to justice.

Whatever the causes of poverty and the poor distribution of food supplies, the view from the bottom must be taken seriously by Christians. There is ample evidence pointing both to poverty as the main cause of malnourishment and to the role of white Westerners in perpetuating structures of poverty. Other factors no doubt are important, but until the role of the rich in maintaining poverty is acknowledged and changed, stressing these other factors, indeed stressing sustainability, is self-serving ideology. In fact, something must be added to the concept of sustainability, for a sustainable world could be a sustainably poor world in which current structures of power and oppression persist. Two concepts must be added: justice and sufficiency. Justice in this context means that the poor should have first access to resources to the point where basic needs are supplied. Sufficiency means the timely supply of basic necessities to all people. Thus our problem of food and population must be expanded to include justice and sustainable sufficiency.

2. *Energy and natural resources.* Between 1950 and 1974, the world's demand for energy tripled.[7] Crises in the Middle East thereafter caused a tapering off of this rate of increase as prices generally rose in response to the rising price of petroleum. Still demand remains high, the price increases have been absorbed for the moment, and newspapers report a glut of oil. The situation seems "normal" again.

One problem is that supplies of oil and natural gas are finite and exhaustible. How long they will continue to serve as major fuels is an open question owing to the speculative and price-sensitive nature of reserves and the impossibility of predicting the costs of substitutes. The nearly unanimous opinion is, however, that oil and gas will be in short supply some time in the next century. Reserves will be dramatically increased if the oil locked up in shale and tar sands can be tapped at a reasonable economic and environmental cost, but these, too, are exhaustible. Oil and natural gas are not sustainable supplies of energy.

Coal reserves are sufficient to last for several hundred years. Of great concern, however, are the serious drawbacks to the increased consumption of coal, notably environmental degradation in mining, the cost of transportation, and the pollution caused by combustion. From an environmental perspective, coal is no bargain. It will help us through a transition to sustainable sufficiency, but it should be used sparingly.

Nuclear energy, once the bright hope for the future, is now so bedeviled with problems that new orders have ceased in the United States. The problems are well known: limited supplies of uranium, radiation, accidents such as Three Mile Island and Chernobyl, waste storage, time delays, high costs, the threat of proliferation, vulnerability to sabotage, and the large scale and complexity of the technology. The most limiting factor at present is cost, but this only reflects efforts to solve the other problems. In any case, nuclear energy is a limited source unless the breeder reactor is developed or it becomes feasible to produce energy from the fusion of hydrogen atoms. Plans to develop the breeder reactor are now on hold. The problems associated with containing a fusion reaction are tremendous because of the high temperatures involved. Experiments with magnetic fields and lasers are proceeding with some success, but containment at a reasonable cost is still far off. Cost may ultimately be the critical factor. Power from the fusion reaction may be too expensive to fuel economic expansion, even if it has potential as a source of almost unlimited energy.

Two other sources of energy, solar and conservation, offer alternatives for sustainable sufficiency, but not for ever-increasing consumption. Solar power comes in many forms, from wind and hydroelectric to passive absorbers and giant reflector farms. All are renewable and some forms are already cost-competitive. Besides being renewable, solar energy technologies have potential for small, local uses where high temperatures are not necessary.[8]

Conservation is the name given efforts to reduce the consumption of energy by cutting back on its use through such simple methods as improving insulation, lowering thermostat settings, designing more gas-efficient automobiles, and constructing energy-efficient buildings. Some estimates place the potential savings for conservation as high as 40 percent.[9]

Conservation and energy from renewable sources, such as solar energy, while not panaceas, are essential elements in any picture of sustainable sufficiency. All other sources are either exhaustible or carry a high economic and environmental price tag or both. Only renewables and conservation offer alternatives. Yet they will not be cheap and will probably not be sufficient to fuel energy-intensive forms of growth.

The situation with mineral resources is such that while a few are scarce, most are in sufficient supply for the short term, given cheap, abundant energy. The question of limited natural resources is inseparable from that of energy. As easy-to-get and rich ore deposits are used up, more energy will be needed to extract the harder-to-get and lower-grade deposits. Mineral availability thus depends on cheap, abundant energy.

Even so, the Bureau of Mines projects a short supply of most minerals within a century if growth continues at its present rate. As for renewable resources, for example, forests, fisheries, and grasslands, there is deep concern about consumption at nonrenewable rates, about using fertile land for purposes other than agriculture, and about the effects of pollution.

In summary, increasing levels of energy and resource-intensive consumption are not sustainable; even if they were, the costs would be great in terms of money and environmental damage. Energy will be the most critical factor both in terms of sufficient supplies and the social structures and technologies that are developed to produce it. The question of social structures is significant, for it leads us back into the second question, the value question. In a very real sense, our choice of energy technologies will go a long way to dictate the style of our social life and the values we hold. Energy is that important.

3. *Pollution.* Of the several potential limits, the earth's pollution absorption capacity is the least pressing. With a combination of capital investment, technological innovation, and changed attitudes about waste, the threat of this limit is already lessening, although local problems persist.

The types of pollution are familiar enough: water, air, radiation, heat, visual, and noise. The climatic effects of pollution are the most worrisome and least understood. Carbon dioxide released in the burning of fossil fuels acts like a blanket, producing a greenhouse, or warming, effect. Countering this, the oceans are capable of absorbing significant amounts of carbon dioxide, and particulate matter suspended in the air by the same combustion processes blocks some of the sun's heat from reaching the earth. The net result may be a balancing of the effects, but the truth is, we really do not know. We do know, however, that a heating up of the earth's atmosphere will cause significant weather changes and that at some point, the polar ice caps will melt, raising ocean levels.

Pollution absorption capacity is an elusive concept. Capacity depends on specific ecological systems. Some systems are extremely fragile at key points, others are more resistant. Absolute levels above which a system is destroyed exist for most organisms, but this level is seldom reached at once by all parts of the system. The relevant question is not always the destruction of entire species, but how many human, other animal, and plant lives are pollution-intensive production and consumption worth. Unfortunately, this trade-off between life and consumption is seldom made explicit.

Most North Americans would like it both ways: low levels of pollution and high levels of consumption. This combination may be possible but not without huge expenditures of money for pollution control. Pollution control is also costly in terms of energy. The most obvious example is the emission control devices on automobiles, which lower gasoline mileage.

Increased levels of consumption will require large doses of energy. Increased energy production does not necessarily mean more pollution, at least in the long run. Conservation, more efficient production methods, and less pollution-intensive forms of energy could allow more production with the same or a smaller amount of energy. But this is not true in the short run. Coal and nuclear power pose serious environmental risks, yet they are counted on by many as the critical fuels in the transition to sustainability.

This linkage between energy and pollution points to another aspect of the sustainability problem: the relatedness of the problems. Limit to growth is not many individual problems lumped under a single heading. The problems are interwoven. Decisions that pertain to one area have an impact on another area. Increased food production, pollution control, and mineral extraction will place a greater demand on energy. Increased energy production in the absence of stringent pollution controls can have deleterious effects on health and food production. The feedback loops are complex and not always well understood.

4. *Social limits.* It is the mind-boggling complexity of the limits problems, especially when superimposed on the everyday problems of inflation, unemployment, budget deficits, and political conflict, that has led some observers to say that the real limits are social. Harvard sociologist Daniel Bell is not so worried about managing physicial limits to growth as he is about the social change that will be demanded in order to manage the increasing scale of technology.[10] This is significant because technological innovation is so often seen as the way around limits. What Bell is saying is that there may be limits to the technological process itself. Bell points to possible management limits. Technology may also increase the occasions for conflict. New technologies increase human interaction but not necessarily harmonious interaction.

Ecologist Barry Commoner argues that our conception of technology is flawed, and as a result, unnecessary problems are created.[11] Too often when technological solutions are sought, problems are defined so narrowly and divided into so many parts that tunnel vision results. We concentrate on the parts or on small problems and miss the whole, the web of many individual technological decisions. We also miss or fail to anticipate negative or unintended side effects. Some technological pessimists, Commoner not among them, have concluded that new technologies on balance create more problems than they solve.[12]

The Desirability Question

The factual debate over limits to growth is critical. Some resolution of conflicting projections is imperative to the material future of human beings. Unfortunately, projections in this debate are not just factual. They are also value-laden. The values involved must be examined, for they predispose individuals to accept certain projections and reject others.

For those who deny that limits can be avoided by technological fixes, substitution, or massive capital investment, the ultimate goal is an "equilibrium" economy in which production levels will depend on the availability of renewable resources and the requirements of ecological support systems. In the transition to equilibrium, the developed countries should gear down their consumption and develop a new value system that has a greater appreciation of nature, sees heavy consumption as materialism bereft of spirituality, and calls technology into play only when it is "appropriate." Many on this side feel alienated from current directions in technological society and are not in positions of great economic power. Others buttress their position with appeals to nature or good stewardship.

On the other side are those who claim that all is well. No change of direction is needed. Technology, substitution, and the price system will allow us to circumvent or push limits back if only we allow them to work. The Edison Electric Institute and Mobil Oil have been prominent in advocacy of this position. In particular, this group extols the virtues of economic growth and technology, rising material standards, national power, political stability, and the extra resources for social programs that growth produces each year. Their most potent argument is that economic expansion is the only feasible way to reduce poverty and to keep employment levels high. In their preference for technological solutions, growth proponents are frequently champions of sophisticated and large-scale forms of technology. They minimize, dismiss, or ignore the problems with these forms. Most growth advocates are ideologically tuned to many of today's dominant values.

These sketchy characterizations give the flavor of the growth debate and its value configurations. It is an ideological struggle reflecting deep differences of opinion about industrialized society and its direction. The debate reflects the cultural polarization of the 1960s and 1970s, which was the occasion for it in the first place. But, to come full circle, we must also insist that the debate is not entirely ideological. It centers on momentous questions that have not gone away even though the polarization has faded.

What may be concluded? For one thing, there are sufficient doubts on the factual question to warrant a change of direction. If immediate movement to sustainable sufficiency is not warranted because of the wrenching social change required, movement to improve the lot of the poor, to promote a policy of food first, to reduce pollution, to shift to renewable resources and conservation, and to concentrate on what the late British economist E.F. Schumacher popularized as "appropriate technology" and Amory Lovins, as "soft technology" is in order.

As for the ideological debate, we fortunately are not left with the either/ or of growth or no growth. Most forms of growth can continue. What matters with technology is its form and direction. Our present form is large scale and complex and has a momentum that appears to have no direction except its own reproduction. Nonsustainable forms of growth, directionless technology, and a value system supportive of undifferentiated growth and technology are the real issues.

In recent years, the World Council of Churches has been a forum for creative alternatives. The vision of the just, participatory, and sustainable society argued in its precincts offers possible directions out of the limits dilemma.

Justice, Participation, and Sustainable Sufficiency

In economic terms, the goals of the World Council's vision are (1) the provision of basic human needs, such as food, housing, clothing, and health at some level above subsistence; (2) the reduction of inequalities in wealth, income, and power; (3) the indefinite sustainability of population and the consumption of energy and resources; (4) more "appropriate" and participatory forms of technology; and (5) environmental soundness.

Three biblically based values provide the name for the vision and are its primary action guides.

1. *Justice.* Justice is put first purposely and the word sufficiency added to the World Council's third value in order to take the view from the bottom seriously. Sustainability without sufficiency and justice is a sham. Survival is important, but once it is assured, the importance of the redeemed life shifts the stress to other action guides.

There is no more prominent social ethical guide in the Bible than justice. It is central to both Old and New Testaments. Justice is the social equivalent of love and means special concern for the poor, a rough calculation of freedom and equality, and a passion for fairness. The ethical aim of justice in the absence of other considerations should be to relieve the worst conditions of poverty, powerlessness, and exploitation; to support programs that help the poor and malnourished to achieve productive, useful, and sharing lives; to avoid coercion; and to narrow inequalities. In questions of energy and resources, it means the provision of sufficient and sustainable energy and resources to all and an equitable distribution of burdens and costs among communities and between generations. It includes the establishment and maintenance of basic human rights.

2. *Participation.* The problems with modern technology, in particular its scale, its complexity, and its resource-intensive and non-participatory character, have been given only cursory attention as the concentration has been placed on limits questions. These problems and the tradition of

close-knit, participatory communities idealized in the Bible have led to the addition of participation as an action guide in World Council discussions. Participation on the social level means having a voice in critical decisions that affect one's life, for example, energy and resource systems, the technologies these resource systems incorporate, and the organization and distribution of food. Participation must sometimes be traded-off for timely decisions, but both require a viable community in which mutuality, solidarity, diversity, and spiritual growth are high priorities.

In the teachings of Jesus on the community of God we find clues for genuine human community. Genuine community is sustained by a different kind of power, God's power of suffering love. This power cannot be engineered. Technologies, material consumption, and economic growth may enhance human power, but they offer little for the realization of God's power of love, and hence for community. Jesus stressed the beginning of community in small things. This does not mean smallness to the exclusion of large size, but it does suggest that our pell-mell rush to larger scales and complexity is misplaced. Small things also include small people, the poor. Genuine community means first priority to those at the bottom.

Early New Testament communities tried to follow these clues. The early community in Jerusalem (Acts 1—5) and the Pauline communities, idealized in Romans 12, all point to the biblical norm of small, holistic, and participatory communities, not isolated individuals whose primary function is to make economic choices. The ideal was never reached, but this may tell us something about a basic human need for small, close-knit groups. Largeness, centralized and impersonal groupings, and too much stress on the individual are contributing factors to modern forms of alienation. Somehow we must learn to put our large productive organizations, with their awesome technologies, together with our need for intimate communities. No sure way to do this on the level of mass societies is now clear, although numerous successful smaller attempts serve as models.

3. *Sustainable sufficiency.* Sufficiency is the timely supply to all persons of basic material necessities defined as the resources needed for food, clothing, shelter, transportation, health care, and some margin above subsistence.[13] The emphasis is on the words basic needs. Sufficiency is not the supply of every human want.

Sustainability refers to the long-range capacity of the earth to supply resources for sufficiency at a reasonable cost to society. Its presence as an action guide means at least partial acceptance of the limits analysis. The concept of sustainability assumes the limited capacity of the earth to yield resources and to absorb pollution. It also assumes the fallibility of human technologies and organizations. Finally, it assumes either that limits are sufficiently near or that the direction of modern technology is sufficiently wrong-headed to warrant corrective action.

The biblical understandings of justice, wealth, consumption, and sharing are the basis for an understanding of sufficiency. Justice and its special concern for the poor means that the poor should have first access to resources to the point where basic necessities are met. The side of the biblical tradition that calls Christians to the radical and rigorous following of Jesus, voluntary poverty, and self-denial points to the satisfaction that is experienced in simple living. From the side of the tradition that argues for contentment with modest consumption, the right use of possessions, and the duty to give liberally comes a call to moderation and sharing. From both sides comes the guidance that sufficiency takes precedence over the piling up of possessions.

The biblical basis for sustainability comes from the notion of stewardship and realism about human sin. Stewardship means care for the earth and care for persons. It embodies Edmund Burke's view of society in which ancestors and posterity are seen as sharing in the decisions of the present. The present generation takes in trust a gift from the past with the responsibility of passing it on in no worse condition. One key text is Genesis 1 and a proper understanding of verses 26 to 28.[14] Genesis 1 presupposes the harmony of the Garden of Eden. In Genesis 3 comes the fall and, according to Paul, the whole creation "[groans] in travail [Rom. 8:22]." But it also "waits with eager longing [Rom. 8:19]" for a renewed and proper stewardship. The shepherd cares for the lost sheep. The earth is the vineyard and we are its tenants. We have betrayed the trust and brought suffering to creation, including the human species. Nevertheless, we are still responsible to God. We are called to exercise dominion with love, justice, care, and nurture, not destruction, rape, and pillage.

Social Policy

The World Council vision of a just, participatory, and sustainable society is not a panacea. It is, however, a way of singing the Lord's song in a strange land of hunger, impersonal technology, and the threat of limits. Certain modest suggestions for social policy flow from its guides for action.[15]

1. The first priority is not immediate transformation, but the beginning of change. The transition to sustainable sufficiency is crucial.

2. In the transition, market forces will be important for the sake of efficiency but should be guided by governmental intervention to speed up and achieve fairness, participation, and sustainable sufficiency.

3. Conservation, an increased reliance on renewable sources of energy, restraint of total energy demand, less consumption of depletable energy

and mineral resources, and strict enforcement of environmental safeguards should be high social priorities.

4. The basic needs of the poor should take precedence. This means a policy of "food first," the cessation of predatory practices, and a shift of resources from rich to poor in a form that encourages self-sufficiency. Increased public and private assistance are a corollary to this.

5. Strengthening the family in its variety of forms, enhancing participation in community, and encouraging the peaceful association of communities are critical as part of the process of reaching sustainable sufficiency. Although nuclear war is the most unsustainable mode of all, the prevention of local wars that may lead to nuclear war and that uselessly consume resources is also important. Modern war is not only unrealistic, but also unsustainable.

6. Education is a necessary component in the social commitment to accelerate the transition. The study of international economics, the social impacts of technology, the environment, and resource consumption should be part of curricula at all levels.

7. Nuclear energy and coal should be energies of last resort, not the primary forms of power for the transition. The ultimate goal should be reduced dependence on conventional nuclear energy and coal, with eventual phase out as conservation and renewable sources are developed. The development of energy from the fusion reaction should continue, although with careful attention to its social and cultural impacts.

8. The churches have a responsibility in education, in the setting of examples, in the stewardship of money, in the showing of solidarity with the poor, and in the exercise of a prophetic role in society.

9. Individuals have personal responsibility. The basis for personal responsibility is faith. God gives the power of love and calls individuals to respond with human love and justice. Understanding the problems, becoming aware of the ethical implications, and probing the tradition for guidelines are key parts of any response. But just thinking about a response is not sufficient. It must be combined with action or it easily becomes implicit support for the status quo. There are enough reasons now for individuals to change their modes of behavior. The vision of the just, participatory, and sustainable society offers a future with great hope. The World Council of Churches and the many Christians who have given their energies to this vision are to be commended for helping us to see a new expression of faith.

PART V.
Business and Labor

ELEVEN

Is an
Economic Apologia Enough
for Business Managers?

James W. Kuhn

*I*n recent years, a variety of groups have increasingly made demands on corporate business managers. They claim to represent such varied interests as those of consumers, racial or ethnic minorities, the elderly, women, employees, conservationists, peace advocates, environmentalists, and the religious. The demands require, at the least, time and consideration of corporate staff advisers and, at the most, may preempt the attention and efforts of a firm's chief officials. The interaction between managers of large companies and the leaders of many of these groups is frequent enough that they can be recognized as corporate constituencies. The leaders may ask managers to change major company policies or reallocate significant resources of the firm. So new are such demands that managers often resent the time and efforts they must devote to what they perceive as the importuning, multiplying groups. They would prefer to give no more than perfunctory attention to them; many believe that they deserve no more than that. Some of the groups enjoy special legal favor or have won governmentally defined or protected rights. Despite such protected status, some managers resent what they consider outside intrusion into their business responsibilities, considering the groups and their demands illegitimate.

An American executive expressed a commonly held judgment: "They have no right to ask us to do anything. They are not the owners; they do not represent the owners. They are elected by nobody and represent no

James W. Kuhn, Courtney C. Brown Professor of Management and Organization, Graduate School of Business, Columbia University, and Adjunct Professor of Christian Ethics, Union Theological Seminary in New York City.

one but themselves." Still other executives see outside protesters as a counterproductive force: "They muddy the waters of decision with foolish arguments and unrealistic objectives."[1] In fact, some constituency demands are foolish and unrealistic; some are little more than publicity gimmicks—advertisements for those involved. More often, though, they involve substantial and, despite managers' doubts, legitimate issues.

Through hard experience and despite their distaste, managers have learned that they had better pay respectful attention and give careful thought to their responses. Some groups can present their cases appealingly to the public, masterfully using television and the press to dramatize their issues. Others have learned how to exert substantial economic pressure, organizing boycotts and even winning legislative action to regulate or restrain business practices. Constituencies may speak as dissident stockholders. Most have discovered the excellent forum of an annual meeting; they have also learned that "ownership" bestows a certain legitimacy on them. Although a group may be small in number, it can nevertheless propose actions large in impact on the corporation.

In presenting their demands to managers, and certainly in displaying them to the public, constituency leaders appeal to as wide a range of interests as they can, supporting their claims with popular and widely held values, including those that managers formally, but not in practice, recognize. Constituency values seldom fit well with business values inherent in managers' conduct of business. They may even contradict business values as pursued and defined in everyday practice. Constituencies usually present themselves as democratic, participative, and egalitarian, even though in fact they may pursue other values. In general, business managers in everyday affairs follow quite different values—authoritarian, elitist, and hierarchical.[2] Within their own organizations, they feel uncomfortable with the approach and challenge of the constituencies.

They can help themselves in dealing with constituencies if, first, they take seriously the ethical nature of some of the constituency values and, second, they prepare themselves to defend the moral relevance of the values on which they base their own policies and actions. They can do so effectively only if they articulate a wise and convincing case that the public has a stake in their values as well.

Can Business Managers Limit Their Justifications to the Economists' Defense of the Market?

Increasingly confronted with critical constituencies able not only to exert some ownership rights, but also to mobilize public opinion and even market power (through boycotts, for example), managers turn to the economists for help. Many managers believe, perhaps naively, that the free *market* apologia will serve as a convincing defense of their own free *enterprise* policies. It is true that, by and large, economists strongly advocate the free, competitive market. They certainly urge its use as the central institution of the economy because they are, in Prof. Amartya Sen's words, "much taken by the notion of private motivation achieving public good through the intermediary of the market mechanism."[3] If this notion is demonstrable and free market arguments are sufficient to defend managerial policies, then economists should be helpful to managers as they contend with their critics. Economics may then provide a powerful case that nonmarket response to constituencies is unnecessary and maybe even harmful. Managers could argue that solving constituency problems through the market is both desirable and appropriate.

Economists offer two major arguments in favor of the competitive market: first, it provides a more effective and efficient allocation of resources than any alternative, and second, it offers more individual freedom than nonmarket systems. Almost all of them emphasize the first. It is a value with which most are technically, as well as philosophically, more comfortable than they are with freedom; efficiency is a value that they confidently believe the market serves exquisitely well.[4] Economists' *efficiency*, however, is not the same as the everyday meaning of the word. It refers to the best allocation of goods and services in accordance with the effective demand of individual consumers. Effective demand is determined by the distribution of income—by consumers' budget limitations. The efficiency of the allocation is not affected by different distributions; incomes may be grossly unequal or rigorously equal, and given either, a free market allocation will be efficient. Further, economists generally assume that the market's efficiency contributes to, but is not the same thing as, increasing productivity and economic growth.

The Defense of Efficiency

By resting their case for the market on efficiency, economists proceed in a "somewhat ethically evasive" way, as Prof. Thomas Schelling notes.[5] They examine ways to secure the largest output but tend to ignore its distribution. Their only professional concern, as economists, is for efficiency, the most production at the lowest cost. As advisers, they can help either private or public policymakers select programs that will minimize waste and maximize return. They can thereby assure their clients that, at any given cost, there will be more goods and services available. With an increasing output, the well-off need not sacrifice, and out of the increase the poor can be made better off. Such a possibility is not fully persuasive to the ethically concerned among the public, however. After all, under what practical conditions will the poor secure any portion of the increase? May not the rich take it all, getting richer, and the poor be left relatively poorer, even if not absolutely worse off?

Furthermore, if the rich are very rich, the poor very poor, and the middle class small or absent, a market system will still produce "efficiently" for economists. Efficient markets may operate, as economists well know, in countries where many people are starving and suffering from acute deprivation while a few families enjoy the good life, as, for example, in an El Salvador or a Zaire, if free markets in fact exist there. The benefits of an efficient market, under such circumstances, may not be impressive to those made uneasy over the social tensions created or may be considered of little consequence for those offended by the political stress within any community suffering a wide gap between rich and poor. Unless the market offers the poor a practical chance to improve their lot, the economists' claims for its efficiency appear hollow and ethically unconvincing.

The market value of efficiency becomes important and worthy of attention when other and more basic community values prevail. The argument for market efficiency is probably convincing to most Americans only if it can assume a general agreement on, or at least movement toward, widely shared notions of social justice. The acceptability of market efficiency in the United States, then, can be seen as dependent on a general social agreement that economic opportunity will be made relatively open and available to all. The acceptance is based only indirectly on the economic abundance that "equal opportunity" appears to encourage. The prior emphasis on "justice" (however defined) that is embedded in our religious and political traditions makes market efficiency a more compelling value and a better defense for business than it is in many poor foreign nations. With some presumption of its validity here, managers may argue that critics should not interfere with market efficiency or, as those in business like to put it, with business efficiency. But managers may emphasize efficiency only insofar and as long as they are first prepared to recognize and deal with issues of social justice. They may involve questions of income distribution or, more likely, matters of equal opportunity.

The Prerequisites of Efficiency

Managers find it comfortable to assume that market efficiencies are but the sum of—the reflections of—their own and their companies' efficiencies. In protecting their policies, company programs, and industry procedures, they convince themselves that they are thereby protecting the efficiency of the economy. The relationship between firm and economy efficiency may, of course, causally run the other way; managerial and firm efficiencies may arise to a significant degree out of such governmental activities as public education; public streets, roads, and highways; and a public court system that protects property and enforces contracts. An increasingly sophisticated public, which has learned in the past two decades to be suspicious about the pronouncements of those in authority, does not necessarily accept managerial assumptions that national productiveness and efficiency arise solely from business practices and the particular, existing production system. It will want to be shown in fact, as well as in theory and after-dinner talks, that firms are truly efficient. As noted later, the facts sometimes reveal something different.

An efficient market in general is no guarantee of efficient markets in particular; business firms do not operate at peak efficiency at all times, and especially so if they are large.[6] Technology continually opens new possibilities for market efficiencies, bringing with them dangers to traditional business practices and standard operating procedures. Business firms do not always produce, nor do business managers always operate, within rigorously competitive markets that continually force efficiencies. Managers are always searching for niches to shield their companies from the fierce, blustery winds of competition; if they do not find them ready made, they are not above constructing shelters if they can. A number of conditions help them in their search and construction.

First, consumers may not be well informed about the products they choose. They may believe that they are buying and paying for a particular good or service but find in its use something quite different. For example, consider a common kind of disappointment with a minor, modern technological item. Advertisement and demonstration may promise that an expensive pocket radio will provide a jogger or biker with stereo FM music wherever he or she goes. When the radio is played, the user discovers that reception is so interrupted by static that listening is not worthwhile. A more serious example is buying an American-built car and then discovering that it is so poorly constructed that the manufacturer must recall it to fix features that endanger driver and passengers. If consumer values are poorly served, then to that degree market efficiency, as defined by economists, is lost. Managers will not fulfill their primary social role through the market, as economists conceive it. They will not be serving customers effectively, for they will be misallocating the resources at their command.

Various conditions bring about a mismatch between what consumers want and what they actually get. On the one hand, technological advances provide goods so intricate in operation and complex in consequence that few consumers can be truly informed buyers. Anyone who has bought a new drug or a recently developed electronic marvel realizes the ignorance with which even an alert and knowledgeable customer must act. On the other hand, the worldwide spread of markets has introduced sophisticated goods and modern selling techniques to peoples of other cultures, new to market ways and unused to their dangers and limits. For example, illiterate mothers living in the rural areas of many African nations may not be experienced in recognizing the wiles of high-pressure hucksterism. Some have been persuaded by companies' exaggerated advertising or misleading claims to buy an infant formula that is more costly than they can afford and even dangerous to their babies' health.

Second, spillover effects of "externalities"—nonmarket costs to the community arising from the production and sale of a good or service—may be significant. If they are, producers do not pay the full costs of production, thus enabling them to charge a lower price and sell more than they otherwise would. The result may be a profitable firm, but an economy inefficiently using its resources. In a world where the spillovers of polluted land, air, and water have become a serious problem, endangering health as well as comforts of life, most people realize that efficiencies of polluters and the rewards they garner for themselves and their customers can mock the larger promises of an efficient market.

Third, the economies of large scale can undermine competitive outcomes, denying efficient allocation in the market.[7] Professors Geoffrey Heal and D.J. Brown suggest that economies of large scale, where costs decline with larger output, are much more common than most economists assume in their analyses of current business practices and policies. Where economies of scale are found, outcomes are quite different from the "normal case" of rising costs, and they invalidate many conventional assumptions about the operations of the market.

Consider the economies of scale in the American automobile industry. In the three decades after the end of World War II, the industry became increasingly oligopolistic, squeezing out the smaller, marginal producers as the largest firms increased their market shares. Given their primary markets in the United States, the oligopolists could produce more cheaply than smaller American auto firms. Once they had achieved their dominating position in the domestic market, the three large firms were under little competitive pressure to increase, or even maintain, their efficiency. The managers no longer carefully tracked the changing demand for their products and left wide markets open for foreign entry. European and particularly Japanese manufacturers offered less costly and higher-quality products. When gasoline prices rose sharply after 1973, and consumers were attracted to fuel-efficient automobiles, the public became aware of the degree to which American producers had long been sheltered from market competition. It increasingly became obvious that they had lost touch with their customers and had too long continued old inefficiencies or slipped into new inefficiencies.

Only when Japanese auto producers captured a significant portion of the domestic market and continued to increase their share did the managers of American firms reluctantly and with difficulty begin to change some of their long-established sloppy and noncompetitive practices. Not until early 1982 did General Motors announce that henceforth it was going to buy steel through competitive bidding, a practice that one might have thought firms in a free market economy would regularly do as a matter of efficient management. The company told its steel suppliers that henceforth it would buy on the basis of price, quality, and timely delivery.[8] Since GM ordinarily purchased more than 7 percent of the steel industry's domestic shipments, the impact of its newfound competitive rigorousness was widely felt. Steven Flax, writing in *Fortune*, made clear the longtime managerial laxness that the change to bidding revealed.

> GM's shift ended an era of stunning complacency. Its steel buying had become an automatic process, conducted with the soothing reassurance of a familiar ritual. At the beginning of each year a supplier would be awarded a fixed percentage of GM's needs for particular steels at particular plants. "We did the same thing the same way every year," says Gus W. Rylander, a 27-year sales veteran at Armco. "We'd go up there [to Detroit] and get our share of the pie." ... As Merrill Lynch steel analyst Charles A. Bradford puts it, "The steel companies' attitude was, 'We make steel. If you want it, you buy it.'" GM, by the same token, didn't want to hear from any steelmaker who thought he might have a better or cheaper way of doing things ... Neither side paid scrupulous attention to quality. ... At the same time GM continued to pay suppliers' list prices even though it had the clout to bargain. Banking on the consumer's willingness to absorb price increases, the company chose to pass costs on rather than disrupt the comforts of doing business as usual. The example of the auto industry indicates that in the long run the market did respond efficiently, but in the short run, consumers paid higher prices and the economy's resources were not efficiently allocated.[9]

Two years later, the American managers were still discovering how inefficient their firms were. They began to seek additional ways to economize and cut costs throughout their operations. They analyzed the way they procured parts from small suppliers as well as steel from the large steel producers. In the easy years before Japanese competition, parts producers usually received a little higher price each year when the new model cars rolled out. They did not have to worry about research and development or quality, simply supplying extra parts as an allowance for defects.

A fourth condition under which the market produces its efficiency is that of uncertainty and instability. The market continually fluctuates. In boom times, output, employment, prices, and incomes tend to rise; in recession, they tend to decline. Popular skepticism focuses on the relatively high and costly unemployment or the periodic recessions. Recession unemployment has seldom involved as many as one out of ten persons in the labor force since the Great Depression, but nonetheless, it burdens millions of people with job losses and disrupted lives. Claims for market efficiency that appear to need or depend on such unemployment—certainly a waste of any society's most valuable resource—are simply not well received by those among the public who care about social justice.

If and when market efficiency is allowed to manifest itself, it will usually benefit consumers to the extent that they enjoy the wherewithal to buy. The links of that general efficiency to the specifics of business efficiency, however, are loose, allowing many a slip. And ironically, when large firms rigorously pursue efficiency, as they were forced to do in response to rising world competition in the early 1980s, they impose heavy costs on their own workers and many of the small producers who have long been associated with them. Of the 30,000 direct and indirect auto parts suppliers, most of them small and owner managed, half are expected to disappear or go into some other line of business before the decade of the 1990s. The pressure on the workers involved—perhaps half a million—will be intense; many will lose their jobs, and those who hold them will find it hard to maintain the industry's high wage levels, let alone win increases.[10] At best, economists offer business managers no more than a contingent argument for their practices, not a compellingly strong moral defense.

Freedom as an Ethically Relevant Market Value

Despite the various qualifications with which they hedge efficiency and their recognition of its conditioned source, economists strongly believe in market allocation of resources.[11] Some, however, do not care to rest their arguments for the free market solely on the contingent case for efficiency. They subordinate it to another value they believe to be of greater ethical worth: *freedom*. They offer business managers the chance to defend their policies, procedures, and positions on the basis of the freedom found in the market.

Two well-known economists, F.A. Hayek[12] and Milton Friedman,[13] both Nobel laureates, have emphasized freedom—or liberty—as the pre-eminent value of the market. Other economists are not unappreciative of the freedom allowed in and encouraged through the market, but most do not find it as compelling as does Hayek. Even Friedman quietly introduces government to qualify market freedom. Economists recognize that an individual's freedom is limited in many ways, and particularly by some of the outcomes of a competitive market. Thus even knowledgeable supporters of the market system, as well as critics, doubt that the freedoms it secures are as significant or as far reaching as Hayek and Friedman presume. Consider the doubts of Arthur Okun:

> Rights in the marketplace represent universal and equal rights to earn unequal incomes. Moreover, the rights of citizens to pick their jobs and to select the items for their market baskets, at least out of some reasonable menu of options, are essential elements of personal freedom. The boundaries around these rights, however, raise intriguing and controversial issues. My right to pick my job is restricted in many ways. ... The scope of private personal property raises even sharper controversies. In order to permit individuals to trade, the law must define a right to private property. ... The big question is where to draw the line. ... The broadest possible scope of private property ... may have seemed natural in a world of yeomen farmers, but it loses meaning in a modern industrial society that rests heavily on wealth in the form of paper claims to assets that owners do not use directly.[14]

An economist of quite a different political persuasion from Okun, Irving Kristol, doubts that many Americans are ready to raise freedom as an ethical value to the highest priority: "Individual liberty is a very fine thing, one of the finest even. But order is also a very fine thing; and justice; and morality; and civility. ... A free market is a superb economic mechanism; but it is not self-justifying."[15]

Both Okun and Kristol doubt that freedom is as available as the market defenders presume because like most people, they find income and wealth setting bounds on it. One's personal household budget obviously sets the range of many of our freedoms. Examples of free choice, often favored in economic texts, focus on common consumer goods, so inexpensive and readily available that choice is an option for all. Typically, Friedman points out that the market allows men to choose among many different colors of ties.[16] He is correct, but surely the choice is not an impressive test of market freedom.

Not only must a variety of goods and services be available if freedom is to be a reality, but one must also enjoy an *effective* choice. With no money in one's pockets, all the variety of the market reduces to a nullity, eliminating freedom of choice. For example, the housing market offers a wide variety in the kind and quality of shelter, but without an adequate income or a good job and suitable credit rating, one may not be able to afford a detached house in the suburbs. Likewise, a supermarket is filled with an amazing variety of foods, but one's selections may be limited to only a small portion of the total. One may prefer prime steak for dinner regularly but have to be satisfied with bologna or chicken wings because the cost of steak is too high for the available paycheck.

Most economists probably agree that the market encourages and allows much individual freedom; unfortunately, the incidence of freedom is as varied as the distribution of income. At best, one can point to no more than a rough and ready relationship of income and merit, and at worst, there is simply no connection.[17] It is hardly surprising, therefore, that a defense of the market based solely on the value of freedom is less than convincing to the public, unless it already has agreed that freedom is the highest of all social values. As already noted, most economists probably agree that the market *can* encourage and even allow much individual freedom, but incomes are far from equal, and consequently, the freedom to choose in the market is exceedingly varied. All people have to live within their budgets, and poor people's choices are relatively, and sometimes seriously, limited.

The Role of Fairness as a Form of Justice

Hayek strongly insisted that those who examine the effects of budget limitations on freedom introduce an irrelevant value into the analysis of the competitive market. They concern themselves with merit or justice— the question of "who gets what"—which, he maintained, is logically separate and categorically different from freedom. Justice introduces an extraneous and irrelevant ethical value into the market system. It is an inappropriate introduction, he argued. Merit applied in the market will confuse those who work within it and can only impair effective market processes.

> In a free system it is neither desirable nor practicable that material rewards should be made generally to correspond to what men recognize as merits and that it is an essential characteristic of a free society that an individual's position should not necessarily depend on the view that his fellows hold about the merit he has acquired. ... The fact is, of course, that we do not wish people to earn a maximum of merit but to achieve a maximum of usefulness at a minimum of pain and sacrifice, and therefore a minimum of merit. Not only would it be impossible for us to reward all merit justly, but it would not even be desirable that people should aim chiefly at earning a maximum of merit. Any attempt to induce them to do this would necessarily result in people being rewarded differently for the same service. And it is only the [market-determined] value of the result that we can judge with any degree of confidence, not the different degrees of effort and care that is has cost different people to achieve it. ... It would probably contribute more to human happiness if,

instead of trying to make remuneration correspond to merit, we made clearer how uncertain is the connection between value and merit. We are probably all much too ready to ascribe personal merit where there is, in fact, only superior [economic] value.[18]

Friedman is not as definitive or as sure as Hayek in excluding merit—or justice—from the market; he neither rejects nor explicitly embraces it. However, he implies and thus assumes a kind of minimal egalitarianism that requires government to redistribute some income. He recognizes that those with no income or wealth possess little freedom within the market. Insofar as they cannot buy or sell, they can cast no "vote" and play no role in the market. He is apparently bothered by the notion that large numbers of individuals might have no market input, and as a consequence, the market will not reflect their preferences.

His illustration of a "free private enterprise exchange economy" is:

in its simplest form . . . a number of independent households—a collection of Robinson Crusoes, as it were. Each household uses the resources it controls to produce goods and services that it exchanges for goods and services produced by other households, on terms mutually acceptable to the two parties to the bargain. . . . Since *the household always has the alternative of producing directly for itself, it need not enter into any exchange unless it benefits from it.*[19]

(Perhaps Friedman meant a Swiss Family Robinson; a collection of Crusoes implies servants or slaves to play the role of Fridays—hardly proper members of a free market society.) Friedman's independent households enjoy some freedom of choice, an ability to enter the market or to stay out. They are not ultimately dependent on an employer, the market, or government. Their basic livelihood is guaranteed by their own separate income and independent wealth. Such a freedom suggests that households in Friedman's market possess some bargaining power. They receive at least a minimum income and are not hand-to-mouth poor.

That he carefully chose his illustration and that it reflects a social value underlying his market notions of efficiency and freedom is clear from the policy recommendations that he later made in *Capitalism and Freedom*. He proposed what many casual readers thought was a "liberal," and thus "un-Friedmanlike," scheme of income redistribution: the negative income tax (NIT). Under NIT, the poor will fill out income tax forms, like everyone else, and if a family's income fell below some predetermined level, the federal treasury would write it a check to bring the income up to a minimum. Other, richer people would pay their graduated taxes to the treasury. His assumption that all members of an economy should have at least some minimum income, and thereby an ability to participate in the market, puts him and his NIT proposal in the earlier classic liberal tradition. He wanted to help the poor to use the market to serve themselves. Then they could choose with some freedom, avoiding a governmental bureaucracy that paternalistically determined the goods and services they would receive. The NIT is therefore not "liberal" in the contemporary political sense. It is a program based on Friedman's free market assumptions. All persons (or families) can participate in the market only if, and insofar as, their incomes allow them to choose to buy and sell in it. To assure full, even if minimal, participation, all families must have at least some income. An NIT would provide that minimum income.

In advocating NIT, Friedman reveals that he had secreted into the very foundation of his market defense a sense of justice—a concern for the poor, who might otherwise be left outside the system. He implicitly recognized that market efficiency and freedom need the accompaniment and fundamental support of at least some sense of fairness. He appears to advocate, with some shyness, a kind of democratic egalitarianism. He does *not* espouse equality of income, and he passes no judgment on the merits of any specifically market return—salary, wages, and earnings—received by managers, workers, or stockholders. Nevertheless, he clearly believes that the market works best only when the poor at the bottom have some assured minimum income. His NIT would provide that minimum, improving the market and serving individual freedom at the same time.

That a popular, learned American economist, widely presumed to be a conservative, should temper his economics with advocacy of a kind of egalitarian minimum is not surprising. Ordinary Americans have long prized fairness, although not many have defined it as equality in the distribution of income.[20] They want a nation in which all may strive for any position and all may participate at least minimally in economic as well as political affairs. They manifest their concern for fair treatment and egalitarian values whenever, as an electorate, they can exert influence on policies and programs. It was revealed in the program of meat rationing during World War II, for example.

American farmers produced more meat than ever before in our history, supplying not only huge quantities for the armed forces and for lend-lease aid to allies abroad, but also more meat for *civilian consumption* than Americans had previously enjoyed. Nevertheless, the government instituted rationing of meat. It was a popular restriction, and generally approved. Chester Bowles, Connecticut's rationing commissioner, and later to become director of the Office of Price Administration and, after the war, an influential senator, explained the need for the rationing despite the ample supplies compared with those of the past. "If uneven or unfair distribution of necessities causes bitterness, then our home morale will suffer drastically."[21]

In time of crisis and emergency, when the whole nation needed to pull together and when most people wanted to emphasize their sense of community, the electorate accepted—even welcomed—shared "sacrifices" (even if only symbolic) on the home front, as well as on the battlefield. There was more meat available than ever before, but Americans found the gross inequalities of a market allocation unsatisfactory. In such a time of national emergency, they preferred an equitable sharing through the use of government ration coupons.

More recently, Americans showed their readiness to turn to equitable sharing through government rationing, when it appeared in the early 1970s that imports of petroleum might be drastically curtailed. Congress approved and the federal government made ready for rationing civilian supplies of gasoline. It even printed millions of coupon books, which eventually were destroyed, unused, and unneeded. Economists then and since pointed out that rationing was not an efficient method of allocating gasoline, but to little avail.[22]

Another indication of public concern for fairness is also relevant. Where a broad electorate can influence pay structures, an element of applied equity is also evident. The salary scales in local, state, and federal governments show a marked egalitarian bias.[23] In a *Business Week* survey, almost half the public believe that elected public officials are either underpaid or worth their pay. Only about a quarter believe that top corporate executives and show business and TV stars are worth their pay; fewer than one out of five (19 percent) believe that professional athletes are worth their pay.[24] Sidney Verba and Gary Orren found in a later survey of American leaders that most agreed those who work in public and nonprofit sectors should be paid more than they presently are. The leaders did not approve of the high pay of those in such occupations as business executive, professional athlete, medical doctor, and engineer.[25]

An additional example of the American electorate's preference for egalitarian pay is found in labor unions. The pay of union leaders, even of officers in the largest unions with up to a million members, is noticeably smaller than that of the top officers in the companies with whom they deal. In 1984, the Teamsters, a union notoriously lacking in democratic control, paid its president in salary and expenses more than half a million dollars, but the more typical large union paid its president between $114,000 and $214,000.

The best-paid business executives, as a group, received an average of $1.1 million in 1984, *excluding* long-term bonuses. That is about eight times more pay than that of the union presidents. If corporate managers were elected to office as democratically as most union leaders, one might well expect their pay to be considerably lower. Professors Verba and Orren concluded from a survey of American leaders that while they do not support radical egalitarianism, "they want to slash earnings at the top of the hierarchy and boost earnings at the bottom. . . . There is a general desire to see a smaller gap [than now exists] between the top and the bottom of the income scale."[26] Having to answer only to members of their boards of directors, whom they appoint, and confronting the electoral power of stockholders only through the less-than-democratic annual meeting procedures, they can largely ignore the widespread American sense of "fair" pay that the opinion surveys indicate.[27]

There is no evidence that the public favors strict equality of pay; in the *Business Week* survey, it approves high pay and large bonuses to managers in industries that appear to be efficient, productive, and innovative. Managers in the computer industry, for example, were adjudged to merit their pay, but those in the telephone, communications, auto, steel, and oil industries understandably ranked near the bottom. Many people perceive those executives as not meriting the pay they granted themselves.

Peter Drucker, a professor and well-known, active business consultant, warned managers that they had better pay attention to the public sense of "fairness" in pay:

> They offend the sense of justice of many, indeed of the majority of management people themselves. They are seen as the embodiment of the ethics and values of American business and management. Few people—and probably no one outside the executive suite—see much reason for these very large executive compensations. There is little correlation between them and company performance.[28]

Drucker's warning is not markedly different from the arguments of business' regular faultfinders, such as those associated with Ralph Nader, in the Democracy Project.[29] That the public generally and both pro and anti business critics should find common ground in deploring the level of executive compensation suggests that there is a general and prevailing American agreement on a standard of "fairness" in the market system. Some form of justice—not just efficiency—should prevail. If business managers are to persuade people that they deserve their compensation, they will at least have to persuade them that they and their companies are truly efficient, contributors to economic welfare. As noted earlier, the managers of a number of the nation's leading and large firms have not been able to provide that persuasion.

Efficiency and Freedom Are Not Enough

Scholars have already warned business managers that they cannot expect to find either capitalism or the business system well defended with the arguments of economists. The values that inform them are too limited ethically to be convincing, and they are too technical to be appealing. Furthermore, they are incomplete and derivative in that they depend on an acceptable and preexisting agreement about some concern for justice. Ernest van den Haag, an ardent supporter of capitalism, has written: "Justice is as irrelevant to the functioning of the market, to economic efficiency, and to the science of economics, as it is to a computer or to the science of meteorology. But it is not irrelevant to our attitude toward these things. People will tolerate a social or economic system, however efficient, only if they perceive it as just."[30]

He argued that there is an uneasy and unstable relation between economic and moral valuation. In the past, the kind of religion that mediated this relationship in the United States was grounded in what is popularly known as "the Protestant ethic." It emphasized the individual, personal values of frugality, industry, sobriety, reliability, and piety, providing a moral justification for even the harshest market outcomes—loss of job, unemployment, or serious injury. These were matters of individual responsibility, not the market's. The ethic also underwrote the notion that there was a direct and causal link between these values and the distribution of power, privilege, and property. Many in the public were willing to believe that economic success might even be a sign of divine approval.

However, another strong and articulate defender of the business system, Irving Kristol, has pointed out that such identification in the past allowed Protestant Christian believers to presume the market to be just, not merely free.[31] He writes, "Samuel Smiles or Horatio Alger would have regarded Professor Hayek's writings as slanderous of his fellow Christians, blasphemous of God, and ultimately subversive of the social order."[32] Kristol doubts that many modern business leaders and rising young managers are as outraged by Hayek's separation of merit and the market as Smiles or Alger; many of them do not possess religious convictions that allow them to find divine sanction for the market. Moreover, he does not find that they possess any other source of justification for their and their corporation's performance. Tradition provides a weak justification; it means simply accepting things as they are because they have been accepted in the past. Unfortunately for those who hope to rely on tradition, they find it is a social asset continuously and rapidly eroded by the dynamism of capitalism.

Managers thus face a serious problem: how can they justify themselves in a society where justice and the market are no longer synonymous? The values of efficiency and freedom, offered by the economists, are problematic from many moral points of view. The justification of the market through religion, which wide acceptance of the Protestant ethic once secured, is no longer convincing to many people. While perhaps a third or more of Americans may still believe in a divine justification of the market and business system, they are probably a far smaller share of the total than they were a century ago, when Andrew Carnegie wrote his widely admired *The Gospel of Wealth*.[33] Managers will have to learn the arguments of fairness and the reasons of equity as they deal with their constituencies. In this endeavor the economists offer little help.

Corporate managers will have to seek their own understanding of, and develop their own sensitivity to, the demands for justice as debated, understood, and practiced in an ethically pluralistic society. They will have to enter into more dialogue with their various constituencies than up to now they have been willing to contemplate. They may well have to learn about the complexities of justice, for contending groups propose different and conflicting definitions. Managers also need to advocate business efficiency with more sophistication and sensitivity to other ethical concerns than they have provided to date. They would be wise to make clear to the public the social and public trade-offs involved in sacrificing business efficiency or market freedom to the demands for equity or fairness; but they may discover that they must support their claims for efficiency and freedom strongly enough to convince skeptical, but not necessarily hostile critics who doubt that the trade-offs are inevitable.

Business managers will continue to enjoy privileged positions, but they will be challenged more sharply than in the past. The world in which they carry out their duties today has changed significantly from that of their parents. They must deal with a well-schooled work force, knowledgeable domestic consumers, a plentiful supply of able, aggressive young professionals available as leadership cadres for new constituencies, and a restless, roving press, omnipresent in its news coverage. They can expect to maintain few organizational secrets, nor are they apt to be able to hide many activities of their firms, inside or out. They will probably continue to exercise great authority, but they may not be able to assume unquestioned prerogatives to which they have aspired in the past. They will have to defend their business and themselves with arguments that are more convincing morally to the public than their arguments of the past have been. There can be little doubt that business managers will increasingly find it desirable to offer the substance, not just the image, of democracy, participation, and egalitarianism to their constituencies.

TWELVE

Capital, Community, and the Meaning of Work

John C. Raines

*I*n the latter part of the twentieth century, a new and powerful form of political economy is emerging that is fundamentally altering the power relationships between management, labor, and local community. This is the emergence of a *global* economy. A revolution in electronic information-processing and rapid international transport has made capital highly mobile and the division of labor international. This means that First and Third World workers compete with one another for available investment. As a result, not only cities and regions, but whole domestic populations are made to compete under the discipline of maximizing profits, and the losers are left with high rates of unemployment and a downwardly mobile pattern of new job creation. The terms of negotiation in this competition range from national and local wage rates, to monetary and taxation policies, to environmental and worker protection laws, and laws regulating the organization of labor. At the same time, all around the world the search for competitiveness and profits is replacing workers with machines.

The result in advanced industrial societies like our own is a new kind of unemployment, unrelated to the normal business cycle. It is an unemployment that is getting worse, not better. After the 1975 recession, unemployment fell to 4 percent; after the 1980 recession, unemployment never got below 6 percent. The recession of 1981-82 left behind an unemployment rate that reached a low point of 7.1 percent and has since gotten worse.[1] Otis Port, an editor at *Business Week* magazine, explains:

John C. Raines, Associate Professor of Religion, Temple University, Philadelphia, Pennsylvania.

We are now on the threshold of a massive transition to robotics. There are industries that are talking about displacing tens of thousands of workers over the next 20 years by robots. I would be surprised if anywhere near half of the people who are now unemployed get their jobs back. American business has learned, is learning rapidly how to increase productivity and do more with less.

All this is inevitable, he concludes, because "that's the only way we're going to survive against the products that are built in low wage-rate countries."[2]

What does it mean, this new survival? Who survives and who gets left behind?

"It affected men terrible. Just all their dreams were in that factory, going to work, supporting their family. It was taken away from them. They felt lost; they were scared; they didn't know what to do." Phyllis Barrett was speaking of her husband, Tom, who had worked for twenty-three years at Eaton Corporation's forklift truck plant in Philadelphia. In the summer of 1982 that plant closed, forever. Eaton continues to make forklift trucks, but in Mexico and Japan. Tom was out of work for two years and went back to work for a third less income and far fewer benefits than he had had before.

"I was working in the plant," Tom said, "and I was complaining about the closing of the plant, and a man named Charlie Miller said to me, 'Tom, don't you realize we're the last of the buffalo?' And I said, 'What the hell do you mean, Charlie, we're the last of the buffalo?' And he said, 'Our type of work is leaving the country and we're just like buffalo—we're the last remaining few people who do this work with our hands and minds, and we're not going to be no more. Maybe in twenty or thirty years our children or our children's children will have prosperity again, but we're the last of the workers.'" For families like the Barretts—and there are millions of them—there has been no recovery. They are the "new poor."

This new, structural unemployment is accompanied by a pattern of downwardly mobile reemployment and a declining standard of living. Many formerly unionized factory workers are driven into nonunion shops with nonunion wages and nonunion benefits, while others are driven into the service economy. Service work may be fine if you are a doctor or a corporate lawyer, but most new jobs being generated in our society are at the lower end of the service economy. The categories of work that will produce the most jobs in our society through the end of the century are, in the order of their rank, building custodians, cashiers, secretaries, office clerks, and salesclerks.[3] What is emerging, whether in Brazil, Western Europe, or the United States and Canada, is a new "dual society," with a minority well paid and many formerly well paid becoming poorly paid or without steady work at all. Boston College economist Barry Bluestone comments:

> What it means to our society is that workers that have always believed in the American way of life, have always believed that if they worked hard, if they played according to the rules of the game, they would have a better life in the future than they have today—for those workers we're finding that the American Dream is shattered.[4]

Workers will want to know why.

One reason is that with the new global economy, yesterday's profits made in America can become today's investment capital creating new jobs in the Third World—jobs that replace those here at home. For example, the same Pittsburgh bank that manages the steelworkers' pension funds lent money to build a new and technologically sophisticated steel mill in South Korea. The delayed wages of the steelworkers built mills abroad that led to the closing of steel mills and coal mines at home. Another example is Singapore, the second largest center of silicon chip production in the world. The investment capital and technical know-how comes from Great Britain and the United States. Clearly, the recovery of capital and of profits does not necessarily mean job security for those who helped to produce those profits.

The Roman Catholic bishops of Canada have spoken of this. "In effect," they say, "capital has become transnational and technology has become increasingly capital-intensive. The consequences are likely to be permanent or structural unemployment and increasing marginalization for large segments of the population in Canada and other countries." The bishops speak of this as a "deepening moral crisis" because "through these structural changes, 'capital' is reasserted as the dominant organizing principle of economic life."[5]

While Third World poverty requires worldwide economic development, this development cannot rest, as it now does, on increasing the social inequalities inside both First and Third World societies. Today, a small piece of the First World is being reproduced in the Third in an affluent elite, while an increasing portion of the First World is growing to be like the Third—people unable to find work or who can find work only at low pay.

Capital disinvestment is not the only cause for this new structural unemployment and underemployment. Another is expanding "paper work" that makes no products, but maximizes short-term profits by diverting capital into mergers and acquisitions and by manipulating tax-saving devices. The result is a pattern of rapid managerial promotion that is completely unrelated—more often antithetically related—to long-term economic productivity. Says David Joys of the Russell Reynolds consulting firm in New York City:

> I know—we all know—people all over this town who are running their companies into the ground, taking huge, quick profits and leaving them a shell. And when you look at their contracts it's easy to see why. What does it matter to them what happens ten years from now? They're building giant personal fortunes, and *appear* to be running their companies terrifically, and in ten years, when there's nothing left, they'll be long gone.[6]

The crisis of productivity and international competitiveness in our nation today cannot be resolved by establishing permanent high unemployment and downwardly mobile patterns of new job creation. Nor can it be resolved by forcing cities and states to bargain away their tax base in the race to attract industry. De-skilling human work through thoughtless technological regimentation, or rewarding socially irresponsible profit speculation with tax breaks may increase profits and bring in jobs in the short run, but in the long run, it undermines both labor and community. And in the long run, productivity rests on human effort that requires *cooperation* between capital owners and managers and workers—a real cooperation, not a false one—a cooperation built on a fair apportioning of the burdens, risks, and benefits associated with their common productive efforts.

But this will not happen without new federal legislation of a kind we have hardly begun to talk about—legislation to make capital investment socially responsible. Such legislation is now a moral necessity because, in the words of the Roman Catholic bishops of Canada, the reassertion of capital as the dominant organizing principle of the economy "directly contradicts the ethical principle that labor, not capital, must be given priority in the development of an economy based on justice."[7] In saying this, the bishops reflect the thought of John Paul II, who wrote in his encyclical "On Human Work": "Labor is always primary efficient cause, while capital, the whole collection of means of production, remains a mere instrumental cause."[8]

Since our reigning economic orthodoxy holds just the opposite, the implications of this ethical claim are provocative. Our economic orthodoxy insists on following the unfettered logic of the free market. If allowed to do whatever it wants wherever it wants, capital will, without conscious moral intention, transform the avaricious pursuit of individual gain into the social benefit of a robust economy. The "invisible hand" of the free market will direct capital investments into the most efficient enterprises and away from the least efficient ones. Although some will get more of the resulting bounty and others less, all will have more in the end.

214

Greed, according to this philosophy, is the guiding virtue, for it alone leads into the promised land of economic efficiency.

The moral reasoning of the pope and the Canadian bishops concerning "the priority of labor" and the ethical preeminence of "the common good" advances notions largely absent from mainstream public discourse and underlines the need to reflect anew on the meaning of human work and on our nation's responsibility to its workers.

A Theology of Work

Who works and who does not, what kind of work is done, and who has a say in the workplace—these are fundamental ethical issues because in work and through work, our species expresses its human essence. Through work we respond to our unique human calling to extend by human creativity the work of God begun in creation. In the opening pages of Genesis, we are told that we are made "in the image of God" and receive therefore a mandate to "be fruitful and multiply and fill the earth and subdue it."

With our new ecological awareness, the idea of subduing the earth is viewed as one-sided. It is helpful, in this regard, to think of work as our species' special way of living with its natural environment. In a real sense, only humans work because only humans make the given social and natural order an object of their reflection and so are not limited to reproducing that world, but can transcend and transform it. In transforming the world, we transform ourselves and our relationship to the world. The tool is thus symbolic of the human, of our special way of being in the world.[9]

It is as beings who work that we become "historical." That is, we transform in a developmental way our natural and social environment, and through this same activity transform ourselves. As humans, we are literally historical; we become. The most graphic example of this can be found in our early evolution as a species. We evolved biologically in a dialectical relationship with our work. The opposing thumb, the expansion of the higher brain, and the increasingly elaborate use of tools all evolved simultaneously, over millions of years. Our working is our species' way of being and of becoming. This is the real meaning of God's command to "subdue" the earth.

Moreover, these creative possibilities inherent in work join us in a special way to our fellow human workers, who also seek to experience themselves and their relationship to others in terms of this transcending and transforming freedom. We remember with gratitude, therefore, the heritage of prior human labor, which, over time, by elaborating its use of tools and organizing in increasingly complex ways its productive activity, has sharply increased the possibilities of our own well-being.

Work, even work distorted by exploitation, reminds us that it is only in joining together with others that we improve that common good through which each benefits by the other's labor and without which all remain alone and destitute. That is why it is wrong to view work solely through the mechanism of the market, where each pursues individually his or her own self-interest. Such calculated bargaining is only a second-order reality and rests necessarily on the division of labor, which permits each to benefit through the work of the other and together to build the common good—what our forebears called the "commonwealth."[10]

In work we discover a profound and necessary mutuality. It is a distortion, therefore, to see fellow workers as competitors to be "beaten" or as impersonal entities in the productive process to be impersonally "planned." Indeed, by our working together, we should be drawn out of our narrow self-preoccupation and excessive self-regard into the clarity of self-perception that sees our common human journey, nourished by the creativity and sacrifice of those who have labored before us. We should be reminded that we, too, are part of this journey—that our time is part of all time and that we have a responsibility to preserve and enhance this legacy built up and made fruitful by human labor.

The gratitude and mutuality that we learn in work and through work is not something merely abstract or naively idealistic. It is something workers actually experience at the workplace. Tom Barrett spoke about his work at Eaton:

> We had a lot of old-timers and they would teach the younger men. They would bring us along. The old-timers would show us how to do the work. And they showed a lot of concern for the product. Many times, in my learning process, if I didn't do the job right, it wasn't the boss that gave me hell, it was my own workers who would tell me that I wasn't doing the job right.[11]

Danny Chmelko, another worker at the Eaton plant, spoke in a similar fashion about workplace companionship. "I walked into that place and I didn't know how to screw a nut onto the end of a bolt. And I was nurtured, I was fostered, not by the corporation, but by the people." That's why the response of many workers to a plant shutdown is grief. Lee Thomas described her husband Jack's response to Eaton's closing:

> I think the company doesn't realize that people are not working together just to earn money. Most working people have two families—the family that they live with and the family they spend their days with, that they work around. It's not the money that you lose or that you miss as much as it is the people. A man has lost the family that he's used to being with. He feels he has done something wrong, that he's being punished.[12]

Displaced workers experience three distinct periods in the grieving process. In the first period, besides the economic loss, there are the physical and mental health injuries documented by Prof. Harvey Brenner, of The Johns Hopkins University. He has shown how job loss is correlated to predictable increases in alcoholism, in wife and child abuse, in stress-related diseases like stroke and heart attack, and in homicide rates and first-time admissions to mental hospitals.[13]

Brenner describes the second stage of grief for workers whose plants shut down:

> As long as they were between jobs, between positions, it was possible to imagine that the recession would go away—that all the bad things, poor income, lowered self-esteem—would go away. They won't go away for many people, because what is left afterward is a lower position socioeconomically than they had before the recession. So what we have is a second period of grief. That loss will be permanent for these people. They will not regain their economic and social position for the remainder of their lives.[14]

Statistics indicate that for unionized factory workers, the wage loss that they must take when they get their next job averages between 25 and 30 percent.[15] Moreover, they will have lost their seniority, and so will be exposed to further layoffs. Indeed, more and more workers are being reduced to a highly transient work pattern. This means that many of them may never be able to vest themselves in a pension.

This happened to Jack Thomas. Before he worked at Eaton, he worked for ITT-Nesbitt, making heating and ventilating equipment. Seven years after he started, the parent company moved Nesbitt to the South. None of the Philadelphia workers were offered positions, and Jack came to Eaton. But after another seven years, Eaton closed. "Sixteen years," Thomas said, "and I have nothing to show for sixteen years anywhere. No pension, no seniority, no vacation time."[16]

The third period of grief happens over time, within families and between the generations. It is the loss of ability to pass on jobs, contacts, communities, to the kids. Jack, for example, got his job at Eaton because his uncle, who worked there, told him about the opening and smoothed the way with the union. Part of being a good American has meant seeing that the next generation does better. Now Don Brady, another displaced Eaton worker, sees that his children may not be able to provide for their families as he provided for his. "You know what?" he asked, his arms extending around the room in his comfortable suburban home. "My son will never be able to afford a house like this." His son pumps gas for $5 an hour. Brady's wife said, "My daughter will never be able to stay at home and raise the kids like I did." Her daughter assembles data machines for $4.35 an hour.[17]

217

The third period means mourning over the passing of a whole way of life. Economist Barry Bluestone notes:

> The traditional industrial America is disappearing. We've seen that in the auto industry, in steel. We've seen it happening in some parts of the petrochemical industry, the tire industry. That was the part of America that was really responsible for what we call "middle America." It was the set of industries that produced a higher standard of living for workers in this country than any set of industries in our history. Now that's disappearing.[18]

For many workers and their families, it's the end of the American Dream. They are confused and hurt. They are not able to parent the way their parents parented them. They can't shelter their children. They are angry. And they want to know why this is happening to them. If the answer to that "why" is to lead us in a positive direction, rather than negatively into scapegoating the poor or blacks or women, we need a firm grasp on how work is being transformed by the new global economy. What does justice mean in this new situation? If work is not so much how we make a living as it is an expression of our unique human dwelling together, then we must ask "How can we protect human community and collaboration, at home and abroad?"

Justice in the Global Economy

Basic human needs, such as adequate food, clothing, shelter, and medical care, are what we usually think of as the minimum criteria for a just economy. They are crucial. They are needs that we have in common with all animals for sustenance, warmth, and health. But we must add to these needs a specifically human need, a need unique to our own species. *Work* for humans is also a basic need because it is in and through work that we take up our residence on the earth and evolve and develop ourselves as a species. Justice in work requires that the economic outcomes of work be sufficient to sustain life. But justice in work also requires that the *structure of work* be suitable to express those virtues unique to our way of living as humans. For there to be justice in work, therefore, the structure of work must be *meaningful*—work must support meaningful community. What are the implications of such a value claim?

"The people live in filth and squalor here. They come from the rural areas thinking their lives will be better, and they end up here." The speaker is Sister Theresee Marques. And the "here" she is speaking of is the Marako slum outside Lagos, Nigeria.[19] Fifty thousand inhabitants live in mud-walled, tin-roofed huts there, and an open sewer runs in front of every house. Planks are thrown across the filth so that people will not have to wade through it. But in the rainy season, when the streets flood, there is no escaping. For all its filth and poverty, Marako has increased its population more than ten times in the twenty years since Sister Theresee first moved in. She explains: "The people do not think of how difficult their lives are or what is happening to their values. They see the riches of the city and hope for them. They think it's progress."

But what is progress whose price is the undermining and overwhelming of people's values? "The basic standards of conduct were swept away," says Stanley Macebuh, editor of the *Guardian* newspaper of Lagos. "We developed a culture of individuals. Add to that the sudden explosion of so-called wealth from oil, and everyone just went mad. We have become a far more vulgar nation, coarse in our moral sensitivities, and cynical. Making money has become the sole and only ambition."

Whether in squalid slums filled with desperate hopes and even more desperate realities, or in high-rise office buildings whose foundations rest on the rapid influx of First World money and technology, whether in Lagos or São Paulo or Manila or Seoul, a strange story is beginning to unfold, a story few anticipated. It is the story of work becoming unjust, in the sense of destroying patterns of human meaningfulness, destroying patterns of dwelling together that secure a place for conscience to take hold.

We forgot, or perhaps never fully understood, that work is, first of all, not a way of making money, but a way of cooperating. *Meaningful community* is what is lost when work is suddenly transformed. In the Bridesburg section of Philadelphia, an old working-class neighborhood that has been devastated by the closing of factories, the same attack on community is evident. Tony Galvin, who worked at the Eaton forklift truck plant with Tom Barrett and Jack Thomas, used to live there. He speaks of his old neighborhood today:

> It looks like . . . ah, hornets—like you see in the movies—have just gone and devastated that particular area, leaving behind people that are unemployed, that can't get jobs. The kids are all drinking beer. I guess it's due to the fact that the father can't provide. And they look at their father and say, "Well, who the hell are you?"—you know. "You're a bum in the park." Consequently, the kids just have no respect. The father can't hold his head with some sort of dignity and say, "Hey, I'm the breadwinner—you do whatever I say."[20]

The ruining of community in Bridesburg, where a First World industrial neighborhood and its culture is staggering toward collapse, is reenacted in Third World cities that thought only benefit would follow from the rapid influx of foreign capital. It is not just Tony Galvin in Philadelphia who complains of the loss of social cohesiveness, but Mutiru Olowu, a third-generation inhabitant of Marako, Nigeria. "Before so many people came, this village was clean. It was because people knew one another and were of one tribe. Now we cannot talk to one another. People do whatever they like."[21] Pointing out the window to an overflowing sewer in front of his house, Olowu remembered better times and how, contrary to expectations, economic development has not brought human development.

> That sewer was clogged long ago. I called a meeting of the people and said, "Let us bring shovels and work together and clean this place." In the village (that Marako was before its rapid growth) we would have worked together and done it willingly. For it would have been for the good of us all. But no one here helped. And now all of us suffer together.

When work becomes unjust, it is not poverty that is its central or necessary symptom, but the collapse of a sense of shared well-being. An isolation and individualism grow up. We do not expect much from others and refuse to have others expect much from us. We lose a sense of common good that encourages moral discipline and obligation. Rather than bind us together, work drives us apart. It "makes sense" to us only as an instrument of individual advancement. We no longer learn from our work that we need and depend on one another.

A New Covenant

More than 300 years ago those who established this country faced the task of building community. John Winthrop, first governor of the Massachusetts Bay Colony, spoke of this task as he sailed to America in 1630.

> Now the only way to avoid shipwreck and to provide for our posterity is to follow the counsel of Micah: to do justly, to love mercy, to walk humbly with our God. For this end, we must be knit together in this work as one man. We must entertain each other in brotherly affection; we must be willing to abridge ourselves of our superfluities, for the supply of others' necessities; we must uphold a familiar commerce together. We must delight in each other, make others' conditions our own, rejoice together, mourn together, labor and suffer together.

But then Winthrop warned, quoting from the biblical book of Deuteronomy:

> There is now set before us life and good, death and evil, in that we are commanded this day to love the Lord our God, to walk in His

ways and to keep His laws and the articles of our covenant with Him, that we may live and be multiplied, and that the Lord our God may bless us in the land whither we go to possess it; but if your hearts shall turn away so that we will not obey, but shall be seduced and worship ... other gods, our pleasures and profits, and serve them, it is propounded unto us this day, we shall surely perish out of the good land whither we pass over this vast sea to possess it.[22]

Today, we are at sea again—as a nation and as a global economy. Our forebears covenanted together in establishing this country. Today, we must establish a new covenant that will restore our sense of common purpose. We've become a nation divided against itself. We've lost the moral basis for our common life. We need a new covenant—a conscious moral relationship between capital and community, between those who make significant economic decisions and those who must live with the consequences of those decisions. True, capital invests in community—producing jobs and income. But equally true, community invests in capital, supporting over time that crucial belief in the work ethic and in the future without which the whole structure of incentive and social discipline breaks down.

Moreover, as a nation among nations, we send capital into communities in the Third World in ways that often destroy the moral and communal values of the host society, even as it leaves devastated working-class neighborhoods behind in the country that first produced the profits. Nationally and internationally, we are undermining our moral dwelling together.

Some don't acknowledge this. They deny that morality is involved. They deny that work is part of an ethical relationship. Free market thinkers claim that economic decisions do not need moral guidance. They trust, instead, the unrestricted pursuit of self-interest. The mentality that separates ethics from economics is perfectly satisfied to leave capital and community to keep two sets of books, where injuries to one do not appear as costs to the other, where workers and their communities can be devastated while capital increases its profits.

This point of view is mistaken. The relationship between capital and community needs to be a covenanted relationship, a conscious and mutually agreed on relationship. Our new, world economy—with its internationalized capital and labor markets, accompanied by the failure of both national and international political institutions to assert effective public discipline on these economic forces—requires the most urgent ethical analysis and corrective action. We are faced with the same task our forebears faced: how to discern and defend our "commonwealth."

Our wealth is our commonwealth. The pursuit of private profit may succeed for a while, but if undisciplined to the common good, it will ultimately destroy its own foundation. Community, whether in the First or the Third World, is the rock on which capital can alone establish a secure future. All else, as the Bible has seen, is sand and will be washed away in the flood of time.

PART VI.

Technology

THIRTEEN

The Ethical Debate About Human Gene Experiments

John C. Fletcher

*M*any Christian ethicists now have turned their attention to ethical implications of technological change. The meaning and application of scientific discoveries create new and sometimes unprecedented choices. My essay describes the main features of the long debate about genetic manipulation,[1] human gene therapy,[2] and the possibility of "human genetic engineering" opened up by work in molecular genetics.[3] Recent contributions by religious and philosophical ethical commentators will be discussed within a methodological approach that presumes an evolutionary perspective on the relationship of ethical thought and social policy. Considerations that should shape church-based approaches to public policy statements also are identified.

The term "applied human genetics" is preferable to "human genetic engineering." The latter term presumes too much, both about current knowledge and skills. More important, decisions to apply genetic knowledge to human needs and problems imply a greater moral freedom than is suggested by the term engineering. The phrase "genetic engineering" is colder, more distant, and more mechanistic than we ever ought to be when reflecting on the *ethics* of intervention in genetics. "Genetic experimentation" will be the most apt term to describe any intervention in human genetic material in the near future. Perhaps it is too late to change popular usage, but we need to recognize that our choice of words is a moral choice.

John C. Fletcher, Assistant for Bioethics, Warren G. Magnuson Clinical Center, National Institutes of Health, Bethesda, Maryland.

In contrast to medical uses, genetic experimentation is much more vigorous in the development of new drugs, hormones, chemicals, foods and feed, agents for environmental protection, and reproductive technologies in animals. Difficult social problems appear in these applied genetic activities, for example, the integrity of academic-industrial relationships, legal issues in patenting and ownership of new life forms, and the potential socioeconomic consequences of a vigorous approach to biotechnology.

The scope of my essay, however, is confined to the debate about human genetic experiments. One context for experimentation may be the treatment of an inherited genetic disorder, such as sickle cell disease. Another may be enhancement of a feature of human physiology, such as extreme short stature. Yet a third (and one that is remoter) may be the alteration of traits influenced by both genetic and environmental causes, such as intellectual capacity or aggression. One ethical objection to all or some gene experiments is the difficulty of "drawing lines" between medical and nonmedical uses of genetic knowledge. I will discuss this objection here and also consider the problem of how respect for moral lines is to be maintained once they are drawn. Some prototypes of moral problems in future genetic therapies can be found in contemporary medical genetics.

Ethics and Ethical Issues Evolve

Descriptively, "ethics" means bodies of critical thought and guidance about the best interests of societies, groups, and persons in moral conflicts. These systems of thought evolve, that is, they grow and change. Originating in older, simpler forms of moral judgment, ethics evolves into newer, more complex forms of thought and guidance. Religious ethics, and the many traditions that constitute it, is only one of many complex ethical systems.

With this guiding assumption regarding the evolution of ethical issues before us,[4] we can observe that such issues generally develop in four stages: threshold, conflict, debate, and adaptation.[5] In the first stage, conditions for moral conflict exist; that is, clear dangers are present and varying convictions about moral obligations may collide. At this stage, leaders or prophetic individuals anticipate ethical problems that only later are more widely appreciated. In the conflict stage, significant or notorious cases arise that epitomize what was predicted and lead to emotional polarization about what practices should be followed. In the third stage, social and ethical debate spreads. Ethical principles are sought, tested, and applied to the problems at hand, while evidence is gathered to support various alternatives. In the fourth stage, moral adaptation occurs and public policies are shaped. If required, fixed administrative procedures and legislative regulations are established.

In applied human genetics, one can trace two streams of evolving ethical issues. The older and wider stream includes moral problems in genetic screening and prenatal diagnosis. The newer stream has emerged with the moral concern about creating new knowledge and new life forms by recombinant DNA (deoxyribonucleic acid) research. The use of human DNA itself in prenatal diagnosis and screening for genetic disorders links the two streams and makes the issues more complex. My interest here is focused on the ethical questions raised about the potential of using strategies of DNA therapy to treat human genetic disorders.

In the past ten years, molecular biologists and geneticists have learned how to alter and recombine fragments of DNA, the basic genetic material in all species, including humans.[6] Beginning in the mid-1960s, obstetricians and medical geneticists have steadily expanded genetic screening and diagnosis. Sensitive tests for carriers, newborns with genetic disorders, and the fetus have been developed.[7] Genetic diagnosis by mid-trimester amniocentesis, the most prevalent contemporary approach to prevention of genetic disorders, may gradually be superceded by first-trimester chorion biopsy[8] and ultrasound imaging of the fetus. Abortion of the affected fetus is the option most frequently chosen, but some parents use the information to prepare for the birth of an affected infant. The newest diagnostic techniques use DNA of individuals and family members to learn who will or will not develop a disorder—for example, Huntington's disease—as well as to make prenatal diagnosis.

The ethical debate about DNA experiments began with a letter to *Science* from eminent scientists[9] about potential and unknown hazards to humans from such experiments. An early, self-imposed moratorium followed, and a Recombinant Advisory Committee (RAC) of the National Institutes of Health (NIH) was established to address regulation of the biosafety of DNA experiments in the laboratory.

A second stage of open conflict and emotional polarization regarding DNA experimentation soon became more evident. University communities, like Cambridge, Massachusetts, were split by controversy about issues of biosafety and the efficacy of the NIH rules, which were formulated to apply to NIH grant recipients but not to private industry. During this period (1976-78), sixteen bills were introduced in Congress to control gene splicing. None passed.

The literature on the ethical and social issues in DNA research and its potential application to humans has become one of the most extensive in the field of bioethics. An important contribution to the debate was a 1980 appeal by religious leaders to a President's commission established to consider the implications of genetic knowledge and experimentation.[10] In their report, *Splicing Life*, the commission acknowledged many serious concerns about undesirable political or social consequences of genetic experiments but found nothing intrinsically wrong with DNA research. At present, the clarification of ethical and social issues is still under way. Congress has continued to receive new bills to establish oversight bodies for genetic research. In terms of the stages outlined earlier, the ethical and social debate continues, while tests for consensus on public policy or other controls are also being applied.

Ethical Views and Human Gene Experiments

The most likely genetic experiments in humans will aim at treating genetic disorders with humanly devised forms of DNA therapy. Current forms of treatment are mainly palliative; none actually cure. Some scientists believe that research with laboratory animals will eventually lead to insertion of genetic material to reduce the harm of genetic defects or replace cells that cause genetic harm. This approach, somatic cell gene therapy, focuses on more than 2,000 of the approximately 3,500 known genetic diseases caused by single-gene defects.[11] The most common genetic disorders in this society are cystic fibrosis, sickle cell disease, Tay-Sachs disease, and the various types of thalassemia. Body (somatic) cells, as distinguished from sex cells (gametes), of the treated individual possibly could function less harmfully, or even be corrected. However, two treated patients would still be able to transmit the disorder to all offspring, since together they have a 100 percent risk. A good contemporary example is parents treated for phenylketonuria, an inherited enzyme deficiency that causes severe mental retardation unless the patient is given a low-phenylalanine diet.

Two ethical arguments are made frequently against present attempts to experiment with somatic cell gene therapy. First, the great majority of physicians and scientists, who are knowledgeable in this field object to experiments because current knowledge is inadequate at three points: (1) how to direct the curative genes to target cells, (2) how to make them remain only where they are placed, and (3) how to regulate curative genes and make them express themselves unharmfully to the patient or future offspring.[12] Real harm could come to patients in a premature experiment, however attractive such experiments are to clinicians who have no other treatment option.[13] Unless progress with laboratory and animal research reduces current difficulties, professional objections will persist.

Most clinicians, however, are prepared to proceed with somatic cell gene experiments as soon as enough progress has been made in research. Such experimentation is supported by ethical principles that are widely enunciated by religious ethicists and ethically informed persons in other disciplines because great human suffering could be relieved and great benefit enjoyed by those who receive treatment. Religious and philosophical traditions alike adhere to the principles of beneficence (the maximization of good) and nonmaleficence (the minimization of harm). In the United States, about one in ten persons, more than 20 million, have either been or will be diagnosed as having genetic disorders. Between 25 and 30 percent of admissions to children's hospitals are for treatment of genetic disorders. Any relief for such children clearly would be warranted by the ethical principle of mercy.

If gene therapy in the fetus were feasible, another benefit would be the avoidance of some abortions for genetic reasons, at least for those parents who understood and were willing to accept the risks of fetal therapy. Abortion is never "therapeutic" for the fetus, as Paul Ramsey has emphasized,[14] and although genetic abortion may prevent lifelong suffering for the fetus and the family, there are negative aspects to this option. Because genetic disease cannot now be diagnosed early, such abortions occur late in gestation. Mid-trimester abortions are several times riskier for mothers than abortions in the first trimester.[15] Furthermore, since most such pregnancies are wanted, to end them often creates difficult psychological problems for parents and families.[16] Earlier diagnosis may ameliorate these factors. However, because there are now more than 3,500 identified genetic disorders, and because most will probably be diagnosable by the end of the century, the incidence of abortion for genetic disease without effective therapies will probably rise.[17] A clear moral obligation exists to treat the fetus, especially if the treatment is well tested and the mother desires it. Gene therapy may be one of several modes of fetal therapy.[18]

Such reasoning is clearly supportable from religious ethical perspectives. In congressional testimony and advice to the President's commission, somatic cell gene therapy was strongly supported by ethicists from Catholic, Protestant, and Jewish traditions.[19]

A second type of ethical argument against human gene therapy proceeds from a different premise. According to a variation of the "slippery slope" argument, inevitable chains of undesirable consequences will flow from the widespread acceptance of gene therapy. In this view, experiments in gene therapy ought not to be done because a process of inevitable escalation will lead to wholesale genetic manipulation. Jeremy Rifkin argues from this "domino theory" premise.[20] For example:

> Once we decide to begin the process of human genetic engineering, there is really no logical place to stop. If diabetes, sickle cell anemia, and cancer are to be cured by altering the genetic makeup of an individual, why not proceed to other "disorders": myopia, color blindness, lefthandedness? Indeed, what is to preclude a society from deciding that a certain skin color is a disorder?

Rifkin's argument does not proceed from a religious view of ethics or morality. To the contrary, he holds that "ethics are designed to be compatible with the way people organize the world around them. Moral codes keep people's future behavior in line with the way society goes about organizing and assimilating its environment." In his view, ethics is already co-opted by a society too influenced by eugenic reasoning. The only remedy is not to step through the door to the brink of the slope. The moral danger is clear to him: "Is guaranteeing our health worth trading away our humanity?"

A less sweeping version of the same argument draws the line at genetic experiments involving cells from the human germ line, that is, cells that result in sperm and eggs. A *New York Times* editorial that appeared late in 1982 proposed a public policy of prohibition of "inheritable alterations to the human gene set."[21] Six months later, a resolution signed by seventy-five prominent Protestant, Jewish, and Catholic clergy, including heads of denominations, requested that the U.S. Senate adopt just such a policy.[22] The resolution cited laboratory experiments in which sex cells of mice are modified by transfer of genes from another species (rabbits). The signers sketched a future in which specific traits might be "engineered" into the gametes or embryos of human beings. Among the ethical objections was that a human germ line experiment "irreversibly alters the composition of the gene pool for all future generations." If adopted, the resolution will ban any germ line genetic experiments involving human cells. There was no objection to human somatic gene experimentation, presumably because of the strong support for this treatment modality already expressed by religious leaders.

How Should Christian Ethicists Weigh These Issues?

The task for the Christian ethicist, up to a critical point, is the same as for moral philosophers,[23] especially when the problem is as specific as the morality of the uses of technology. The first step is to present the problem in a factual and logical way, showing clearly that it is (or could be) a moral problem. If no viable approach exists to resolve the moral conflict, a second step is needed. A search for basic ethical principles, widely accepted in the society as well as in religious tradition, must be made to help guide the formation of a viable ethical approach. An argument must show that to follow these principles, and the approach recommended, is in the best interests of the persons or groups involved. The last step, where Christian ethics diverges from moral philosophy, is to show that the approach and principles are accountable to tests of scripture and tradition.[24] The remainder of this essay addresses this task and responds to some of the objections to gene experiments noted earlier.

Moral Conflicts and Ethical Reasoning

The terms moral and ethical often are used interchangeably. However, important differences exist between the meanings of the words. It is therefore best to respect a distinction between them. Failure to do so may result in collapsing two interdependent levels of moral reasoning.[25] Distinguishing them enables more logical and self-critical ethical discussion.

On the moral level, human responses have evolved that are aimed at guiding and increasing the ability to resolve conflicting desires, especially those that arise in the face of danger to persons or to groups themselves. Morality emerged primarily to protect humans and other species from danger and is structured by action guides (or rules) perceived as acceptable to the group as a whole. One learns these rules by being "well brought up" in the ways of families, groups, and the society. To act morally means to make choices guided by such action guides and to praise or blame choices in terms of these standards. So to act is presumed to strengthen bonds that protect self, kin, and the group from threats to survival, cooperation, and cohesion.

But problems arise that cannot be resolved simply in terms of received moral guidance. First, human beings can stand partially outside morality and ask "Why?" We learn that morals differ in various cultures and especially between religious groups. Second, we are often faced with choices in which two or more duties required by the same general moral code are in conflict. How can the conflict be resolved without undermining respect for morality?

Gradually, newer human responses evolved that invoke a different level of reasoning, a more general and critical level. Ethics in the West evolved to protect in-group partiality and overdependence on rigid morality that lacked resources to adapt to new challenges or overcome internal conflicts. Excessive loyalities to special interests create a need for a more generalized level through which the "best" interests of persons and societies can be considered. On this level of reasoning, basic ethical principles are formulated as expressions of broadly accepted definitions and tests of best interest, and clarifying and relating such principles to our acts becomes the main modes of ethical reasoning. Such principles also provide ideals and incentives to find new approaches to moral conflicts. To do ethical reflection is to use this more general form of reasoning to reduce the dangers of ethnocentric or ideological moral reasoning. Ethics increases our ability to give a morally persuasive account to others.

Ethics also enables us to decide those moral conflicts that arise when choices bring moral duties into conflict. To choose to act on a duty, however praiseworthy that duty may be in some situations, will increase harm or danger in others. The example of children with serious genetic disorders may be such a situation. Parents and physicians confront the danger of such diseases to the lives of such children. They have a moral duty to relieve or prevent suffering. Experiments in somatic gene therapy may lead to relief. But another duty enters here—to protect a child from harm as the subject of an experiment.

At present, the most viable moral approach has two features. First, given the uncertainty of present knowledge, the duty to relieve suffering ought to include all current therapies except gene experiments. Until parents and physicians are persuaded that there is a reasonable chance that failure to try the experiment adds to the danger and burden of suffering of the child, they have no duty to permit experimentation. The restraint of somatic cell gene experiments is now justified in part because authorities in medicine object to trials as premature and dangerous.[26] Also, the best interests of children and society are not served by unjustly pressuring vulnerable parents to cooperate in experiments.

The second feature of the best moral approach is local and national review of experiments *before* requesting parental or pediatric consent.[27] In these reviews, the best medical interests of the children involved and the scientific interests of experimenters must be weighed and sifted. Morally, the interests of subjects are weightier than those of science. Such impartial reviews do not eliminate the risks of harms or medical experiments, but such "rehearsals" are proven ways to minimize risks and increase learning otherwise lost for lack of foresight. Wide support exists among authorities in medicine and ethics for such reviews. Further, the basic ethical principles we have discussed support the use of somatic cell gene experiments when these can be more safely carried out.

Rifkin's "slippery slope" objection to somatic cell gene experiments is not focused on the potential harm to particular subjects of gene experiments. His main concern is *eventual* danger to the values of "companionship and belonging" that he claims will follow from these experiments. He fears the systematic dominance that future genetic engineers would have over human reproduction. Others, such as the signers of the resolution to the Presidential commission, share his concern about potential abuses of gene technology but do not see somatic cell experiments as dangerous to society. Both Rifkin and these signatories commit mistakes in ethical reasoning, however. If such errors are allowed to guide, confusion and injustice to many who will suffer from genetic disorders could follow.

Rifkin draws the moral line so as to prevent any somatic cell experiments and is willing to forego all health benefits from gene technology to prevent a *Brave New World*.[28] This position is sustained by three assumptions: (1) that gene technology *is* the moral problem, (2) that no meaningful distinctions can be made between medical and eugenic uses of gene technology, and (3) that ethical decisions always will be overridden by the technological imperative "If it can be done, it must be done." None of these assumptions is sound or supportable by evidence or past experience.

The first assumption locates the moral problem in the technology itself and exaggerates the impact of somatic cell gene therapy on social values. Technology is often an occasion for moral conflicts and may create moral problems. But the moral problem is in the clash of moral duties that technology gives rise to, not literally in the technology itself. To make technology the problem is to "objectify" the problem and locate it in a thing or person. Doing this suggests that moral problems can be easily addressed, and results in simple moralizing rather than differentiated moral reasoning.

Are DNA experiments in single-gene disorders a threat to social values? Approaching disease through DNA therapy is morally no different than using any other drug or agent to treat disease. Other human products, like blood, organs, hormones, and bone marrow, are well-established avenues to therapy. DNA has no special ontological status compared with other human products. It is true that gene experiments in clinical settings will create choices that pose difficult problems. Many moral conflicts lie uncharted in the future of gene technology and will need to be brought to tests of moral adequacy. Even so, to ban gene experiments that may help existing children in the name of protection from unclarified dangers to tomorrow's society is to act irrationally and unfairly. Rifkin's argument denies the possibility of more "companionship and belonging" to persons whose suffering makes them deserving now.

Second, Rifkin holds that "there is no logical place to stop" after gene therapy experiments prove successful, a view shared by *New York Times* editorialists.[29] This assumption casts doubt on two common human traits: the logical capacity to make meaningful moral distinctions and the readiness of societies and their members to invoke them. The contrary evidence about moral restraint in recent evolution of medical and research ethics is legion. Doubt about line-drawing always asserts itself in the early stages of moral conflict. In the 1950s and 1960s, a favorite retort of those who opposed any change in research practices was, "Where do you draw the line between research and practice?" Yet many effective lines have been drawn in contemporary research ethics. Today, a body of morally viable practices exists in human research that is respected in many nations.[30] In medical ethics, for example, a recent study by the President's commission on choices in health care of the terminally ill[31] demonstrated a capacity for moral reformulation. This work demonstrated that many older distinctions, such as acting/refraining or withholding/withdrawing treatment, are no longer viable in many medical settings. A new moral distinction was outlined between harms and benefits to the patient's best medical interests.

Societies differ in the energies and creativity given to these moral labors, but many societies are at work today on critical reform of medical and research ethics.[32] The United States has had two distinguished national bodies for such work. Neither has been criticized for any failure to make logical moral distinctions between beneficial and harmful uses of technology.

Morally revelant lines can and will be drawn in uses of gene technology. The most relevant moral distinction is between uses that may relieve real suffering and those that alter characteristics that have little or nothing to do with disease. Real suffering involves morbidity and mortality. A condition that so impacts lives as to keep persons in various degrees of imprisonment, accompanied by pain and foreshortened life expectancy, should be alleviated or prevented in the name of mercy. Of course, not all ways to accomplish this end are of equal moral worth, but once accomplished, the result could be compared with emancipation from unjust imprisonment. Severe genetic disorders evoke this analogy of unjust imprisonment and undeserved suffering that can inspire wide social support for emancipation. Severe mental retardation and extreme short stature clearly fall within the scope of the morally acceptable side of the distinction.

There is also clear guidance here as to what constitutes the other, normally unacceptable side of the distinction. Eugenic uses of gene technology are clearly precluded. The term eugenic refers to biological measures to improve characteristics of persons who are generally viewed as "normal" and who fall within the normal range of functioning abilities within a society. Eugenics intends to add a "plus," assigned by someone's group or private decision, to change human characteristics presumed invidious by *cultural* rather than biomedical standards. Aims to increase the capacity for intelligence in the "average" person, to alter the sex ratio deliberately, or to measure height to fit someone's notion of a more desirable range are hypothetical examples of eugenic uses. Rather than the principle of mercy, some debatable standard of self-realization would need to be invoked to support such measures morally. Each proposal would also be vulnerable to criticism by the principle of justice. Why should the preferences of some be imposed on all? Why should precious resources be used to promote the interests of normal persons when so much remediable suffering exists? Such measures could indeed be controlled by special interests or by repressive governments, which does give some credibility to the worst fears of those who oppose the relatively primitive gene experiments of today. However, such actions would also be clearly objectionable on moral grounds.

Meanwhile, these protests about the difficulties of making moral distinctions should be assessed in the context of what has actually occurred in evolution of ethical issues in gene technology. Why should establishing

234

moral lines here be more difficult than any moral labor societies have undertaken in the past? Genetics must not be mystified or treated differently than any other branch of science or medicine. A more realistic problem is whether lines, once drawn, will be respected. Will physicians and parents have enough self-restraint to maintain and encourage the distinction already described? This question is addressed in the final section of this essay.

The reasoning of signatories to the anti-germ line resolution commits two similar mistakes. Future human germ line experiments are defined as *the* problem, and there is exaggeration of the danger of current animal experiments to human social values. The resolution rests on a distinction between somatic cell and germ line research. A better line would be one that differentiates preventative gene therapy and any eugenic uses of germ cell alteration.

The resolution's objection to germ line experiments on grounds that there would be irreversible evolutionary changes in the gene pool has been analyzed by Bernard Davis.[33] He reminded us that there are clear examples of the desirability of germ line therapy in Tay-Sachs disease and showed that each available option has evolutionary consequences. The carrier of one gene for the disease inherits one recessive gene from a parent in exactly half of all pregnancies involving carriers. Today, prenatal diagnosis and abortion can prevent the birth of an affected infant, but because parents are encouraged to use this method, more carriers will eventually be born, increasing the genes for the disorder in the population.

If somatic therapy were possible, affected infants could be treated, but with the added effect of increasing the harmful genes in the population. However, therapy in the germ line eventually could both prevent the disease in persons and reduce the incidence of harmful genes. Such therapy may also lower the incidence of abortion for this disorder, if parents opposed to abortion would be willing to accept the accompanying risk. If a morally viable form of somatic cell therapy opens up and works, many more treated persons will desire children of their own. In short, the same reasoning that supports somatic cell experiments also supports germ line experiments in humans, assuming that all other questions about inheritable harms have been answered in prior animal research. The issue of inheritability of mistakes poses a crucial and morally relevant difference between somatic cell and germ line human experiments. This difference alone should sharply demarcate the ethical evaluation of germ line experiments but is not sufficient to warrant a total ban before much more data are available on this type of research.

Rifkin's third assumption, surely not shared by the clergy signatories, is that ethics is merely a passive servant of a technological determinism that dominates American culture. Many believe in the softer version of this theory, that at least in this society "if it can be done, it will be done." A look at some past historical examples does not support this outlook. In medical research, much could be done that is not done for ethical reasons. Fetal research is a good example; much could be learned from uninhibited research on fetuses destined for abortion. Perhaps fetal research is the most convenient way to learn about environmental and genetic harm to human life. But a principle of equal treatment of all fetuses in research effectively restrains some morally objectionable research, while enabling some to do research that could benefit fetal life and obtain valuable knowledge.[34]

A second example of restraint is demonstrated in refusal to require mandatory genetic screening before marriage and in every pregnancy, even though screening could prevent much disease. No nation has so violated the autonomy of persons or families. A last example is from the selection of subjects for research. Prisoners, the poor, and the mentally retarded were once convenient subjects for risky research. Their powerlessness meant that it could be done. This situation has radically changed, primarily because of protest on ethical grounds.

Our ethical traditions sometimes are but pale reflections of the status quo, but they need not be. Ethical thought is influenced by technological possibilities, but ethics does not have to be determined by technology or by the way a society currently defines its needs. Ethics poses a "Why and wherefore?" and asks, "What are the consequences of our actions?" to science, technology, and the wider society. It must ask such questions of each institution with which it co-evolves, including morality and law. Our society, when its best interests are at stake, has and can continue to give a "no" to some uses of technology that violate precious values and principles. Contemporary societies are not as passive in the ethical analysis of technology as Rifkin portrays them. Human ethics never stands completely outside its cultural setting, but it can be and frequently is much more critical and creative than his view suggests.

Future Human Gene Experiments: The Search for Principles

Sufficient ethical consensus exists to support somatic cell experiments, but a viable moral approach for preventative gene therapy experiments or alteration of physiological or other characteristics that may be a source of real suffering has yet to be fully charted. In this situation, the task is to search widely for basic ethical principles by which to evaluate the moral problems that will arise. A viable moral approach must be constructed from these principles if real moral choices are to be made regarding more complex human gene experiments in the future. The two principles

236

invoked here, mercy (love) and justice, count heavily in the definitions and tests of best interests applied in religious and Christian ethics. But many other ethical traditions and principles have a constructive role to play in defining the limits and possibilities of gene technology.

Some noteworthy contributions have recently been made to this debate. *Splicing Life*, mentioned earlier, is an able current description of the issues related to the topic, but it falls short in the search for relevant ethical principles. The document stresses a consequentialist thesis that selection between desirable and undesirable outcomes is the most important ethical task. Unlike its other reports, the President's commission did not, in this instance, formulate any ethical principles to guide its consequentialist analysis.

An important work on ecological ethics[35] informed by process theology has been written by Charles Birch and John Cobb. They select "richness of experience" as their central ethical criterion. This "richness" principle, however, appears less truly explored in the context of genetic technology than in other parts of this book. In their discussions of "genetic engineering," they mention only "reducing human suffering by control of genetic disease" as an example of such enrichment. Could it be that their criterion, "richness of experience," would allow for more eugenically aimed experiments than the authors' other ethical principles, like justice and mercy, would legitimate?

Although process theology has been helpful in reconstructing outworn and unintelligible theological arguments within Christian tradition, I have not found its expressions in ethics to be as forceful and persuasive. "Richness of experience" suggests an aesthetic standard rather than an ethical principle commanding wide loyalty from persons in many ethical traditions. However, the "richness" principle may provide a source of supplementary arguments for assessing gene technology where severe retardation or extreme short stature are at issue.

An Oxford moral philosopher who has probed as far into ethical evaluation of genetic experiments as anyone to date is Jonathan Glover.[36] His basic interest is testing for values which would be most at stake in genetic technology that moves beyond gene experiments. He assumes that the technical skills to alter normal state characteristics may be forthcoming and poses several intriguing, imaginative experiments to have his readers think the unthinkable. He finds much to reject, but something to desire, about conceivable technologies that would monitor thoughts, create mood-altering drugs, create behavior control, and enable machines to create experiences. When considering gene technology, he argues for cautious willingness "to change what we are like." He is open-minded about some gene experiments to alter intellectual capacity or aggression. The value system that is central in his work is personalistic, that is, "self-development and self-expression; certain kinds of contact with other people; the development of consciousness."

Glover does persuade the reader to see some potentially desirable features of genetic engineering. Human nature is not fixed. Perhaps in the distant future the cool confidence of his hopes will be realized. But the ethicist must be wary. Arguments for gene experiments to alter characteristics that have no relation to disease, especially those derived from the principle of autonomy, do not survive tests grounded in a commitment to justice, at least as long as there are people who suffer from biologically inherited disorders. Their needs come first. Also, in more self-critical moments, Glover concedes that his argument is vulnerable to a criticism that it is elitist.

Moral Integrity
in Current Moral Distinctions

In addition to searching for principles to guide new moral approaches, the practitioners of Christian ethics must be vigilant about the integrity of current moral distinctions. They should also aim to influence the moral climate in which future gene experiments will occur.

Today, medical genetics is the main arena in which physicians and parents confront human genetic problems. Most genetic centers set forth criteria for prenatal diagnosis that distinguish medical from nonmedical indications, a distinction consistent with the principles of mercy and justice. Medical indications include a family history of genetic disease, a previous child with a disorder, or patients who have a proven risk factor, like advanced maternal age. Two controversial types of requests for diagnosis fall outside the medical category: requests aimed at sex choice that are unrelated to a history of sex-linked disease, and maternal anxiety.

Most ethical guidance and professional consensus rules out sex choice as a morally acceptable indication for genetic testing.[37] In my experience, this line of restraint is observed with integrity, a judgment confirmed by literature in nations that encourage reportage of controversies in medical ethics. Now that fetal sex can be revealed by chorion biopsy at eight to ten rather than sixteen to eighteen weeks of pregnancy, a new reason to be vigilant about sex choice exists. There has been a problem, however, in centers serving cultural groups at high risk for genetic disorders who also have pronounced cultural preferences for males.[38] Prenatal diagnosis for gender choice is ethically objectionable for two reasons. It violates the principle of fairness between the sexes. Also, it is clearly eugenic, since gender is a characteristic that has nothing to do with disease, except in transmission of X-linked genetic disorders. Any practice of sex choice abortion or inability of medical geneticists to resolve such conflicts in keeping with their standards would set a foreboding precedent for future decisions about genetic experiments. Good studies of the incidence of this request have not been made and records of the responses of medical geneticists have not been kept. Such data are needed.

Maternal anxiety as an indication for genetic diagnosis is a more complex moral problem. Some women are anxious because they fear that they have been exposed to drugs or environmental hazards during the earliest stage of pregnancy. Some cases involve women over thirty-five years of age in nations that set the age cutoff for genetic testing as high as thirty-eight years. If a Norwegian woman of thirty-seven years, eleven months knows that the service is routinely provided to thirty-five-year-olds in neighboring Denmark and Sweden, she has a rational reason to be anxious about a 1.5 percent risk of a chromosomal abnormality of her fetus.

However, most pregnant women experience anxiety in pregnancy. Some who are younger than thirty present themselves in genetic centers. They want to rule out an abnormality like Down's syndrome, for which the statistical risks are significantly lower than in pregnancy over thirty-five years of age. They might have been close to friends with an affected child or work in jobs where they see retarded persons. Some are wives of physicians or themselves scientists or laboratory workers. A few are morbidly anxious because of problems in their lives or are expressing pre-existing mental illness that fixes anxiety on the pregnancy rather than on the emotional problem. Wide variation exists between nations and between centers in the same nation in counseling such women and in providing prenatal diagnosis to "allay anxiety."[39]

Some geneticists have great difficulty saying "no" to women who are anxious and persistent. A few make exceptions on request from other physicians. The ethical objection to agreeing to fetal testing where no reasonable justification exists is clear. To sample amniotic fluid or chorionic villi with a risk of fetal loss significantly higher than the statistical benefit of diagnosis violates the principle of nonmaleficence so central to medical ethics. Further, to give a valuable resource to a less deserving person is unfair and violates the principle of justice. Although not a strictly ethical reason, there is also the dubiousness of "treating" anxiety with amniocentesis in many of these cases. If a much safer approach to fetal diagnosis were ever developed, such a line would need reexamination.

To the extent that the line of reasonable justification is broken in today's genetic practices, we have reason to be concerned about the ability of future physicians and parents to maintain cogent moral distinctions in gene experiments and in relation to the future medical possibilities that may emerge. Medical geneticists have much work to do to clarify their standards and the ethical principles that guide them and to develop a more open process for determining exceptions to policies once established.[40] In some nations, efforts are made to publish regularly the number of prenatal genetic studies performed and the indications that led to them.[41] Such efforts will help to reveal contradictions or lapses that set dubious precedents and thereby may help to prevent breaches of moral standards in future human gene experiments.

Conclusions

Church groups that develop social policy statements about human gene experiments should consider six questions to test the adequacy of their moral labors. These questions embody the central claims of this essay about the role of Christian ethics in moral conflicts about technology.

1. Do we have the best available essential facts about the problem?
2. Have we defined a real moral problem or displaced it abstractly onto technology itself?
3. Have we outlined one or more morally relevant distinctions to use in constructing an approach to resolution of the problem?
4. Have we selected and discussed the relevance of widely accepted basic ethical principles for the problem at hand? Do the principles support the distinctions (or lines of logical analysis) that we want to make?
5. Are the principles and the approach taken accountable to tests of scripture and tradition?
6. What moral dangers exist in current practices, if left uncorrected, that could weaken the probability of sustaining the most desirable moral approach in the future? What facts support our alerting others to these dangers?

FOURTEEN

The Moral Assessment of Computer Technology

Edward LeRoy Long Jr.[1]

The development of the computer, which is having a profound effect on many aspects of our lives, has received relatively little attention from Christian social ethicists.[2]

Some quickly gathered statistics indicate in gross comparisons the rise of interest in computers since 1970, and a corresponding lack of attention to them on the part of Christian social ethicists. For example, in the volume of *The Reader's Guide to Periodical Literature* covering the period from March 1970 to February 1971, there are about three and one-quarter pages, with about sixty entries per page, dealing with computers. In the volume covering the same period five years later, there are about the same number of entries. The volume covering the period from March 1980 to February 1981 contains five and one-half pages, with about seventy entries per page, and the volume for the same period three years later has nearly fourteen pages of entries, with about eighty entries per page. Similarly, the *Cumulative Book Index*, in its subject listings, has about one and one-quarter pages for 1970; two and one-quarter for 1975; three and one-half for 1980; and five and three-quarters pages for 1983. Although there has been a nearly tenfold growth in the periodical literature about all matters related to computers, and almost a fourfold growth in book materials about them, *The Index to Religious Periodical Literature* shows no such pattern. In 1970, there were ten articles listed (five under computers, five under cybernetics), and of these, only two dealt with ethical implications

Edward LeRoy Long Jr., James W. Pearsall Professor of Christian Ethics and Theology of Culture, The Theological School and the Graduate School, Drew University, Madison, New Jersey.

of the emerging technology. In the volume covering both 1975 and 1976, there was one entry dealing with the use of the computer in biblical research. In the 1981-82 years, only five entries are shown, with two of them having possible implications for thinking about the role of the computer in society. The 1983 year shows four articles, with only three of them having possible implications for understanding the role of the computer in society.

The Place of the Computer in Society

The place of the computer in society deserves more attention than it has been given. The computer has arrived in the laboratory, in the classroom, in industry, and even in the home without creating quite the trauma associated with the splitting of the atom. Yet the implications may be no less momentous. The purpose of this essay is to outline some of the issues that may be involved in the moral assessment of computer technology. It is probably too early in the discussion to form many definitive conclusions about the impact of computers on our lives, but that does not make the exploration of the issues unimportant.

The discipline of Christian social ethics examines relevant social data from the standpoint of a theological stance. This stance helps to formulate the questions that must be asked and to suggest what values ought to be kept in mind in making judgments about the social consequences of particular events or processes. Christian social ethicists do not come to such subjects with a ready-made set of principles that can be simplistically applied to judge what is right or wrong about technical developments. Rather, they wrestle from a position of informed concern with the interface between the problems as they unfold in their concrete particularity and the perennial concerns that a people seeking to be faithful to God must keep in the forefront of their consciousness. The computer poses a number of issues about what it means to be human and what is necessary to have a society in which human existence can be most richly nurtured.

In a book written many years ago, Norbert Wiener spoke of "The First and Second Industrial Revolution."[3] The categories used in that book would probably not be found in a discussion framed in light of our contemporary knowledge, but Wiener's early attempt to assess the changes he saw coming is significant in helping us to perceive how these matters have been discussed. The first industrial revolution greatly aided (through its advances in time-keeping) the arts of navigation and saw the development of the steam engine. The steam engine was employed first to replace the human labor used to pump water out of mines and then to advance mechanical means for making textiles and to replace sails as the power for moving boats. Although in time the electric motor replaced the steam engine as the main device for producing rotary motion at the point of application, much of the electricity needed to supply such motors was—and still is—produced in generators driven by steam engines, steam turbines, or internal combustion engines. Most of the developments associated with the first industrial revolution aided or extended the work performed by human muscles.

Wiener associated the development of "the second industrial revolution" with the vacuum tube, which was first put to use in the communications industry and had a central role to play in the development of radar during World War II. Putting the vacuum tube and related electronic devices to use in computing machines, made possible the development of much faster and more manageable versions of the calculating and stored program machines that had been pioneered in mechanical versions by Charles Babbage. One of the first applications of machines that could respond to feedback was to control the power-amplifying machines of the first industrial revolution. Whereas, "except for a considerable number of isolated examples, the industrial revolution up to the present has displaced man and the beast as a source of power, without making any great impression on other human functions,"[4] the new machines could do something different—they could perform functions that were more similar to the functions performed by the people who controlled the machines. Although circumspect in his description of the possibilities inherent in the development of computing machines, Wiener did see them as promising to aid in management tasks normally done by white-collar employees, even as the machines of the first industrial revolution had greatly aided in the kind of manual labor done by blue-collar employees.

The cover of Christopher Evans' paperback *The Micro-Millennium*[5] draws the same comparison used by Wiener, but in a more cryptic way and with a different use of terms. It says: "The industrial revolution harnessed muscle power; the computer revolution is harnessing the power of the brain." Evans believes that it is almost impossible to overestimate the extent and the significance of the developments taking place. He argues that changes of even greater magnitude will come about as a result of the computer revolution as came about as a result of the industrial revolution. These changes will come about, in his judgment, with remarkable and ever-increasing speed as the ability to exchange information electronically and process data with computers is advanced in ways that help to lower costs.

David J. Bolter, in his recent book *Turing's Man: Western Culture in the Computer Age*,[6] provides a more highly developed schema for thinking about the rise of technology and the place of computers in Western culture. Bolter understands Western culture as having been shaped by four "defining technologies," each of which "develops links, metaphorical and otherwise, with a culture's science, philosophy, or literature; and each of

243

which is always available to serve as metaphor, example, model, or symbol."[7] The four successive "defining technologies" of Western culture identified by Bolter are (1) the Greco-Roman technology of craftsmanship (from the Bronze Age to the fifth millennium A.D.), the technological achievements of which were extensions of human hands; (2) the technology of the medieval world based on the invention of the mechanical clock, which emphasized the regularity in the created order and portrayed that regularity as an important model for rationality; (3) the industrial revolution, the central characteristic of which was the harnessing of power on a massive scale; and (4) the computer as the technological paradigm. According to Bolter, "we now have [in the computer] an inanimate metaphor for the human mind as compelling as the clock was for the planets."[8]

These different characterizations of the computer revolution all draw a contrast between computer technology and the technology associated with the industrial revolution. The contrast may not be as complete or as compelling as it is sometimes made out to be. Certainly not all the technology of the past has been a technology that merely magnifies the power of human hands. For instance, although agricultural technology has had its tractors and threshing machines, which do the work that hands can do but on a more massive scale, it has also had its agronomy, its horticulture, and similar sciences. These technologies are technologies of the head and involve the use of knowledge to transform processes rather than merely to amplify power. The hand/head division cannot be applied unequivocally as the distinguishing difference between the pre-computer and post-computer periods.

Another reason to hesitate in making the contrast between a technology of power and a technology of knowledge too complete is that the two can often be used in concert. One use to which computers have already been put has been to control the machines of the industrial revolution. The role of the computer in guiding space vehicles is an important case in point, as has been the development of the guidance system for the cruise missiles system. All through industry, cybernetics has proven to be a significant science, putting computers to use for directing complex industrial processes performed by machines. The development of computer technology does not abrogate the technology of power and replace it with another entirely different technology, but gives the technology of power new dimensions by controlling power machinery in new and more complex ways.

One of the most frequently and hotly debated issues concerning computers is whether, given sufficient development and refinement, they can entirely duplicate and perhaps even excel the working of the human mind. Sherry Turkle, in her study on the effect of computers on the thinking of those who use them,[9] has reported that some members of the computer community think of their minds in terms of the computer as a model even more than they think of computers as extensions or variations of their minds. Although this observation suggests how pervasive the computer may already have become as the defining technology of our era, it also introduces a new discussion—whether computers can be said to be "intelligent" and, if so, in what sense.

The contention that the computer will eventually think as human beings think, and do so with something that approaches the independent initiative of a human will, is a matter of serious and intense debate. In his book *What Computers Can't Do: The Limits of Artificial Intelligence*,[10] Hubert Dreyfus expresses a deep skepticism about whether computers can ever be designed or programmed to acquire anything that can plausibly be considered akin to the mental capability of the human person. In a similar line of argument, J. Weizenbaum, in *Computer Power and Human Reason: From Judgment to Calculation*,[11] has taken the stance that computers should be thought of strictly as "unthinking tools," and that they do not, and never will, have the capacity to respond to persons as, for instance, therapists respond to their patients. In contrast, Geoff Simons, of the National Computing Centre in England, in his book *Are Computers Alive?: An Essay in Emergent Systems*,[12] argues that computers actually represent a new life form—a kind of progenitor of a new and as yet unimagined species of life that will eventually come to inhabit Earth. His case is based in part on the experience of computer users who sense that they confront a device that is capable of making independent responses—a device with which some form of cognitive, and maybe even emotional, intercourse is experienced.

The usual hypothesis used for judging whether computers can duplicate human intelligence is the "Turing Test." This test imagines a computer terminal wired to receive responses from a hidden human person and the same terminal connected to a computer having the alleged capabilities of a human mind. The two connections can be switched back and forth without the knowledge of the operator. If the computer can make responses so that the operator of the terminal cannot distinguish between the personal respondent and the computer, then the computer can be alleged to have artificial intelligence.

The discussion of artificial intelligence will gain clarity if we become clearer about the role and functions of human reflection. If, for example, we mean by the term intelligence the capacity to memorize (store) information, then it does make sense to think about artificial intelligence. There is no question about the capacity of computers to store data; indeed, they can or certainly will be able to store data on a scale that dwarfs the capacity of the human memory. Within a decade, even home-sized computers may make available to every person all the known information of the human species. But memory is useless without recall. The data in computers can be used only if it can be accessed. The program that makes accessing possible is devised by the natural intelligence of the programmer, not by the machine. A technology may arise that changes this, but it is hard to imagine, from what we now know, that any computer will be so constructed or so completely self-programmed that no human agency is involved in either initiating or guiding its accessing of information.

If by intelligence we mean the capacity to compare two items, or two groups of items, then as far as those items can be represented in ways that can be programmed into a computer, it is also legitimate to speak about computers as having this aspect of intelligence. Indeed, computers can greatly extend the range of data that may be compared—not because the human mind is necessarily slower in forming a judgment when evidence is before it, but because our ordinary means of bringing data to awareness are more limited than computerized means. But the making of comparisons is dependent on the capacity of the programmer to define and direct the making of those comparisons. Programming, which is done by human intelligence, determines what will be compared and how it will be compared. It is hard to project a situation in which such matters will not depend on the way machines are programmed by human intelligence. A similar set of considerations relates to the function of the human intelligence that enables recognition. Recognition may be only a complex form of comparison, but some of the same possibilities and limitations that apply to the first apply to the second as well.

Still another function of the natural intelligence is to foresee and, to a limited degree, anticipate future events. Computers can be programmed to assist certain kinds of predictions. They can be used to predict the movement of the stars, galaxies, and planets that operate according to known natural laws; they can be programmed to predict the outcomes of certain logistical matters, such as how the budget of an institution will be affected by changes in factors like tuition adjustments, student body size, and inflation rate. Computers are enormously helpful in such functions, but they only shorten the time needed to make calculations that could be made more laboriously by the natural intelligence. They can do so only because they can be programmed by an intelligent human who understands the complexities involved.

Computers may make it possible to predict natural happenings that cannot as yet be "called" because the causative factors are too complex. Long-range weather forecasts, the paths of hurricanes or tornadoes, and the number of degree days that will be experienced in a particular winter season—the sort of things that are now called "acts of God"—may become more comprehensible if the capacity to coordinate the myriad influences that produce them becomes more manageable with the use of the computer. But will it not be necessary for natural intelligence first to understand the many factors involved before computers can be programmed to make such predictions?

Will computers ever be able to predict the ways in which human agents will make decisions in historical situations? Will they ever be able to predict events in the life history of individuals, as they now can predict actuarial averages of group experience? Could they predict where a conflict might break out, where a terrorist is going to strike next, what the stock market will do, or a host of similar matters that cannot now be predicted with the natural intelligence?

A still more complex level of human thinking that we are able to do naturally, perhaps even more readily than we can predict future events, is evaluation. How the human mind makes evaluative judgments is not clear. People come to different evaluations of the same factors—whether engaged in aesthetic judgments, strategic judgments, moral judgments, or judgments that enter into the forming of contrasting world views. But suppose that we could agree on what factors are involved in making evaluative judgments, and suppose that these could be defined in ways enabling them to be programmed into computers. Such programs as might be devised would depend on the exercise of the natural intelligence of those who construct them. Those using computer programs capable of making evaluative judgments would be using a matrix created by a human intelligence, rather than a thought process originating in the machine.

These several considerations are raised to suggest the complexity of the discussion that is required in order to understand the challenges that computers create, not to provide a philosophical or theological preemption of the possibility that computers can or will be able to do things that the human mind can do, or even things qualitatively beyond what the human mind can do. It is not required that computers prove capable of doing all these things in order to contend that it is possible to speak of artificial intelligence. However, some commentators on these matters believe that the time will come when computers can do qualitatively different things than the human mind can do, and that artificial intelligence will, in time, go beyond human capacity and in effect become a new level of being. When such an inflated contention is used to define artificial intelligence, the concept becomes problematic.

Even if computers do turn out to be a higher form of cognitive life, no effort to prevent that from occurring will be permanently effective. Prior restraints on scientific developments have never been successful and can hardly be expected to be so in this instance. One development, however, needs to be avoided. The computer must not become such an all-controlling paradigm that it is permitted to be the model into which all thinking about the nature and limits of human intelligence is forced. Human intelligence includes the capacity to wonder, even to wonder about what computers will do, to discern meanings in facts and interpret the significance of events, as well as to gather information. Human intelligence continuously transcends itself and even asks what selfhood is. It is by no means clear that computers will ever do those things, and even less clear that they will do them as acts of independent initiative, rather than as responses to programmed commands. Only a completely self-programming computer would have the self-transcending quality that is associated with human agency in its broadest and most valuable dimensions, and there is no such computer in actual or foreseeable existence.

The Impacts of Computers

Regardless of the nature and limits of the computer's capability, it has already had tremendous impacts on our lives. We have all begun to sense the impact of these changes: computerized banking, computerized mailing lists used by commercial and philanthropic organizations, identification cards that can be instantly changed or voided at a central control station, and computerized reservation systems that deal with our travel needs with incredible speed. Many of us are also using the word-processing techniques that are proving more efficient (and also more expensive) than the typewriters on which we depended for decades. Many pharmacists now keep records of drugs dispensed, to prevent the giving of medicines in the wrong combinations. In time, such records might be interlocked with one another so as to prevent innocent people from taking dosages of medicines that would produce adverse side effects and less innocent people from maintaining dependency on drugs through misuse of the prescription process. A clerk at the local office of a mail order house can now punch a few buttons and report instantly on the inventory status of an item in a warehouse many miles away or place an order almost as rapidly. The mails, dependent on the machines of the first industrial revolution, don't bring an item any faster, but the ordering process has been revolutionized, and computers may soon offer a solution to the mail problem as well. In the "office of the future," communication will be by electronic device rather than by courier, and documents will be transmitted across the country in minutes rather than in days.

Many of the things that computers can do are quite amazing, and we have reason to be excited about the future. But there are sobering contrasts in our use of computers that give us cause for concern. For instance, computers have been programmed to teach young people, even very young people, to play war games but not to engage in conflict resolution. They have been put to use guiding space flight but not in resolving disputes at the United Nations. They can quite easily be programmed to make out payrolls but not to solve labor disputes. Although computers have been used to up the efficiency of tax enforcement, they have not been as extensively used to create more efficient welfare systems. It may be that our natural ways of thinking understand how to do the one set of things better than the other—but it may also be that the uses to which we have put computers reveal the things about which we as a society care most and are willing to budget resources to accomplish. Perhaps in time, computers will be programmed to do the now neglected things with dispatch, but that remains to be seen. Indeed, the extent to which it is possible to regard the computer as making a contribution to humanity may depend on whether we come to stress some of the things we now neglect and to neglect some of the things we now stress.

There are some interesting contrasts between the trends in the development of computers and in the development of industrial machines. Industrial machines tend to become bigger and bigger as their capacity for work is increased. The technology of computers has become smaller and smaller, even as capacity has been increased manyfold. We may approach a threshold at which it is no longer possible to shrink the size of computers drastically while increasing capacity. There are theoretical limits that may become practical problems. It takes electricity a certain time to travel along a conductor ($10-^9$ seconds to travel 11 inches), but the limits in the size reduction of machines imposed by this consideration do not yet stare us in the face.

Moreover, the machines and the mechanical and chemical processes that are associated with the industrial revolution have frequently produced adverse consequences on the environment. Computer technology does not seem to have these side effects on the massive scale that many industrial technologies do. The use of computers does not produce harmful toxic wastes and gobble up nonrenewable resources in massive quantities. There are some hazards to the workers and to the environment involved in the manufacturing of computer equipment, however. The chemicals used in the making of microchips are toxic, and workers are often women in Third World settings who are not fully protected by health and safety laws. In other words, the computer revolution is not problem free, although it poses issues of a somewhat different order—not necessarily less momentous—than those of industrial technology. It is these problems to which attention is now turned.

Most of us probably think first of the problems raised by computers in relationship to events that have been journalistically reported in recent months—events such as the unauthorized penetration of data bases by "hackers" doing so more for the lark than for criminal purposes. If such persons can get information out of Pentagon files or the programs of major corporations for "playful" purposes, then it must also be possible for those with malicious objectives to gain access to information in confidential files, to balances in private bank accounts, or to any other data that identifies a person or controls significant processes.[13] The accumulation of information about persons who take unpopular stands or do unpopular things poses a possible threat to civil liberties, particularly when there is no way to verify such information.[14] Is it wise or legitimate to allow large amounts of data to be accumulated in the first place? What social pressures and legal mandates will be needed to see that the users of computers are adequately zealous in protecting people from unauthorized intrusion into or from the misuse of the information that is collected about them?

The responsibility for preventing unauthorized access to information stored in computer systems must be placed on the owners and users of those systems. It is not sufficient simply to make it illegal for the general public to intrude. Just as many states require people to remove the ignition keys and lock the doors of their cars to prevent thefts, so the makers of data banks must be required to take adequate measures to safeguard privacy. The use of access code words alone is not a sufficient safeguard, since these break down or can be circumvented by human cleverness. For instance, a code of three or four letters can be broken with little effort, particularly if a computer system is not designed to reject all but a correct first entry of the password. Security must be more stringent when public phone lines are used to carry information to and from outside stations. One way to do this is with a call-back arrangement that requires users to identify themselves and their locations. Some of these arrangements are relatively simple and require only a deliberate decision to install them and require their use. But others can be more costly, and more than voluntary good will may be necessary to see that they are followed. Computer privacy cannot be assured merely by condemning unauthorized access if the technological arrangements "leave the keys in the ignition."

A second kind of problem is the mistakes that creep into the accumulation of data. Errors occur at every level—in collecting data, in key punching, in running programs, etc. James Martin and Adrian R.D. Norman, in their book *The Computerized Society: An Appraisal of the Impact of Computers on Society over the Next Fifteen Years,*[15] have a long section entitled "Alarm" that is sandwiched between a section called "Euphoria" and a section called "Protective Action." The "alarms" these authors sound include the invasions of privacy associated with computer use and the dangers involved in collecting unsubstantiated and trivial information from numerous sources, the activity that has come to be known as *cyberveillance.* In addition, they cite the errors that programmers and machines can make, the possibility for harassment that stems from the possession and control of such information, the possibility that computers can be used by criminals, and the occurrence of billing errors. They could also have considered the effects of computer use on the engineering of election campaigns and even the premature identification of winners.

The greatest possibilities for mistakes are probably located in the data-gathering and data-entering processes, rather than in the running of programs. Groups collect such vast amounts of data, often without the knowledge of those about whom the data is gathered, that the possibility of error is enormous and the opportunity to detect and correct it, minimal. The corner grocer who knew each customer on an intimate basis could spot a billing error without much difficulty, but the computer that spews out major accounts from a data-processing unit halfway across the country has no way of picking up flukes. Moreover, it is not always to the self-interest of those who operate computers to ferret out such errors, even if they are detected and reported. Almost everyone has heard about some failure to make corrections, even when they have been pointed out. Why should a company go to great expense to seek perfection in its records if general accuracy seems to suffice?

All these are real problems. Many of them can be overcome but only if there is a deliberate public will to require it. The problem for society is to understand such dangers and devise ways of creating and sustaining the public will to counteract them. The responsibility for correcting such misuse must be put on the users of computers. It is not enough to punish misappropriation of information; it is also important to prevent its unauthorized or accidental dissemination. Those who decide to use computer billing procedures, for instance, should be forced to accept the cost of seeing that such possibilities are minimized and of redressing the damage done if they occur. If the cost of doing these things offsets the savings from installing a computer system, the use of the computer should probably be abandoned. Court actions under tort law and legislative mandates against particular practices are both possible ways of requiring those who use computers to accept the responsibilities for dealing with information about individuals. The precedents for this are not good. For decades, those who use the machines and processes of the industrial revolution have been allowed to pass along ecological damages as "external costs" borne by the public. It will be unfortunate to repeat that error with respect to computers.

Still another set of problems needs attention, and that is, "How general should computer use become?" A certain liberal arts college has decided that computer literacy is an essential aspect of a liberal education, and therefore has decided to require all students to purchase and use computers in their learning. This "computer-initiative" has been quite consciously used as a selling point in the scramble for students, but it has a more thoughtful justification. It is based on a belief that a person will not be able to function adequately in the world of the future without some computer literacy.

This requirement raises several issues. Why is computer literacy more a requisite for students than good penmanship? Why have students never been required to own typewriters? To be sure, computers do many things that typewriters cannot, and they do facilitate learning, particularly in mathematics and engineering. But should students who, on other grounds, qualify for an advanced education be required to learn how to use the computer? Will, or should, it become a requirement for faculty advancement, and if so, will all faculty members be required to qualify as programmers as well as operators of word processors? Can everyone learn to use a computer productively? Not all computer experts believe that computer literacy is universally possible. (Alas, sometimes one comes to wonder if ordinary literacy is universally possible.) What would be the social consequences if every college required computer literacy for a degree? What poetic spirits with tendencies to be electronic Luddites would be excluded from education were that to happen? Is not the presence of such spirits an enrichment to the community of general learning? Or, suppose we were eventually to computerize the voting process. Would it be proper to make the capacity to use a computer a test for voting, even as literacy was once made a test? To expect too high a level of computer skill among a whole population could be to require a conformity that is incompatible with a society that honors and cultivates freedom and a variety of talents.

Moreover, it must be recognized that computer literacy can easily become another means for exacerbating social inequalities. When public school financing is done by local districts, the affluent districts will have the resources to purchase computers, whereas the marginal districts will not. Privileged groups will be given the opportunity to learn the skills that make advancement possible, while impoverished groups will not. Such a consequence can be counteracted by intentional social policy, but the ideological climate in which we find ourselves seems adverse to the idea that the affluent should help the impoverished.

A not unrelated question concerns the portion of social resources that ought to be expended on computers. This question arises on an intramural basis in many educational institutions today. Should a college spend as much, or more, on computing facilities as it does on library services? The question needs to be answered by different institutions in different ways, but it should not be swept under the administrative rug. It deserves better answers than those that emerge from a balancing of contending claims based on internal campus power struggles.

In business, where monetary balances are the "bottom line," questions of resource allocation can possibly be resolved by a cost/benefit analysis, although it is quite essential to be hard-nosed about the counting of costs. For instance, now that I have an office computer, I make my syllabi ready for photocopying whereas before I only made good enough copy for a secretary to type from. It may be that I am saving the time of a secretary rather than my own, but the other possibility is that I will contribute to "pink-collar" unemployment. Or, where before the business office went on a computer, we could requisition travel advances or reimbursements on short notice, now we have to wait at least forty-eight hours for a check to be mechanically written. The school computer is a marvelous help to the financial officers in ascertaining the status of school expenditures at any given time, but the less obvious costs to faculty members or employees who must do things according to a more complex routine or have to wait longer for certain things to get done can be too easily overlooked. Perhaps the question is less "Do computers save time?" than "Whose time do they save, and whose time is it most important to save?" The hard-nosed asking of such questions may be far wiser than odes of ecstasy about the promise of computers for eliminating drudgery from the modern world.

Another inquiry that needs to be pursued, although with great care, concerns the effects that computers have on the quality of the lives of those who use them. Is there an experience with computers that carries the self beyond a good healthy relationship to a tool into a level of interaction that is quasi-addictive? To be sure, that question does not need to be asked only about computers. It needs to be asked about cars and other kinds of inventions. Sherry Turkle has examined this matter in her book *The Second Self: Computers and the Human Spirit.*[16] A "hacker" may be as psychically enthralled with the computer as the drug addict or alcoholic is dependent on the intake of chemicals, although the consequences may be somewhat more socially productive. If a person comes to relate only to computers, eschewing all interaction with other persons and all other kinds of experiences and interchanges, that person can well be said to be deprived of those dimensions that make for humanity. Even though the problem, in most circumstances, involves a personality defect, rather than being a function of the computer, the computer becomes no longer a tool, but an addiction. Computers are fascinating devices; they provide feedback that makes them seem highly interactional. That raises the need to take the possible consequences of using them into account so that we remain masters rather than becoming mastered.

A number of educators have been concerned about an overemphasis on the use of the computer in education, particularly at too early an age.[17] They have charged that an experience at the keyboard—before which one sits almost motionless—is a poor substitute for real-life experiences. Birds and flowers on a screen are not the birds and flowers of smells and tastes, of song and motion. This could also be said of birds and flowers on a printed page, but the possibility of deception may not be as great. One educator has gone so far as to suggest that a computer-dominated school would produce a generation of psychopaths because computers give a false sense of ease. There are contrasting judgments about the nature and possibility of computer learning. Some observers are impressed with the ways in which it frees students to let their imagination soar by lightening the drudgery of learning.

Computers may also have a tendency to change the patterns of interaction between members of organizations. Some departments in educational institutions have tried dispensing with face-to-face faculty meetings and have attempted to transact business through interlocked terminals. Those who have sat through long faculty meetings understandably entertain prospects of relief when first hearing about such arrangements. But if decisions come to be centered entirely in keyboards, an element of communal identity and interpersonal interaction could be lost. The use of interkeyboard communication in industry may have a profound effect—even a healthy effect—on the traditional hierarchical lines of authority, since entries into keyboards can be made anonymously or without the direct interaction between people having different levels of authority. But is not face-to-face interchange as valuable to the working world as to the leisure world?

The mere ownership of or ready access to a computer has become a kind of status gambit in certain circles. (I have not one, but two at my disposal!) Within proper bounds, prestige games are fun to play, but they can also become a source of rancor and estrangement, like other tests of status. In group terms, as sociological studies of the culture of "Silicon Valley" and "Route 128" show, certain attitudes develop in high-tech culture that need to be watched with care for personal strain. According to Everett M. Rogers and Judith K. Larson, in *Silicon Valley Fever: Growth of High-Technology Culture,*[18] there is a dark side to high-tech—professional burnout, exploitation of assembly line workers, pollution, technological espionage, and alienated wives and children. These problems may reside more in the socioeconomic system of fierce competitiveness than in computers as such, but they bear investigation and examination on a continuing basis.

Conclusion

One of the vexing things about technology assessment is the difficulty in foreseeing what the consequences of particular inventions or of new ways of doing things will be. We usually learn what the problems are only after new discoveries have been made and put to use on a wide scale. We can make some efforts through a process of imaginative investigation to avoid being caught off guard. Computers may well help in assessing the possible consequences of further developments in the technologies of power. But we will learn about their benefits and costs mainly from trial and error as they come to have a larger and larger place in our lives. We can try to be aware of some of the possibilities and avoid the sanguine naiveté that has allowed us to stumble into some technological developments that have proven more costly to habitate than beneficial to humanity. Only as we are sensitive and concerned will we get the maximum benefits from the revolutionary developments in computerization that are taking place all about us.

PART VII.

Family
and Women's Lives

FIFTEEN

Conflict over Sexuality: The Family

John R. Wilcox

*T*he family embraces many areas of concern within the field of Christian social ethics. This chapter deals with two of these areas: the manner in which the family is defined and the formalism of role assignment. Because moral normativity is given to the traditional nuclear family, other types of families or alternate ways of living are ignored, disdained, or excluded: the single person, cohabiting couples, gay marriages, childless couples, single-parent families, and blended families. A focus on roles becomes formalistic, since personhood is blurred when the emphasis in on identification as wife, husband, mother, father, daughter, son. An approach to family that affirms respect for the dignity of the person is needed. To a great extent, this essay is about women. Their liberation from a restrictive place in the family traditionally understood has broad implications for the enhancement of life in the last part of the twentieth century. These considerations about the family conclude with policy recommendations for church and state that will increase the stability of family life and be responsive to changes taking place in American society.

Introduction

A recent newspaper article highlights the need for a reassessment of our ethical analysis of the family: "Nearly 50 percent of black families are headed by women . . . , and 5 percent of black children are born to single

John R. Wilcox, Director of the Center for Professional Ethics and Associate Professor of Religious Studies, Manhattan College, Bronx, New York.

mothers. Many of them are raised in poverty because women, and particularly black women, on the average earn less than men."[1]

Although the article points out that many households headed by black women are healthy and stable, it is a fact that many others only survive. This marginalization and feminization of poverty is a scandal in our society, but the problem also raises searching questions about the family, questions involving personal values as well as the larger social context within which individuals and groups live and act. For instance, do these groupings headed by women truly constitute a family? If so, are they the exception? Where are the fathers, and what are they contributing to family maintenance? If these women work, who takes care of the children? Is there adequate care if the mother is away for long periods of time? What obligations does the larger community have to these families?

Repealing Reticence

The example chosen to begin this discussion of the family is indicative of several of my own presuppositions in writing about social ethics. First, personal ethics and social ethics cannot be compartmentalized. They interact and overlap. The family, a school for intimacy, is a set of intensely personal relationships; at one and the same time it constitutes a fundamental social institution, since it is the usual context for species survival. These personal and social dimensions are not isolated one from the other; the quality of species survival is closely connected with the quality of intimacy; in humans they go hand in hand. Thus, the quality of social life is greatly affected by the quality of life in the black families headed by women.

Christian social ethics takes seriously the questions of domestic virtue and personal sexual ethics but also sees them as integrally linked to the structural problems in which the family has been enmeshed in the recent past. Can one speak of family tranquillity without considering high continuing rates of unemployment, rates that are clearly related to domestic violence, health problems, and family stress?[2] Can familial well-being endure when functional power remains vested in the husband because of pervasive patriarchy? Can there be true marital fidelity as long as women are not treated justly and as equal partners, as long as they are abused physically in the home as well as symbolically in pornography? To press the issue even further, what definition of family is used in formulating public policy and what type of sexual ethics dictates guidelines for contraceptive availability and access to abortion? This issue of definition leads to another belief about social ethics.

A second presupposition is that care must be given to the definitions used in social ethics because the definitions themselves are often loaded with moral norms. Does family have a morally normative content so that it is understood as constituted by husband as breadwinner, wife as homemaker, and children? Or does the term family begin with an understanding of how individuals experience relationships and intimacy and then proceed to the construction of a formal definition? Thus, in the example provided, do we indict the single-parent family because of values implicit in our definition of the family?

A third presupposition is that social and behavioral sciences play a significant role in ethical analysis. Christian social ethics assesses the family as an institution that can only be understood by evaluating the social context within which the family exists. A subspecialty of general Christian ethics, Christian social ethics seeks to evaluate the good and bad in human activity, as well as structures developed in society, bringing to such evaluation the normative criteria of individual dignity rights and social justice demands. Christian social ethics views human activity in the light of gospel values and the wealth of teaching and tradition in the churches.

Because its area of concern is social structure, institutions, and human interaction, social ethics relies heavily on the social and behavioral sciences in its method. This is clearly the case in the analysis of family life. Reliance on these sciences does not guarantee truth or "objectivity." They, too, are open to bias and self-serving justifications, as much victims of a time period as they are identifiers of change and social problems.[3] Of course, Christian social ethics is equally susceptible to being as self-serving, rationalizing, and ideological as any empirically based science. For instance, racism and sexism, endemic and pervasive as they have been in American society, have not always been identified by political scientist, sociologist, or ethicist. Examination of one's own premises, world view, or self-interest is integral to doing Christian ethics honestly.[4] Thus, the ethical analysis of the family must be done courageously but critically, realizing the tendency to blindness and rationalization.

Closely related to these three presuppositions are the norms used in this discussion of family life. A governing principle in this chapter is that individuals must be treated with respect and dignity. This fundamental ethical norm is bound up with the theological understanding that God is closest to us in our human experience. Revelation comes to us through our personal and social history. Practically speaking, this means accepting people as they are, embracing them compassionately, and assisting them in ways that will enhance their human dignity and heighten their capacity for intimacy. This principle clearly enters the discussion of family and the analysis of role assignment as these are developed in this chapter.

Thus, we seek to discern what God is saying to us in the many forms in which people express their intimacy and continue the species. We bring to this process the norm of respect for the dignity and rights of the person,

261

especially of those who are powerless and suffering. Although all may agree with this approach, not all will assent to the conclusions drawn after assessing the family today in the light of the presuppositions and principles laid out here, especially in terms of public policy recommendations.

The Family: Respect for Women and Diversity of Form

Family means many things to many people. Families take many shapes and configurations, function differently, and relate in varied ways to the society at large. Despite the diversity of family life, one form—the traditional nuclear family—has had a morally normative status. The Christian ethicist can neither ignore the diversity of family life nor simply accept the elevated moral status ascribed to the nuclear (breadwinner+homemaker+children) family. Why is this so? Ethical analysis cannot fly in the face of human experience. If we take seriously the God of history, then God is speaking to us through the events, the strivings, the commitments of people's lives. In that light, the ethicist cannot afford to make judgments about the moral worth of individuals based on a particular family category. The ministry of all Christians begins with the compassionate embrace of the person in all of his or her wholeness or brokenness. If the Christian ethicist does not begin there, individuals will find the compassion of God elsewhere.

When Margaret Mead was asked if she thought equality between the sexes would ever be achieved, she immediately responded: "It depends on who takes care of the children."[5] That remark brings to the fore one of the central issues we face today: the changing role of women in the family. Although long hours and hard work have been the enduring characteristics of women working at home, in agriculture, or in industry down through the centuries,[6] the numbers pursuing work for hourly wages or in career tracks away from home for significant periods of time have had a profound impact on the contemporary family.[7]

A second income does allow for some families to hire help for child care and domestic work such as cooking and cleaning, but in the majority of cases, this income is insufficient for those purposes, since it is necessary for basic income maintenance.[8] Women traditionally earn less than men, even for comparable work, a fact that compounds the financial problem and takes its own psychological toll on women.[9] Thus, it does often come down to "who takes care of the kids?" If the mother is working all day, away from the home for eight or more hours, who will be the primary agent of socialization during that time, since the father usually works also? What type of attention can be given to the children if both parents arrive home in the evening having to cook meals, do housework, shop? Statistics indicate that these tasks still fall generally to the women.[10] Will parents who have spent the better part of their day at work be able to fulfill the intimacy needs of children, assist with homework, and prepare them for bed with sufficient energy and concentration?

If all goes well in the marketplace, then these tasks may well be accomplished with finesse. If work is a place of tension and competitiveness, these problems compound the difficulties experienced in a two-paycheck family. There is no doubt that women are even more vulnerable to difficulties in the workplace than men are. Discrimination in hiring, treatment, promotion, and wages cannot be left in the office at five o'clock. They inflict wounds to be carried home. And for many women, there is resentment at having to work, since they make so little money.[11] Along with the additional burdens of homemaker that most women bear, the psychological burdens of work can contribute to an unpleasant atmosphere at home.

The foregoing description presumes a certain definition of the family: father, mother, and children. Family is such a common word that definitions are passed over all too quickly. In the social and behavioral sciences, as well as in Christian ethics, what is empirically descriptive often becomes morally normative without acknowledgment of the transformation. The definition presumed here of father, mother, and children, commonly called the nuclear family, is complicated because a further qualification is frequently added—"traditional."[12] The traditional nuclear family too easily becomes morally normative for all people. It is a powerful symbol influencing us in many ways, even though not statistically preponderant.

The traditional nuclear family, consisting of father (= breadwinner), mother (= homemaker), and children living together as an economic unit, plays an important role in American self-understanding, if not in actuality.[13] Put another way, 29.4 percent of husband-wife families fit the category of being nuclear. Of this percentage, 10.1 percent have no children, thus reducing the "typical American family (with children)" to 19.3 percent.[14] Given the small number of such traditional nuclear families, one must ask why it has such importance.

One possible explanation for the definition of family taking on tones of moral normativity can be found in the dominance of patriarchalism or male sexism, both of which have provided a social framework for Western society and the United States in particular.[15] The traditional nuclear family protects male identity and the economic power base of the male spouse, since that family form contains the expectation that the husband is breadwinner and everyone else is dependent on him.[16] It thus becomes obvious that any discussion of family life immediately raises ethical issues relative to the status of women and the presumed superior status of males.

As a result of this nuclear normativity, a judgment is made on other ways of living: "remaining single is immature, cohabitation is immoral, homosexual marriages are perverse, childless marriages are selfish, families with more than four children are irresponsible, single-parent families are broken homes, blended families are unhappy."[17] The fact that the lack of social support for any of these alternatives in life-style might actually cause problems is often overlooked. Finally, the ultimate stamp of condemnation for many of these forms comes from the religious traditions that view them as being against God's (= His) will. The religious traditions in the West, moreover, are themselves patriarchal, thus such a condemnation also protects male domination of social structure.

James Nelson reminds us, however, that Jesus relativized every human institution (as in Mark 2:27). "He taught us, in effect, that form follows function. If the function of marriage, family, and home is to serve authentic human needs, then forms should adapt to serve precisely that."[18] How significant, then, are alternatives to the traditional family?

The Single State

The Census Bureau reported that "in 1982, almost 12 percent of women and 17 percent of men aged 30 to 34 had never married. . . . That was almost double the percent of never-married single people in 1970, when 6 percent of women and 9 percent of men had never married."[19] What is significant is that the Bureau interprets these changes as the choosing of a permanent life-style. A similar trend was noted among the mid-to-late twenties group. "Twenty-three percent of women and more than a third of men in that age group were still single in 1982, compared with 11 percent of women and 19 percent of men in 1970."[20] Although single individuals are not considered family units, the increase in their numbers must be taken into account in assessing the family.

Cohabitation

Understood as unmarried heterosexual union, cohabitation has also increased significantly. The U.S. Bureau of the Census reported in June 1982 that the number of couples went from 523,000 in 1970 to 1,808,000 in 1981, a 246 percent increase.[21] These statistics might be somewhat misleading, since they include nonintimate relationships, such as an elderly woman renting to a male college student. However, "enough couples are openly living together in intimate relationships that some theorists now consider living together an ongoing part of the mate selection process for a growing minority of couples."[22]

Gay Marriages

Homosexual couples exist, but their numbers are hard to determine because little research has been done in this area. Social disapproval makes it more difficult for such relationships to continue.[23] The point here is not so much an accurate statistic, but the more open, nonjudgmental discussion that is becoming more prominent, thus overshadowing the disapproval of this alternative life-style. In fact, authors John Scanzoni and Letha Scanzoni refer to the "Gay Marriage Alternative" in one of their books.[24] Researchers point out that, regardless of sexual orientation, most people desire close loving relationships.[25]

Childless Couples

Childless couples sometimes are confused with couples who delay having children. Census Bureau statistics for 1983 indicate that the median age for women marrying in 1982 was 22.5, up from between 20.2 and 20.4 for women between 1950 and 1969.[26] "The best current estimates of childlessness and parenthood in the United States among currently married women ages fifteen to forty-four are: 2 percent are voluntarily childless, 2 percent are involuntarily childless."[27] However, "the Census Bureau reported that three times as many wives under thirty expected to remain childless in 1975, 4.6 percent, as in 1964, 1.7 percent."[28]

Single-Parent Family

The single-parent family has increased significantly since the 1970s. Statistically, there has been a 66 percent increase between 1970 and 1982. In the latter year, 25 percent of all children, or about 13.7 million, lived with one parent, as opposed to 12 percent in 1970. The overwhelming majority (90 percent) live with their mothers, a constant pattern since early in this century.[29] Significantly, 53 percent of black households and 31 percent of Hispanic homes had one parent, compared with 19 percent for white families.[30]

The Blended Family

There is little research available on the blended family, that is, remarriage involving the uniting of two families.[31] The high rate of divorce, however, will certainly influence the number of blended families. "Between 1955 and 1965 ... about 1 percent of all married couples divorced. Between 1965 and 1975, however, the divorce rate rose to 2.2 percent of all married couples."[32] Although this does signify that marriage is quite durable, the number of children involved in divorce has increased from 261,000 in 1956 to 1,123,000 in 1975. "If the current divorce rate does not decline, there is a 50 percent probability that a person will be a member of a blended family (stepfamily) as a child, parent, or stepparent."[33] The divorced do not remain in that state. Many remarry and do so quickly.

The Family: Roles and Persons

The family understood in terms of children, or in the traditional nuclear sense, is exclusionary. This problem is compounded by another highly formalistic definition of the family, one that defines people according to roles played. In focusing on roles, the traditional definition of family reinforces patriarchal attitudes and values. Thus, in a text on marriage and family from the 1950s we read: "We may define the family structurally as a systematic aggregate or organized unity of persons carrying basic social roles. These are husband and wife; parent and child."[34]

An emphasis on relationship between or among people is not only more inclusive than an emphasis on role, but it also does not necessarily include children. Rather, it gives pointed recognition to the centrality of person and intimacy.[35] One can protest that this is really a discussion of marriage as opposed to family. If family automatically implies children, then significant ways of relating, as previously described, are excluded. Why is that important? Because the definition of family that must include children all too easily becomes ethically normative, as already seen. This does not mean that children are unimportant or that most families will have none in the future. It is just that there must be great sensitivity to those who have intimacy needs that do not include offspring.

Not only is it a question of sensitivity to variation, but also an issue of justice toward and equality for women. The traditional definition of family reinforces patriarchy and the denigration of women, which is the central ethical issue facing the family. Furthermore, an emphasis on spousal relationships counteracts the child-centered marriage, in which parents live for their children and find themselves with little in common when their offspring are born and much disillusionment when the children become independent and leave home. In many instances, parents then must painstakingly rebuild their marriage.[36]

In contrast to the traditional definition of family the following is offered:

> A family is any sexually expressive or parent-child relationship in which (a) people live together with a commitment, in an intimate, interpersonal relationship; (b) the members see their identity as importantly attached to the group; and (c) the group has an identity of its own.[37]

Respect for the Dignity of the Person

The enduring and constant ethical issue in family life across the variations in form is the need for a nonexclusionary and dynamic respect for the person. The impetus to overcome the traditional family's patriarchal structure and its concomitant abuse of power derives from this respect. It is difficult even to focus on this patriarchal structure as an ethical question because it is so pervasive, widely accepted as natural, and seen as ordained by God (a masculine deity). As long as the churches are built on this same model, whether in theology or in practice, religion will continue powerfully to reinforce an unjust social situation.

The family has been defined in such a way that one type—the traditional nuclear—has become morally normative. Furthermore, the family has been defined in terms of roles fulfilled within a patriarchal society. Role subsumes person, leading to a formalistic understanding of family life. These exclusionary, formalistic approaches, often unspoken, enter our social ethics, church policy, and public policy. Policymakers in the church and in public life must examine their individual and collective consciences. Respect for the person should impel them to accept the diverse form of family life chosen. Such acceptance will demonstrate itself in policies and programs that are profoundly shaped by this fundamental principle of ethics. Within the family, this same respect should be evident in a focus on the person and his or her self-actualization, especially needs for a sense of self-worth and intimacy. To a large extent, women would be the beneficiaries of such change.

This essay is written in the belief that God is calling us to respond to the times in both a personal and a social way. At the core of this response lies the fundamental ethical principle: respect for the dignity of the person. This unprovable yet foundational dimension of moral behavior and ethical reasoning is the starting point for choosing the good and doing what is right.

Because it is fundamental but unprovable, we take the dignity of the person for granted, frequently trivializing it. This statement can be made without hesitation when one studies, for instance, Western Christianity. In the name of God and civilization, whole classes of persons have been systematically denied their dignity: women, blacks, Indians, the poor. Thus, the irony: while affirming this most fundamental principle in ethics and religion, it has been systematically and flagrantly abused in practice, as if that which is closest and most important to us is repelled the most violently or ignored with the greatest indifference and callousness. "Because persons are so valuable," says Daniel Maguire, "we owe them fidelity and truth and justice."[38] Although this obligation is honored more in the breach than in the observance, the justified anger at sinfulness here must be directed at all, for all have failed in this regard. Repentance begins with the "utterance of awe before the phenomenon of personhood."[39] This is the foundation for approaching family life and for a renewed definition of this keystone of society. It is "a mystical perception of the inviolable sanctity of human life."[40]

Although this mystical perception is greatly assisted by reason and the deliberation of ethicists in both the religious and the philosophical traditions, it is a perception grounded in our experience of the other as person.[41] The scales must drop from our eyes in the continual interaction with others. We must behold the person, so that "hearing we may hear, and seeing we may see." But this affirmation must lead as well to acts of respect and justice toward others. As Christians, we believe that God is known in the midst of history, in our experience of other people.[42] In this sense, the basic tenet of Christianity and the first principle of ethics meet and reinforce each other. A true believer acts on his or her faith. In the first instance, this means respect for the dignity of others, but this is a matter of seeing, a matter of faith.

A renewed definition or understanding of family depends on conversion that gives birth to interpretive frameworks sufficiently awe-inspired of persons. The very nature of patriarchy, our dominant social structure, opposes the dignity of persons as described here. Thus, family life will not be enhanced on the personal level by individuals, the churches, or society until we radically alter our perception of persons, seeing God in them as they exist and not in some idealization of what the person should be. In other words, we must work at the development of a consciousness whereby the person is valued. On this basis, the institution of the family will take on new meaning and be understood in terms of a new definition, one that is inclusive and person-oriented.

Policy Recommendations

In view of the emphasis on a nonexclusionary, person-cente. approach to the family, an approach based on the fundamental ethic. principle of respect for the dignity of the person, the following policy recommendations with regard to the family are offered to church and government:

1. Church committees and synods as well as governmental agencies should examine their working definitions of family and how those definitions affect different groups of people. Do the churches and government use the traditional nuclear family as an operative, normative definition?

2. A clear commitment to justice and equality for women in the workplace must be felt in both church and government policy. The correction of pay disparity, in particular, will enhance self-esteem and power among women, with important implications for greater equality in family life.

3. Guaranteeing equal rights for homosexuals in housing and employment should be the policy of both church and government on all levels. A clear manifestation of such commitment would be the legal protection of gay/lesbian couples in the same way that heterosexual relationships are protected.

4. Providing enough day-care centers with quality programs should become a high priority. The churches often have facilities that can provide the first step in developing such centers. Government can give tax incentives to companies that institute on-site child-care programs. Local school boards should be lobbied so that all-day kindergartens and meaningful after-school programs become a reality.

5. Whatever can be done to keep families, defined as broadly as possible, intact should be given precedence by church and state. To what extent are divorces preventable? Would not government actually be saving money if qualified counselors were available to distressed families? If the dissolution of the marriage is inevitable, what resources do the churches offer the spouses and the children, if any, so that the emotional pain can be salved and new beginnings can be made?

6. What outreach do the churches have for the single person? Is there a well-thought-out pastoral program and understanding of the spiritual needs of such people? How much is known about the single life?

7. Single parents, most of whom are women, along with their children, need the greatest help. Poverty has been feminized, for it is the single mothers who are most vulnerable to unemployment, inflation, inadequate child care and housing. They are subjected to fathers who

cease child-care payments, and women find remarriage more difficult than men do.

Near the beginning of this essay I quoted from an article about households headed by black women. Many of these households are strong and enduring, signifying the depths of commitment in family life within the black community. Many others in that community live on the razor's edge. It often takes only minimum instability in one facet of the family system to fragment the life of the mother and her children. A mother's serious cold can diminish earning power, affect mealtime regularity, and weaken discipline over the children. Many, if not most, of us know of these problems only in a theoretical sense. Do we have a responsibility to do anything about feminized poverty or any of the other problems raised in this essay? The answer to this question depends on the presuppositions about society and government that each person holds.

For the Christian, society is the Body of Christ. Each is related to all and bears responsibility for all. Government, as the expression of society's will, plays a central role in the welfare of all, not simply in the negative sense of noninterference through freedom of association or religion, but in a positive sense of entitlement to education or health care. For the Christian, life is not the survival of the fittest, but the healing and redeeming of all people. This belief calls for public policy that is compassionate and caring, policy based on a rethinking of the family, so that those who choose to live together may receive social support and be accorded personal dignity and a "recognizing that at the heart of the matter we are bound to one another."[43]

SIXTEEN

To Make a Seamless Garment, Use a Single Piece of Cloth: The Abortion Debate

Christine E. Gudorf

*T*his essay is an attempt by a Catholic feminist to sort through the contemporary controversy over abortion from within a Catholic understanding of morality. Although the argument can be valuable for non-Catholics, it has been constructed using exclusively Catholic moral argumentation. Respect for human life has a long history in Catholicism. It has been treated most extensively within the context of the debates over the morality of war, specifically in the development of the just-war teaching, which distinguishes at great length combatants from noncombatants who are to be preserved inviolate. In the abortion decision, I begin with the Catholic premise that the fetus is innocent human life and urge the separation of the decision that abortion kills innocent human life from the decision that abortion must be made illegal. Separation can be justified by examination of Catholic teaching on war, especially the pastoral letter of the U.S. bishops on nuclear war. This examination demonstrates that we have in Catholic teaching on war and abortion two very different methods of moral decision-making, despite claims of and calls for a consistent ethic of life, a "seamless garment."

The distinction between a personal moral decision against abortion and a political decision by the individual to make abortion illegal is under a great deal of attack, especially in New York, where the moral integrity of prominent Catholic politicians, such as Geraldine Ferraro, has been called into question by the bishops of New York, who believe the distinction to be illegitimate.[1]

Christine E. Gudorf, Associate Professor of Theology, Xavier University, Cincinnati, Ohio. This essay has been published in *Cross Currents* 54:4. Copyright © 1985 by *Cross Currents*.

271

One must agree with the bishops, on the one hand, that personal moral conviction cannot be legitimately divorced from one's political decisions; in fact, it should not only inform, but be the foundation for those decisions. To the extent that Ferraro and others have defended their abortion positions by indicating that personal and political moral decisions are not synonymous without specifying if or how they are related, they are at fault. On the other hand, the bishops are remiss in writing glib statements that seem to equate moral principles with specific legal applications of those principles.

A legislator should not merely bow to the wishes of the majority when those wishes contradict his or her conscience, as Mario Cuomo has attested in thrice vetoing capital punishment laws desired by the majority in New York State. At the same time, when fundamental moral values are in conflict, as they are in the abortion instance, and in the absence of strong popular support for the conclusion reached by the legislators' conscience, a strong case can be made for Catholic legislators refusing to impose the conclusions of their conscience on others. The more difficult a moral decision is to reach, the less ready we should be to choose legislation as the means to promote moral change.

Sanctions for Killing
Innocent Life Directly

The similarity in Catholic teaching on war and abortion is based on the principle that one may never morally kill innocent life directly.[2] Fetal life is innocent. The debates within Catholic thought about abortion have centered traditionally on whether abortion could ever be justified as indirect, as in the case of tubal pregnancy (allowed under the principle of double effect), or whether self-defense could be used to justify abortion when the fetus constituted a threat to the life of the mother (traditionally not allowed).

It is not at the level of moral principle that our Catholic position is inconsistent. It is at the level of political application. For the direct taking of innocent life in war has always been condemned by the Church. One of the *jus in bello* conditions of just-war theory is noncombatant immunity. This is a major difficulty that the U.S. bishops have with nuclear war in the pastoral letter: it cannot be discriminate enough to preserve noncombatant immunity.

And yet the application of this principle in real life is not treated by the magisterium with any consistency. We do not have religious sanctions for those who destroy innocent life in war. How many soldiers, bomber pilots, or generals who order or carry out the destruction of villages, towns, and cities have ever been excommunicated, or even threatened with excommunication? Warfare in the twentieth century is technological, with weapons so destructive that even what we designate "conventional war" is indiscriminate. In total war, which war has been since World War I, the purpose is not merely to defeat the enemy by killing its army, but to use one's technological power to destroy the enemy's ability to make war by demolishing factories and transportation systems and breaking the will of the civilian population to support the war by destruction of civilian centers, as was done in World War II in Hamburg, Dresden, London, Tokyo, Hiroshima, and Nagasaki.[3] It is not just world wars that demonstrate this total war concept, as the bombing of Hanoi, the defoliation of South Vietnam, and the destruction of entire villages made clear in Vietnam.

Even when it is not the intention to make war on civilians (presumably because it is not thought necessary for victory), our technological systems are still prone to human error, as we saw in our bombing of the mental hospital in Grenada. In the military resistance to guerrilla warfare that the U.S. government supports in El Salvador, we are constantly reminded of Vietnam because of the difficulty in distinguishing guerrillas from innocent civilians—a difficulty so great as to erode whatever effort the military might have otherwise inclined to make.

Some will surely say that the reason the Church imposes sanctions on women who kill innocent life in abortion and not on men who kill innocent life in war is that war is so complex that it is difficult to judge individual guilt—there are orders to obey, decisions as to self-defense, and other considerations. But this is not an adequate answer. Is it so clear that the abortion decision is never complex, that women are not facing authorities with orders (employers who will fire them, men who will leave them, parents who will eject them from their homes)? Are these never situations of self-defense? Surely if the direct taking of innocent life is always immoral, and women who take one such life are subject to excommunication for mortal sin, then we would expect to find at the very least a threat of such sanctions for government figures and members of the military who might be responsible for initiating full-scale nuclear war that would kill millions of innocent lives. But we find no such threat.

Women are threatened with dire sanctions; men in the military are treated to an exercise in persuasion. To illustrate the difference, I have taken the following section from the U.S. bishops' pastoral letter but altered it to refer to pregnant women rather than members of the military. Have we heard such a message?

> 311. We remind all pregnant women and all in the medical profession that medical training and manuals have long prohibited, and still do prohibit, certain actions, especially those actions which inflict harm on persons. The question is not whether certain measures are lawful

or forbidden, but which measures: to refuse to take such measures is not an act of cowardice or blind obedience, but one of courage and responsibility.

312. We address particularly those involved in pregnancy counseling and those with responsibility for health programs. We are aware of your responsibilities and impressed by the standard of personal and professional duty you uphold. We feel therefore that we can urge you to do everything you can to insure that every other alternative is exhausted before abortion is even remotely considered. In developing plans in individual cases, and in planning social policy, we urge you to try to insure that these are designed to reduce violence, suffering and death to a minimum, remembering the innocence of the unborn.

313. Those who train medical personnel must remember that the individual does not lose his or her basic human rights either by becoming a patient or by becoming a member of a medical team. No one, for whatever reason, can justly treat a patient or a health worker with less dignity and respect than that demanded for and deserved by every human person. One of the most difficult problems with abortion involves supporting a free society wherein patients make their own choices, without endangering the right of health care workers to choose in accordance with their own values. Dehumanization of patients or health workers by removing from them decision making responsibility, or by generating hatred toward those who oppose their stance, robs them of basic human rights and freedoms, degrading them as persons.[4]

In the pastoral, we find no judgment on persons, no condemnation of those who make the wrong choice, no outlining of specific circumstances under which a pilot can decide to bomb or not to bomb a target, or a soldier to shoot or not. Instead we read:

Our pastoral contact with Catholics in military service, either through our direct experience, or through our priests, impresses us with the demanding moral standards we already see observed and the commitment to Catholic faith we find. We are convinced that the challenge of this letter will be faced conscientiously.[5]

Indeed, the bishops wrote the pastoral letter to provoke reflection and discussion on the issue of war and the taking of life in war in the conviction that such reflection and discussion is the only way to end war.[6] This choice of reflection and discussion rather than coercion as the means to affect social policy was chosen not only with reference to non-Catholics, whom the bishops do not have the power to coerce, but also with reference to Catholics, whom they do not order to conscientious objection either. Why is persuasion, rather than coercion, appropriate for dealing with one kind of social policy regarding the taking of innocent life and not appropriate for another social policy regarding the taking of innocent life?

Our Church has not been pacifist since the third century, and in fact, as late as the 1950s, we find a pronouncement by Pius XII that conscientious objection is forbidden to Catholics as irresponsible[7]—long after it was clear that modern warfare necessarily kills the innocent with the military. Why can some things be more important than preserving innocent life in war but not in reproduction? Why no primary emphasis on helping women themselves to choose to support life, rather than coercing them into parenthood? Have women so much worse a record at preserving life than the military the bishops praise?

Of course not. The historical reasons for this inconsistency lie in the separation of reality into two spheres, the public and the private, and the unconscious acceptance by the Church at the end of the nineteenth century of the notion that religion's home is in the private realm, the realm of compassion, humaneness, morality, the realm of the family, of personal relationships and faith. It is only since Vatican II that the Church has seen the public realm as an appropriate realm for full-scale mission and has begun regularly to address such issues as poverty, disarmament, human rights (other than religious), capital punishment, racism, capitalism, and others.[8] In addressing these issues, the Church still sees itself as a relative newcomer who must convince the principals of its right to participate and of the worth of its contribution. The Church speaks to persuade because it cannot coerce. It uses reason; it is careful to consult many other views and to refer deferentially to some. The process for the "Challenge of Peace" is instructive here, for before writing a word, the bishops invited to the hearings almost every political name ever associated with U.S. defense policy and most groups that deal with it. Can we assume that a letter on family policy or marriage law, or any other private realm issue, would be preceded by hearings in which half or more of the witnesses were non-Catholics, or even unchurched experts? No. The difference is that in the private realm, the Church feels that it owns the turf, that moral principles are sufficient, that social analysis, while sometimes helpful, is not necessary because the principles are absolute and practical applications are obvious.

The Catholic Church uses proportional consequentialism in public realm issues and a deontological natural law approach in private realm issues. It has been rumored that some bishops were upset at the consequentialism (to which they are in principle opposed) of the pastoral letter on nuclear war—and well they might be, in view of the case I am attempting to make here. What is astounding is that they had not already noticed their heavy reliance on consequentialism in addressing public realm issues, for example, in capital punishment.[9]

The fact is that since the political stance of the Church on public realm issues has been seemingly irrevocably set in terms of gaining a hearing from the existing power structures, the bishops could not use a deontological approach based on New Testament or early Church pacifism, or even a strict just-war application, which would necessitate the outlawing of all modern weapons of war and all participation in such wars as indiscriminately killing the innocent. Either of these approaches would have set the Church all over the world back in a new version of the nineteenth-century church vs. state situation—with the Church outside the political community, seen as the political adversary of the modern nation-state. Given this, consequentialism was necessary. The fact that many bishops who in principle oppose consequentialism as a moral method tend to support American wars and military interventions, and to disavow pacifism, no doubt influenced the final result also.

The move to consequentialism is limited to public realm issues. The Church is attempting to retain a deontological, law-centered approach to the private realm—which includes not only personal morality (especially sexual), but also intra-ecclesial questions. It is difficult not to conjecture that consequentialism is perceived as relatively harmless as well as necessary in the public realm that has already passed beyond the control of the Church, a realm characterized in general by democratic give-and-take and acceptance, at least in principle, of egalitarianism. But consequentialism in the private realm is perceived as dangerous to the power structure in the Church, in that consequentialism, because it requires a more rigorous contextual analysis best done by persons immersed in the specific context, would pass the power of moral decision-making from the almost exclusive control of the magisterium to include the laity at large.

Women as Decision-makers

Considering this methodological inconsistency in the Church's treatment of war and abortion, is it any wonder that feminists charge the Church with misogyny in the face of an apparent inability to trust women to be moral decision-makers? Is a woman with the medical option of abortion so much greater a danger to life than men armed with tanks, missles, and bombs?

I do not believe that the *source* of the inconsistency is misogyny, but I am forced to agree that the *continuation* of methodological inconsistency that discriminates against women as moral persons is only possible in a climate of misogyny. In a society where many, and potentially all, women are not in control of their own bodies, but are raped, beaten, and molested by fathers, husbands, and strangers, as well as subjected to medical care that often treats care of women's bodies as if they were not women's to control[10]—in such a society we move in entirely the wrong direction when we refuse to allow women final responsibility for their bodies' reproduction.

Much present thinking among Catholics on this issue is reprehensible, especially new voices which maintain that since the courts may use state equal rights amendments to support abortion funding, Catholics are morally obliged to oppose equal rights laws.[11] Women should not be granted equality because it might be misused. How is this different from the arguments in the past for not freeing the slaves or not giving the vote to the unpropertied because these rights might be misused? Freedom cannot be refused to whole classes of persons on the ground that some of them might, or even probably would, use that freedom to commit grievous sin.

Church and Politics

These reflections are relevant to another related difference between treatment of war and abortion by the bishops, and that is the use of the political realm as an instrument of the Church's moral policy. The Church is involved in politics and always has been,[12] although it has fairly consistently in this country abstained from electoral politics (supporting particular candidates and parties). Attempts by the Church to safeguard religious practice have always involved the Church in politics. For example, the 5D exemptions for priests, ministers, and seminarians in the World War II draft law were the result of the lobbying efforts of the Catholic bishops of the United States, efforts that set precedents for similar laws in subsequent wars.[13] Regardless of the oft-heard charge that the Church should stay out of politics, or did stay out of politics until recently, we have, even here in the United States (the case being easier to make in Europe, where the Church has concordats with nations), a rather consistent record of Church involvement in politics, not only regarding war, but also other aspects of social policy, such as the right of labor to organize. Today the Catholic Church, as do many other churches, cooperates with federal and local governments in administering a great deal of government money and agricultural surpluses in the areas of foreign aid (especially under P.L. 480, Food for Peace) and local and regional social welfare programs.

The new element in the abortion issue is not the involvement of the Church in politics. The new element is the type of political involvement: political involvement aimed at extending rights to persons unrecognized by law by limiting what are regarded as vital rights of others—rights vital both morally and legally. Anti-abortion action is aimed at protecting the right of the unborn to life through limiting the right of women to control their bodies' reproduction.

All action aimed at protecting some human lives or rights involves placing limits on the lives and rights of others. For the most part, we understand the limits placed on us to protect others as minimally harmful: limits on our rights to pollute our common water or air, to drive as fast as we wish, to hire and fire on the basis of racial, sexual, or religious considerations, among others.

The problem with the limits proposed in anti-abortion action is that those limits consist of a denial of bodily integrity. Bodily integrity is a rather basic human right, certainly more basic than the right to pollute, or speed, or hire whom we wish. Many wonder whether real personhood is possible without a sense of bodily integrity. The body constitutes, in a concrete way, the limit of the self; an inability to control one's body because of the power of (an)other(s) over it can easily prevent one from developing the ability to draw the boundaries of the self, to know at what point a self exists for whom the individual is responsible. Women, as remarked earlier, already live in a context that unsubtly conveys the message that women's bodies are not their own, but are to be used by individual men and by advertising, that women's bodies are, to some extent, not personal, but public property like the flag, to be displayed and enjoyed at the will of men. Women have not been taught, for the most part, to know and use their own bodies, but to save them for men who will bestow on women knowledge and appreciation (even if impersonal) of their female bodies. Women have been taught to see their bodies as commodities, not as intrinsic to self, not as their functioning, active self. To remove legally the ability to decide for or against nurturing another human life in one's body surely confirms the social message that women's bodies are not personal, but public.

Bishops and many Catholics have not recognized that they propose any real restrictions on women in their support for anti-abortion legislation. The Catholic bishops of New York wrote:

> We fail to see how officeholders can escape their responsibility in this grave matter. Particularly we fail to see the logic of those who contend "I am personally opposed to abortion, but I will not impose my personal view on others." That position is radically inconsistent because a third party's right is at stake. It is the same as a 19th century legislator saying "I am personally opposed to slavery, but I support the right of others to hold slaves if they choose." The analogy is all the more appropriate when we recall that the Supreme Court, in its Dred Scott decision, said the slaves were not citizens with rights. If people of influence had not acted on their moral conviction to oppose that decision, slavery would still be the law of the land.
> *It is no exercise of civil liberty to own a slave, nor is it an exercise of civil liberty to destroy an unborn child.*[14]

Is it not an exercise of civil liberty to decide to become or not to become a parent? This failure to see the serious conflict of rights involved in the abortion question is telling. I am forced to agree with many in the women's movement that it is the result of not taking women seriously as full human persons, but understanding them solely in biological terms as created for the purpose of reproduction. Only if women's purpose is reproduction can one assert that forcing pregnant women into motherhood is not depriving them of liberty. Bodily integrity is recognized by the Church as a basic human right in other contexts; we have condemnations of slavery, forced labor, and torture, for example. That the right of fetal life to continue living must be defended should not, and ultimately cannot, mean that we exclude from the discussion the rights with which that right conflicts.

Some say that women themselves choose parenthood when they engage in sexual intercourse, knowing that pregnancy could result. It should be immediately clear, though, that this defense for ignoring the rights of women (that such rights were voluntarily surrendered by the women themselves) cannot apply in rape cases. This is why some anti-abortion advocates want to make exceptions for rape cases. From a Catholic perspective, this exception is not defensible, for the life to be terminated is still itself innocent, and its right to life is absolute. A similar problem exists with proposed exemptions for cases in which pregnancy endangers the mother's life: Catholic teaching holds that no direct killing of innocent life is permissible. Every effort must be made to save both lives, the final decision resting in the hands of God. To agree to *either* of these exceptions should bring down the wrath of the bishops on the heads of anti-abortion Catholic legislators—for would *they* not be inconsistent in voting for legislation contrary to their religious/moral stance? And yet *this* inconsistency does not seem to bother the bishops, or Catholics in the right-to-life movement. Either fetal life is real human life above which no other life, and certainly no right less than life itself, should ever be preferred—as Catholic moral tradition maintains, or else, we turn to consequentialism and do the best job we can of preserving the greatest mix of respect for human life, dignity, and responsibility that we can. Attempting to defend a political action as necessitated by an absolute moral principle, when that political action contains aspects that contradict the absolute principle in question, is patently dishonest.

Dismissing the right of women to bodily integrity on grounds that women surrender that right with intercourse has two chief problems. The first is that the very social attitudes toward women's bodies described earlier have created a situation in which one must question to what extent women freely choose to engage in sexual intercourse. For many women, and at least at times for most women, intercourse is not a fully chosen moral act. Rather, women's acquiescence is taken for granted, both within and without marriage. The attitude that women's bodies are for the perusal and possession of men, where it does not lead to total disregard of the wishes of women altogether, frequently leads to the idea that once a woman has "given" herself to a man either in sex or in marriage vows, she has surrendered her rights to her body forever. Many women do not have, even within marriage (and many would say *especially* within marriage), any control over how often, when, where, or how intercourse takes place or whether it will be open to the possibility of pregnancy or not. This is one of the worst problems with the natural methods of family planning, as many poverty workers and multitudes of poor women in this country and around the world attest—natural methods require cooperation, the agreement of the husband to forego intercourse. The anger of many men at discovering a wife on the pill is not necessarily anger aimed at the decision not to have another child, but at the audacity of women to presume that they can make any decisions about sexuality at all. The simple fact is that women do not, in many, many cases, have the ability to make moral choices with regard to intercourse.

"A conservative estimate is that, under current conditions, 20-30 percent of girls now twelve years old will suffer a violent sexual assault during the remainder of their lives," writes Allen Griswold Johnson.[15] Some studies indicate that as many as 14 percent of women have been violently sexually assaulted by their husbands[16]; 33 percent of women in some random studies have been the victims of completed rapes, 44 percent the victims of completed or attempted rape.[17] And the figures for such sexual crimes against women go up every year, as do the figures for wife-battering, which, depending on the study, occurs in 10 percent to 25 percent of all the families in the nation.[18]

The lack of freedom of women to control their participation in intercourse far exceeds these statistics, for the existence of the 14 percent, or the 33 percent, or 44 percent, provides a climate of intimidation that affects *all* women. To say that only these women of the statistics are unable to control their sexual behavior is to place women in a no-win situation—either they are abused and not responsible, or they must assert responsibility at the risk of abuse.

A second problem with maintaining that women agreed to parenthood when they agreed to intercourse is that the equation of intercourse and procreation in popular attitudes is no longer true. The two are still related as cause and result, of course, but pregnancy is possible without intercourse today (and although not the usual way, this is increasing) and individual acts of intercourse seldom lead to pregnancy today. This separation is not something that the Church can readily deplore, for it has had a hand in this change. When the Church admitted that (1) procreation is not the only or the single primary purpose of the marriage act, but shares the role with nurture of the marital relationship, and (2) that natural methods of contraception were morally acceptable, it effectively severed the equation of intercourse with procreation.

Agreeing to intercourse is not to be equated with agreement to parenthood. Methods of contraception fail, partners are sometimes dishonest about contraceptive coverage, and ignorance about procreation is still rampant, especially among the young. Less than five years ago in my parish school I conducted a sex education program for seventh- and eighth-graders, some of whom were sexually active, and found that the girls were unanimous in insisting that they didn't need to worry about pregnancy because one can only get "caught" during one's period—and they didn't do it then.

In addition to the special problems of conflict between crucial human rights in the abortion situation—problems difficult for the traditional Catholic mentality, which understands reality as basically harmonious order, disorder being caused by sin—there are other problems in the attempt to reflect religious/moral value in civil law on abortion. Chief among these problems is, of course, that many persons do not recognize the fetus as a human person, and so understand anti-abortion law as limiting the rights of women over their bodies illegitimately, with no corresponding social gain.

Regardless of the analogy of the New York bishops, when representatives of the Church have championed in the past the rights of other groups whose humanity was not recognized, such as native Americans, or blacks, or women, the laws that recognized their humanity and established (?) their protection did not cut so deeply into the rights of others in the society. Slaveowners lost property, slave dealers lost their livelihood, landowners lost some control over Indian peasants, men lost control over women's property and person (?), but no one was legally deprived of rights over their own person. For those who do not see the fetus as human life, a law with such a cost for a disputed gain is extremely coercive, even tyrannical.

What is the possibility for effectiveness of such a law? The enforceability of anti-abortion laws is questionable. Although abortion mills can be closed down or chased undercover, the abortion procedure is so simple that many relatively untrained persons will undoubtedly go into business. After all, such persons have always been in business, even before the maternal risks were so drastically lowered and the demand for abortion became so high. Relevant to enforceability is whether the law would be seen as useful to the common good. On the one hand, majority acceptance is in doubt, for most people seem to favor many fewer abortions than go on at present but want abortion available for rape, birth deformities, the very young, incest, and danger to the mother's life and health. On the other hand, most do not favor expensive and unwieldy systems of appeals hearings for abortion. What the majority want is for women *them-*

selves to choose fewer abortions.[19] What is not clear to most is how that can be done.

We have learned what happens to laws that do not have popular support. Prohibition in this country has long stood as an example of this. The failure of such laws to be obeyed makes citizens less respectful of law in general and more cynical about the possibility of achieving the ideal the law aimed at. We do not need further disrespect for law, nor can we afford more cynicism about the human capacity to respect life.

Our Church cannot merely *use* government to achieve its ends without taking seriously the effect such use has on the ability of government to protect the common good. Law can itself change social attitudes over time by affecting social structures, as most of us would agree has happened in this country in the area of civil rights for blacks. While minorities are not by any means treated justly or equally by all, there is virtually no social legitimacy anymore for the public denial of equality—a very different situation from thirty years ago.

Abortion is not amenable to the same kind of treatment. The absence of a social group to represent to society those protected by the law is critical. (When abortion is illegal, what parent would admit, what child know, that the parent would have had an abortion if it had been possible?) This absence will lead to the public's understanding the law chiefly in terms of its limitations on women. We can imagine which women will be used as illustrations of the injustice of the law: fifty-year-old welfare mothers of ten whose last five children had Down's syndrome, and other such cases. Furthermore, there would certainly be severe dissatisfaction about the 1.5 million unwanted children every year. I am sure that many parents would become reconciled to these children and come to love and care for them, but it would be naive not to expect that enforcing parenthood will swell the rates of child abuse and neglect, as well as the number of children given up to or taken by state welfare agencies. As a twice-adoptive parent, I have seen some of the thousands and thousands of children who are shuffled from institution to foster home and back again and have seen how few people ever consider adoption. What is to happen to those unwanted children? Many of them will inevitably end up dead—from the violence of abuse or, more probably, from the violence of neglect. And the nightly news will lay the fate of these at the doors of anti-abortion laws, never considering that the death toll would be even higher otherwise.

Law works best to change social attitudes when the benefits are clearly visible, represented by direct beneficiaries who exert support for the law. Law itself will not change the minds of those who do not recognize the fetus as human, but it will create other major problems.

Church Politics and War

With all these difficulties, why has the Church chosen the civil law as the mechanism for creating social recognition of fetal life? Has it turned to civil law, either its passage or enforcement, in order to protect other innocent life? Certainly not to protect innocent life in war. The Church has not pressed any legislation aimed at forcing government to disarm, or even to outlaw/forego particular weapons systems that violate noncombatant immunity. The bishops backed off from explicit support of the nuclear freeze movement in the pastoral letter and have neither endorsed nor funded any campaign to lobby against indiscriminate weapons systems. Although the bishops have urged negotiation over military solutions to problems in Central America, there has been no mobilization of clergy and laity, no financial support for any specific program to change foreign military policy involving the killing of innocent civilians, either in Central America, East Timor, the Philippines, or anywhere else. The bishops did not take the United States to task for failure to satisfy *jus ad bellum* conditions before invading Grenada in 1983, where there was innocent life taken—although "minor" by the standards of mass murder to which we have become accustomed. Concerning war, the bishops state principles and rely on persuasion and do not mobilize the laity for political/legislative action.

Why is organization of mass lobbying on foreign and military policy "political," and therefore to be avoided, but lobbying for an end to abortions within the legitimate mission of the Church? Why does morality require outlawing clinics that provide services which result in the death of innocents and not require the outlawing of sales of products and services which are designed to bring about the same results?

Many persons seem to assume that these deaths, this killing, is indirect, as opposed to direct killing in abortion. I disagree. The object of both abortion and military policy is territorial integrity, control of one's body or nation's land. Action designed to produce this effect also has the effect of killing. We have in the Catholic tradition a principle for deciding the morality of action with two effects, one good and the other evil, and that is the Principle of Double Effect.[20] The Principle of Double Effect states that in order for the action to be moral, it must satisfy four conditions. The first is that the intention be the good effect, which both abortion and war can meet. The second is that the action itself must not be intrinsically evil. Some acts of war can meet this: attacks on military targets and personnel, for example, are allowed with *jus in bello* conditions of just-war theory, provided they meet proportionality conditions.

An examination of the morality of the act of abortion requires first that we do not immediately place abortion in the category known as intrinsically evil acts. It makes no pedagogical sense in the contemporary theological scene to assert that abortion is intrinsically evil because it thwarts God's will, as expressed in human biology, that intercourse be open to procreation—too many have opted for a broader understanding of God's will than physicalism can provide. Rather than classifying abortion with artificial contraception, we should understand it as we do killing. Killing is not intrinsically evil; murder is. Abortion as an act that kills must meet the same criteria that other kinds of killing do. It must be subjected to the Principle of Double Effect to determine whether this killing can be justified as other kinds of killing can be justified: by self-defense, the demands of a just war, or capital punishment.

The third condition is that there be sufficient reason for tolerating the evil effect. This is the equivalent of the principle of proportionality in just-war theory. It is questionable whether most cases of abortion, or most causes of war, meet this condition. The fourth condition of the Principle of Double Effect most directly illuminates the question of directness when it requires that the good effect cannot result from the evil effect. And here again, war seems to have the same difficulty that abortion does, in that both achieve the good effect through, or at least simultaneously with, the evil effect. Can one defend one's nation's interests in war any way but through the destruction of innocent life? Perhaps in the past—but with bombers and missiles? It would seem not. If waging war to win (any other way being contrary to just-war theory) requires demolishing the enemy's civilian support and will to fight through mass destruction, is this not direct killing, achieving the good through the evil effect? Or is it not direct killing because it does not matter to the planners or war wagers *which* thousands of the enemy die?

Even more, when we sell, or even buy for ourselves, huge expensive weapons systems, have we not *first* chosen that the world's hungry die? It is not accidental that using more than $595 billion of the world's resources on military preparation—125 percent of the world's health budget—leaves much of the world hungry, so that 40,000 children die *every day* of hunger and hunger-related causes.[21] The rise in military spending under President Reagan has fed a huge national deficit, which has in turn raised interest rates on the debt of developing nations, so that larger and larger proportions of their national budgets go to pay interest on external debt. Many of these nations, who have massive hunger problems, then use remaining income to purchase weapons from the United States and other developed nations.[22] When the two effects—death by hunger and military arming—are linked so causally, can we really maintain that the killing is not direct? If, in medical ethics, it is immoral to deprive the dying of food because food is accounted an "ordinary means of preserving life" (as opposed to optional "extraordinary measures of preserving life"), surely such deprivation—depriving those who are not dying *except* for lack of food—in economic situations is immoral.

It is undeniably true that in abortion, the good achieved—the termination of an undesired physical and emotional strain from hosting in one's body a biological parasite—is achieved at the cost of the death of an innocent life. But war also fails the Principle of Double Effect. Why do we only see moral inadequacy in abortion?

What obligations do we have toward innocent life beside not desiring its death and not choosing goods that can only be achieved through its death? Innocent life perishes in tremendous numbers constantly. What are we required to sacrifice to preserve innocent life? We do not require nations to sacrifice any of their national interest, neither military nor economic interest, to protect innocent life. What obligations does our faith place on us to preserve the children dying of hunger in the world? Are we obliged to lobby for more foreign aid, to forswear unnecessary luxuries in order to share the resources of the world with the hungry? Are we obliged to house, at the risk of imprisonment, the illegal aliens fleeing death in El Salvador and Guatemala? Are we obliged to adopt the innocent, homeless children of our own country and of the world, the thousands and millions of unwanted children who suffer from physical, emotional, and mental disability resulting from their lack of care? Are we obliged to give up parts of our bodies—a kidney, for example—to preserve the life of dying innocents? No, we are not. These are good deeds, but they are not obligatory, just as it is not required of us that we rescue the drowning or those trapped in burning buildings or wrecked cars. We are not obliged to put ourselves out, much less to risk our freedom and our lives, to protect threatened innocent life. And we do not see any campaign in our Church to change civil law to make such actions obligatory.

Yet women—and not only Catholic women, but all women—are to be forced to sacrifice in order to protect innocent life. And there is no question about this raised within the Catholic community. Do we really have a consistent ethic of life when we mobilize our laity, commit our economic resources, and command the obedience of our faithful with the most serious religious sanctions in support of the legal protection of only one group of threatened innocents, and at the expense of only one group in our society?

I second Cardinal Bernardin's call for a consistent ethic of life, a "seamless garment." But that ethic's consistency must go beyond the level of principle to embrace the entire area of application so as to treat persons, both the varied groups of threatened innocents and those groups who should protect the innocent, consistently. We will never convince those involved in the taking of one and a half million aborted lives a year to consider the life of the unborn reverently if we do not evince reverence for the mothers of those unborn, for the starving millions of the world, the hundreds of thousands of innocent civilians threatened by death in war. We will be accused of romanticizing the unborn out of disdain for the already born, of ignoring the personhood of women, and of passing the burdens of protecting life onto the shoulders of pregnant women rather than accepting the very real burden belonging to all of us to protect all human life.

PART VIII.

The Work
of Roger Lincoln Shinn

SEVENTEEN

The Quest for Justice

Beverly Wildung Harrison

Introduction

It is too soon to take the measure of Roger Lincoln Shinn's intellectual
legacy. Those of us blessed to be his students, colleagues, and friends
anticipate further enhancement of his already prodigious contributions to
Christian social ethics in the years of his active retirement, as he continues to devote himself to research, teaching and writing.[1] Yet no volume
conceived to honor him, and influenced by his work, would be complete
without an interim review and preliminary assessment. Something, however brief and inadequate, must be said in celebration of the integrity,
quality, and impact of his labors.

A systematic review of his writings and professional career is a moving
experience. Although I have been a longtime student of his work,
rereading many of his books, articles, and reviews and discovering numbers of his published and unpublished manuscripts for the first time have
provided unexpected revelatory moments.[2] It has been an occasion not
only for remembrance and awareness of continuities, but also for new
insight and discovery of subtle nuance or of change insufficiently appreciated or inadequately savored. Research in preparation for writing this
essay has reconfirmed my conviction that Roger Shinn deserves to be
numbered among those who have most artfully and systematically con-

Beverly W. Harrison, Carolyn Williams Beard Professor of Christian Ethics, Union Theological
Seminary in New York City.

tributed to the formation of contemporary Christian ethics, to its substance and its methodological and normative clarity.

In introducing the aims of this volume, my coeditors and I have identified already several basic convictions and intentions that characterize his Christian ethical stance and give distinctive nuance to it.[3] We have underscored his ecumenical concern, both within Christianity and beyond it,[4] along with his ever-growing awareness that Christian ethical discourse must express a mode and range of cultural sensibility beyond that envisaged by post-Enlightenment Euro-American perspectives.[5] We have stressed that Roger Shinn's central animating vision of Christian ethics requires us to focus on basic public policy issues while speaking from immersion in and accountability to biblical and Christian theological traditions. He has modeled a form of normative Christian ethical discourse that both reiterates central concern for a Hebraic and Christian prophetic ethic of public righteousness and mercy and incorporates dimensions of new knowledge.[6] "The vocation of the Christian ethicist is to maintain conversation between the biblical heritage and the contemporary world ..." for ". . . the Church cannot claim holiness by escaping the common life."[7] Few have matched the standard he sets for speaking both with confidence in the relevance of biblical faith and with humility and openness toward the wisdom that others bring to contemporary moral dilemmas.

We have also observed the importance to his conception of Christian social ethics of being a *teacher* of ethics *within* the churches. Much more could be said about this close correlation in his life between normative public policy analysis and his work as a church-educator-ethicist. Merely to skim his remarkable bibliography makes one aware how much of his research and writing (not to mention the teaching and lecturing not captured in print) aims to encourage Christians and their churches toward more adequate ethical engagement, which is always simultaneously public engagement.

Roger's workaday schedule regularly finds him preaching and teaching in parish churches, consulting with ecumenical and denominational bodies on social issues, discussing ethics with governmental and nongovernmental organizations. He has rapport both with groups that formulate public policy and with those who challenge such policy. His agenda has included lecturing at the Army and Air War colleges, West Point, and other military schools. Simultaneously, he was providing testimony in defense of conscientious objectors in courts and before congressional committees.

All of this is to say that if his work is assessed only in singular terms, from an academic locus, or in terms of its public policy context, or from the standpoint of contributions within an ecclesiastical setting, much will be missed. Few of his contemporaries would be judged so appreciatively in each of these arenas; far fewer can count equivalent impacts in all of them. It is this multifaceted capacity to work as an ethicist on this variety of fronts that accounts for his influence as a scholar and graduate teacher in the field of Christian social ethics. Many of us were drawn to study with him—and his work as doctoral mentor is legendary—precisely because of his capacity to hold together the competencies required to do all of this work well.[8]

Anyone concerned for the full vocation of Christian ethics is bound to find his contributions impressive, and he has a deservedly broad spectrum of admirers within his own discipline and in numerous church constituencies, clerical and lay, as well as in other disciplines. Even so, it may well be that in some respects, Roger Shinn is an underappreciated figure in contemporary Christian ethics. An unassuming man whose balanced and reticent style sometimes belies his extraordinary wit and incisive turn of mind, he is infrequently numbered either among the contemporary polemicists within the discipline or among those who have a specific methodological axe to grind. Associated neither with exotic fixed opinion nor with dramatic innovation, he seems a bit like the long-distance runner whose strong and steady pace often is taken for granted as others spurt or lag. Yet reflection on the quality of his labors in relation to the circumstance of the period in which he has come to maturity as a Christian ethicist makes it clear that the very range of his talents actually makes full appreciation of his disciplinary contribution more difficult.

In a field not overly endowed with gifted writers and where obtuse or highly technical prose has occasionally been adjudged a mark of profundity, the clarity, conciseness, and readability of what he writes, while making him the envy of some of us, seems at times to mislead others into characterizing him merely as "a generalist." His audiences are indeed diverse, and he has published in an almost bewildering array of scholarly and popular journals.[9] However, his readable prose, provided for both technical and nontechnical audiences, invariably bears the mark of deep learning. His conceptual clarity and stylistic simplicity reflects neither oversimplification nor lack of specialization, but the gift of artful communication.[10]

In his early career, particularly, he provided several of what he has termed his "small books,"[11] specifically to introduce college students or church laity to intellectual movements or critical theological-ethical themes and issues. One discovers in these volumes a pervasive concern for the nuance of changing sociocultural ethos and a deep desire to enable people, particularly the young, to discern the theological import of and need to respond to such shifts. He also has responded repeatedly to a call to write study material and reports for his own denomination, the United Church of Christ, and for ecumenical bodies. He is coauthor, with his friend and former colleague Daniel Day Williams, of a moving book-length exposition of the theological confession of the United Church of

Christ and has authored a substantive theological and methodological guide to a new educational program of his church.[12] His ease as a writer has enabled him to provide regular copy for religious and secular journals, and during many years his editorials (often unsigned) and columns have appeared regularly, especially in *Christianity and Crisis* and in several journals of his denomination.

Many of the most important of his scholarly pieces are published in books now long out of print. Some appeared in festschrifts and collections of mixed caliber, and his important contributions were forgotten as works went out of print.[13] I have been struck by the number of substantive and instructive essays he has penned, particularly regarding the state-of-the-art of Christian theology and social ethics, that are seldom cited in literature of the field.[14]

His prodigious work as an editor of innumerable volumes has also been inadequately weighed for its impact on the discipline. He is editor or coeditor of many works in theological and social ethics and is the editor of several important ecumenical studies for the National and World Council of Churches.[15] Undoubtedly, he is asked to do such editing because of his reputation for productivity and fairness, and for his marked ability to provide accurate characterization of conflicting viewpoints and positions with which he disagrees. An excellent recent example of this important skill is reflected in the first volume of *Faith and Science in an Unjust World*. Published in 1980, this work contains papers given at the important and controversy-filled World Council of Churches-sponsored "Conference on Faith, Science and the Future."[16] Certainly, for those of us who did not participate, Roger Shinn's brief and unobtrusive introductions and summaries of issues provide a clear sense of the ethos of the conference and of the theoretical issues that deeply divided a meeting itself reflective of the global and cross-cultural tensions to which he alludes so frequently.

Stunning as this range of contributions is, then, its variety and style also contribute to the difficulty of adequately appreciating his total contribution. Because of his disparate audiences and given his commitment to reach a wider, nonacademic public, few of his professional peers, or others for that matter, have read and pondered the full range of his writing. One will want to read Roger Shinn's work for a myriad of reasons, but few think to pursue it systematically. Many of his constituencies have *some* appreciation for the breadth of his work, but it is difficult to appropriate the whole of it. And some of his finest scholarship has been executed in writing books aimed not for professional peers, but for a general public. One thinks, for example, of one of his numerous "little books," *The Sermon on the Mount*, a work continuously in print since he first wrote it in 1954 and revised it in 1962.[17] With well over a quarter million copies sold, it is, by any standard, a religious best-seller in this culture, yet it is infrequently cited in scholarly discussions of biblical ethics. Few works by Christian ethicists hold up so well in terms of substantive textual scholarship and sensibility to using scripture to illumine the moral life.[18] Similarly, his study *The New Humanism*, written to highlight the challenges that post-World War II philosophical movements addressed to Christian theology, remains as useful today as when it was written.[19] In fact, save for the use of more inclusive language, much that Roger Shinn has written in the past, if published today, would require little or no revision or apology.[20]

The quite formidable array of intellectual interests and competencies that shape his theological and ethical work may also be a source of the underappreciation of his work. Here again, the label "generalist" may be too readily invoked for this sort of wide-ranging competence. (I should hasten to add that Roger uses this label quite proudly to describe himself and the work of his field, but when he does, he is merely being modest.) Few can match his continued attention to method in ethics or his command not only of Christian intellectual history, but also of Western philosophy and history, of several behavioral sciences, of modern art and culture. Throughout his career he has taught ethical method and the history of Christian and philosophical ethics.[21] His knowledge of the natural sciences, several major world religions, and social and cultural traditions remote from our own is also impressive. Yet how many of those who appreciate his work as a biblical exegete and expositor of ancient and modern theological and ethical thought also appreciate fully his gifts as an interpreter of secular philosophical movements or his provocative wrestling with classic and modern theories of history?[22] It is not always remembered, either, that he warned of the failure to take modern humanism and the confrontation with radical unbelief seriously. Nor is it always understood that as long as twenty years ago, he was clear that the neoorthodox renaissance of the 1930s and 1940s had largely failed in its theological program, in part because it did not take the widespread existence of radical doubt seriously enough.[23]

Similarly, how many who commend his grasp of political theory and practical politics are also cognizant of his career-long interest in theories of perception, psychological and social, and of his concern to approach systematically the relationship of belief to ethical perception and sensibility? Psychological and educational studies and, since the late 1960s, sociological theory, particularly approaches to the sociology of knowledge, have supplemented his already considerable research in political and economic theory.[24] Increasingly, this issue of perception informs all of his scholarship, including his work on technological ethics, in a substantive way.[25]

Furthermore, how many of those who credit his mastery of several broad streams of social science also know of his serious interest in educational theory and his career-long concern for educational method, for understanding learning processes and religious education and the moral formation of the young? How many know that for several years he penned a regular column in a church journal on the challenges of parenting?[26] Or again, who of those appreciative of his wide-ranging discussions of technological ethics or of ecological and bioethical issues also think of him as one of the premier interpreters of the role of the arts and culture in Christian ethics? How many are aware that for years he regularly offered courses in theology and literature, and that his writings abound not only in literary reference, but also in explicit discussion of the role of literature and the visual arts in theology and ethics?[27] Recently in Christian ethics, there has developed a great deal of concern for the role of story, narrative, and ritual in Christian theology and moral awareness. Words he wrote on these matters in 1958 are surely prophetic:

The artist does not set out to prove a moral principle. He does not choose as his subject a general truth, then pick his characters and plot to illustrate it. ... And on exactly this issue, I fear, many people will say that Christian declaration departs completely from the manner of the artist.

But that claim shows a disastrous misunderstanding of the Christian message. When the basic mood of Christian enunciation becomes, "You ought," the meaning of Christian testimony is lost. Then the preacher has lost kinship with the artist and—still more important for his purpose—with the New Testament. For the New Testament ... centers in a Gospel (Good News). The appropriate literary form of news is narrative. The Christian Church has communicated its message through the ages by two main methods. One has been to tell "the old, old story" ... the other has been to re-enact and relive the same story—whether in the sacraments, or the Christian year with its fasts and festivals, or the life which St. Paul calls life "in Christ."

None of this means to deny that one proper function of church and pulpit is ... instruction. ... Yet in the Christian message the proper setting and framework for all communication is narrative. ... It tells of a manger in a stable, and a mother now thrilled and now perplexed, of the self-questioning of a man about his mission, of temptation and conflicts, of fishermen and soldiers and housewives and shepherds, of high hopes and insidious plots, of cruelty and death, of a new life and a new community. And this sharply-focused narrative is set within a more sweeping one—the grand epic or drama or story of a beginning, of a creation of heaven and earth and man, of sin and a fall, of strife and pain and mercy and new opportunity, of incarnation and atonement and resurrection, of a new people and their struggles, of a last judgment and an eternal life.

If the basic literary form of Christian faith is narrative-dramatic, the typical form of theology is exposition. The best theology (if I may express a prejudice) never leaves entirely behind the narrative-sequence. . . . It relates the biblical drama to the experiential drama of . . . human relations and man's inner life.[28]

What is also so striking about Roger Shinn's work is the ease with which he has moved from preoccupations central to theological ethics in the period when neoorthodox confessionalism set the agenda to greater specialization and issue-concentration that characterizes most Christian ethicists' work today. At a time when most practitioners of the discipline elect *either* to concentrate on theological ethics or methodological questions, *or* to focus on a cluster of issues raised by one or two other disciplines, he continues to address the full spectrum of matters that press themselves on the churches, including issues that must be addressed because of public controversy.

It would be a serious error to presume that this impressive interdisciplinary scope of Roger Shinn's labors is only a happy accident, the product of an admittedly formidable and wide-ranging intellectual curiosity. For more than three decades, the message screams out from his texts that not only philosophical sensibility, but also some substantive engagement with the social and natural sciences is a *basic competency requirement* of modern Christian social ethics.[29] As I have already noted, he believes that "the short career of neo-orthodoxy" succumbed to "a built-in instability" born in part of its disinterest ("not hostility, but lack of interest") in human science and world religions, and of its refusal to recognize that the truth claims that confronted an earlier theological liberalism are not solved by a simple reassertion of biblicism.[30] Nothing so typifies the concern that informs his mature work than this conviction that there are "genuine difficulties to working out a Christian social ethic,"[31] and that the neoorthodox renaissance of interest in theological tradition, although important, had not removed these difficulties. Our approach, he repeatedly contends, *must* be open to the wisdom of other forms of human inquiry beyond theology, and our enunciation of our own perspective must be modest in the face of the many new insights and challenges we confront. From the period of the 1960s, the name he used to characterize this approach was "the ethics of ambiguity."[32]

Roger Shinn's Association with "Christian Realism"

This characterization of contemporary Christian ethics as inherently "an ethics of ambiguity" coming from a then "younger scholar" usually was heard as reiteration of a theme familiar to Christian realism, that movement in the discipline initiated by his famous teacher, Reinhold Niebuhr. His close association with, and regard for, Niebuhr is well known. He has been the active Reinhold Niebuhr Professor of Christian Social Ethics at Union Seminary since John C. Bennett's retirement. (By recent action of the seminary's board of directors, he will share that title, emeriti, with Dr. Bennett.) No doubt it is all but inevitable that Roger Shinn should be counted as an exemplar—by some, the leading currently active exemplar—of realism in Christian social ethics.

There are obvious and important continuities with Niebuhr's ethics that justify this characterization. I will identify some of these in what follows. Yet at a time when invocations of the term Christian realism have become particularly ambiguous, and when there are numerous appeals to realism or to Niebuhr's "authority" by the political right of the discipline,[33] it is important to assess how Christian realism has affected Roger Shinn's position.[34]

There are continuities with realism in his work that were forged out of his own life experience and independent scholarship, but there are also differences with Niebuhr that are more than merely superficial. What is surprising, on the whole, is how unpredictably distinctive Roger Shinn's style of Christian ethics has become in contrast to others who invoke the Niebuhrian heritage. In reviewing his writing, I also have been struck again by the absence of an uncritical "familial piety" toward Christian realism in his work. We need to recall that Roger Shinn, for all his appreciation for Niebuhr, does *not* promote the Christian realist label, nor could I locate any text in which he explicitly applies the term to himself.

To be sure, he often pleads for "realism" in our Christian ethical deliberation, but this is far from a technical invocation of a Niebuhrian stance. One recent interpreter has correctly suggested that such appeals will be explicit in any approach that acknowledges a considerable role for human rational deliberation in Christian ethics, and Roger Shinn's surely does.[35] However, his concern that our ethical life live close to the concrete substance of its historical context is one that can be as much credited to his appreciation of the American pragmatist tradition, of which he is a more judicious interpreter than Niebuhr ever was, than to any deference to Niebuhr per se. It needs always to be remembered that Niebuhr, unlike Shinn, came to social Christianity from a deeply embedded epistemological idealism.[36] Niebuhr's lingering idealism sometimes led him to treat human selfhood as a transcendental a priori, untouched by human sociality.[37] No such assumption presents itself in Roger Shinn's work. Furthermore, the much celebrated triumph of empiricism in Niebuhr's thought was ad hoc and, at points, somewhat inconsistently applied. Roger Shinn recognized this. He suspected that despite an antiperfectionist intent in Niebuhr, there was also a lingering element of perfectionism in the latter's work.[38] He concurred with John C. Bennett's assessment that Christian realism in ethics might too readily degenerate into expediency.[39] As we review the developing shape and substance of Roger Shinn's own ethic, we shall see how mindful he has been to make explicit the continuing normative force and role of ethical values within every political process. Hence he can never be read, as one might occasionally be justified in reading Niebuhr, as treating politics in abstraction from the norms of ethics.

Because both theological neoorthodoxy and Christian realism (Roger Shinn emphasized that Niebuhr was not neoorthodox)[40] were shaped by the traumas surrounding the rise of Nazism, and because this same context shaped Roger Shinn's life experience, we would expect continuities with these movements. Urgent as this engagement with totalitarianism was for Niebuhr's generation, it posed even more existential issues for those younger, like Roger Shinn, who had personal decisions to make about military involvement and who were to live through a direct personal engagement with combat. As the prospects of U.S. participation in World War II heightened, Roger Shinn and many of his friends in the student community at Union Seminary wrestled with these personal dilemmas. He chose to enter the Army, while several close to him chose the path of conscientious objection and, for several, imprisonment.[41]

Roger Shinn's different choice also led to imprisonment. As an army officer, he participated in some of the most ferocious engagements of the war and was captured by the Germans during the Battle of the Bulge. His journal of his internment in a Nazi prison camp and his subsequent writings on the experience and meaning of war, on its costliness and complexity, must be consulted by those who too quickly discount the values that led to military participation or by any inclined to romanticize even this "good war."[42]

After the war, his first "little book" poignantly challenged Christian readers both to understand its costs and to seek a faith that could speak to and confront its appalling continuing legacy:

The memory of America is short. . . . No one will ever know the total number of military casualties in this slaughter. Far less will we know the numbers of civilians killed by the twentieth century war-god who spares no one. Nor can we conceive of the children who must grow up without parents, of the wives who lost husbands, and the husbands who lived in battle while their wives were killed at home. It makes no difference that we do not know the number. What we know is already beyond our comprehension. . . . The cost is not reckoned only in destruction to life. Many who still live are forced to wonder whether life was worth snatching from destruction. *A second great entry in the cost ledger of the war must be disillusion and despair. . . .* The third great cost will be the worst. *For it seems sometimes that even the ideals of civilized men must be written among the casualties of war. . . .* The question is whether we can find any meaning in the confusion and conflict of this age—whether God is here.[43]

In quoting him here I have excised some of the most moving passages that make concrete these somber observations. Yet *Beyond This Darkness* is, above all, an affirmation of the *meaningfulness* of biblical faith, a call to continue the struggle for justice and peace through confidence in God's self-revelation in Jesus Christ.

Clearly, the tenor of this and other of Roger Shinn's early writing is in no way merely a product of the academic influence of teachers, even teachers so powerful and affecting as Niebuhr. The tone and themes that tie him to the mood of Christian realism in the post-World War II period were born of what he had lived.

Several convictions forged in this time do indeed converge with Niebuhr's emphases and come to shape Roger's continuing conception of the work of Christian ethics. The first of these involves an explicit and clear-cut break with any evolutionary view of historical change, or any assumption of irrevocable and unalterable moral progress in human history. Social evil—the inhumanity and suffering that human beings inflict on their enemies and on themselves and their communities—has a force and reality for him that makes expectation of perfection in history unthinkable. In his earliest work, and through the 1950s, his elaboration of this theme, of moral evil in history, often was cast as a discussion of theological anthropology or philosophy of history, characteristically Niebuhrian rubrics. Convictions about the reality of moral evil in history and of moral ambiguity as a condition of our action never cease in his work. These themes are as poignantly affirmed in his recent work as in his early writing:

A world accustomed to believe that good was overcoming evil responded at first with unbelief to the vicious regime bent on slaughter of the Jewish people, conquest of neighbors, and the glorification of blood and soil. Later the time came when militant evil haunted our own national consciousness and we wondered how it could be that in this society racists massed ugly power to torment their fellow human beings and infantrymen "wasted" Vietnamese villages while airmen bombed them from the skies. We went on to wonder about evil in the White House, where straight-laced advocates of "law and order" violated the constitution and the traditions of fair play in politics. These events made us wiser, if they showed us the persistence of cruelty and fraud in a world that calls itself civilized. But they deceived us if they led us to think that evil can be localized in a foreign dictator or an American conspiracy, somehow "out there," waiting only to be exposed and defeated by the righteous.

For now our society and world are as uneasy as at any time in this century. Yet we cannot identify some single criminal or some center of power that needs to be overthrown. The world still has a fairly rich sprinkling of villains. You can make your list as easily as I. But the fears and anxieties, the resentments and frustrations that haunt this world cannot be tracked down to some one festering malignancy that spews poison through the system. The problem is more diffuse, more chronic, more enervating.[44]

Yet while Roger Shinn shares Niebuhr's suspicion of approaches to history that looked to its perfectibility, and interprets history as an arena in which human "grandeur and misery" are exemplified in full array,[45] there has been little reliance in Roger's mature writing either on specific Niebuhrian phraseology or on linkage to "*the* Christian *doctrine* of man." Clearly, Roger Shinn heard more clearly than many of Niebuhr's present-day advocates the reservations that Niebuhr himself expressed at the end of his life about the terms he relied on to commend his message to his contemporaries. In Roger's work, one finds no evidence for those convictions some now parody as "realistic." There is no highly predictable appeal to the invariants of human pride and power-seeking in his work, no suggestion that "modern man" would find his way back to Christian faith if "he" looked unromantically at the dramas of history.

None who read Roger Shinn's work only as a gloss on Niebuhr's have taken into account the points at which his assessment of historical reality explicitly differs from Niebuhr's. On this point, it is urgent to remember that much that Roger Shinn wrote in his early career focused on an examination of "the new humanism," those emphases in postwar philosophy and intellectual life that demonstrated contemporary people's capacity to take history seriously despite the depth of evil within it. He read the existential philosophers and the emergent continental philosophical traditions as demonstrating that despair had not led to a Christian renaissance, but to human capacity to act responsibly in the face of radical unbelief. Because of this he urged that post-neoorthodox theology had to approach its task even more modestly, for secular humanism had not crumbled in the light of the sobering exemplifications of evil in history.[46]

Furthermore, he was not tempted, as Niebuhr seemed sometimes to be, with the option of finding the full theological meaning of history "above" or "at the edge" of history.[47] As I read the record, the transcendental element in Niebuhr's approach, signaled by his lingering perfectionism, meant that at times he bracketed history and presumed that divine fulfillment made sense only within a transhistorical realm.[48] Although Roger Shinn consistently presumes an eschatological dimension to the Christian ethic, his formulations unambiguously affirm the possibility of divine presence and fulfillment within historical life itself. Furthermore, he does not rely so exclusively on the correlation of historical ambiguity with moral ambiguity as compared with Niebuhr. Aware to a degree that many theologians of Niebuhr's generation were not of the range of cultural pluralism and human diversity characterizing human reality, he gives more emphasis to these *positive* sources of complexity and ambiguity than Niebuhr sometimes seemed to do.

Most important, in contrast to purported realists on the current scene, Roger Shinn avoids using an "ethics of ambiguity" and awareness of history's moral complexity in a way that cuts the nerve of moral imperative. He recognizes that Christian realism has, under "tepid" circumstances, led to severing the nerve of moral commitment:

> Christian realism [made] two simultaneous assertions. First, human conflict never sets perfect righteousness against total evil. But second, social life requires moral choices and commitments, even among ambiguous causes. Aware of both of these, a generation of Christians learned to make decisions among relative goods and evils. ... Frequently in the tepid post war years, when heroes were few and leaders often faltered, society drifted into moral malaise. ... Awareness of the rents and patches in all garments of righteousness gave many the excuse for noncommitment.[49]

It also has resulted in an attempt to silence dissent from the status quo by those who do not participate in its advantages. "The privileged person, confronted by injustice, does not like to defend his privilege. He prefers to defend peace or law and order."[50] All of this is relevant to assessing his work vis-à-vis newer appeals to "Christian realism" that embrace it precisely to challenge persistent calls for change. While rejecting a *nonreflective* activism, Roger also has affirmed consistently an action-centered understanding of the Christian moral life.[51] It is this emphasis on the human necessity of moral choice and decision, continuous throughout his career, that provides the second major continuity with Niebuhr's ethics. Even here, however, we may detect a nuance that corrects against any perfectionism that intrudes reservations against acting in the world as it is. Roger Shinn frequently quotes the words of William Temple, former Archbishop of Canterbury, who denied the possibility of knowing what "a perfect social order" might be:

> But it is very difficult to know what a "perfect social order" means. Is it the order that would work best if we were all perfect? Or is it the order that would work best in a world of men and women such as we actually are? If it is the former, it certainly ought not to be established; we should wreck it in a fortnight.[52]

In any case, what is noteworthy throughout Roger Shinn's writings is his insistence that Christian realism stands in *positive* continuity with

Social Gospel Christianity. It represented a continuance of activism for love and justice.

> This quality of restraint (in Realism) might have led to suspension of judgment and inactivism, but Christian love and concern for justice drove the Christian realists to urgent activity. This ethical passion, in itself, might have led to dogmatic fury if it had not been qualified by the awareness of the fallibility of men.[53]

If it recognized that the "old love affair" between Christianity and society had been too simple,

> the love was right too. . . . The church could claim no right to reject a world that God loved. It could claim no superiority, no aloofness to God's world. Its mission was to live in this world and serve this world, as God had done in Jesus Christ and as God was continuing to do.[54]

Niebuhr, the Social Gospel's most penetrating critic, had also been the "one most indebted to it."[55]

When one compares the sort of intense focus on social justice and the necessity of reflection on action, the chasm that separates his approach from many of today's self-espoused "Christian realists" is once again obvious. Christian theological tradition provides no justification for standing apart from the existing world, no source of effacement of the "merely secular." This passion for addressing "the policies and programs of the real world"[56] is always, simultaneously, a call for engagement that has a real feel for the concrete character of problems and a sense of modesty in relation to "the art of the possible": "an ethic . . . must try to get from here to there."[57] But it could never be read as justification for Christian contempt toward the world.

A final, career-long formative continuity with a Niebuhrian ethic is the consistent attention he gives to the dynamics of political power in analyzing moral issues and public policy dilemmas. The reality of power, and the resultant inevitable presence of elements of restraint and coercion in all social life, had made it impossible for the young Roger Shinn to choose the pacifist option or to rest easy with a radical, utopian, or perfectionist ethic.[58] Nor could he treat any social-ethical question without central attention to the institutional context in which dilemmas are set.

Here, however, there is no disposition to treat "the many forms of social power"[59] in terms of a unilateral historical dynamic that is predictable. Not all assertions of power are morally equivalent. While none were more mindful that "unaccountable power" in human history is power to be distrusted, he is equally aware that absolute power*lessness* is a condition of degradation. Whereas Niebuhr quoted Lord Acton repeatedly to the effect that "power tends to corrupt and absolute power corrupts absolutely," Roger Shinn as frequently quoted Adlai Stevenson: "Being out of power corrupts and being clear out of power corrupts absolutely."[60] By comparison to Niebuhr, whose sharp distinction between interpersonal and collective power seems at times to result in neglect of the positive meaning of power in life, Roger Shinn affirms its basic goodness.[61]

> Let us look at the meaning of the word, power. We can start with an ordinary dictionary definition: "Power is ability to do or act; capacity of doing or accomplishing something." This means immediately, I should think, that power is basically good. It is a blessing in life. This does not mean that power is always used well or that all concentrations of power are good for society. But most of us, if we had the choice, would like to increase power—the capability of doing or accomplishing something—rather than diminish it. We might also choose to redistribute it. But who wants to live without the ability to do or act? In the Christian tradition, power is basically good, in the same sense that creation is good; it is divine in origin.[62]

He stresses that this affirmation of the goodness of power must precede insistence on the multifaceted corruptions and abuses of power that render political life so ambiguous morally. Roger Shinn also warns against reducing politics to compromise prematurely:

> Politics is frequently defined as the art of the possible. I do not want to acquiesce too easily in that. How do we ever know the limits of the possible unless we sometimes strain for the impossible? Surely we do not want a world without prophets, poets, and visionaries who raise our aspirations beyond achievable mediocrity. Somebody should always "dream the impossible dream." Political leaders should have their visions, too. But they must ask: how can we make these dreams functional? . . . Is there a coalition of interests that can be assembled to support this project? If I cannot attain all my goals, what compromises are justifiable in order to attain some?[63]

And there is a strong current in his ethics, so lacking in many unimaginative appeals to Christian realism, that affirms the continuous need for change and places the onus of resistance to change on the powerful. Some have more power than others, and it is the powerful who are most unlikely to acquiesce to desirable change. "Major social change requires pressure, especially pressure on the privileged who do not want to give up what they have."[64]

Roger Shinn's desire to do justice in Christian social ethics to the realities of power and to be faithful to the best of Christian realism on this matter is obvious. Yet the careful observer will recognize that this concern did not lead him, as it has led some realists, to focus exclusively on formal political problems or to be preoccupied chiefly with questions relating to international relations. Roger Shinn remains an informed and competent sympathetic interpreter and critic of this nation's foreign policy stances, but the center of his ethical interests lies elsewhere. His current interests in perception and ideology and his work on technology and ecology are distinctive, concerns not reflected in most realists' agenda. Attention to the dynamics of power is always present in these analyses, but Roger Shinn has broadened the questions to which such insight is relevant. When he does discuss international relations in the narrower sense, he is rather more consistently skeptical than was the mature Niebuhr of the benevolent uses of power on the part of the U.S. government.

Although his early work occasionally voiced an element of cold war, anti-Communist rhetoric, he was, even then, averse to and concerned about the persistent Russia-baiting in this society.[65] Like Niebuhr, he recognizes that much of the moralizing done in international relations is not clarifying. Moral rhetoric in international affairs, he argues, can be a form of sloganeering unrelated to actual political options.[66] In such instances, rhetoric is hypocritical and frequently aimed at the sort of "image-making" that has become a "monstrous industry" in the present world. Furthermore, such moralizing in foreign relations may intensify rather than resolve conflict. Nevertheless, he is forthright in identifying the role that moral factors have to play in foreign relations. He has specified four ways in which these factors always operate.[67]

For one thing, questions about means/ends relationships can never be suspended in foreign affairs. "Nations can choose better or worse means for pursuing their interests: they can even restrain their interests rather than resort to vicious means." A second dimension of morality enters foreign relations as "the art of finding mutually advantageous solutions to conflicts." Morality also shapes foreign affairs in the way that nations *perceive* their self-interest. Nations *misperceive* their interests, not merely because they lack accurate information, but because ideology functions as a blinder: "there is an ethical quality in the perception of the world. And there are kinds of fanaticism that blind people to realities, including even self-interest." And finally, because national interest "is not, in fact, a self-defining term," the most far-reaching impact of ethical sensibility in foreign policy actually arises at the point of defining "the national interest" itself. "National interest evokes deep loyalties only if it represents the meaning, the values, and the self-image of a people. Thus the national interest is subverted whenever a nation acts to destroy a valued identity." He quotes with appreciation Hans Morgenthau's words: "The real power of a nation consists not in the number of nuclear warheads it holds . . . but in the moral image it presents—not only in words, but, more particularly, in deeds—to the rest of the world."[68]

For Roger Shinn, then, appeals to national interest set certain parameters to foreign policy debate, but he remains a skeptic toward morally insensitive interpretations of what such interest involves. Furthermore, even when his ethical assessments lead him to policy options convergent with those of other realists, one does not find Roger Shinn urging such courses of action on grounds of national interest. His reasons appeal to substantive moral concerns to which political realists seldom attend. Just as often he has departed from policies that most realists embrace. His sensibility to injustice has led him, especially in the past decade, to stress the moral legitimacy of many social revolutionary movements.[69] His position on nuclear disarmament is a further case in point. Over the years, his position has evolved, and he has urged increasingly that the United States take unilateral initiatives on disarmament. Even at the height of the cold war of the 1950s, he consistently pointed to the need for vigorous and careful negotiation.[70] He was explicit that a Christian perspective must include awareness of possible irresponsibility on the part of *both* the United States and the Soviet Union. Those uncritically supportive of U.S. moral superiority have found no resonance in his position.[71]

On the related issue of nuclear energy development, a question also bitterly disputed within the Christian social ethical community, Roger Shinn has given qualified support to such development. On the face of the argument, his position correlates with many whose invocation of U.S. national interest is strong. Yet a careful reading of the record indicates that the morally relevant reasons he elaborates for his stance have nothing to do with endorsement of U.S. economic interests. Rather, as he analyzes the global situation, curtailment of production of nuclear energy will result in even greater economic pressure on poor nations already severely disadvantaged in the global competition for energy resources.[72] Whether one agrees or disagrees with these policy stances—and on these issues, Roger Shinn and I hold different positions—it is a misreading of his position to classify it as an archetypical expression of political realism.

Despite the many continuities with the concerns of the Christian realist movement in social ethics, then, Roger Shinn's work deserves appreciation at least as much for its innovation as for its continuities with that approach. In the last analysis, it is possible to fully appreciate the distinctive development of Roger Shinn's work as an heir of and innovator in relation to Christian realism only if one takes into account the active and independent theological dynamics that have operated over time in his work. It is of special importance to weigh and appreciate his strong conviction about the need to let "biblical faith" and the reality of Christian gospel inform contemporary issues and dilemmas.

The Theological Grounding
of Roger Shinn's Social Ethic

Today's new "realism" in Christian ethics is articulated and espoused by spokespersons who classify Christian realism as a postliberal movement in Christian theology, and who affirm neoorthodoxy as a successful alternative to liberalism. I have already observed the extent to which Roger Shinn dissents from such an interpretation, regarding neoorthodoxy as inadequate and emphasizing realism's continuity with Social Gospel sensibilities. There is in his own theological formulation too much of concern for the ethical substance of biblical faith for him to permit a reading of Christian revelation placing ethics in subordination to theology.

It was Roger Shinn's beloved colleague and collaborator Daniel Day Williams who insisted that theological liberalism cannot be dismissed or downgraded precisely because it was the theological movement that secured the centrality of *ethics to Christian theology.*[73] Liberals were insistent that no reading of the meaning of Christian theology is admissible that does not place ethical vision at the center of Christian self-understanding and faith definition. Read this way, it is possible to say that Roger Shinn's work has always sustained the best heritage of theological liberalism. For him, biblical faith and Christian gospel involve an experience of divine righteousness and mercy that is *utterly* inseparable from the call to human righteousness and mercy. This ethical meaning of faith inherent in Christian theological utterance was reflected in the title of his inaugural address at Union Seminary, "Some Ethical Foundations of Christian Theology."[74] Even when, as in his early work, there was a sense of the distance between divine transcendence and judgment and human struggle for meaning in history, there was no disposition to acquiesce in God's transient absence from the world and history. Always for him, to be a Christian has meant to enter an *active* vocation of love and justice within the common life. The Christian moral heritage is central to faith and it is radical: Christianity begins with a declaration of "good news to the poor," "release of the captives," and "liberty for the oppressed."[75]

His is a faith confession strongly centered in Jesus as the Christ, but for him this means trust in one who keeps faith with his own ethical-prophetic heritage, extending the vocation of righteous love that is always simultaneously a demand for human love and justice and confidence in a mercy that sustains us when we fall short in that effort.

> Our future will require many a surrender of privilege, many a change in familiar life styles, but these threats, if we read them as the prophets do, may have hidden promises. Christians have always said that God's judgment, even when severe, is gracious. ... That kind of belief comes out of a faith that looks neither to Prometheus nor to

Atlas—though it might appreciate both these myth heroes—but to Jesus Christ. In him there is more of fun and delighted contemplation, more of fervor for justice, more of joy in sharing.[76]

Admittedly, to live such a vocation, to embody biblical faith, involves a delicate balancing of challenge and forbearance. It is certainly not Christian to express prophetic witness untouched by priestly and pastoral concern. Restraint is frequently a mark of faith.[77] At the same time, it is not Christian to eschew conflict in the face of injustice:

> Some of us, from time to time, feel obliged to say of policies and actions, not simply that we think they are misguided, but that we think them morally wrong, cruel, or oppressive. If we are silent, the reason will be lethargy or cowardice. ... Even as we accuse the opposition, we are likely to recognize that we are not entirely righteous. ... We need not be sentimental on this point. There is a kind of driveling masochism that does nobody any good. The Jews slaughtered by Hitler were not guilty of genocide. The black people oppressed in South Africa and in this country are not exercising massive tyranny. I, on occasion, have refused to repeat liturgical confessions in which I was supposed to bemoan my guilt for public policies that I had opposed with considerable energy. It might be said that there was always more that I could have done, but I am not always going to crawl because I am not a moral giant. Sometimes I have a right and duty to denounce wrong-doers.[78]

Grace and judgment are inseparable in his theological vision because—as I have already observed—divine presence in human history is real and unbridgeable. To embrace an "eschatological ethic" is to embrace, not the limits of history, but Godly presence and

> an open future. It is the Christian vocation to keep the faith even in the absence of any clear, adequate plans. Fatalism is not the last word. Neither is the last word, "The wages of sin is death." God's last word has *not* been spoken, his last deed not done. ... Christians ... may not succumb to fatalism, may not cease to hope, may not cease ot look for new alternatives that are not yet evident."[79]

Nor is any virtue of the Christian life commended more often in his writing than courage.[80]

Because there is no irrevocable division between God's love for humanity and our human capacity for love and justice here, agape is relevant to all of life. God's love or agape is neither so remote from us nor so discontinuous from our own capacity to love that it renders our action extrinsic to the divine vocation within history.[81] We are to love as God in Christ has loved us, which means that our bonds to others are not conditional on agreement or lack of enmity. For the Christian, "enemies are never just enemies, but those who share a common origin, a common nature, a common sin and at least some common hopes."[82] Nor can we permit our theological ethic to construe the demands of love as so radical that justice becomes discontinuous with it:

> Many theologians insist that (Christian love) ... cannot be applied in any meaningful sense to social and political problems. Instead, we are told, justice must rule in this area. Furthermore, justice is defined, not in the ancient and biblical tradition to mean a full righteousness, but in the more limited sense of rendering to each man his due. That is, the make of justice is its impartiality, its refusal to be a respecter of persons ... if the Christian accepts such a dichotomy between love and justice. ... It would mean that a most important area of life is beyond the influence of Christian love. It would bring an almost intolerable tension into the life of the Christian. He would find himself acting upon Christian principles with his right hand and with sub-Christian principles with his left hand. Even if one could live this kind of schizophrenic life without serious damage ... to ... Christian faith, where does one draw the line between the areas ruled by justice and those ruled by love? ... It does not appear, however, that we need to or can separate the realms of love and justice. ... In short, our concept of what things are just has become filled with the contact of Christian love. Consequently, we must reject the sharp division between love and justice. Love has influenced and ought to influence our concept of what is just. Even if Christians should decide to deal with the social realm by justice, it would be justice that has been remoulded in the spirit of love.[83]

This refusal of dualism with respect to history and the transhistorical, with respect to divine and human action, and with respect to love and justice has characterized all of Roger Shinn's work. However, there has been a growing emphasis in his theological affirmations on the meaningfulness of creation, the value and beauty of the cosmos, and the full integrity of secular and worldly existence. Here, one cannot overlook the evidence that the later writings of Dietrich Bonhoeffer have touched him deeply,[84] or that Paul Tillich's discerning elaboration of the spiritual dimensions of culture has left its mark.[85] In his most recent work, Roger Shinn's exposition of the meaning of biblical faith gives equal stress both to the *eschatological* character of our hope and the *incarnational* character of our historical engagement:

> In its incarnational faith, the Church will seek to identify with the just needs of a society, especially an oppressed society and the oppressed people within any society. Recognizing its incarnational vocation, the Church will not treasure security or aloofness. It will

share in the sufferings and struggles of peoples. It will be, like its Lord, a partisan of the needy. Whatever "separation" there may be of Church from state, there can be no separation of the Church from God's people or from those processes in social and political life that seek to enact justice and love.

Simultaneously, in its eschatological faith, the Church will act for a kingdom that is yet to come. It will recognize that its responsible commitments to political movements are never its total commitment to God's kingdom. It will keep alive that eschatological sensitivity that gives it a leverage on all human political structures, a possibility of judgment on all human organizations including its own. While looking for the activity of God in human history, including movements that do not acknowledge God, it will never get so coopted to any movement that it forgets the God who is judge and saviour of creation and history.[86]

Not surprisingly, greater emphasis on the creation and incarnational motifs in the exposition of "biblical faith" has also led to even greater emphasis on the constructive role of vision and imagination in the Christian moral life.

This, then, is the theological matrix that provides the backdrop to much of Roger Shinn's writings in the most recent decade. It is a rather typical fate of social ethicists within the Christian community to be evaluated and remembered more for the positions they take on specific issues, and the normative judgments they make on them, than for the substantive and basic convictions that inform those judgments.

Because Roger Shinn has elected to take on the really hard questions— the "forced options" now facing our planet, because he has insisted that we are on a trajectory of perpetual crisis and that the supply of natural resources and overpopulation are real problems that cannot be wished away, because he has suggested that our "addiction for growth" is not consistent with the long-term well-being of the human community and "the ecological system that sustains our life," his recent voice might be heard and remembered chiefly for its pessimism. To read him this way, however, is to miss the deepest convictions that hold him to his course of doing Christian ethics close to the nerve of real problems. He understands that life is not given as curse, but as blessing, and as a result, he has no taste for "a riskless world, a world without insecurity,"[87] and he has little patience for those who will not own the ethical challenge of living in this "tangled world."[88]

It is, I submit, his own exemplification of biblical faith that enables his own most recent characterization of what the Christian ethic must be as a "*venturing* ethic."[89] It is this theological conviction that enables such relentless probing of complex dilemmas that some others in his discipline hardly acknowledge or recognize.

Conclusion

So brief a review of Roger Shinn's still dynamic intellectual legacy does not begin to do justice to the riches embedded in his work. The intricate texture of his thought lends itself neither to easy generalization nor to adequate summary. Nor is it possible to highlight all the major themes that pulsate through his teaching and writing. To review his work is to be confronted with a rich array of choices, both methodological and substantive, about what to celebrate in brief compass.

The light he has shed on many urgent specific moral questions also has been neglected here.[90] For example, reviewing Roger Shinn's writing has reminded me of the extent to which the personal passion for racial justice that animates his daily life has also shaped his written work throughout his career. Few of his professional peers have focused so consistently and perceptively on the dynamics of racism and anti-Semitism as has Roger Shinn. These are matters that command his heart and conscience, for he grasps profoundly the extent to which racism has blighted our personal and public lives. He has targeted racism and anti–Semitism as *the* measure of all of our moral and theological failures; he has challenged the churches, government, and other public institutions to accelerate action against them.[91] No assessment of his work, however provisional, should neglect this contribution.

The term one often hears applied to Roger Shinn, the man and his work, is "prudent." The appropriateness of the term depends on the connotation intended. Roger Shinn's friend and professional colleague Karen Lebacqz has reminded us that "prudence" in modern parlance too often is taken to mean only "a utilitarian weighing of benefits and harms, and a willingness to compromise benefits in order to avoid harm." The classic meaning that made prudence a cardinal moral virtue is more relevant. It means one who has "vision or accurate perception. . . . Prudence involves both *deciding* (not being irresolute) and *deliberating* (not being impetuous. . . . Sufficient attention must be given to the truth of real things so that we may perceive what is required."[92]

It is in this classic sense, then, that we may say that Roger Shinn is a prudent man, and that his intellectual legacy as an ethicist bears, and will continue to bear, the mark of Christian prudence. It is not caution about risk, but "the feel for complexity" that leads him to insist on living close to the actual reality of situations. Only so can the cause of justice, the substance of the Christian public vocation, be served.

Because he has taken on a full measure of the really tough questions, even those who share his vision of this vocation will find occasions to differ with him, sometimes strongly. Yet all who have worked closely with him will attest that he is a man of grace and forbearance. Given his irenic style, it is less often recognized that he is also a man who thrives on strong reasoned debate. In a time marked by polemics that are full of moral import, he has ducked neither the issues nor the controversies that are inevitable to the engaged. Yet he has set a high standard in reasoned argument, one that exemplifies the qualities he urged on our discipline when he was president of the Society of Christian Ethics:

> I am not rejecting the dynamic of polemics, but recognizing a comparable dynamic of grace. The influence of such grace will not be to make our polemics mild and ineffectual, but to raise them to a more penetrating and compassionate style. . . . Whatever the practical effectiveness, the notion of a polemic with compassion is consistent with the theological conviction that judgment and grace are not totally opposites, that there is a judgment in grace and a grace in judgment. . . . An appropriate ethical response, at least on occasion, is to engage in irenic polemic.[93]

Those of us who have shared directly in *his* irenic polemics have every reason to await, with anticipation, their further unfolding.

EIGHTEEN

Bibliography of Writings

Compiled by E. Richard Knox

*R*oger Lincoln Shinn's ecclesiastical and academic writings often have crossed the traditional lines of intellectual discourse. These interdisciplinary works have been published in a wide forum, making it difficult to find all his articles. Therefore, any claim to offer a bibliography as definitive would be foolhardy. Roger Shinn continues to write and publish at a steady pace, again making this listing incomplete. In this bibliography, emphasis has been given to published material. This collection does not include manuscripts and other material that were designed for limited circulation. Also, in general, the articles listed are in English unless a specific writing appears only in another language. No attempt has been made to catalogue the numerous translations of Roger Shinn's books and articles.

Books

Beyond This Darkness: What the Events of Our Time Have Meant to Christians Who Face the Future. A Haddam House Book. New York: Association Press, 1946.

Christianity and the Problem of History. New York: Charles Scribner's Sons, 1953; St. Louis: Bethany Press, 1964.

The Sermon on the Mount. Philadelphia: Christian Education Press; Boston: Pilgrim Press, 1954. Revised edition, Philadephia: United Church Press, 1962. Latest printing, New York: The Pilgrim Press, 1984.

E. Richard Knox, Doctoral Student, Christian Ethics, Union Theological Seminary in New York City.

Citizens of God's Kingdom: A Study Guide to the Sermon on the Mount. New York: United Student Christian Council, 1955; New York: National Student Christian Federation, 1963.

Life, Death, and Destiny. Layman's Theological Library. Philadelphia: Westminster Press, 1957.

Great Phrases of the Christian Language: A Devotional Book, with others. Philadelphia: United Church Press, 1958.

The Existentialist Posture: A Christian Look at Its Meaning, Impact, Values, Dangers. New York: Association Press, 1959. Revised edition, 1970.

The Educational Mission of Our Church. Boston: United Church Press, 1962.

The Fellowship of Prayer: Lenten Season 1963. Boston: The Pilgrim Press; St. Louis: Eden Publishing House, 1962.

Moments of Truth: A Devotional Book for Lent. Philadelphia: United Church Press, 1964.

The Search for Identity: Essays on the American Character, editor. Religion and Civilization Series. New York: The Institute for Religious and Social Studies; distributed by Harper & Row, 1964.

Tangled World. New York: Charles Scribner's Sons, 1965.

We Believe: An Interpretation of the United Church Statement of Faith, with Daniel Day Williams. Philadelphia: United Church Press, 1966.

Man: The New Humanism, vol. 6 of *New Directions in Theology Today*. Philadelphia: Westminster Press, 1968.

Restless Adventure: Essays on Contemporary Expressions of Existentialism, editor. New York: Charles Scribner's Sons, 1968.

To Love or to Perish: The Technological Crisis and the Churches, with J. Edward Carothers, Margaret Mead, and Daniel D. McCracken, editors. A Report of the U.S.A. Task Force on the Future of Mankind in a World of Science-based Technology, cosponsored by the National Council of Churches and the Union Theological Seminary of New York. New York: Friendship Press, 1972.

Unity and Diversity in the United Church of Christ. Royal Oak, MI: Cathedral Publishers, 1972.

Wars and Rumors of Wars. Nashville: Abingdon Press, 1972.

Plenary Presentations, vol. 1 of *Faith and Science in an Unjust World: Report of the World Council of Churches' Conference on Faith, Science and the Future*, editor. Philadelphia: Fortress Press, 1980.

Forced Options: Social Decisions for the 21st Century, vol. 27 of *Religious Perspectives*. San Francisco: Harper & Row, 1982. Second edition, New York: The Pilgrim Press, 1985.

Genetics, Ethics and Parenthood, contributor. Edited by Karen Lebacqz. New York: The Pilgrim Press, 1983. All the contributors take equal responsibility for the book, but Professor Shinn was instrumental in the writing of Chapters 5 and 9.

The Thought of Paul Tillich, with James Luther Adams and Wilhelm Pauck, editors. San Francisco: Harper & Row, 1985.

Essays and Articles

1935

"Sifting the Week's Headlines." *The Kilikilik* 42, nos. 1-11. This weekly summary of national and international news appeared in the Heidelberg College student newspaper.

"First Reports Indicate Ohio College Enrollments Above 1934-35 Figures." *The Kilikilik* 42, no. 2 (26 September):1.

1936

"Sifting the Week's Headlines." *The Kilikilik* 42, nos. 13-22:1.

"Political Views Through the States." *The Kilikilik* 42, no. 23 (31 March):1.

"Student Opinion Polled at Convention." *The Kilikilik* 42, no. 24 (9 April):1.

1939

"Hollywood Hops the War Bandwagon." *The Union Review* 1, no. 1 (December):4.

"Making No Promises." *The Union Review* 1, no. 1 (December):1.

1940

"Canon Raven's Pacifism." *The Union Review* 1, no. 2 (March):1-2.

"The Pacifist Apostasy." *The Union Review* 1, no. 2 (March):2-3.

" 'Ye Cannot Serve . . .' " *The Union Review* 1, no. 3 (May):2-3.

"Conscription Is America's Best Choice." *Peace Bulletin* No. 1, issued by the Peace Commission of the Intercollegiate Christian Council, October 6, pp. 2-3.

"Volume II." *The Union Review* 2, no. 1 (November):1.

"Faith for Action." *The Union Review* 2, no. 1 (November):1-2.

1941

"A Buck Private's Look at the World." *Christianity and Society* 7, no. 1 (Winter):24-27.

"On the Other Hand . . ." *The Union Review* 2, no. 2 (March):3-4.

"Guilty." *The Union Review* 2, no. 2 (March):24-25.

"Dialogue: Between Two Young Men Caught in a Historic Struggle." *Motive* 1, no. 3 (April):16-18.

"Dialogue in Letters: Between Two Young Men Caught in a Historic Struggle." *Motive* 1, no. 4 (May):21-22, 55-57.

"Uncle Shylock Still?" *The Union Review* 2, no. 3 (May):3-4.

"Christian Faith and Historical Decision." *The Union Review* 2, no. 3 (May):23-25.

"Why I Entered the Ministry in a World Gone Mad: Faith Cannot Be Destroyed." *New York Journal American* (Sunday, 27 July):5.

1942

"Because of My Faith I Must Fight." *Motive* 2, no. 7 (March):24-25, 28.

Excerpts from letters dated Christmas Day, 1941, Fort Ord, California; and February 12, 1942, Marysville, California. *Alumni Bulletin of Union Theological Seminary, New York City* 17, no. 2 (March):13-14.

"A Soldier Does Some Preaching." *The Union Review* 3, no. 2 (March):8-11.

"Men Are Greater and Worse Than They Seem." *Motive* 3, no. 4 (December):16-18.

1943

"Where Men May Walk Humbly . . ." *Motive* 4, no. 2 (November):9.

1945

"Men Under Fire." *The Intercollegian* 62, no. 12 (September):4-5.

"War Wounds in Europe." *Christianity and Crisis* 5, no. 15 (17 September):2-5.

"Recollections of War." *Christianity and Society* 10, no. 4 (Fall):12-19.

"The Failure of Protestant Worship." *Union Seminary Quarterly Review* 1, no. 1 (November):19-23.

1946

"American Failure of Nerve." *The Messenger* 11, no. 21 (15 October):10-13.

1947

"Is It Time to Preach Optimism?" *Christianity and Crisis* 7, no. 8 (12 May):4-6.

"Confusion in the Colleges." *The Christian Century* 64, no. 25 (18 June):762-64.

"Christian Thought Confronts the Atomic Bomb." *Christianity and Society* 12, no. 3 (Summer):14-17.

"For Crisis—A Creative Politics." *The Messenger* 12, no. 17 (19 August):12-14.

"Confusion in the College." *HIS* 7, no. 9 (September):28-32. Reprinted from *The Christian Century.*

1948

"The Relation of Religion to Democracy and Communism in the Writings of John MacMurray: A Review Article." *The Review of Religion* 12, no. 2 (January):204-15.

"The Relation of Religion to Democracy and Communism in the Writings of John MacMurray: A Review Article." In *Religion and Democracy*, edited by Horace L. Friess, 204-15. Papers from the University Seminar on Religion, 1946-47. New York: Columbia University. Reprinted from *The Review of Religion*.

"Plans for the Future." *Christianity and Society* 13, no. 2 (Spring):19.

"Ultimate Loyalties and Our Pragmatic Mentality." *Christianity and Society* 13, no. 3 (Summer):21-25.

1949

"1949 May Be the Year of Destiny for America." *Motive* 9, no. 4 (January):12.

"Must Theologians and Educators Fight?" *The Christian Century* 66, no. 1 (5 January):12-14.

"What Will History Say?" *The Intercollegian* 66, no. 6 (February):8, 24.

"News of the Fellowship." *Christianity and Society* 14, no. 3 (Summer):25.

"Augustinian and Cyclical Views of History." *Anglican Theological Review* 31, no. 3 (July):133-41.

"Social Evils and the 'Mystery of Iniquity.' " *Christianity and Society* 14, no. 4 (Autumn):19-21.

1950

"Comments on 'The Religious Imagination' by Richard Kroner." In *Perspectives on a Troubled Decade: Science, Philosophy, and Religion, 1939-1949.* Edited by Lyman Bryson, Louis Finklestein, and R.M. Maciver. New York: Conference on Science, Philosophy and Religion in Their Relation to the Democratic Way of Life, Inc.; distributed by Harper & Brothers, p. 618.

"A Survey of Recent Theological Literature: Theology and Philosophy of Religion." *Union Seminary Quarterly Review* 5, no. 2 (January):34-39.

"Another View." Letter to the Editor. *Commentary* 9, no. 3 (March):290.

"Religion Again Basic Part of Curriculum in Many Leading Colleges." *The Advertiser-Tribune*, Tiffin, Ohio, 10 November, p. 5.

"Courses in Philosophy Aim at Understanding." *The Advertiser-Tribune*, Tiffin, Ohio, 10 November, p. 11.

1951

"Religious Faith and the Task of the Historian." In *Liberal Learning and Religion*, edited by Amos N. Wilder. New York: Harper & Brothers, Publishers, pp. 56-77.

"Dangerous Absurdities." *Christianity and Crisis* 11, no. 13 (23 July):101-3.

"The Problem Beneath the Problem of Christian Living." *Christianity and Crisis* 11, no. 15 (17 September):117-20.

"Things a Calf Can't Do Better." *The Messenger* 14, no. 21 (6 November):8-9.

"Letter to the Editor." *The Advertiser-Tribune*, Tiffin, Ohio, 19 December.

1952

"The Colleges of the Christian Churches." *Christianity and Crisis* 12, no. 2 (18 February):14-16.

"The Heavens Declare the Glory of God." *Children's Religion* 13, no. 3 (March):5-6.

"The Theology of Political Campaigns." *Christianity and Crisis* 12, no. 15 (15 September):114-117.

"Corruption in Government." Letter to the Editor. *The Advertiser-Tribune*, Tiffin, Ohio, 28 October.

"Comment on Corruption." Letter to the Editor. *The Advertiser-Tribune*, Tiffin, Ohio, 31 October.

"Can God Speak to Joe College?" *Motive* 13, no. 2 (November):1-3.

1953

"The Christian Gospel and History." In *Christian Faith and Social Action*, edited by John A. Hutchison. New York: Charles Scribner's Sons, pp. 23-36.

"Is Politics a Religious Problem?" *The Messenger* 18, no. 4 (24 February):13-15.

"Is Economics a Religious Problem?" *The Messenger* 18, no. 10 (19 May):11-13.

Letter to the Editor. *Time* 62, no. 21 (28 November):8.

1954

"Neutrality Impossible—Christian College Affirmed." *The Christian Scholar* 37, no. 1 (March):23-27.

"We Have A Savior." *The Messenger* 19, no. 5 (9 March):3.

"A God Who Suffers and Saves." *The Messenger* 19, no. 6 (23 March):3.

"The Christian Hope." *The Pastor* 17, no. 8 (April):3-5.

"God Reconciles." *The Messenger* 19, no. 7 (April 6):3.

"Our Ministry of Reconciliation." *The Messenger* 19, no. 8 (20 April):3.

"Power to Become Children of God." *The Messenger* 19, no. 9 (4 May):3.

"A Transforming Power." *The Messenger* 19, no. 10 (18 May):3.

"Religion and Education Have a Major Stake in an American Heritage of Freedom." *Ohio State University Monthly* 45, no. 8 (15 May):7-10.

"Comment on 'The Theology of Education.' " *The Christian Scholar* 37, no. 2 (June):150-51.

"Still Working Miracles." *The Messenger* 19, no. 11 (1 June):3.

"We Can Count on Him." *The Messenger* 19, no. 11 (1 June):8-10. First Appeared in *The Pastor*.

"Polysyllables: Pro and Con." *Christianity and Crisis* 14, no. 11 (28 June):84-86.

"The Parents' Class." *Program Manual* (Fall):13-29. Boston: Pilgrim Press.

Letter to the Editor. *The Messenger* 19, no. 22 (30 November):33.

1955

"Arnold Toynbee: The Long and Short of It." *The Intercollegian* 72, no. 6 (February):3.

"Preaching Hope During Lent." *Pulpit Digest* 35, no. 202 (February):11-15.

"To the Editor." *The Reporter* 12, no. 4 (24 February):12.

"The Religious Vision of Arnold Toynbee." *Christianity and Crisis* 15, no. 6 (18 April):43-46.

" 'Though the Mountains Shake.' " *Children's Religion* 16, no. 5 (May):12-13.

"The Parents' Class in Pilgrim Series." *Program Manual* (Summer):14-30. Boston: Pilgrim Press.

"Teetering on the Edge of a Precipice." *The Messenger* 20, no. 14 (26 July):10-12.

"What's the Use?" *Youth* 6, no. 17 (21 August):8-10.

"Evangelism, Stewardship, and Social Action." *Social Action* 22, no. 1 (September):6-18.

"The Partiality of God." *The Intercollegian* 73, no. 2 (October):14-17.

"Neither Defeatist nor Silent." Letter to the Editor. *The Christian Century* 72, no. 48 (30 November):1402.

1956

"Theological Insights into Self-identity." *The Chicago Theological Seminary Register* 46, no. 2 (March):58-65.

"Three Snapshots of the South." *Christianity and Crisis* 16, no. 8 (14 May):60-61.

"Time Is a Mystery." *Children's Religion* 17, no. 6 (June):3-4.

"The 'Fanaticism' of Christianity." *Christianity and Crisis* 16, no. 15 (17 September):116-19.

"No One Can Tell You Why to Pray." *Children's Religion* 17, no. 11 (November):3-4.

1957

"The Artist as Prophet-Priest of Culture." In *Christian Faith and the Contemporary Arts,* edited by Finley Eversole. Nashville: Abingdon Press, pp. 72-79.

"The Stories Jesus Told." *Children's Religion* 18, no. 3 (March):3-4.

"Religion, Stewardship, and Social Action." *The New Christian Advocate* 1, no. 7 (April):74-80. Condensed from *Social Action.*

"Sacred Images of Man—Protestant." *The Christian Century* 74, no. 50 (11 December):1478-81.

1958

"The Holy." In *A Handbook of Christian Theology: Definition Essays on Concepts and Movements of Thought in Contemporary Protestantism,* edited by Marvin Halverson. New York: Meridian Books, pp. 167-70.

"Imperatives and Motivations for Church Unity." In *Christian Unity in North America: A Symposium,* edited by J. Robert Nelson. St. Louis: Bethany Press, pp. 33-42.

"God's Power and Our Weakness." In *Streams of Healing: A Book of Comfort,* compiled by Lester R. Liles. Westwood, NJ: Fleming H. Revell Co., p. 19.

"To Magnify His Holy Name." In *Great Phrases of the Christian Language: A Devotional Book,* by Roger L. Shinn and others. Philadelphia: United Church Press, pp. 1-18.

"Service in the Armed Forces: Resources for Study in the Christian Round Table." *Crossroads* 8, no. 2 (January-March):55-64.

"Resources for the Leader of the Christian Round Table: Service in the Armed Forces." *Westminster Adult Leader* 1, no. 2 (January-March):35-40.

"Who Killed Jesus?" *Parish School* 37, no. 5 (February):4-6.

"Symbolic Roles in Little Rock and Nashville." *Christianity and Crisis* 18, no. 1 (3 February):4-6.

"The Story of Man and the Image of Man." *Religious Education* 53, no. 2 (March-April):108-13.

"What Can Easter Mean to Children?" *Baptist Leader* 19, no. 12 (March):20-21. This article, one of a series planned by the Committee on Children's Work of the Division of Christian Education of the National Council of Churches, was published by several cooperating denominations. Some include *Children's Religion* 19, no. 3 (March):14-16; *Church School Worker* 8, no. 6 (March):53-56; *Presbyterian Action* 8, no. 3

(March):12-13; *Growing* 11, no. 2 (January-March 1959):70-72; *The Cumberland Presbyterian Worker* 17, no. 3 (March 1961):1, inside back cover; *Christian Growing* 10, no. 3 (Spring 1962):20-23; *Child Guidance* 21, no. 4 (April 1962):1-2; *Resources* 2, no. 8 (April 1963):4-7; *Crossroads* 13, no. 3 (April-June 1963):78-80; *The Methodist Teacher—Kindergarten* 1, no. 3 (Spring 1965):2-4; *The Christian Home* 27, no. 8 (April 1968):38-40; and *The United Methodist Pupil—Kindergarten* 3, no. 3 (Spring 1971):52-54.

"A Note on Art and Religion." *Koinonia* 2, no. 2 (Spring):3-7.

"The Adventure of Self-discovery." *Children's Religion* 19, no. 8 (August):3-4.

"Saying Good-Bye to God." *The Pulpit* 29, no. 9 (September):4-5, 15.

"Churchman as Citizen." *Social Action* 25, no. 2 (October):5-12.

"Comments on 'Prologue to Involvement.' " *Motive* 19, no. 3 (December):31.

"The Star and the Satellite." *Christianity and Crisis* 18, no. 21 (8 December):169-70.

1959

"Die christliche Ethik in der industriellen Gesellschaft." In *Hamburger Jahrbuch für Wirtschaft- und Gesellschaftspolitik,* herausgegeben von Heinz-Dietrich Ortlieb, übersetzt von Ingeborg Fleischmann. Festausgabe für Eduard Heimann. Tübingen: J.C.B. Mohr, pp. 288-97.

"The Story of Man and the Image of Man." In *What Is the Nature of Man? Images of Man in Our American Culture,* by Kenneth Boulding and others. Philadelphia: Christian Education Press, pp. 118-31.

"The Service of the Christians." *Theology and Life* 2, no. 1 (February):41-48.

"Ancient Faith, Modern Testimony." *The Christian Century* 76, no. 15 (15 April):448-50.

"The Lordship of Christ—and American Society." *Encounter* 20, no. 4 (Autumn):459-69.

"The Affair Between Church and Culture." *Social Progress* 50, no. 1 (October):17-30.

"Time for Self-criticism." *Christianity and Crisis* 19, no. 16 (5 October):134-35.

"A Good Word for Some Southern Ways." *Christianity and Crisis* 19, no. 17 (19 October):148-51.

"The X Factor in the New Church-School Curriculum." *United Church Herald* 2, no. 20 (29 October):15, 34.

"God's Gift at Christmas." *Church School Worker* 10, no. 3 (November):60-61, 64.

"The Rumpus About Highlander." *Christianity and Crisis* 19, no. 20 (30 November):170-71.

"New Questions." *The Southern Patriot* 17, no. 10 (December):4. Reprinted from *Christianity and Crisis.*

"A Good Word for Some Southern Ways." *Concern* 15, no. 8 (25 December 25):9-11.

1960

"Sünde und Schuld." In *Weltkirchenlexikon,* herausgegeben von Franklin H. Littell und Hans Hermann Walz. Stuttgart: Kreuz-Verlag, pp. 1411-15.

"Bibliography for Ministers: Christian Ethics," with John C. Bennett, *Union Seminary Quarterly Review* 15, no. 2 (January):137-42.

"Conversations Between Athens and Jerusalem." *Resource* (January):1-9.

"Some Ethical Foundations of Christian Theology." *Union Seminary Quarterly Review* 15, no. 2 (January):99-110.

"Fear in Deerfield." *Christianity and Crisis* 19, no. 24 (25 January):211.

"What Does Christian Education Aim to Do?" *Church School Worker* 10, no. 6 (February):9-11.

"New Questions." *Social Progress* 50, no. 4 (February):31. Reprinted from *Christianity and Crisis.*

"The Importance of the Right to Vote." *Christianity and Crisis* 20, no. 4 (21 March):25-26.

"What Next at Vanderbilt?" *The Grain of Salt* 13, no. 12 (31 March):1, 5.

"The Vanderbilt Fracas." *Christianity and Crisis* 20, no. 5 (4 April):34-35.

"To the Editor." *The Reporter* 22, no. 9 (28 April):10.

"Curious Comrades." *Christianity and Crisis* 20, no. 9 (30 May):74.

"The Negro Communicates." *Christianity and Crisis* 20, no. 10 (13 June):83.

"A University in Conflict." *Christianity and Crisis* 20, no. 11 (27 June):91.

"Ethics Requires Faith." *Christianity and Crisis* 20, no. 14 (8 August):123.

"Civil Rights in the Election." *Christianity and Crisis* 20, no. 15 (19 September):126-27.

"The Parents' Class." *Church School Worker* 11, no. 2 (October):25-31.

"Interview ... with a Theologian." *Youth* 11, no. 21 (9 October):18-23.

"The Parents' Class." *Church School Worker* 11, no. 3 (November):27-30.

"What the Campaign Did to Religion." *Christianity and Crisis* 20, no. 19 (14 November):161-63.

"The Parents' Class." *Church School Worker* 11, no. 4 (December):42-46.

"Beats and the Squares." *The Intercollegian* 78, no. 4 (December):18-19.

1961

"The Parents' Class." *Church School Worker* 11, no. 5 (January):22-28, 68.

"Statistics: Important But Not Enough." *Christianity and Crisis* 20, no. 24 (23 January):213-16.

"The Parents' Class." *Church School Worker* 11, no. 6 (February):26-30.

"The Parents' Class." *Church School Worker* 11, no. 7 (March):33-37.

"The Parents' Class." *Church School Worker* 11, no. 8 (April):27-33.

"Fools—and Fools." *Motive* 19, no. 7 (April):4-7.

"The Parents' Class." *Church School Worker* 11, no. 9 (May):26-29, 33.

"Leaders in Communication Speak . . ." *The Christian Broadcaster* 9, nos. 2-3 (May-September):24-29.

"The Burning Issue." *Christianity and Crisis* 21, no. 9 (29 May):83.

"The Parents' Class." *Church School Worker* 11, no. 10 (June):42-46.

"The Parents' Class." *Church School Worker* 11, no. 11 (July-August):16-27.

"The Parents' Class." *Church School Worker* 12, no. 1 (September):34-37, 64.

"Does Christian Faith Change?" *Children's Religion* 22, no. 10 (October):5-6.

"The New Era in Economic History." *Christianity and Crisis* 21, no. 17 (16 October):170-71.

1962

"Responses of Protestant Ethics to Political Challenges." In *The Ethic of Power: The Interplay of Religion, Philosophy, and Politics,* edited by Harold D. Lasswell and Harlan Cleveland. New York: Conference on Science, Philosophy and Religion in Their Relation to the Democratic Way of Life, Inc.; distributed by Harper & Brothers, pp. 143-59.

"Social Ethics." In *New Frontiers of Christianity,* edited by Ralph C. Raughley Jr. New York: Association Press, pp. 63-80.

"Faith and the Perilous Future." In *Nuclear Weapons and the Conflict of Conscience,* edited by John C. Bennett. New York: Charles Scribner's Sons, pp. 173-88.

"An Invocation" and "For Better Understanding." In *Worship Services for Church Groups,* by Friedrich Rest. Philadelphia: Christian Education Press, pp. 134, 137-38.

"Human and Divine: The Encounter with Humanism." In *Proceedings of the Ninth International Congregational Council,* Rotterdam, The Netherlands, 4-12 July. London: Independent Press, Ltd., pp. 70-78.

"Education for an Unknown Future." *Perspective* 3, no. 1 (March):41-51.

"Non-Partisan Piety of the Right." *Christianity and Crisis* 22, no. 3 (5 March):22-23.

"Christian Education as Adoption." *Religious Education* 57, no. 2 (March-April):88-90.

"What I Believe About Life After Death." *Union Seminary Quarterly Review* 17, no. 4 (May):311-15.

"Tragicomedy in New Orleans." *Christianity and Crisis* 22, no. 8 (14 May):70.

"Who Crows Last on Jim Crow?" *Christianity and Crisis* 22, no. 13 (23 July):126.

"The Highlander Spirit." *Christianity and Crisis* 22, no. 14 (6 August):134.

"Planning for Christian Education." *United Church Herald* 5, no. 15 (23 August):10-11.

"Hopes for the Second Vatican Council." *Christianity and Crisis* 22, no. 16 (1 October):157-59.

"The Ethics of Affluence." *The Nation* 195, no. 10 (6 October):199-201.

"Protestant Reconstruction in Urbanized Culture." *Christianity and Crisis* 22, no. 20 (26 November):203-4.

"The Student Interracial Ministry: A Venture of Faith." *The Interseminarian* 1, no. 4 (December):25-26.

"The Strange New Economy." *Christianity and Crisis* 22, no. 22 (24 December):231.

1963

"Neoorthodoxy." In *The Westminster Dictionary of Christian Education*, edited by Kendig Brubaker Cully. Philadelphia: Westminster Press, pp. 461-63.

"Military Technology and Human Hopes." *Christianity and Crisis* 23, no. 1 (4 February):1-2.

"Do We Really *Want* Christian Education?" *Church School Worker* 13, no. 7 (March):7-9.

"The Ministry to Persons in a Time of Social Change." *Pulpit Digest* 43, no. 297 (March):15-20.

"A Protestant Looks at Religious Liberty." *Union Seminary Quarterly Review* 18, no. 3, Pt. I (March):223-34.

"Taxes, Economics and Morals." *Christianity and Crisis* 23, no. 4 (18 March):33-34.

"The Churches and Taxation." *Christianity and Crisis* 23, no. 4 (18 March):34-35.

"Conversation Between Athens and Jerusalem." *Universitas* 1, no. 2 (Spring):62-71.

"The Impact of Rapid Economic Change upon the Churches." *Social Action* 29, no. 8 (April): 16-30. Also appeared in *Social Progress* 53, no. 6 (April): 11-21.

"The New Economy." *Christianity and Crisis* 23, no. 7 (29 April):63.

"The Pathological Right." *Christianity and Crisis* 23, no. 10 (10 June):102.

"The 'Corrupt Society.'" Letter to the Editor. *The Nation* 196, no. 24 (22 June):inside cover, opposite 517.

"The Testing of the Church." *Christianity and Crisis* 23, no. 12 (8 July):122-23.

"The Meaning of the Bible for Children." *Church School Worker* 13, no. 12 (August):54-55, 58.

"1963 First Amendment Conference: Response of the Discussants." *Catholic World* 197, no. 1, 181 (August):308-10.

"Faith for Critical Times." In *The Church and Culture in Crisis*, report of the Town and Country Convocation of the United Church of Christ, held at Heidelberg College, Tiffin, Ohio, August 27-29, pp. 78-84. Published by the Department of the Church in Town and Country, Division of Church Extension, United Church Board for Homeland Ministries.

"Juniors and the Bible." *Church School Worker* 14, no. 1 (September):51-53.

"La question raciale dans le christianisme américain." *Christianisme Social* 71e Année, No. 9-12 (Septembre-Décembre):641-52. Trad. Christiane Allenbach.

"Study the Bible with New Depth." *United Church Hearld* 6, no. 16 (5 September):12-13.

"Axioms for White Liberals." *Christianity and Crisis* 23, no. 16 (30 September):167.

"The Shattering of the Theological Spectrum." *Christianity and Crisis* 23, no. 16 (30 September):168-71.

"Jesus—As He Was and as He Is." *International Journal of Religious Education* 40, no. 2 (October):14-16. Reprinted in *The Methodist Teacher III-IV* 2, no. 2 (Winter 1965-66):2-4.

"The Church and Technology." *Monday Morning* 28, no. 18 (4 November):5-7. Also appeared in *The Interchurch News* 5, no. 4 (December):2, and *The Witness* 48, no. 42 (12 December):12-13.

"Civil Rights: Morality and Practical Politics." *Christianity and Crisis* 23, no. 19 (11 November):197-98.

"To Be Bold or Timid?" Letter to the Editor. *Christianity and Crisis* 23, no. 22 (23 December):243.

1964

"Many Perspectives Needed." In *Religion and International Relations*, by Kenneth Thompson. New York: Council for Christian Social Action—United Church of Christ, pp. 32-36.

"Preface," "The American Search for Self-understanding," and "Is This a Time of Crisis for the American Character?" In *The Search for Identity: Essays on the American Character*, edited by Roger L. Shinn, Religion and Civilization Series. Published by The Institute for Religious and Social Studies; distributed by New York: Harper & Row, pp ix-xi, 1-13, 181-93.

"The President's Budget." *Christianity and Crisis* 24, no. 2 (17 February):9-10.

"Come Creator Spirit—For the Redemption of the Secular World." *Theology and Life* 7, no. 1 (Spring):112-19.

"Prejudice Feeds on Falsehoods." *The Link-Wagner College Alumni News* 15, no. 2 (April):10-11.

"The Changing Tides of History." *Christianity and Crisis* 24, no. 6 (13 April):58-59.

"Come Creator Spirit—For the Redemption of the Secular World." *Theology and Life* 7, no. 2 (Summer):112-19.

"The Moral Duty to Obey—or Disobey—Law." *Christianity and Crisis* 24, no. 13 (20 July):142-43.

"Election Issues—1964." *Social Action* 31, no. 2 (October):4-15.

"Rejoinder." *Social Action* 31, no. 2 (October):26.

"The Campaign and the Candidates." *The Intercollegian* 82, no. 2 (October-November):6-11.

"The Old Question: Politics and Religion." *Christianity and Crisis* 24, no. 18 (2 November):205, 207.

"The Urgency of Congressional Reform." *Christianity and Crisis* 24, no. 22 (28 December):257-58.

1965

"Discussion: Christianity and Other Faiths." *Union Seminary Quarterly Review* 20, no. 2 (January):178-79.

"The State of the Culture." *Christianity and Crisis* 24, no. 24 (25 January):281-82.

"The Assassination of Malcolm X." *Christianity and Crisis* 25, no. 4 (22 March):46-47.

"Dietrich Bonhoeffer: 1906-1945." *Christianity and Crisis* 25, no. 6 (19 April):75.

"Law and Behavior." *Youth* 16, no. 9 (25 April):16-22.

"Negotiation Without Capitulation." *Christianity and Crisis* 25, no. 7 (3 May):89-90.

"Ferment on the Campus." *Christianity and Crisis* 25, no. 10 (14 June):126-27.

"The Christ of Many Faces." *Christianity and Crisis* 25, no. 13 (26 July):157-58.

"Sex Is Not God—Agora." *United Church Herald* 8, no. 16 (15 September):3.

"In Our Time." *The American Scholar* 34, no. 4 (Autumn):632-34.

"Living in a World That Won't Stand Still." *Motive* 26, no. 1 (October):49-52.

"A New Era of Self-understanding." *Youth* 16, no. 18 (10 October):8-13.

"How Free Can a Free Society Be?" *Christianity and Crisis* 25, no. 18 (1 November):224-25.

"The Need to Keep Moving." *Christianity and Crisis* 25, no. 22 (27 December):277-78.

1966

"The Educational Ministry of the Church." In *An Introduction to Christian Education*, edited by Marvin J. Taylor. Nashville: Abingdon Press, pp. 11-20.

"Unsettling Problems." In *Reform and Renewal: Exploring the United Church of Christ*, by Douglas Horton and others. Philadelphia: United Church Press, pp. 24-31.

"The Old Question: Politics and Religion," "How Free Can a Free Society Be?" and "Axioms for White Liberals." In *Witness to a Generation: Significant Writings from Christianity and Crisis 1941-1966*, edited by Wayne H. Cowan, with a preface by Herbert Butterfield. New York: Bobbs-Merrill Co. pp. 65-67, 72-74, 201-3. Reprinted from *Christianity and Crisis*.

Population Crisis. Pt I. Hearings before the Subcommittee on Foreign Aid Expenditures of the Committee on Government Operations. U.S. Senate. Eighty-Ninth Congress, Second Session. Washington, DC: Government Printing Office, pp. 171-76.

"The Church in an Affluent Society." In *Christian Social Ethics in a Changing World: An Ecumenical Theological Inquiry*, edited by John C. Bennett. New York: Association Press, pp. 266-85.

" 'God is Dead' Theology: One Assessment." *The Episcopalian* 131, no. 1 (January):32-33. An interview with Shinn.

"Pathways of Miscalculation." *Christianity and Crisis* 25, no. 23 (10 January):289-90.

"Education Will Change." *The Presbyterian Outlook* 148, no. 12 (21 March):1. Reprinted from *An Introduction to Christian Education*.

"A Theological Perspective of Communication." The Christian Broadcaster 13, no. 1 (April):27-28.

"In a Time of Tragic Conflict." *Social Action* 32, no. 8 (April):19-27.

"Lippmann—Kennan Realism." *Christianity and Crisis* 26, no. 6 (18 April):76-78.

"Persecution of the Homosexual." *Christianity and Crisis* 26, no. 7 (2 May):84-85.

"Toward Responsible Parenthood." *United Church Herald* 9, no. 11 (1 June):17-18, 32.

"Justice and Selective Service." *Christianity and Crisis* 26, no. 11 (27 June):139-40.

"The Attraction and Offense of the Ministry." *Religion in Life* 35, no. 3 (Summer):344-52.

"Human Responsibility in the Emerging Society." In *Prospective Changes in Society by 1980: Including Some Implications for Education,* reports prepared for the First Area Conference. Denver: Designing Education for the Future, July, pp. 243-59.

"Form and Reform." In *Proceedings of the Tenth Assembly of the International Congregational Council,* Swansea, South Wales, 7-11 July, pp. 35-37.

"The American Economy—The Next Ten Years." *Christianity and Crisis* 26, no. 14 (8 August):181-82.

"Agora." *United Church Herald* 9, no. 15 (September):29.

"The Moral Meaning of Transportation." *Christianity and Crisis* 26, no. 16 (3 October):209-10.

"How Not to Conduct a Poll." *Christianity and Crisis* 26, no. 18 (31 October):234-35.

1967

"The Public Responsibility of Theology." In *America and the Future of Theology,* edited by William A. Beardslee. Philadelphia: Westminster Press, pp. 174-91.

"Anti-Semitism," "Apartheid," "Collectivism," "Colour Bar," "Individualism," "Race Relations," "Racism," "Segregation," and "Slavery," In *Dictionary of Christian Ethics,* edited by John Macquarrie. Philadelphia: Westminster Press, pp. 14-15, 16, 60-61, 61, 164-65, 285-87, 287-88, 314, 321-22.

"The Church in an Affluent Society." In *The Church Amid Revolution: A Selection of Essays Prepared for the World Council of Churches Geneva Conference on Church and Society,* edited by Harvey G. Cox. New York: Association Press, pp. 70-89.

"Agnosticism" and "Atheism." In *The Encyclopedia Americana,* New York: Americana Corporation, 1:337, 2:604-5.

"Harry F. Ward—1873-1966." *The Union Seminary Tower* 14, no. 1 (Winter):1, 5.

"Current Movements in Christian Ethics—An Annotated Bibliography." *Social Action* 33, no. 5 (January):27-30.

"Christian-Communist Dialogue." *Christianity and Crisis* 26, no. 23 (9 January):301-2.

"Discussion: Communist—Christian Dialogue." *Union Seminary Quarterly Review* 22, no. 3 (March):213-17.

"The House vs. Powell." *Christianity and Crisis* 27, no. 4 (20 March):46-47.

"The Selective Conscientious Objector Again." *Christianity and Crisis* 27, no. 5 (3 April):61-63.

Amending and Extending the Draft Law and Related Authorities. Hearings before the Committee on Armed Services. United States Senate. Ninetieth Congress, First Session. April 12, 13, 14, 17, 18, and 19, 1967. Washington DC: Government Printing Office, pp. 598-602.

"Respect for Dissent." *Council Journal* 5, no. 8 (May):10-12.

"Some Meanings of Sex in Western Culture." *Coker College Alumnae Magazine* 2, no. 3 (Summer):6-9.

"The New Wave in Christian Thought." *Encounter* 28, no. 3 (Summer):219-56.

"The Hate-Johnson Syndrome." *Christianity and Crisis* 27, no. 12 (10 July):157-58.

"Whom the Gods Would Destroy . . ." *Christianity and Crisis* 27, no. 15 (18 September):197-98.

"Is Racial Hostility Ever a Gain?" *Christianity and Crisis* 27, no. 17 (16 October):225-26.

"Paul Ramsey's Challenge to Ecumenical Ethics." *Christianity and Crisis* 27, no. 18 (30 October):243-47.

"Ethical Perspectives on the Guaranteed Annual Income." *Social Action* 34, no. 3 (November):37-49.

"Soviet Russia—After 50 Years." *Christianity and Crisis* 27, no. 20 (27 November):271-75.

1968

"The Lover's Quarrel of the Church with the World." In *Crisis in the Church: Essays in Honor of Truman B. Douglass*, edited by Everett C. Parker. Philadelphia: The Pilgrim Press, pp. 15-27.

"Bonhoeffer, Dietrich," "Brunner, Emil," and "Bultmann, Rudolf Karl." In *The Encyclopedia Americana.* New York: Americana Corporation, 4:208, 4:654, 4:768-69.

"Editor's Introduction: A Rebellion and Its Career" and "Theology—The Prodigal Son of Biblical Faith." In *Restless Adventure*, edited by Roger L. Shinn. New York: Charles Scribner's Sons, pp. 11-22, 53-89.

"The Gift of Sex." In *Tune In*, edited by Herman C. Ahrens Jr. Philadelphia: The Pilgrim Press, pp. 18-19. Reprinted from *Youth.*

"The President and His War Critics." *Christianity and Crisis* 27, no. 23 (8 January):309-10.

"Congress Is Important, Too." *Christianity and Crisis* 28, no. 2 (19 February):16.

"How Do We Recognize God's Action?" *Bulletin of the Department of Theology of the World Alliance of Reformed Churches and the World Presbyterian Alliance* 8, no. 3 (Spring):2-3.

"Lent in an Age of Satire." *Christianity and Crisis* 28, no. 5 (1 April):53.

"The Trial of Captain Dale E. Noyd." *Christianity and Crisis* 28, no. 5 (1 April):63-66.

"Education: The Mediator of Conflict." Interview. *Colloquy* 1, no. 6 (June):6-7.

"Guilt: Personal and Social." *Christianity and Crisis* 28, no. 13 (22 July):161-62.

"Christian Realism: A Symposium." *Christianity and Crisis* 28, no. 14 (5 August):175-90.

"Fellowship Funds Cut." Letter to the Editor. *The New York Times* 118, no. 40, 426 (Sunday, 29 September):Sec. 4, 11.

"Election Issues 1968." *Social Action/Social Progress* 35/59, nos. 2/1 (October/September-October):5-19.

"Election '68: A Symposium, The Election Is Important." *Christianity and Crisis* 28, no. 17 (14 October):237-38.

"Discussion: Communist-Christian Dialogue." *Social Action* 35, no. 3 (November):12-17.

"Severe Time of Testing Ahead!" *Tempo* 1, no. 4 (1 December):2.

"After Viet Nam, What Next?" *Christianity and Crisis* 28, no. 21 (9 December):293-94.

1969

"Paul Tillich as a Contemporary Theologian." In *The Intellectual Legacy of Paul Tillich*, edited by James R. Lyons. Detroit: Wayne State University Press, pp. 57-77.

"Homosexuality: Christian Conviction and Inquiry." In *The Same Sex: An Appraisal of Homosexuality,* edited by Ralph W. Weltge. Philadelphia: The Pilgrim Press, pp. 43-54.

"The New Administration Moves In." *Christianity and Crisis* 28, no. 24 (20 January):337-38.

"God—War—Love—The Church Morality—Sin—Christ: Questions and Answers from a Theologian." *Youth* 20, no. 4 (23 February):5-16.

"The Identity Crisis of Theology." *The Tower Alumni Magazine,* Union Theological Seminary, Spring, pp. 3-4.

"End the Draft? Yes, But ..." *Christianity and Crisis* 29, no. 6 (14 April):79-80.

"The Reformed Position in an Ecumenical Age." *Bulletin of the Department of Theology of the World Alliance of Reformed Churches and the World Presbyterian Alliance* 9, no. 4 (Summer):9-13.

"Reflections on Recent Elections." *Christianity and Crisis* 29, no. 13 (21 July):197-98.

"Apollo as Ritual." *Christianity and Crisis* 29, no. 14 (4 August):223.

"The Tragic Middle East." *Christianity and Crisis* 29, no. 15 (15 September):233-36.

"A Policeman's Lot." *Christianity and Crisis* 29, no. 16 (29 September):243-44.

"Genetic Decisions: A Case Study in Ethical Method." *Soundings* 52, no. 3 (Fall):299-310.

"More Than Survival." *Commonweal* 91, no. 5 (31 October):148-49.

". . . to Bind Up the Nation's Wounds." *Christianity and Crisis* 29, no. 19 (10 November):277-78.

"Together in Ministry: Opportunities for the 70s." *Lutheran Teacher* 44, no. 11 (December):26-27.

1970

"Heim, Karl," and "Incarnation." In *The Encyclopedia Americana.* New York: Americana Corporation, 14:57, 14:838-39.

"Ethics and the Family of Man." In *This Little Planet,* edited by Michael Hamilton, with an introduction by Edmund S. Muskie. New York: Charles Scribner's Sons, pp. 127-59.

"Theological Ethics: Retrospect and Prospect." In *Theology and Church in Times of Change: Essays in Honor of John Coleman Bennett,* edited by Edward LeRoy Long Jr. and Robert T. Handy. Philadelphia: Westminster Press, pp. 117-41.

"Agenda for the 70s—Radicalizing Theological Education." *United Church Herald* 13, no. 1 (January):15.

"Hans Morgenthau: Realist and Moralist." *Worldview* 13, no. 1 (January):9-12.

"Together in Ministry." *Findings* 18, no. 1 (March):16.

". . . On the Way to Desegregation." *Christianity and Crisis* 30, no. 5 (30 March):53-55.

"Population and the Dignity of Man." *The Christian Century* 87, no. 15 (15 April):442-48.

"What Price Reversal?" *Current* no. 118 (May):29-30. Reprinted from *Christianity and Crisis.*

"Christianity and the New Humanism: Second Thoughts." *Review and Expositor* 67, no. 3 (Summer):315-27.

"Prophecy and Politics in Search for Peace." In *The Reformation and the Revolution,* Monograph Series no. 3 (July):107-14. Sioux Falls, SD: The Augustana College Press.

"The Gift of Sex." *Youth* 21, no. 14 (July):26-27. Reprinted from *Tune In.*

"Together in Ministry—Christian Education Emphasis—1970." *Spectrum* 46, no. 4 (July/August):2.

"Chasms in Communications." *Christianity and Crisis* 30, no. 13 (20 July):153-54.

"Social Principles Draft—II." *Engage* 2, no. 20 (1 September):13-15.

"Response to Albert van den Heuvel's 'Letter to a White South African Friend.' " *Christianity and Crisis* 30, no. 21 (28 December):287-88.

"To Wait and to Do: A Response to Roland Murphy." *Continuum* 7, no. 4 (Winter):596-604.

1971

"God" and "Tillich, Paul Johannes Oskar." In *The Encyclopedia Americana,* New York: Americana Corporation, 12:835-38, 26:747-48.

"The Locus of Authority: Participatory Democracy in the Age of the Expert." In *Erosion of Authority,* edited and with an introduction by Clyde L. Manschreck. Nashville: Abingdon Press, pp. 92-122.

"A Paradigm of Decision-Making." In *Public Policy and the Expert: Ethical Problems of the Witness,* by Daniel D. McCracken, Special Studies #212. New York: The Council on Religion and International Affairs, pp. 114-25.

"Human Freedom and the SST." *Christianity and Crisis* 31, no. 1 (8 February):1-2.

"Our Crisis of Authority." *United Church Herald* 14, no. 3 (March):20-22.

"The Court Coerces Conscience." *Christianity and Crisis* 31, no. 5 (5 April):53-54.

"Education Is a Mystery." *Colloquy* 4, no. 6 (June):4-7.

"The Mass Psychology of Army Life." Interview with Cornelius Cooper Jr. *Christianity and Crisis* 31, no. 13 (26 July):151-56.

Letter to the Editor. *Commentary* 52, no. 2 (August):12, 14.

"Humanity and the Future." *New World Outlook* New Series 32, no. 2, Whole Series 61, no. 10 (October):30.

"The Court and Social Change." *Christianity and Crisis* 31, no. 17 (18 October):210.

"Who Am I?" *Youth* 22, no. 11 (November):42-43.

1972

"Education Is a Mystery." In *A Colloquy on Christian Education,* edited by John H. Westerhoff III. Philadelphia: United Church Press, pp. 18-24.

"Science and Ethical Decision: Some New Issues." In *Earth Might Be Fair: Reflections on Ethics, Religion, and Ecology,* edited by Ian G. Barbour. Englewood Cliffs, NJ: Prentice-Hall, pp. 123-45.

"Existentialism" and "Logos." In *The Encyclopedia Americana,* New York: Americana Corporation, 10:762-63, 17:691-92.

"Political Theology in the Crossfire." *Perspective* 13, no. 1 (Winter):59-79.

"Confronting Moral Realities." *Social Action* 38, no. 6 (February):25-30.

"Survival Ethics: Toward a Zero-Growth Economy." *Christianity and Crisis* 32, no. 4 (20 March):56-60.

"Political Theology in the Crossfire." *Journal of Current Social Issues* 10, no. 2 (Spring):10-20.

"Statement at the Funeral of Adam Clayton Powell, The Abyssinian Baptist Church, April 9, 1972." *UTS Journal,* May, p. 14.

"The P.O.W. Diaries of Roger L. Shinn." *United Church Herald* 15, no. 7 (July/August):12-17.

"Wars and Rumors of Wars." *Together* 16, no. 7 (July):36-40.

"Response to 'The Just Revolution.'" *Christianity and Crisis* 32, no. 12 (10 July):168.

"What's at Stake in '72?" *Christianity and Crisis* 32, no. 17 (16 October):227-28.

"Quotas: The Arithmetic of Justice." *Christianity and Crisis* 32, no. 18 (30 October):238-40.

"Our Cause Is Not Just." *The Christian Century* 89, no. 39 (1 November):1099-103.

"A Divine Gift." *Engage* 5, no. 3 (December):16-18.

"Dialogue on the Future." With Margaret Mead. *Youth* 23, no. 12 (December):2-15.

"Our Technological Time of Troubles." *Religion in Life* 41, no. 4 (Winter):450-61.

1973

"Population and the Dignity of Man." In *Ethical Issues in Biology and Medicine,* edited by Preston N. Williams. Cambridge, MA: Schenkman, pp. 78-93.

"Jesus." In *The McGraw-Hill Encyclopedia of World Biography.* New York: McGraw-Hill, 5:557-61.

"Religious Communities and Changing Population Attitudes." In *The Population Crisis and Moral Responsibility,* edited by J. Philip Wogaman. Washington, DC: Public Affairs Press, pp. 299-319.

"How Do You 'Cultivate the Spirit'?" *Lay Leaders Bulletin,* United Church of Christ, Council for Lay Life and Work. No. 37 (Spring):1.

"How People Make Moral Decisions." *Colloquy* 6, no. 5 (May-June):19-21.

"Personal Decisions and Social Policies in a Pluralist Society." *The Perkins School of Theology Journal* 27, no. 1 (Fall):58-63.

"Barmen and Ourselves." *Christianity and Crisis* 33, no. 22 (24 December):266-67.

1974

"Ethical Aspects of the Exercise of Command." *Military Chaplain's Review* DA PAM 165-100 (Winter):67-76. Reprinted in *Journal of Professional Military Ethics* 3, no. 2 (December 1982):1-9.

"Perilous Progress in Genetics." *Social Research* 41, no. 1 (Spring):83-103.

"The Impact of Science and Technology on the Theological Understanding of Social Justice." *Anticipation* No. 17 (May):52-59.

"Morality and the President's 'Amnesty.' " *Christianity and Crisis* 34, no. 10 (10 June):122-23.

"Scenario: Petrol for the Future." *Engage/Social Action* 2, no. 8 (August):18-29.

"The Population Crisis: Exploring the Issues." *Christianity and Crisis* 34, no. 14 (5 August):170-75.

"Realism, Radicalism, and Eschatology in Reinhold Niebuhr: A Reassessment." *The Journal of Religion* 54, no. 4 (October):409-23.

"Vietnam Amnesty: What Would *You* Have Done?" with others. *The Christian Century* 91, no. 34 (9 October):926.

"The President's Page." *UTS Journal* (December):3-4.

"Amateur and Professional." *UTS Journal* (December):12-14.

"Asceticism for Our Time." *A.D.—United Church of Christ* 3, no. 12 (December):42-46.

"Christmas 1974: Time for a Turnaround." *Messenger* 123, no. 12 (December):16-19.

1975

"Realism, Radicalism, and Eschatology in Reinhold Niebuhr: A Reassessment." In *The Legacy of Reinhold Niebuhr,* edited by Nathan A. Scott Jr. Chicago: University of Chicago Press, pp. 85-99. Reprinted from *The Journal of Religion.*

"The Style of Christian Polemics." In *American Society of Christian Ethics Selected Papers,* edited by Franklin Sherman. Missoula, MT: Scholars Press, pp. 1-14.

"Foetal Diagnosis and Selective Abortion: An Ethical Exploration." In *Genetics and the Quality of Life,* edited by Charles Birch and Paul Abrecht. Elmsford, NY: Pergamon Press, pp. 74-85.

"Discussion: Are There Ethical Limits to Scientific Discovery?" In *The Nature of Scientific Discovery: A Symposium Commemorating the 500th Anniversary of the Birth of Nicolaus Copernicus,* edited by Owen Gingerich. Washington, DC: Smithsonian Institution Press, pp. 596-604.

"The President's Page." *UTS Journal* (April):3-4.

"Report to the Board of Directors—February 4, 1975." *UTS Journal* (April):5-7.

"Reviewers' Choice: Summertime Reading." *The Christian Century* 92, no. 16 (30 April):449.

"Whatever Happened to Theology?" *Christianity and Crisis* 35, no. 8 (12 May):112-13.

"Science and Ethics," with others. *The American Scholar* 44, no. 3 (Summer):439-56.

"Continuing the Discussion on Intervention in the Middle East." *Christianity and Crisis* 35, no. 11 (23 June):162-63.

"A Prayer for a Hungry World." *Youth* 26, nos. 7 and 8 (July-August):90-91.

"Litany for the Hungry." *Youth* 26, nos. 7 and 8 (July-August):90.

"The Churches and Nuclear Energy." *Ecumenical Courier* 34, no. 3 (July-September):2.

"Ethical Reflections on the Use of Nuclear Energy." *Anticipation* No. 21 (October):40-45.

1976

"Ethical Reflections on the Use of Nuclear Energy." In *Facing Up to Nuclear Power: Risks and Potentialities of the Large-scale Use of Nuclear Energy,* edited by John Francis and Paul Abrecht. Philadelphia: Westminster Press, pp. 137-55. Reprinted from *Anticipation.*

"Foreword." In *The Sustainable Society: Ethics and Economic Growth,* by Robert L. Stivers. Philadelphia: Westminster Press, pp. 9-11.

"Lifeboat Ethics: A Response," "Panel on the Human Future," and "The Wind and the Whirlwind." In *Finite Resources and the Human Future,* edited by Ian G. Barbour. Minneapolis: Augsburg Publishing House, pp. 48-54, 168-73, 176-84.

"The Population Crisis: Exploring the Issues." In *Moral Issues and Christian Response,* edited by Paul T. Jersild and Dale A. Johnson. New York: Holt, Rinehart & Winston, 1976, 1983, 2d ed. 221-28; 3d ed. 234-41. Reprinted from *Christianity and Crisis.*

"The Baffling Mix of Confusion and Guilt." *Union Seminary Quarterly Review* 31, no. 2 (Winter):126-36.

"Who Should Decide?: The Karen Quinlan Case." *Christianity and Crisis* 35, no. 22 (19 January):328-29.

"The Books That Shape Lives." *The Christian Century* 93, no. 7 (3 March):202.

"Continuing the Discussion on the NCC and Nuclear Power." *Christianity and Crisis* 36, no. 8 (10 May):105-6.

"What's at Stake in '76?" *Christianity and Crisis* 36, no. 15 (4 October):217-18.

1977

"Ideals, Maxims, and Deeds." In *Morality and Foreign Policy: A Symposium on President Carter's Stance,* edited by Ernest W. Lefever. Washington, DC: Ethics and Public Policy Center, Georgetown University, pp. 53-56.

"Living with Scarcity." In *Small Comforts for Hard Times: Humanists on Public Policy,* edited by Michael Mooney and Florian Stuber, introduction by Florian Stuber, with a foreword by James Gutmann. New York: Columbia University Press, pp. 137-51.

"Realism and Ethics in Political Philosophy." In *Truth and Tragedy: A Tribute to Hans J. Morgenthau,* with an intellectual autobiography by Hans J. Morgenthau, edited by Kenneth Thompson and Robert J. Myers. Washington, DC: The New Republic Book Co., pp. 95-103.

"Biblical and Theological Perspectives on Peace." *Bulletin of the Peace Studies Institute* 7, no. 1 (January):35-40.

"Language and Communication: On Words, Music and Math." *The New Review of Books and Religion* 1, no. 10 (June):3.

"Nuclear War in the Mideast—Part II: Ethical Questions to the Pranger Scenario." *Worldview* 20, nos. 7 and 8 (July-August):45-47.

"Paying for Abortion: Is the Court Wrong? A C&C Symposium." *Christianity and Crisis* 37, no. 14 (19 September):202-3.

1978

"Church and State: Some Convictions and Perplexities Coming Out of Experiences of the United States of America." In *Church and State: Opening a New Ecumenical Discussion,* edited by Lukas Vischer, Faith and Order Paper No. 85. Geneva: World Council of Churches, pp. 29-39.

"Gene Therapy: VI. Ethical Issues." In *Encyclopedia of Bioethics,* edited by Warren T. Reich. New York: The Free Press, 2:521-27.

"Harry Emerson Fosdick, Religious Reformer." In *The Riverside Preachers: Fosdick, McCracken, Campbell, Coffin,* edited by Paul H. Sherry. New York: The Pilgrim Press, pp. 171-76.

"Crisis of Energy, Crisis of Faith." *A.D.—United Church of Christ* 7, no. 2 (February):22-27. Also published in *The Lutheran* 16, no. 4 (March):15-17, and *The United Church Observer* New Series 43, no. 5, Old Series 150, no. 5 (November 1979):15-17.

"Energy: Lurching to Jerusalem." *Christianity and Crisis* 38, no. 4 (3 April):66-68.

"An Awakening of Freedom." *Journal of Current Social Issues* 15, no. 2 (Summer):14-16.

"A Prayer for a Hungry World." *Concern* 20, no. 8 (July):30.

"How Far Have Christians Come to Terms with the Nuclear Debate?" *One World* No. 38 (July/August):7-9.

"Perception and Belief." *Union Seminary Quarterly Review* 34, no. 1 (Fall):13-21.

"Liberation, Reconciliation and 'Just Revolution.'" *The Ecumenical Review* 30, no. 4 (October):319-32.

"Beyond the Horizon: A Prayer." *Youth* 29, no. 11 (November):68-69.

"Covenant: Heritage and Responsibility." *Reformed World* 35, no. 4 (December):174-79.

"I Miss You, Margaret." *Christianity and Crisis* 38, no. 19 (11 December):304-6.

1979

"The Technological Explosion." In *Great Decisions '79: Identifying Human Values.* Supplement issued by the Council on Religion and International Affairs (CRIA): 3 pages, not paginated.

"Education in Values: Acculturation and Exploration." *Teachers College Record* 80, no. 3 (February):507-18.

"Faith, Science, Ideology and the Nuclear Decision." *Christianity and Crisis* 39, no. 1 (5 February):3-8. Reprinted in *The South African Outlook,* June, pp. 83-86.

"Continuing the Discussion: 'A Political Christ.'" *Christianity and Crisis* 39, no. 4 (19 March):54-57.

"Continuing the Discussion: 'Faith, Science, Ideology and the Nuclear Decision.'" *Christianity and Crisis* 39, no. 9 (28 May):139-42.

"Faith, Science, Ideology and the Nuclear Decision." *Anticipation* No. 26 (June):53-57.

"Forum: An Educational Impossibility: The Value-Free Classroom." *Columbia* 5, no. 1 (Summer):26-30.

"How to Control Technology: An Overview of the Faith-Science Conference." *Christianity and Crisis* 39, no. 16 (29 October):266-69.

"Books That Make a Difference." *The New Review of Books and Religion* 4, no. 3 (November):24.

1980

"Education in Values: Acculturation and Exploration." In *Education and Values,* edited by Douglas Sloan. New York: Teachers College Press, pp. 111-22. Reprinted from *Teachers College Record.*

"International Agreements and Unilateral Initiatives: A Response." In *Faith and Science in an Unjust World: Report of the World Council of Churches' Conference on Faith, Science and the Future,* vol. 1: Plenary Presentations, edited by Roger L. Shinn. Philadelphia: Fortress Press, pp. 323-24.

"Toward a Post-Enlightenment Doctrine of Human Rights." In *History, Religion, and Spiritual Democracy: Essays in Honor of Joseph L. Blau,* edited by Maurice Wohlgelernter. New York: Columbia University Press, pp. 294-316.

"Homosexuality: Christian Conviction and Inquiry." In *Homosexuality and Ethics,* edited by Edward Batchelor Jr. New York: The Pilgrim Press, pp. 3-13.

"The World Energy Crunch." In *Great Decisions '80: Identifying Human Values,* Supplement issued by the Council on Religion and International Affairs (CRIA), pp. 35-39.

"Mission and Unity: How Are They Related?" *Encounter* 41, no. 1 (Winter):1-13.

"WCC Conference on Faith, Science, and the Future." *Journal of Ecumenical Studies* 17, no. 1 (Winter):206-7.

"Competence and Participation." *The New Review of Books and Religion* 4, no. 6 (February):3, 26.

"How to Be Fighters and Healers." *The Bulletin of the American Protestant Hospital Association* 44, no. 1 (Spring):19-22, 31-32.

"Is Noble Sperm So Special?" *Christianity and Crisis* 40, no. 10 (9 June):171-73.

"Abortion: An Unhappy Stand-Off." *Christianity and Crisis* 40, no. 13 (18 August):219, 31.

"Our Creative Opportunity." *RCAgenda* (September-October):21-25.

"Our Creative Opportunity." *Journal of Current Social Issues* 16, no. 4 (Winter):4-6.

1981

"High Technology—Its Human Problems and Benefits." *The Bulletin of Science, Technology, and Society* 1, nos. 1/2:43-48.

"Social Ethics: The Roman Catholic Church and the World Council of Churches." *Mid-Stream* 20, no. 1 (January):41-59.

"The Energy Question: The Theological Issues." *Journal for Preachers* 4, no. 2 (Lent):4-8.

"No More Painless Progress: The End of a Liberal Dream." *Christianity and Crisis* 41, no. 4 (16 March):52-57.

"Moral Majority: Distorting Faith and Patriotism." *A.D.—United Church of Christ* 10, no. 6 (June/July):15-17.

"A Search for Faith: Questions and Answers from a Theologian." *Youth* 32, no. 7 (July):10-25.

"The Career of a Scholar-Teacher: James Alfred Martin, Jr." *Union Seminary Quarterly Review* 37, nos. 1/2 (Fall/Winter):5-12.

1982

"Personal Decisions and Social Policies in a Pluralist Society." In *Abortion: The Moral Issues,* edited by Edward Batchelor Jr. New York: The

Pilgrim Press, pp. 166-74. Reprinted from *The Perkins School of Theology Journal.*

"Ethical Responsibility and the Corporate World: An Educational Experiment." In *The Annual of the Society of Christian Ethics,* edited by Larry L. Rasmussen. Dallas: The Society of Christian Ethics, pp. 217-27; distributed by The Council on the Study of Religion.

"Niebuhr, Reinhold" and "Niemoller, Martin." In *The Encyclopedia Americana,* Danbury, CT: Grolier Inc., 20-324, 20-326.

"WCC Disarmament Hearings: Reflections on the Meeting in Amsterdam." *The Union News* Issue No. 1:8-9.

"A Dilemma, Seen from Several Sides." *Christianity and Crisis* 41, no. 22 (18 January):371-76.

"Letters: The Meaning of Our Years." *A.D.—United Church of Christ* 11, no. 6 (June):47.

"Cloak This Blessing in Some Safeguards." *USA Today* 1, no. 50 (23 November):10A.

1983

"Ethical Dilemmas of Deterrence." In *Before It's Too Late: The Challenge of Nuclear Disarmament,* edited by Paul Abrecht and Ninan Koshy. Geneva: World Council of Churches, pp. 59-71.

"The Story of Man and the Image of Man." In *Wholeness and Holiness: Readings in the Psychology/Theology of Mental Health,* edited by H. Newton Malony. Grand Rapids, MI: Baker Book House, pp. 31-40. Reprinted from the March-April 1958 issue of *Religious Education.*

"Die schwierigen Partner: Deutsch-amerikanische Belastungen." *Evangelische Kommentare* 16, no. 3 (März):148-49.

"Ecumenism and Advocacy: The UCC's Prophetic Witness." *Keeping You Posted* 18, no. 3A (1 March):1, 4.

"Faith and Politics: The Mission to Speak." *Christianity and Crisis* 43, no. 4 (21 March):85-88.

"What Will You Read This Summer?" *Christianity and Crisis* 43, no. 11 (27 June):256.

Human Genetic Engineering. Hearings before the Subcommittee on Investigations and Oversight on Science and Technology. U.S. House of Representatives, Ninety-Seventh Congress, Second Session, November 16, 17, 18, 1982 (No. 170). Washington, DC: Government Printing Office, pp. 301-41.

"The Dilemma of Likely Uses." *Christianity and Crisis* 43, no. 19 (28 November):459.

1984

"The Days After 'The Day After.' " *Bulletin of the Atomic Scientists* 40, no. 2 (February):43-44.

"The Candidates: Walter Mondale." *Christianity and Crisis* 44, no. 3 (5 March):56.

"The Churches' Search for a Peace Policy: Two Approaches Compared." *Christianity and Crisis* 44, no. 5 (2 April):105-11.

"Changing with Tradition." *Church Leaders Bulletin for Laity & Clergy* no. 32 (Summer):4.

"Law as a Structure for Freedom." *Seventh Angel* 1, no. 4 (20 July):17-18, 22.

"Celebrating the Birth of a Baby." *Christianity and Crisis* 44, no. 20 (10 December):459-60.

1985

"Preface." *The Ecumenical Review* 37, no. 1 (January):ix-x.

"A Venturing Social Ethic." *The Ecumenical Review* 37, no. 1 (January):133-39.

"Memories of Margaret Mead." *Christianity and Crisis* 45, no. 3 (4 March):66-70.

Reviews by Roger Lincoln Shinn

1947

"Truth from Harry's Bar?" *The Intercollegian* 64, no. 8 (April):21.

"Tragedy and Anxiety in Human Existence." Review of *The Meaning of Existence*, by Charles Duell Kean. *The Woman's Press* 41, no. 6 (June):38.

Review of *The Meaning of Existence*, by Charles Duell Kean. *Christianity and Society* 12, no. 3 (Summer):27-29.

Review of *God in History*, by Sherwood Eddy. *Christianity and Society* 12, no. 3 (Summer):30-31.

Review of *Report on the Germans*, by W.L. White. *Christianity and Society* 12, no. 4 (Autumn):28-29.

Review of *Freedom and Order: Lessons from the War*, by Eduard Heimann. *Union Seminary Quarterly Review* 3, no. 1 (November):47, 49.

"Faith of a World Christian Leader." Review of *The Kingship of Christ*, by W.A. Visser't Hooft. *The Woman's Press* 42, no. 3 (March):34.

1948

"Conceptual Theologizing in a Desperate Day." Review of *The Christian Doctrine of Grace*, by Oscar Hardman. *Christendom* 13, no. 2 (Spring):250-51.

Review of *The Kingship of Christ*, by W.A. Visser't Hooft. *Christianity and Society* 13, no. 2 (Spring):28-29.

Review of *Christianity and Civilisation*, by Arnold J. Toynbee. *Christianity and Society* 13, no. 2 (Spring):30-31.

Review of *God Confronts Man in History*, by Henry Sloane Coffin. *Union Seminary Quarterly Review* 3, no. 4 (May):42-43.

Review of *The Kingship of Christ*, by W.A. Visser't Hooft. *Union Seminary Quarterly Review* 3, no. 4 (May):46-47.

Review of *The Church, The Gospel and War*, edited by Rufus M. Jones. *The Westminster Bookman* 8, no. 1 (September-October):30.

1949

Review of *William Temple, Archbishop of Canterbury: His Life and Letters*, by F.A. Iremonger. *Union Seminary Quarterly Review* 4, no. 3 (March):47, 49.

Review of *Meaning in History*, by Karl Löwith, *Christianity and Society* 14, no. 3 (Summer):29-30.

Review of *Man's Disorder and God's Design*, an omnibus volume of the Amsterdam Assembly Series, prepared under the auspices of the First Assembly of the World Council of Churches. *Christianity and Society* 14, no. 3 (Summer):30.

Review of *Notes Towards the Definition of Culture*, by T.S. Eliot. *Christianity and Society* 14, no. 4 (Autumn):29-30.

Review of "Religion and the State," vol. 14, no. 1 of *Law and Contemporary Problems*. *Christianity and Society* 14, no. 4 (Autumn):30.

Review of *Christianity and Civilization*, First Part: Foundations, by Emil Brunner. *Union Seminary Quarterly Review* 5, no. 1 (November):53-54.

Review of *God's Boycott of Sin: A Consideration of Hell and Pacifism*, by Rachel H. King. *The Review of Religion* 14, no. 1 (November): 103-4.

Review of *The Holy Imperative: The Power of God and the Good Life*, by Winston L. King. *The Westminster Bookman* 9, no. 2 (November-December):20-21.

Review of *A Short History of Existentialism*, by Jean Wohl and *Existentialism*, by Jean-Paul Sartre. *Christianity and Society* 15, no. 1 (Winter):29-30.

Review of *Kierkegaard's Philosophy of Religion*, by Reidar Thomte. *Christianity and Society* 15, no. 1 (Winter):32-33.

1950

Review of *Christianity and Civilization*, Second Part; Specific Problems, by Emil Brunner. *Union Seminary Quarterly Review* 5, no. 3 (March):52-53.

Review of *Existentialisme théologique*, by Enrico Castelli. *The Review of Religion* 15, no. 3 (March):324-25.

Review of *A Free Man's Faith*, by D. Luther Evans. *Religious Education* 45, no. 3 (May-June):188.

Review of *The Christian Demand for Social Justice*, edited by William Scarlett, *Christianity and Society* 15, no. 3 (Summer):29.

"For Modern Doubters." Review of *The Gospel and Modern Thought*, by Alan Richardson. *The Pastor* 13, no. 11 (July):30.

Review of *Psychotherapy and a Christian View of Man*, by David E. Roberts. *The Westminster Bookman* 10, no. 1 (September-October):19-20.

Review of *Modern Arms and Free Men*, by Vannevar Bush. *Christianity and Society* 15, no. 4 (Fall):23-24.

Review of *Call to Christian Action*, by Dores R. Sharpe. *Christianity and Society* 15, no. 4 (Fall):29.

Review of *Catholic Radicalism*, by Peter Maurin. *Christianity and Society* 16, no. 1 (Winter):25-26.

1951

Review of *The Belief in Progress*, by John Baillie. *Christianity and Society* 16, no. 2 (Spring):27-28.

"This Is Man's Destiny." Review of *Catholicism*, by Henri de Lubac, translated by Lancelot C. Sheppard. *The Pastor* 14, no. 9 (May):40.

Review of *The Theology of Reinhold Niebuhr*, by Edward J. Carnell. *Theology Today* 8, no. 2 (May):284-85.

Review of *Christian Love*, by Paul E. Johnson. *The Westminster Bookman* 10, no. 5 (September):7-8.

Review of *Faith and Duty*, by N.H.G. Robinson. *The Journal of Religious Thought* 9, no. 1 (Autumn-Winter):61-62.

1952

Review of *Protestant Thought in the Twentieth Century*, edited by Arnold S. Nash. *The Student World* Serial Number 177 (Third Quarter):296-97.

Review of *The Irony of American History*, by Reinhold Niebuhr. *Religious Education* 47, no. 5 (September-October):358-59.

"Faith and History: A New Approach." Review of *History and Human Relations*, by Herbert Butterfield, and *Christianity in European History*, by Herbert Butterfield. *Christianity and Society* 17, no. 4 (Fall):27.

" 'Unfuzzy' Mysticism." Review of *Time and Eternity: An Essay on the Philosophy of Religion*, by W.T. Stare. *The Pastor* 16, no. 3 (November):39-40.

Review of *Christ and Time*, by Oscar Cullmann. *The Review of Religion* 17, nos. 1-2 (November):96-97.

Review of *The Scriptures of Mankind: An Introduction*, by Charles S. Braden. *The Westminster Bookman* 11, no. 4 (December):20-21.

1953

Review of *Nietzsche and Christian Ethics*, by R. Motson Thompson. *Theology Today* 10, no. 2 (July):275-76.

1954

Review of *God Hidden and Revealed*, by John Dillenberger, foreword by Paul Tillich. *The Student World* Serial Number 183 (First Quarter):112.

Review of *Criticism and Faith*, by John Knox. *Union Seminary Quarterly Review* 9, no. 3 (March):48-49.

"Prisoner for God." Review of *Dietrich Bonhoeffer*, edited by Eberhard Bethge, translated by Reginald H. Fuller. *The Intercollegian* 71, no. 9 (May):21.

Review of *Introduction to Religion*, by Winston L. King. *The Westminster Bookman* 13, no. 2 (June):10-11.

Review of *Christianity, Communism, and History*, by William Horden. *Religious Education* 49, no. 5 (September-October):363.

Review of *Against the Stream; Shorter Post-War Writings 1946-52*, by Karl Barth, edited by Ronald Gregor Smith. *Theology Today* 11, no. 3 (October):415-16.

1955

"An Appeal to Americans." Review of *Tomorrow Is Today*, by James H. Robinson, *Christianity and Society* 20, no. 2 (Spring):26.

Review of *Early Christian Interpretations of History*, by R.L.P. Milburn. *The Westminster Bookman* 14, no. 2 (June):9-10.

"Boomerang." Review of *The Tyranny of Progress—Reflections on French Sociology*, by Albert Salomon. *The Christian Century* 72, no. 27 (6 July):792.

"Symposium." Review of *The Idea of History in the Ancient Near East*, edited by Robert C. Dentan. *The Christian Century* 72, no. 42 (19 October):1209-10.

Review of *The Bent World: A Christian Examination of East-West Tensions*, by J.V. Langmead Casserley. *Religion in Life* 25, no. 1 (Winter):137-38.

1956

Review of *Reinhold Niebuhr: His Religious, Social, and Political Thought*, edited by Charles W. Kegley and Robert W. Bretall. *The Messenger* 21, no. 8 (17 April):26.

"Restless Pioneer." Review of *Reinhold Niebuhr: His Religious, Social, and Political Thought*, edited by Charles W. Kegley and Robert W. Bretall. *The Pastor* 19, no. 10 (June):40.

Review of *Christian Eschatology and Social Thought*, by Ray C. Petry. *Religion in Life* 25, no. 4 (Autumn):624-25.

"Stimulating Thomism." Review of *The Social and Political Philosophy of Jacques Maritain: Selected Readings*, edited by Joseph W. Evans and Leo R. Ward. *Interpretation* 10, no. 4 (October):469-71.

"No Historians' Historian?" Review of *Toynbee and History: Critical Essays and Reviews*, edited by M.F. Ashley Montagu. *The Christian Century* 73, no. 40 (3 October):1133.

"The Religion of Arnold Toynbee: A Review Article." Review of *An Historian's Approach to Religion*, by Arnold Toynbee. *The Christian Century* 73, no. 41 (10 October):1166-67.

"No Unthinking Faith." Review of *Faith, Reason, and Existence*, by John A. Hutchison. *The Christian Century* 73, no. 42 (17 October):1201-2.

Review of *Christianity and the Existentialists*, edited by Carl Michalson. *The Chaplain* 13, no. 6 (December):32-33.

"Back-Talk." Review of *Debates with Historians*, by Pieter Geyl. *The Christian Century* 73, no. 51 (19 December):1480.

1957

Review of *The Idea of Revelation in Recent Thought*, by John Baillie. *Chicago Theological Seminary Register* 47, no. 1 (January):19-20.

Review of *Sin and Science: Reinhold Niebuhr as Political Theologian*, by Holtan P. Odegard. *The Journal of Religion* 37, no. 1 (January):57-58.

Review of *God's Way with Man: Variations on the Theme of Providence*, by Roger Hazelton. *Interpretation* 11, no. 2 (April):236.

"Revivals in U.S. Studies." Review of *Revivalism and Social Reform*, by Timothy L. Smith. *The Nashville Tennessean*, 14 July, p. 3-E.

"Societies and Symbols." Review of *Israel and Revelation*, vol. 1 of Order and History, by Eric Voegelin. *The Christian Century* 74, no. 30 (24 July):894.

"Sex Study Draws Ire." Review of *The Decline and Fall of Sex*, by Robert Elliott Fitch. *The Nashville Tennessean,* 11 August, p. 9-C.

1958

Review of *The Dynamics of World History*, by Christopher Dawson, edited by John J. Mulloy. *The Journal of Religion* 38, no. 1 (January):70-71.

"History and Eternity." Review article of *The Presence of Eternity: History and Eschatology*, by Rudolf Bultmann; *Christianity Among the Religions of the World*, by Arnold Toynbee; *On the Philosophy of History*, by Jacques Maritain; *The Dynamics of World History*, by Christopher Dawson, edited by John J. Mulloy; and *Israel and Revelation*, vol. 1, *The World of the Polis*, vol. 2, and *Plato and Aristotle*, vol. 3, by Eric Voegelin. *Saturday Review* 41, no. 10 (8 March):26-27.

"U.S. Church in Society Examined." Review of *American Protestantism and Social Issues 1919-1939*, by Robert Moats Miller. *The Nashville Tennessean,* 11 May, p. 6-H.

Review of *Christianity Among the Religions of the World*, by Arnold Toynbee. *The Westminster Bookman* 17, no. 2 (June):24-25.

Review of *The Presence of Eternity: History and Eschatology,* by Rudolf Bultmann. *The New Christian Advocate* 2, no. 7 (July): 87-88.

Review of *Christian Commitment: An Apologetic*, by Edward John Carnell. *Theology Today* 15, no. 2 (July):278-79.

"Another 'Leap of Being.'" Review of *The World of the Polis* and *Plato and Aristotle*, vols. 2 and 3 of Order and History, by Eric Voegelin. *The Christian Century* 75, no. 38 (17 September): 1053-54.

Review of *Patterns of Faith in America Today*, edited by F. Ernest Johnson. *United Church Herald* 1, no. 1 (9 October):27.

1959

Review of *Judgements on History and Historians*, by Jacob Burckhardt, translated by Harry Zohn. *The Christian Century* 76, no. 5 (4 February):135-36.

Review of *Christians and the State*, by John C. Bennett. *United Church Herald* 2, no. 4 (12 February):31.

Review of *Maker of Heaven and Earth*, by Langdon Gilkey. *Prospectus* 2, no. 20 (6 March):1-2.

Review of *Christian Theology: An Ecumenical Approach*, by Walter Marshall Horton. *Religious Education* 54, no. 3 (May-June):313-14.

Review of *Christian Affirmations in a Secular Age*, by Giovanni Miegge, translated by Stephen Neill. *Religious Education* 54, no. 3 (May-June):314.

Review of *The Crucial Task of Theology*, by E. Ashby Johnson. *The Journal of Religion* 39, no. 3 (July):216-17.

Review of *An Analytical Philosophy of Religion*, by Willem F. Zuurdeeg. *Theology Today* 16, no. 2 (July):272-74.

Review of *The Case for Theology in Liberal Perspective*, by L. Harold DeWolf; and *The Case for a New Reformation,* by William Hordern. *Religious Education* 54, no. 5 (September-October):475-77.

Review of *Religious Experience and Other Essays and Addresses*, by William Temple, collected and edited with an introduction by A.E. Baker. *The Journal of Religion* 39, no. 4 (October):291.

"Contemporary Relevance of Plato." Review of *Therapeia: Plato's Conception of Philosophy*, by Robert E. Cushman. *Interpretation* 12, no. 4 (October):475-76.

"On Rendering to Caesar and to God." Review of *How to Serve God in a Marxist Land*, by Karl Barth and Johannes Hamel; and *Communism and the Theologians: Study of an Encounter,* by Charles C. West. *Worldview* 2, no. 12 (December):10-11.

1960

Review of *Protestant Thought from Rousseau to Ritschl,* by Karl Barth, translated by Brian Cozen, translation revised by H.H. Hartwell and others. *Union Seminary Quarterly Review* 15, no. 2 (January):170-72.

Review of *The Population Explosion and Christian Responsibility,* by Richard M. Fagley. *United Church Herald* 3, no. 3 (4 February):23.

Review of *Sexual Relation in Christian Thought,* by Derrick Sherwin Bailey: *Sex and Family in the Bible,* by Raphael Patai; and *Sex and Love in the Bible,* by William Graham Cole. *Union Seminary Quarterly Review* 15, no. 3 (March):260-61.

Review of *The Hinge of History,* by Carl Michalson. *The Westminster Bookman* 19, no. 1 (March):13-14.

Review of *Poems,* by Boris Pasternak, translated by Eugene M. Kayden. *United Church Herald* 3, no. 5 (3 March):22.

Review of *The Faith We Proclaim,* by Elmer J.F. Arndt. *United Church Herald* 3, no. 10 (12 May):30.

Review of *A Mirror of the Ministry in Modern Novels,* by Horton Davis. *Review of Religious Research* 2, no. 1 (Summer):39-40.

Review of *The Spiritual Legacy of John Foster Dulles,* edited by Henry P. Van Dusen. *Union Seminary Quarterly Review* 16, no. 1 (November):51-52.

Review of *Christianity and Communism Today,* by John C. Bennett. *Union Seminary Quarterly Review* 16, no. 1 (November):52-53.

1961

Review of *Christian Attitudes Toward War and Peace,* by Roland H. Bainton. *The Westminster Bookman* 20, no. 1 (March):18-19.

Review of *Protestant Thought and Natural Science,* by John Dillenberger. *Review of Religious Research* 3, no. 1 (Summer):45-46.

Review of *The Sense of History in Greek and Shakespearean Drama,* by Tom F. Driver. *Union Seminary Quarterly Review* 17, no. 1 (November):108-10.

Review of *Searchlights on Contemporary Theology,* by Nels F.S. Ferré. *Religious Education* 56, no. 6 (November-December):461-62.

1962

Review of *Symbolism in Religion and Literature,* edited by Rollo May. *Union Seminary Quarterly Review* 17, no. 2 (January):198.

"Further into Idealism." Review of *Radical Monotheism and Western Culture with Supplementary Essays,* by H. Richard Niebuhr. *Interpretation* 16, no. 2 (April):197-99.

"Heresy—or Academic Orthodoxy?" Review of *The Faith of a Heretic,* by Walter Kaufmann. *The Christian Scholar* 45, no. 3 (Fall):248-52.

Review of *God and the Rich Society,* by D.L. Munby. *Union Seminary Quarterly Review* 18, no. 1 (November):108-10.

Review of *Christ and Selfhood,* by Wayne E. Oates. *Religious Education* 57, no. 6 (November-December):459.

1963

Review of *The Role of the Self in Conflicts and Struggle,* by Edward LeRoy Long Jr. *The Westminster Bookman* 22, no. 1 (March):27-28.

Review of *Reinhold Niebuhr: A Prophetic Voice in Our Time,* essays in tribute by Paul Tillich, John C. Bennett, and Hans J. Morgenthau, edited by Harold R. Landon. *Union Seminary Quarterly Review* 18, no. 4 (May):426.

Review of *War and Christian Conscience: How Shall Modern War Be Conducted Justly,* by Paul Ramsey. *Union Seminary Quarterly Review* 18, no. 4 (May):426-29.

Review of *Science and Religion: An Interpretation of Two Communities,* by Harold K. Schilling. *United Church Herald* 6, no. 10 (16 May):25.

Review of *Conscience and Its Right to Freedom,* by Eric D'Arcy. *Religious Education* 58, no. 5 (September-October):481-82.

Review of *Honest to God,* by John A.T. Robinson. *Union Seminary Quarterly Review* 19, no. 1 (November):83, 85.

1964

Review of *Second Chance for American Protestants,* by Martin E. Marty. *Union Seminary Quarterly Review* 19, no. 2 (January):181-83.

Review of *For Christ's Sake,* by O. Fielding Clarke, and *The Honest to God Debate,* edited by David L. Edwards. *Union Seminary Quarterly Review* 19, no. 4, Pt. 1 (May):371-73.

Review of *The Responsible Self: An Essay in Christian Moral Philosophy,* by H. Richard Niebuhr. *Religious Education* 59, no. 6 (November-December):518.

"Concerned Critics." Review of *What's Ahead for the Churches?* edited by Kyle Haselden and Martin E. Marty. *The Christian Century* 81, no. 53 (30 December):1625-26.

1965

Review of *The Ethics of Sex,* by Helmut Thielicke. *Union Seminary Quarterly Review* 20, no. 2 (January):203-5.

Review of *The New Creation as Metropolis,* by Gibson Winter. *The Journal of Religion* 45, no. 1 (January):69-70.

Review of *Towards a Theological Understanding of History,* by Eric C. Rust. *Review and Expositor* 62, no. 2 (Spring):225-27.

Review of *Christian Sex Ethics,* by V.A. Demant, and *Love and Sexuality,* by Robert Grimm. *United Church Herald* 8, no. 16 (15 September):32.

"Paperbacks: Paul Tillich." Review of *Dynamics of Faith; The Courage to Be; Love, Power and Justice; Christianity and the Encounter of World Religions; The Religious Situation; Theology of Culture; The Shaking of the Foundations; The New Being; The Eternal Now; Biblical Religion and the Search for Ultimate Reality,* and *The Protestant Era. The New York Times Book Review,* (19 September) Sec. 7, 30. Distributed in 115, no. 39,348 (17 October) because of a strike from 17 September to 10 October. Reprinted in *Church Social Worker* 16, no. 10 (June-July 1966):46-47, 54.

1966

"The Dialogue Between the Theologian and the Historian." Review of *Christianity and History,* by E. Harris Harbison. *The Ecumenical Review* 18, no. 1 (January):107-8.

Review of *The Secular Promise,* by Martin Jarrett-Kerr. *Union Seminary Quarterly Review* 21, no. 2, Pt. 2 (January):258-59.

Review of *Freedom and Man,* edited by John Courtney Murray. *Commonweal* 83, no. 17 (4 February):538-39.

Review of *Man's Nature and His Communities,* by Reinhold Niebuhr. *Union Seminary Quarterly Review* 21, no. 3 (March):350-51.

Review of *The Insecurity of Freedom: Essays on Human Existence,* by Abraham J. Heschel. *Conservative Judaism* 21, no. 1 (Fall):83-84.

1967

Review of *Shantung Compound,* by Langdon Gilkey. *Religion in Life* 36, no. 4 (Winter):615-16.

1969

"Rethinking the Unthinkable." Review of *War and/or Survival,* by William V. O'Brien. *Worldview* 12, no. 10 (October):17-19.

1970

Review of *Humiliation and Celebration: Post-Radical Themes in Doctrine, Morals and Mission,* by Gabriel Fackre. *Religious Education* 65, no. 1 (January-February):72-73.

Review of *Technology and People,* by Cameron P. Hall. *Tempo* 2, no. 15 (15 May):8.

Review of *Abortion: Law, Choice and Morality,* by Daniel Callahan. *Theological Studies* 31, no. 4 (December):782-84.

1971

Review of *The Experience of Nothingness,* by Michael Novak. *The Journal of Religion* 51, no. 4 (October):307-8.

Review of *The Power to Be Human: Toward a Secular Theology,* by Charles C. West. *The Princeton Seminary Bulletin* 64, no. 3 (December):116-17.

Review of *Responsible Freedom: Guidelines for Christian Action,* by L. Harold DeWolf. *Commonweal* 95, no. 13 (24 December):306-8.

1972

Review of *Christian Ethics and the Community,* by James M. Gustafson. *Commonweal* 96, no. 2 (17 March):42-43.

Review of *Reinhold Niebuhr: Prophet to Politicians,* by Ronald H. Stone. *Union Seminary Quarterly Review* 27, no. 4 (Summer):250-51.

1973

Review of *Things to Come: Thinking About the 70's and 80's,* by Herman Kahn and B. Bruce-Briggs. *Theology Today* 29, no. 4 (January):430-31.

1974

"A Potential for Influence." Review of *American Religious Groups View Foreign Policy: Trends in Rank-and-File Opinion 1937-1969,* by Alfred O. Hero Jr. *The Christian Century* 91, no. 6 (13 February):185-86.

1975

Review of *Justice and Mercy,* by Reinhold Niebuhr, edited by Ursula M. Niebuhr. *Union Seminary Quarterly Review* 30, nos. 2-4 (Winter-Summer):231-32.

1976

"American Ideology and the Bible." Review of *The Captain America Complex: The Dilemma of Zealous Nationalism,* by Robert Jewett. *Interpretation* 30, no. 3 (July):303-5.

1977

Review of *The Just War in the Middle Ages,* by Frederick H. Russell; *Ideology, Reason, and the Limitation of War: Religious and Secular Concepts, 1200-1740,* by James Turner Johnson; and *War and Christian Ethics,* edited by Arthur F. Holmes. *Religious Studies Review* 3, no. 3 (July):157-61.

Review of *On Synthesizing Marxism and Christianity,* by Dale Vree, and *Culture and Practical Reason,* by Marshall Sahlins. *The New Review of Books and Religion* 2, no. 2 (October):24, 26.

1978

Review of *Once to Every Man,* by William Sloane Coffin Jr. *Union Seminary Quarterly Review* 33, no. 2 (Winter):101-2.

Review of *Young Reinhold Niebuhr,* edited by William G. Chrystal. *Union Seminary Quarterly Review* 33, nos. 3-4 (Spring-Summer):199-201.

Review of *Scientific Man: The Humanistic Significance of Science,* by Enrico Cantore. *Theological Studies* 39, no. 4 (December):808-10.

1982

Review of *The Human Center: Moral Agency in the Social World,* by Howard L. Harrod. *Interpretation* 36, no. 3 (July):328-29.

"Calvin Revisited, Revised." Review of *Ethics from a Theocentric Perspective,* vol. 1, *Theology and Ethics,* by James M. Gustafson. *Christianity and Crisis* 42, no. 12 (12 July):218-20.

Review of *The Liberation of Life: From Cell to the Community,* by Charles Birch and John B. Cobb Jr. *The Christian Century* 99, no. 35 (10 November):1143-44.

1983

Review of *Where Faith and Economics Meet: A Christian Critique,* by David M. Beckmann. *International Bulletin of Missionary Research* 7, no. 1 (January):36.

"The Struggle for Clarity: What to Do About the Arms Race." Review of *The Game of Disarmament,* by Alva Myrdal; *Beyond the Cold War: A New Approach to the Arms Race and Nuclear Annihilation,* by E.P. Thompson; *Nuclear Illusion and Reality,* by Solly Zuckerman; and *The Nuclear Delusion: Soviet-American Relations in the Atomic Age,* by George F. Kennan. *Christianity and Crisis* 42, no. 22 (24 January):449-52.

Review of *A Matter of Hope: A Theologian's Reflections on the Thought of Karl Marx,* by Nicholas Lash. *The Christian Century* 100, no. 5 (16-23 February):161-62.

"Bulwarks Against Faith Erosion." Review of *A Church to Believe In: Discipleship and the Dynamics of Freedom. The Review of Books and Religion* 11, no. 7 (Mid-April):7.

Review of *The Liberation of Life: From the Cell to the Community,* by Charles Birch and John B. Cobb Jr. *Anticipation* No. 30 (July):35. Reprinted from *The Christian Century.*

Review of *Ethics and Nuclear Deterrence,* edited by Geoffrey Goodwin, and *Nuclear Deterrence—Right or Wrong?* by Roger Ruston. *The Modern Churchman* New Series 25, no. 3:56-57.

"A New Kind of History Casts Light on the First Christians." Review of *The First Urban Christians: The Social World of the Apostle Paul,* by Wayne A. Meeks. *Christianity and Crisis* 43, no. 15 (3 October):364-66.

Review of *Biomedical Ethics Review, 1983,* edited by James M. Humber and Robert F. Almeden. *The Quarterly Review of Biology* 59, no. 2 (June):212-13.

Review of *Research Ethics,* by Kåre Berg and Knut Erik Tranøy. *The Quarterly Review of Biology* 59, no. 3 (September):305.

"The Manifold Forms of Revelation." Review of *Models of Revelation,* by Avery Dulles. *The Review of Books and Religion* 12, no. 10 (September/October):3.

"Engaging Gandhi." Review of *Fighting with Gandhi: A Step-by-Step Strategy for Resolving Everyday Conflicts,* by Mark Juergensmeyer. *Christianity and Crisis* 44, no. 15 (1 October):355-56.

Review of *Coping with Genetic Disorders: A Guide for Clergy and Parents,* by John C. Fletcher. *Christianity and Crisis* 44, no. 17 (29 October):408.

Electronic Media Works by Roger Lincoln Shinn

The Relentless Quest. Series includes "Can God Be Justified?" 50 minutes; "Absurdity, Compassion and Exile," 51 minutes; "Inscrutable Power and the Mystery of Iniquity," 52 minutes; "Nothing or Christ?" 52 minutes; and "Is Anything Not Phony?" 52 minutes. Recordings taped at Riverside Church in New York City, n.d. Richmond, VA: Reigner Recording Library, Union Theological Seminary in Virginia.

Theology Today. "The Meaning of Christian Ethics," 14 minutes. Faith in Action radio program taped 26 March, 1961. Richmond, VA: Reigner Recording Library, Union Theological Seminary in Virginia.

Theology Today. "Some Problems of Contemporary Christian Ethics," 14 minutes. Faith in Action radio program taped 2 April, 1961. Richmond, VA: Reigner Recording Library, Union Theological Seminary in Virginia.

Christian Unity. "Difference and Similarities," 42 minutes. Taped at Riverside Church in New York City on 19 April, 1961. Richmond, VA: Reigner Recording Library, Union Theological Seminary in Virginia.

Tangled World. 16mm film, black and white, sound, 28:30 minutes, 1962-66. Series includes "The Procession," "Tomorrow?" "The Captive," "The Affluent Society," "The City," "International Affairs," "Law and Behavior," "Organization," "Politics," "Racial Tension," "Science," "Self-understanding," and "Sex and the Family." Produced by the United Church of Christ (Office of Communication and Board for Homeland Ministries) for the National Council of the Churches of Christ in the U.S.A.

How Free Can a Free Society Be? 16mm film, black and white, sound, 28 minutes, 1966. Available from the Reigner Recording Library, Union Theological Seminary in Virginia, Richmond.

Crisis and Reconstruction in Christian Ethics. Series includes "Alienation as a Phenomenon of Our Time," 50 minutes; "Will Constitutional Government Remain Possible?" 55 minutes; "Sex Ethics: A Case Study," 50 minutes; and "Towards a Method of Reconstruction," 55 minutes. Cassettes taped at Phillips University in Enid, OK, on 12-13 November, 1968. Richmond, VA: Reigner Recording Library, Union Theological Seminary in Virginia.

"Ethics, Aesthetics and Scientific Endeavor," with Victor Weisskopf. University Lecture Series. Ames, IA: Iowa State University, 1970. Audio cassette, 56 minutes.

"The Implications of Genetic Engineering." University Lecture Series. Ames, IA: Iowa State University, 1970. Phonotape cassette, 28 minutes.

"Social Responsibility and the Goals of Science." University Lecture Series. Ames, IA: Iowa State University, 1970. Phonotape cassette, 58 minutes.

"Political Theology in the Cross Fire." *Thesis Cassettes* 2, no. 3 (1970). Pittsburgh: Thesis Cassettes.

"Learning to Live with Scarcity." *Thesis Cassettes* 6, no. 9 (1975). Pittsburgh: Thesis Cassettes.

"Whatever Happened to Theology?" with others. *Catalyst* 7, no. 8 (August 1975). Waco, TX: Word, Inc.

"Nuclear Arms Proliferation," with Michael P. Hamilton and Robert Pranger. Conference on Nuclear Proliferation and Terrorism sponsored by the Washington National Cathedral. Atlanta: Catacomb Cassettes, 1977. Sound recording, 76 minutes, 43 seconds.

Interpreting the Faith. "Forced Options: Theology, Ecology, Social Justice," five cassettes. Taped at Union Theological Seminary in Virginia on 3-7 July, 1978. Richmond, VA: Reigner Recording Library, Union Theological Seminary in Virginia.

"Fetal Diagnosis and Abortion." *Thesis Cassettes* 10, no. 1 (1979). Pittsburgh: Thesis Cassettes.

"Some Questions the Coming Years Will Throw at Us." Charles E. Spahr Lecture taped 29 January, 1981. Rochester, NY: Colgate-Rochester Divinity School/Bexley Hall/Crozer Theological Seminary. Sound recording, 75 minutes.

Reviews of Shinn Works

Beyond This Darkness

Bulletin from Virginia Kirkus Bookshop Service 14, no. 19 (1 October, 1946):494.

John Dillenberger. *Union Seminary Quarterly Review* 2, no. 2 (January 1947):46-47.

Hugh Peterson. *Review and Expositor* 44, no. 1 (January 1947):97-99.

Harold W. Fildey. *The Presbyterian Tribune* 62, no. 19 (8 February, 1947):22.

Richard W. Day. *The Journal of Philosophy* 44, no. 4 (13 February, 1947):109.

Roger Shaw. *The Churchman* 161, no. 4 (15 February, 1947):17.

The Christian Century 64, no. 8 (19 February, 1947):240.

Frederick B. Igler. *Crozer Quarterly* 24, no. 2 (April 1947):188-89.

Isaac K. Beckes. *International Journal of Religious Education* 23, no. 8 (April 1947):32-33.

Charles L. Copenhaver. *Advance* 139, no. 8 (August 1947):23.

John Philip Lindsay. *The Journal of Bible and Religion* 16, no. 2 (April 1948):124.

Christianity and the Problem of History

Bulletin from Virginia Kirkus' Bookshop Service 21, no. 2 (15 January, 1953):48.

Andrew D. Osborn. *Library Journal* 78, no. 5 (1 March, 1953):442.

William H. Bernhardt. "Meaning in History?" *The Pastor* 17, no. 1 (September 1953):42-43.

The United States Quarterly Book Review 9, no. 3 (September 1953):310.

A. Roy Eckardt. *Religion in Life* 22, no. 4 (Autumn 1953):619-21.

Cross Currents 4, no. 1 (Fall 1953):77.

H.W.H. *Church Management* 30, no. 1 (October 1953):82-83.

John W. Suter Jr. *The Journal of Bible and Religion* 21, no. 4 (October 1953):272-73.

John McIntyre. *Union Seminary Quarterly Review* 9, no. 1 (November 1953):50-53.

W.E. Garrison. *The Christian Century* 70, no. 47 (25 November 1953):1360.

Paul L. Ward. *The Christian Scholar* 36, no. 4 (December 1953):305-9.

Robert T. Handy. *Christianity and Society* 19, no. 1 (Winter 1953-54):23-24.

E. Harris Harbison. *Theology Today* 10, no. 4 (January 1954):571-73.

Guy H. Ranson. *Review and Expositor* 51, no. 1 (January 1954):108-9.

W. Norris Clarke. *Social Order* 4, no. 2 (February 1954):80-81.

Robert Paul Mohan. *The American Ecclesiastical Review* 130, no. 3 (March 1954):213-14.

Thomas P. Neill. *The Historical Bulletin* 32, no. 3 (March 1954):182-83.

J.J. Murray. "The Sovereignty of God." *Interpretation* 8, no. 2 (April 1954):245-46.

J. William Lee. *Religious Education* 49, no. 3 (May-June 1954):234.

Charles D. Kean. *Anglican Theological Review* 36, no. 3 (July 1954):235-37.

Howard J.B. Ziegler. *The Review of Religion* 19, nos. 1-2 (November 1954):78-80.

Edward Daub. *The Japan Christian Quarterly* 21, no. 2 (April 1955): 177-78.

Arthur Carl Piepkorn. *Concordia Theological Monthly* 29, no. 1 (January 1958):65.

Lester G. McAllister. *Encounter* 26, no. 3 (Summer 1965):405-6.

Life, Death, and Destiny

Ruth P. Tubby. *Library Journal* 82, no. 5 (1 March 1957):664.

Anglican Theological Review 39, no. 4 (October 1957):383.

Richard F. Beyer. *Advance* 149, no. 18 (4 October 1957):23.

C. Milo Connick. *The Journal of Bible and Religion* 25, no. 3 (July 1957):270.

Great Phrases of the Christian Language

Luther A. Weigle. *United Church Herald* 1, no. 1 (9 October 1958):27.

David Dunn. *Theology and Life* 2, no. 2 (May 1959):170-71.

The Existentialist Posture

J. Kenneth Kohler. *United Church Herald* 2, no. 18 (1 October 1959):30.

P.M. *The Personalist* 41, no. 3 (Summer, July 1960):376.

The Church School 15, no. 6 (March 1962):17.

The Christian Century 87, no. 18 (6 May 1970):570.

The Educational Mission of Our Church

Virgil E. Foster. "The Local Church's Educational Pilgrimage." *United Church Herald* 5, no. 13 (28 June 1962):16.

Virgil E. Foster. *International Journal of Religious Education* 39, no. 1 (September 1962):38.

Findley B. Edge. *Review and Expositor* 60, no. 2 (Spring 1963):256-57.

Oscar J. Rumpf. *Theology and Life* 6, no. 1 (Spring 1963):80-81.

Gerald H. Slusser. *The Hartford Quarterly* 3, no. 3 (Spring 1963):110-11.

Oscar J. Hussel. *Union Seminary Quarterly Review* 18, no. 4 (May 1963):429-30.

William D. Streng. *The Lutheran Quarterly* 15, no. 2 (May 1963):190-91.

William B. Kennedy. *Religious Education* 56, no. 6 (November-December 1963):556, 558.

The Search for Identity

Leon J. Putman. *United Church Herald* 7, no. 21 (1 December 1964):33.

Choice 2, no. 1 (March 1965):59.

Edwin S. Gaustad. *Union Seminary Quarterly Review* 20, no. 4 (May 1965):399-401.

Stanley J. Rowland Jr. *The Christian Century* 82, no. 37 (15 September 1965):1131-32.

Tangled World

Bulletin from Virginia Kirkus Bookshop Service, Inc. 33, no. 2 (15 January 1965):101.

Robert E. Wagenknecht. *Library Journal* 90, no. 4 (15 February 1965):889.

The Booklist and Subscription Books Bulletin 61, no. 14 (15 March 1965):683.

H.M. Warehime. *The Presbyterian Outlook* 148, no. 12 (21 March 1966):15.

Lyle E. Schaller. *The Christian Century* 82, no. 22 (2 June 1965):711.

Ethics 75, no. 4 (July 1965):309.

Clyde A. Holbrook. *Religion in Life* 34, no. 4 (Autumn 1965):629-30.

Quentin L. Quade. "Social Man and Ethics." *The Review of Politics* 28, no. 2 (April 1966):248-49.

Charles P. Taft. *Union Seminary Quarterly Review* 21, no. 4 (May 1966):469-72.

John H. White. *The Westminster Theological Journal* 28, no. 2 (May 1966):227-28.

Nolan Howington. *Review and Expositor* 63, no. 3 (Summer 1966):355.

We Believe

Jack Edward Yates. *United Church Herald* 10, no. 2 (February 1967):52.

Man: The New Humanism

The Kirkus Service 36, no. 5 (1 March 1968):251.

Herman J. Ridder. *The Reformed Review* 21, no. 4 (June 1968):27-28.

George H. Bricker. *Religion in Life* 37, no. 4 (Winter 1968):633-34.

F.W. Dillistone. "A New Humanism." *Frontier* 11, no. 4 (Winter 1968-69):314.

David L. Mueller. *Review and Expositor* 66, no. 1 (Winter 1969):84-85.

Thomas Sluberski. *Lutheran World* 16, no. 2 (1969):200.

Harold B. Kuhn. *Christianity Today* 13, no. 9 (31 January 1969):44(420).

Frederic Greeves. "Looking Ahead in Theology." *The Expository Times* 80, no. 6 (March 1969):174.

Larry Rasmussen. *Social Action* 35, no. 9 (May 1969):32-34.

Franklin M. Segler. *Southwestern Journal of Theology* 13, no. 1 (Fall 1970):88.

Restless Adventure

Harold B. Kuhn. *The Asbury Seminarian* 22, no. 3 (July 1968):21-22.

Maureen Sullivan. *Jubilee* 16, no. 3 (July 1968):44.

H. Dermot McDonald. *Christianity Today* 12, no. 21 (19 July 1968):43(1051).

Robert L. Perkins. *Library Journal* 93, no. 14 (August 1968):2878.

James A. Capo. "Philosophy's Elusive Child." *The Catholic World* 208, no. 1,246 (January 1969):190-92.

Thomas S. Champness Jr. *The Westminster Theological Journal* 31, no. 2 (May 1969):226-30.

William H. Becker. *Interpretation* 23, no. 4 (October 1969):499-502.

Paul L. Homer. *Religious Education* 65, no. 3 (May-June 1970):82, 84.

Wars and Rumors of Wars

Publishers Weekly 201, no. 9 (28 February 1972):66.

Helen Johnson. *Together* 16, no. 4 (April 1972):60.

J. Glenn Gray. *America* 126, no. 14 (8 April 1972):381-82.

Martin Marty. "Religious Books." *The Critic* 30, no. 5 (May-June 1972):85.

Peter Rowley. "The Ethics of Battle: A Soldier's Memoir." *The Christian Century* 89, no. 18 (3 May 1972):520, 522.

Berchmans Downey. *Best Sellers* 32, no. 5 (1 June 1972):124.

Paul D. Simmons. *Review and Expositor* 69, no. 3 (Summer 1972):396.

Francis Breisch. *Eternity* 23, no. 10 (October 1972).

Prentiss L. Pemberton. *Theology Today* 29, no. 3 (October 1972):336, 338.

Choice 9, no. 9 (November 1972):1170.

James H. Forest. *Commonweal* 97, no. 6 (10 November 1972):140-42.

Richmond N. Hutchins. *Religious Education* 68, no. 6 (November-December 1972):485-86.

Dale G. Lasky. *The Cresset* 36, no. 2 (December 1972):24, 27.

Charles P. Lutz. *Lutheran World* 20, no. 3 (1973):287-89.

Larry Rasmussen. *Dialog* 12, no. 1 (Winter 1973):76-78.

Ronald Stone. *Religion in Life* 42, no. 2 (Spring 1973):270-71.

Beverly Harrison. *Union Seminary Quarterly Review* 28, no. 2 (Winter 1973):182-86.

Pat Ryan Greene. *Cross and Crown* 25, no. 2 (June 1973):198-99.

Patrick P. McDermott. *Theological Studies* 34, no. 2 (June 1973):347.

Ronald E. Santoni. *Anglican Theological Review* 56, no. 1 (January 1974):105-7.

Faith and Science in an Unjust World

Eric Jenkins. *New Scientist* 7, no. 1213 (7 August 1980):467.

Ronald Preston. *The Ecumenical Review* 32, no. 4 (October 1980):456-58.

Choice 18, no. 4 (December 1980):543.

William A. Mueller. *Journal of Church and State* 23, no. 2 (Spring 1981):339-40.

John A. Radano. *Religious Studies Review* 7, no. 3 (July 1981):240-41.

Duane E. Priebe. *Zygon* 18, no. 2 (June 1983):201-3.

Forced Options

Kirkus Reviews 50, no. 14 (15 July 1982):856.

Paul Knitter. *Library Journal* 107, no. 16 (15 September 1982):1759-60.

Choice 20, no. 6 (February 1983):845.

Daniel Callahan. "Shinn on Faith and Science: Sane, Sober, Disappointing." *Christianity and Crisis* 43, no. 3 (7 March 1983):67-69.

Edward A. Malloy, C.S.C. *Theology Today* 40, no. 1 (April 1983):74-76.

Marlin Jeschke. "Decisions for the Next Century." *The Review of Books and Religion* 11, no. 7 (mid-April 1983):4.

John Langan. *New Catholic World* 226, no. 1353 (May/June 1983):136.

Keith Bridston. *Anticipation* No. 30 (July 1983):35.

Thomas A. Shannon. *Horizons* 10, no. 2 (Fall 1983):396-97.

Robert L. Stivers. *Religious Studies Review* 9, no. 4 (October 1983):366.

Raymond A. Schroth. "Ethics and Isolation." *Commonweal* 111, no. 2 (27 January 1984):57-60.

Ralph M. Moore Jr. *The Annals of the American Academy of Political and Social Science* 473 (May 1984):233-34.

Notes

Introduction

1. For a useful way of conceiving the meaning of "public" that is consistent with our usage, see Parker Palmer, *The Company of Strangers* (New York: The Pilgrim Press, 1982). Palmer defines "the public" as the place where strangers meet and engage their common or shared interest. He contends that concern for public issues, that is, those shared by Christians and others, is *intrinsic* to an adequate normative Christian understanding of both personal and churchly responsibility.

2. Most of the contributors believe that *all* ethical reflection is intrinsically social, and therefore that the frequently made distinction between theological and social ethics is suspect. Here "social ethics" refers to concern for the implications of ethical reflection for both Christian communal and institutional life, and for the shape of public policy in the wider society.

3. Roger Shinn was born in Germantown, Ohio, January 6, 1917, was educated at Heidelberg College and Union Theological Seminary (M.Div. 1941), and holds his doctorate from Union-Columbia University (Ph.D. 1951). He was an officer in the U.S. Army during World War II, and a prisoner of war. Later he taught at Heidelberg College and Vanderbilt University Divinity School before joining the faculty of Union Theological Seminary. He is an ordained clergyman of the United Church of Christ, has held numerous Distinguished Lectureships, and has three honorary doctorates. He belongs to numerous professional scholarly organizations and is past president of the American Theological Society and the Society

of Christian Ethics. His wide-ranging ecumenical involvements are referred to in the text below.

Roger has been a contributing editor to *Christianity and Crisis* and a consultant to numerous state, federal, and international projects. He and his wife, Katherine, are the parents of two daughters, Carol and Marybeth. Katherine and Roger are also active members of the Riverside Church in New York.

4. Other exceptions to the traditional festschrift style have been usefully made before in the case of other distinguished Christian ethicists. See, for example, Paul Deats, ed., *Towards a Discipline of Christian Social Ethics: Essays in Honor of Walter Muelder* (Boston: Boston University Press. 1972).

5. This theme of unprecedented moral dilemmas and of the urgency of comprehending the technical aspects of ethical issues runs through innumerable writings of Roger Shinn. These concerns are well illustrated in his recent *Forced Options* (2d ed.; New York: The Pilgrim Press, 1985).

6. "Christian Realism"—the name given to the approach to Christian ethics generated by Reinhold Niebuhr and often also associated with many of Niebuhr's colleagues and students, including John C. Bennett and Roger Shinn himself—is today a much controverted topic. See John C. Bennett, "Realism and Hope After Niebuhr," *Worldview* 15 (May 1972):4-14; Beverly W. Harrison, "Social Justice and Economic Orthodoxy," *Christianity and Crisis*, 21 January 1985, pp. 513-15, and "The Role of Social Theory in Religious Ethics," *Making the Connections: Essays in Feminist Social Ethics*, ed. Carol Robb (Boston: Beacon Press, 1985), pp. 54-64; Ronald Stone, *Reinhold Niebuhr: Prophet to Politicians* (Washington, DC: University Press of America, 1981), and *Realism and Hope* (Washington DC: University Press of America, 1977).

The Next Stage of Christian Ethics as a Theological Discipline

1. Emil Brunner, *The Divine Imperative* (Philadelphia: Westminster Press, 1947), ch. 35. Brunner later became so concerned about the threat of communism that his emphasis changed.

2. Reinhold Niebuhr, *Moral Man and Immoral Society* (New York: Charles Scribner's Sons, 1932).

3. Paul Tillich, *Systematic Theology* (Chicago: University of Chicago Press, 1951), I:31.

4. Bruce C. Birch and Larry L. Rasmussen, *Bible and Ethics in the Christian Life* (Minneapolis: Augsburg Publishing House, 1976).

5. Elisabeth Schüssler Fiorenza, *In Memory of Her* (New York: Crossroads-Seabury Press, 1983). Professor Fiorenza shows that women had a high place in the Jesus movement, and she finds a great deal of evi-

dence for this in the New Testament accounts of the early church, despite patriarchal attempts to cover it up.

6. H. Richard Niebuhr, *Christ and Culture* (New York: Harper & Row, 1951).

7. Roland Bainton, *Christian Attitudes Toward War and Peace* (Nashville: Abingdon Press, 1960).

8. Roland Bainton, *The Travail of Religious Liberty* (Philadelphia: Westminster Press, 1951).

9. Roger L. Shinn, *Forced Options* (2d ed.; New York: The Pilgrim Press, 1985).

10. John Howard Yoder, *The Politics of Jesus* (Grand Rapids, MI: Eerdmans, 1972): Stanley Hauerwas, *A Community of Character* (Notre Dame, IN: University of Notre Dame Press, 1981) and *The Peaceable Kingdom* (Notre Dame, IN: University of Notre Dame Press, 1983). Although he is difficult to classify and would certainly reject the sectarian label, Jacques Ellul sometimes has a similar influence. See Jacques Ellul, *Violence* (New York: Seabury Press, 1969).

11. John Calvin, *The Institutes of the Christian Religion,* ed. John T. McNeill, trans. Ford Lewis Battles (Philadelphia: Westminster Press, 1960), Bk. 4, ch. 20 para. viii.

12. Reinhold Niebuhr, *The Children of Light and the Children of Darkness* (New York: Charles Scribner's Sons, 1944).

13. Walter M. Abbott and Joseph Gallagher, eds., *The Documents of Vatican II* (New York: Corpus Books, 1966), p. 666.

14. Benjamin Mays, *Born to Rebel* (New York: Charles Scribner's Sons, 1971), p. 141.

15. I describe the conflict between the social and the ethical assumptions of the Reagan Administration and the thought of all persons who have influenced this chapter in John Bennett, "Reaganethics," *Christianity and Crisis,* 14 December 1981.

16. Beverly Wildung Harrison, *Our Right to Choose* (Boston: Beacon Press, 1983). The subtitle of the book is "Toward a New Ethic of Abortion." Professor Harrison argues powerfully that the availability of abortion is essential as a matter of justice for women. She does not regard abortion as a desirable form of birth control, and she greatly stresses preference for early abortion, although abortion in the second or third trimester may be necessary in certain situations.

1. The Nuclear Dilemma

1. Cited by Alan Geyer in *The Idea of Disarmament: Rethinking the Unthinkable* (Elgin, IL: Brethren Press, 1982), p. 33.

2. Reported by John C. Bennett in "Nuclear Deterrence Is Itself Vulnerable," *Christianity and Crisis* 13 August 1984, p. 296. This may well be

one of the most important articles on the subject in recent Christian ethics, not least because it includes the evolution of Bennett's steady attention to nuclear deterrence issues over nearly forty years.

3. Beverly Woodward, "The Abolition of War," *Crosscurrents* 33, no. 3, 267. For a helpful contrast of the dynamics of arms control and those of disarmament, see Geyer, *Idea of Disarmament*, pp. 21ff.

4. Woodward, "Abolition of War."

5. The discussion here cannot include what should be undertaken, a scrutiny of targeting doctrines, such as counterpopulation, counterforce, and schemes of limited nuclear war. See Geyer's discussion in *Idea of Disarmament*, and the Roman Catholic bishops' peace pastoral, U.S. Catholic Conference, *The Challenge of Peace: God's Promise and Our Response* (Washington, DC: USCC, 1983), Pt. II.

6. See the summary of testimony reported by the Catholic bishops, *Challenge of Peace*, Pt. II, Sec. C. See also David Hollenbach, *Nuclear Ethics: A Christian Moral Argument* (New York: Paulist Press, 1983), p. 53 and n. 19.

7. Even the most dramatic of the public efforts to portray the eery aftermath have not communicated the totality of this particular peril—a dying ecosystem winding down to extinction of life in any form we could appreciate if we were around. The TV film *The Day After*, portraying Kansas after a nuclear attack, concluded the drama at a time relatively soon after the explosions. It didn't show the long-term outcome of such possibilities as a shattered ozone layer, as sudden, extended winter, or as poisoned land, air, and water. All such would fall on the just and the unjust alike. Neither would survive, nor their children, except possibly in grotesque forms amid indescribable conditions. To show the full consequences of a 10-megaton holocaust, the film would, in Jonathan Schell's words, have to "display nothingness on the screen, and last forever." *The Abolition* (New York: Alfred A. Knopf, 1984), p. 10. The scientific findings are gathered in such books as Jonathan Schell, *The Fate of the Earth* (New York: Alfred A. Knopf, 1982); Richard Turco, Carl Sagan, et al., "Nuclear Winter: Global Consequences of Multiple Nuclear Explosions," *Science*, December 1983; Michael Riordan, ed., *The Day After Midnight: The Effects of Nuclear War* (Palo Alto, CA: Cheshire Books, 1982); or the studies from several countries, including those of U.S. and USSR scientists, published in *Aftermath—The Human and Ecological Consequences of Nuclear War* (New York: Pantheon Books, 1983).

8. "Tapes Pick Up Reagan Joke About Soviets," *Washington Post*, 12 August 1984, p. 1.

9. George Kennan, *The Nuclear Delusion: Soviet-American Relations in the Atomic Age* (New York: Pantheon Books, 1983), p. xxvii. Emphasis added.

10. See the argument of Richard Barnett in *Real Security: Restoring American Power in a Dangerous Decade* (New York: Simon & Schuster, 1983), especially pp. 25-26, 39.

11. At the time of this writing, the Reagan Administration continues to argue that this is the way, the only way, to a tolerable peace with the Russians. Without the buildup, negotiations will not be taken seriously. I think John Bennett is exactly right in his judgment: "Reagan can change his rhetoric without notice, but I believe that he has one settled conviction: Our own increased strength can prevent nuclear war whether we have arms control or not." See Bennett, "Nuclear Deterrence," p. 298.

12. Cited by Edward LeRoy Long Jr. in *Peace-Thinking in a Warring World* (Philadelphia: Westminster Press, 1983), pp. 32-33.

13. *USCC, Challenge of Peace*, p. 69.

14. *USCC, Challenge of Peace*, p. 43.

15. Do I misread the bishops? If the weapons must never be used, and certainly not as first use, and that is to be declared as public policy, as the bishops seem to insist, then deterrence unravels, since deterrence rests in genuine retaliatory capacity and the threat to use it. But if the bishops count on sheer possession of these weapons to carry a perception of possible use (i.e., the bishops calculate the enemy believes use *is* possible, whatever the declared policy), then the bishops are effectively advocating deception and bluff. If this reading is correct—we must never intend to use or actually use these weapons and should make that known, but we hope the enemy thinks we might—the bishops are in a curious position as teachers of the church in moral matters. On the basis of their own premises, should they not conclude, as one of the generals did in a letter to one of the bishops, that the heart of deterrence—the threat of mutual assured destruction—is a "failed and basically immoral" concept that should be rejected? (A letter from Lt. Gen. Daniel O. Graham, ret., to Bishop William D. Borders, 2 November 1982, cited by Patricia M. Mische in "National Security and Nonviolence: The New Moment," *Crosscurrents* 33, no. 3, 305-6.

16. Geyer, *Idea of Disarmament*, pp. 58-59.

17. The phrases are Jonathan Schell's, *Fate of the Earth*, p. 71.

18. USCC, *Challenge of Peace*, pp. vii and 46, respectively.

19. Michael Walzer, *Just and Unjust Wars: A Moral Argument with Historical Illustrations* (New York: Basic Books, 1977), p. 274.

20. The Harvard Nuclear Study Group, Albert Carnesale, et al., *Living with Nuclear Weapons* (Cambridge, MA: Harvard University Press, 1983), p. 268. This is an appropriate point at which to mention what ought to be obvious. Moral judgments about deterrence policies—or any other—are inextricably tied to empirical and political judgments and "readings" of history on the matter at hand. In the case of the discussions here, moral judgments are inseparable from judgments about, for example, the rea-

sonably expected outcomes of specific deterrence policies, about disarmament prospects, about arms race outcomes. The moral is submerged in the technical, institutional, and historical. But the judgments are not a whit less "moral" for all that. They are only more complex, since sound moral judgment then includes sound factual, political, and technical judgments.

21. A particularly eloquent volume of scripturally grounded pacifism with strong "Christian realism" perspectives on human behavior is Dale Aukerman's *Darkening Valley: Biblical Perspectives on Nuclear War* (New York: Seabury Press, 1981). On the presentation of Jesus and the early church as a movement of messianic nonviolence, John Howard Yoder's *The Politics of Jesus* has become something of a classic (Grand Rapids, MI: Eerdmans, 1972).

22. Vladimir Ilyich Lenin in *Letters of Modern Atheism*, cited in *Sojourners*, December 1981, p. 17.

23. See especially the works of Gene Sharp, in particular his opus, *The Politics of Nonviolent Action* (Boston: Porter Sargent, 1973).

24. Augustine, *City of God*, Book IV, ch. 15. I draw on two translations and adapt them so as to avoid sexist language. Readers probably have easiest access to this passage in the Pelican Classics series (New York: Penguin Books, 1981), p. 154. While it does not belong to the discussion directly at hand, it is worth noting that although Augustine held killing in defense of others to be justifiable in some circumstances, he found killing in self-defense morally proscribed for Christians.

25. Roger Shinn, *Wars and Rumors of Wars* (Nashville: Abingdon Press, 1972), p. 260. Shinn here is talking about his own choice to enlist in the Army during World War II. But the description of his feelings and choice is a precise one for many "just-war" Christians facing participation in war.

26. See Shinn's testimony, *Wars and Rumors of Wars*, especially pp. 183-93, "Conscience and History." This volume, as well as his other writings on social conflict, shows Shinn to be a personification of the just-war subtradition described earlier.

27. See Matthew 22:37-40; Mark 12:28-31; see also Matthew 5:43-48 and Luke 6:32-36.

28. The phrase is James Turner Johnson's in "On Keeping Faith: The Use of History for Religious Ethics," *Journal of Religious Studies* 7 (1979):113. See Johnson's books for a nuanced treatment of just-war traditions not possible here: *Just War Tradition and the Restraint of War* (Princeton, NJ: Princeton University Press, 1981) and *Ideology, Reason and the Limitation of War* (Princeton, NJ: Princeton University Press, 1975). The reading of traditions by Johnson supports the contention that nonviolence is the norm and "selective conscientious participation" in violence is a carefully limited exception to that norm.

29. Thomas Aquinas, *Summa Theologiae,* II-II, p. 40, cited by J. Bryan Hehir in "The Just-War Ethic and Catholic Theology: Dynamics of Change and Continuity," *War or Peace? The Search for Answers,* ed. Thomas A. Shannon (Maryknoll, NY: Orbis Books, 1980), p. 18.

30. These three comments, as well as the discussion of just war as a whole, are indebted to John Howard Yoder, *When War Is Unjust* (Minneapolis: Augsburg Publishing House, 1984). The phrase "national interest wars" is Yoder's.

31. Space limitations prevent discussing the full list of just-war criteria. But at least the list can be included here, drawn from Yoder, *When War Is Unjust,* p. 18: (1) The authority waging the war must be legitimate. (2) The cause being fought for must be just. (3) The ultimate goal ("intention") must be peace. (4) The subjective motivation ("intention") must not be hatred or vengefulness. (5) War must be the last resort. (6) Success must be probable. (7) The means used must be indispensable to achieve the end. (8) The means used must be discriminating, both quantitatively, in order not to do more harm than the harm they prevent ("proportionality"), and qualitatively, to avoid use against the innocent ("immunity"). (9) The means used must respect the provisions of international law. Yoder's volume includes excellent discussions of the criteria, as do the following: James F. Childress, "Just-War Criteria," *Moral Responsibility in Conflicts* (Baton Rouge: Louisiana State University Press, 1982), pp. 63-94; Ralph Potter, *The Moral Logic of War* (Philadelphia: United Presbyterian Church, n.d.); Paul Ramsey, *The Just War: Force and Political Responsibility* (New York: Charles Scribner's Sons, 1968); and *War and the Christian Conscience* (Durham, NC: Duke University Press, 1961). Ramsey is probably the most prolific and influential Christian ethicist on this subject.

32. The German city of Dresden was fire-bombed by the Allies near the end of the war. Dresden was militarily meaningless for both the Nazis and the Allies. It was not an industrial center but had long been the city of German arts, culture, and learning. It was also a "free" city to which thousands of refugees had come to escape the ravages of war. They were incinerated in the bombing. Speculation is that the deed was undertaken by some of the Allies to impress the other ally, the Soviet Union, and thereby show the relative strength of the Western Allies, for the sake of postwar relations.

33. See USCC, *Challenge of Peace,* for the important point that pacifist and just-war orientations complement and correct each other.

34. Aukerman, *Darkening Valley,* p. 42.

35. See Douglas John Hall, *Lighten Our Darkness: Towards an Indigenous Theology of the Cross* (Philadelphia: Westminster Press, 1976), especially chs. 1 and 2.

36. The phrase is Hunter Brown's in "The Nuclear Mirror and the Will to Identity," *Crosscurrents* 33, no. 3, 351.

37. See the essay by John Howard Yoder, "The Lordship of Christ and the Power Struggle," in *The Lordship of Christ: Proceedings of the Seventh Mennonite World Conference*, ed. Cornelius J. Dyck (Elkhart, IN: Mennonite World Conference, 1962).

38. Kennan, *Nuclear Delusion*, p. 7.

39. A word coined, to the best of my knowledge, by George Will and part of the title of his book *Statecraft as Soulcraft* (New York: Simon & Schuster, 1984).

40. See Max Weber's famous essay *Politics as a Vocation* (Philadelphia: Fortress Press, 1965).

41. The discussion here is indebted to the good work of Beverly Woodward, "Abolition of War," 269-70.

42. Kennan, *Nuclear Delusion*, p. xxiii.

43. Kennan, p. 49. Quotation altered slightly, to avoid sexist terms.

44. See the presentation of Long, *Peace-Thinking in a Warring World*.

45. Cited from Evans, *Crosscurrents* 33 no. 3, 260.

46. A fruitful discussion of the role and dynamics of an eschatological community in North American society is found in Thomas W. Ogletree, *The Use of the Bible in Christian Ethics* (Philadelphia: Fortress Press, 1983), especially pp. 175-206.

47. The term nonviolence is no more satisfactory as an adequate description than is "just war." Indeed, it is worse in that it defines a reality by saying what it is not. That is akin to calling "light," "undarkness." We do not mean by nonviolence the absence of violence. An alternative might be the phrase "active, dehostilizing love and justice," but that obviously has its own problems. Reluctantly, nonviolence is retained for the time being.

48. See Walter Brueggemann, *Living Toward a Vision: Biblical Reflections on Shalom* (New York: United Church Press, 1976), and Bruce C. Birch and Larry L. Rasmussen, *The Predicament of the Prosperous* (Philadelphia: Westminster Press, 1978), especially chs. V and VII.

49. USCC, *Challenge of Peace*, p. 70. The use of the terms violence and nonviolence is without nuance in this essay. In a fuller treatment they would need specification and elaboration. I am aware in particular of a region of moral ambiguity in which their realities overlap. Nonviolence, for example, has often relied on legal instrumentalities that used the threat of violence themselves—police and national guards protecting nonviolent protesters from angry crowds, for example. Nonviolence has also counted on the adversary to expect violence if the "nonviolent" demands were not met, even when nonviolent leaders did not use the threat of violence per se—the British acquiesced to Indian demands in part because the alternative threatened greater civil unrest, probably violent unrest. Too, the case

can be made, and often has, that the controlled use of violence has sometimes resulted in less suffering and degradation overall than nonviolent actions did and could have—the Nicaraguan overthrow of the Somoza regime comes to mind. All this is to recognize that there is no refuge from difficult choices and moral ambiguity. Those *are* sometimes masked by too simple a contrast of "violence" and "nonviolence." It is also to recognize, in passing, that nonviolence is evidently capable of real elements of social coercion and power, or it would not elicit the response it sometimes gets. Finally, it is *more* important, not less, to be clear about what is the norm, and what is the exception, when there is moral ambiguity. This essay argues for publicly engaged nonviolence as the Christian norm.

50. See the work of Sharp, *Politics of Nonviolent Action*; also Robert C. Johansen, *Toward a Dependable Peace* (Princeton, NJ: Institute for World Order, 1978); Schell, *The Abolition*; and the discussion and resources suggested in Ronald J. Sider and Richard K. Taylor, *Nuclear Holocaust and Christian Hope* (Downers Grove, IL: InterVarsity Press, 1982).

2. Christian Realism and the Russians

1. Report of study by the Harvard Medical School's Department of Psychiatry and the International Physicians for the Prevention of Nuclear War, *The New York Times*, 13 October 1983.

2. Kenneth W. Thompson, *Political Realism and the Crisis of World Politics* (Princeton, NJ: Princeton University Press, 1960), pp. 50-61.

3. *The Literary Digest* 62 (6 September 1919): 60. Quoted by George F. Kennan, *Russia and the West Under Lenin and Stalin* (Boston: Little, Brown, 1960), p. 112.

4. Roger L. Shinn, "Soviet Russia—After Fifty Years," *Christianity and Crisis*, 27 November 1967, p. 274.

5. "An Interview with Reinhold Niebuhr," *Christianity and Crisis* 29 (17 March 1969): 51.

6. "Peace Through Cultural Co-operation," *Christianity and Crisis*, 17 October 1949. Reprinted in Ernest W. Lefever, *The World Crisis and American Responsibility* (New York: Association Press, 1958), pp. 111-12.

7. Hans J. Morgenthau, *Politics Among Nations: The Struggle for Power and Peace* (New York: Alfred A. Knopf, 1967), pp. 540-50.

3. Making the World Safe for Transnational Capitalism?

1. For a critical discussion of the social role of the conservative Central American Protestant church in Costa Rica, its theological and ideological characteristics, and its dependence on its North American "parents," see Jane Cary Peck, "Reflections from Costa Rica on Protestantism's Dependence and Non-Liberative Social Function," *Journal of Ecumenical Studies* 21, (Spring 1984):181-98.

2. Right social relations are marked by justice, mutual respect, and dignity. It is within this "labor of justice/love," within social and ecclesial movements engaged in the righting of morally wrong and distorted relationships of domination and dependence, that the tasks of Christian ethics are properly undertaken. An adequate method for Christian ethics includes four steps: (1) critical awareness of the dialectic between personal suffering and social injustice; (2) analysis of the conditions that produce and sustain oppression, the forms of complicity in *and resistance to* the oppression, and projections of constructive alternatives; (3) engagement in movements for emancipatory sociocultural transformation; and (4) theological reflection and celebration. These steps are analyzable as discrete moments within the moral life, but they seldom proceed in a strictly linear sequence.

3. John C. Bennett, *The Radical Imperative: From Theology to Social Ethics* (Philadelphia: Westminster Press, 1975), pp. 156, 154.

4. By the "socialist option," I understand what British socialist Tony Benn describes by his definition of economic democracy: "To secure for the workers by hand or by brain the full fruits of their industry and the most equitable distribution thereof on the basis of the common ownership of the means of production, distribution, and exchange, and the best obtainable means of popular administration and control of each industry and service." Benn's definition is found in Alexander Cockburn and James Ridgeway, "Talking to Tony Benn: Can European Socialists Teach Americans Anything?" *The Village Voice* 25 (10-16 December 1980):28.

5. Bennett, *Radical Imperative*, p. 155.

6. For a full-length analysis of this debate and its implications for Christian ethics, see my *The Center Cannot Hold: The Search for a Global Economy of Justice* (Washington, DC: University Press of America, 1983).

7. Beverly Wildung Harrison, "The Dream of a Common Language: Towards a Normative Theory of Justice in Christian Ethics," *The Annual of the Society of Christian Ethics* (1983), p. 7. My emphasis.

8. Michael Novak, "The Case Against Liberation Theology," *The New York Times Magazine*, 21 October 1984, pp. 51, 94, 85.

9. Michael Harrington, *The Vast Majority: A Journey to the World's Poor* (New York: Simon & Schuster, 1977), p. 103.

10. These criteria are discussed, for example, by C. Dean Freudenberger and Joseph C. Hough Jr., in "Lifeboats and Hungry People," in Dieter T. Hessel, ed., *Beyond Survival: Bread and Justice in Christian Perspective* (New York: Friendship Press, 1977), especially pp. 30-43. Generally speaking, there are two "quick" tests to use in determining whether a social order is just or not: (1) find out how the least well-off and most vulnerable members of the society are faring (ask, e.g., how the unemployed woman of color, single head of household, with dependent children is faring these days), and (2) ask whether you are willing, at least

in principle, to trade places with those least well positioned, in this case with the above-mentioned woman.

11. For a compilation of recent Catholic social teaching on economic development, see Joseph Gremillion, ed., *The Gospel of Peace and Justice: Catholic Social Teaching Since Pope John* (Maryknoll, NY: Orbis Books, 1976). A critical appraisal of Catholic perspectives is found in Christine E. Gudorf, *Catholic Social Teaching on Liberation Themes* (Washington, DC: University Press of America, 1980). For a review of both Catholic and Protestant perspectives, especially from the World Council of Churches, see Robert McAfee Brown, *Theology in a New Key: Responding to Liberation Themes* (Philadelphia: Westminster Press, 1978), chs. 1-2, and my *Center Cannot Hold*, ch. 2, "The Development Debate Within the Ecumenical Church Movement."

12. Irma Adelman and Cynthia T. Morris, *Economic Growth and Social Equity in Developing Countries* (Palo Alto, CA: Stanford University Press, 1973), p. 189.

13. Adelman and Morris, *Economic Growth*, p. 192. My emphasis.

14. *North-South: A Programme for Survival; Report of the Independent Commission on International Development Issues*, under the chair of Willy Brandt (Cambridge, MA: MIT Press, 1980), p. 32.

15. Sergio Torres, "Introduction," in *The Emergent Gospel: Theology from the Underside of History*, ed. Sergio Torres and Virginia Fabella (Maryknoll, NY: Orbis Books, 1976), p. xiv.

16. Richard J. Barnet and Ronald E. Muller, *Global Reach: The Power of Multinational Corporations* (New York: Simon & Schuster, 1974).

17. In Robert McAfee Brown's phrase, we ought to move "onward and leftward." Brown notes that this leftward movement involves both the identification of poverty as an issue of social injustice and a strategic shift from alleviating the results of poverty (symptoms) exclusively to altering the underlying structural dynamics and power inequalities (causes) that produce poverty.

18. Hugo Assmann, *Theology for a Nomad Church*, trans. Paul Burns (Maryknoll, NY: Orbis Books, 1976), p. 54. Assmann's emphasis.

19. Herman Kahn, with the Hudson Institute, *World Economic Development: 1979 and Beyond* (New York: Morrow Quill, 1979), p. 62.

20. Kahn et al., *World Economic Development*, p. 61; Max Singer and Paul Bracken, "Don't Blame the U.S.," *The New York Times Magazine*, 7 November 1976, p. 120.

21. Barnet and Muller, *Global Reach*, p. 151.

22. Herman Kahn, William Brown, and Leon Martel, *The Next 200 Years: A Scenario for America and the World* (New York: William Morrow & Co., 1976), p. 1, and Kahn et al., *World Economic Development*, p. 2. For an ethical analysis of the social structural limitations to economic growth and the need for a political struggle to redistribute economic goods

and resources more equitably, see Roger L. Shinn, "The End of a Liberal Dream: No More Painless Progress," *Christianity and Crisis* 41 (16 March 1981): 52-57. Shinn rightly places the debate over natural limits to growth within a broader analysis of social policy and political constraints on distributive justice.

23. A liberation historical project, varying in programmatic and strategic application in differing social situations, includes the social appropriation of the means of production, of political power, and of freedom, as well as the creation of a new social consciousness. Such a project envisions a cultural revolution that is dynamic and open-ended. See Gustavo Gutierrez, *A Theology of Liberation*, trans. and ed. Caridad Inda and John Eagleson (Maryknoll, NY: Orbis Books, 1973), p. 237, and José Míguez Bonino, *Toward a Christian Political Ethics* (Philadelphia: Fortress Press, 1983), p. 77.

24. Brian Wren, *Education for Justice: Pedagogical Principles* (Maryknoll, NY: Orbis Books, 1977), p. 97.

25. Theotonio Dos Santos, "The Crisis of Development Theory and the Problem of Dependence in Latin America," in Henry Bernstein, ed., *Development and Underdevelopment: The Third World Today* (Baltimore: Penguin Books, 1973), p. 77.

26. Bennett, *Radical Imperative*, p. 164.

27. Harrington, *Vast Majority*, p. 16.

28. Daniel Lerner, "Comparative Analysis of Processes of Modernization," in Horace Miner, ed., *The City in Modern Africa* (London, 1967), p. 24.

29. W.A. Visser't Hooft, ed., *The New Delhi Report* (New York: Association Press, 1962), p. 107.

30. Visser't Hooft, *New Delhi Report*, p. 275.

31. Arend Theodoor van Leeuwen, *Development Through Revolution* (New York: Charles Scribner's Sons, 1970), p. 108.

32. ISAL (Commission on Church and Society in Latin America), "Christians, Churches and Development," *Risk* 5 (1969): 44.

33. Julio de Santa Ana, "What Development Demands: A Latin American Position," in Richard D.N. Dickinson, *To Set at Liberty the Oppressed* (Geneva: World Council of Churches, 1975), p. 143.

34. Gutierrez, *Theology of Liberation*, p. 174.

35. Henry Bernstein, "Modernization Theory and Sociological Study of Development," *Journal of Development Studies* 7 (January 1971): 153.

36. Harrington, *Vast Majority*, p. 102.

37. Harrington, *Vast Majority*, p. 137.

38. Celso Furtado "Elements of a Theory of Underdevelopment—the Underdeveloped Structures," in Bernstein, ed., *Development and Underdevelopment*, pp. 35, 37.

39. Samuel Parmar, "Self-reliant Development in an 'Interdependent' World," in Guy F. Erb and Valeriana Kallab, eds., *Beyond Dependency: The Developing World Speaks Out* (Washington, DC: Overseas Development Council, 1975), p. 13.

40. Bernstein, "Modernization Theory," p. 154.

41. Jose Miguez Bonino, *Doing Theology in a Revolutionary Situation* (Philadelphia: Fortress Press, 1975), p. 16.

42. Osvaldo Luis Mottesi, "Doing Theology in the Latin American Context," *Church and Society* 68 (January-February 1978):9.

43. Phillip E. Berryman, "Doing Theology in a (Counter-) Revolutionary Situation: Latin American Liberation Theology in the Mid-Seventies," in Sergio Torres and John Eagleson, eds., *Theology in the Americas* (Maryknoll, NY: Orbis Books, 1976), p. 58.

44. Barnet and Muller, *Global Reach*, p. 163.

45. Jose Comblin, *The Church and the National Security State* (Maryknoll, NY: Orbis Books, 1979), p. 84.

46. Robert L. Heilbroner, *The Great Ascent* (New York: Harper & Row, 1963), p. 28; *An Inquiry into the Human Prospect* (New York: W.W. Norton & Co., 1975), p. 110.

47. Sylvia Ann Hewlett, *The Cruel Dilemmas of Development: Twentieth-Century Brazil* (New York: Basic Books, 1980), p. 6.

48. Hewlett, *Cruel Dilemmas*, p. 11. My emphasis.

49. Helio Jaguaribe, quoted in Penny Lernoux, *Cry of the People: The United States Involvement in the Rise of Fascism, Torture, and Murder and the Persecution of the Catholic Church in Latin America* (Garden City, NY: Doubleday & Co., 1980), p. 172.

50. Samuel L. Parmar, "Issues in the Development Debate," in Dickinson, *To Set at Liberty*, p. 177.

51. Miguez Bonino, *Toward a Christian Political Ethics,* p. 78.

52. Bonino, *Toward a Christian Political Ethics*, p. 76.

53. See, for example, Immanuel Wallerstein, "The USA in Today's World," in Marlene Dixon et al., eds., *World Capitalist Crisis and the Rise of the Right* (San Francisco: Synthesis Publications, 1982).

54. Penny Lernoux, *Fear and Hope: Toward Political Democracy in Central America* (New York: Field Foundation, 1984), p. 8.

55. Comblin, *Church and the National Security State*, p. 175.

56. Novak, "Case Against Liberation Theology," p. 51. For an illustration of the reactionary dismissal of liberation theology, see Rene de Visme Williamson, "The Integrity of the Gospel: A Critique of Liberation Theology," published and distributed by the Presbyterian Lay Committee. Neoconservative Williamson, as Novak, characterizes liberation theology as distorted by a "naive idealism" that refuses "to accept the fact that injustice is built into the very structure of human personality" and faults it for offering "bad social science and bad theology" (p. 3). For a construc-

tive perspective on the necessary "politicization" of faith and elaboration of criteria for choosing among conflicting options, see Roger Shinn, "Faith and Politics: The Mission to Speak," *Christianity and Crisis* 43 (21 March 1983):85-88, and also Miguez Bonino, *Toward a Christian Political Ethics,* esp. ch. 3, "From Praxis to Theory and Back," and ch. 6, "Justice and Order."

4. Democracy in Argentina

1. Enrique D. Dussel, "Church-State Relations in Peripheral Latin American Societies," in *Church and State,* Faith and Order Paper No. 5 (Geneva: World Council of Churches, 1978), pp. 69-72.

2. José Míguez Bonino, *Toward a Christian Political Ethics* (Philadelphia: Fortress Press, 1983), pp. 54-78. Hereafter this book will be referred to as *CPE.*

3. Míguez, *CPE,* pp. 58-64.

4. Míguez, *CPE,* p. 65.

5. Míguez, *CPE,* pp. 75-77. I will return to his thesis later.

6. Roberto Calvo. "Doctrina de la seguridad nacional," in *Iglesia y seguridad nacional,* ed. Equipo Seladoc (Salamanca: Sígueme, 1980), p. 15.

7. "Introduction," *The New Authoritarianism in Latin America,* ed. David Collier (Princeton, NJ: Princeton University Press, 1979), p. 5; Irving Louis Horowitz, "Military Origins of Third World Dictatorship and Democracy," *Third World Quarterly,* January 1981, p. 38. Horowitz rejects both Western modernization theory and Soviet socialization theory because both deny the "thirdness" of the Third World.

8. The dominant methodological principle found in Latin American liberation theology writings translated into English is to treat the continent as a whole. Brief references to particular situations are used to illustrate a continentwide reality. This approach has helped to make Christians in the USNA more aware of the suffering, oppression, and dependence of all of Latin America. I wonder, however, if it has not also served to reinforce the ignorance that tends to see the continent as a monolithic, homogeneous block. This approach was perhaps valuable in the first stages of liberation theology, but I question its adequacy for the future. A contextual, political theology, to remain true to its own starting point, needs to show how its thinking relates to the actual political options in the situation from which it arises.

9. Reinhold Niebuhr, *Moral Man and Immoral Society* (New York: Charles Scribner's Sons, 1966), p. 163. (The book was first published in 1932.)

10. Míguez, *CPE,* p. 108.

11. Reinhold Niebuhr, *The Children of Light and the Children of Darkness* (New York: Charles Scribner's Sons, 1960), p. xiii. (The book was first published in 1944.) I have altered text to avoid language now recognized as sexist.

12. Juan J. Linz, *The Breakdown of Democratic Regimes, Crisis, Breakdown and Reequilibration* (Baltimore: The Johns Hopkins University Press, 1978), p. 5.

13. Cf. John C. Bennett, "Reflections on Democracy," *Christianity and Crisis*, 16 August 1976, pp. 183-86.

14. Cf. Roger Lincoln Shinn, *Forced Options* (2d ed.; New York: The Pilgrim Press, 1985), pp. 226-34.

15. The writings of liberation theologians are both well known and extensive. Gustavo Gutiérrez's *A Theology of Liberation* (Maryknoll, NY: Orbis Books, 1973) remains a classic presentation of Latin American liberation theology. Míguez's *Doing Theology in a Revolutionary Situation* (Philadelphia: Fortress Press, 1975) is an important introduction to the theme that both summarizes the general movement as well as offers his own theological thinking. Robert McAfee Brown's *Theology in a New Key* (Philadelphia: Westminster Press, 1978) is a sympathetic treatment and response "to liberation themes." Brown's book contains a helpful bibliography. I will refer especially to the writings of the Argentine theologian Míguez. Although I will indicate my differences with certain texts from his books, I have nothing but admiration for his clear, constant, and courageous democratic commitment in Argentina.

16. Samuel Silva Gotay, in his lengthy study of Christian revolutionary thinking in Latin America and the Caribbean, presents Cuba as "the only alternative" and "the only hope" for Latin America. *El pensamiento cristiano revolucionário en América latina y el caribe* (Salamanca: Sígueme, 1981), p. 35. Míguez, on the other hand, writes, "While socialism is a common feature [of the project of liberation], the amount of 'heterodoxy' in socialist terms varies greatly all the way from the Peronist 'third way' to the Peruvian socializing military regime, to the communist Moscow- or Peking-type parties" (*Doing Theology*, p. 40). These two references show that it is difficult to define precisely the political position of liberation theology. The first reference is too specific and would exclude the position of many liberation theologians, and the second is so general that it is hard to know what socialism means. In broad terms, one can say that the position is a Marxist-oriented revolutionary socialist option that seeks to be authentically Latin American. Cf. Míguez, *Christians and Marxists the Mutual Challenge to Revolution* (Grand Rapids, MI: Eerdman's 1976), p. 19. Because of this imprecision, I will, as much as possible, refer to specific texts in discussing its political position.

17. I know of no discussion by liberation theologians of the "democratic" political structure that is to replace "liberal democracy." Míguez

recognizes that there is "the problem of the control of power." He rejects for the postrevolutionary period "an empty pseudo-democratic affirmation of 'fair play' and 'equality' " as "sentimentalism and shallow humanitarianism" that "can only be instruments of reaction and the cause of even greater suffering." He admits, however, "that Marxist political thinking has not yet developed adequate forms of control of the exercise of power in order to prevent arbitrariness" (*Christians and Marxists*, p. 19).

18. I dedicate this article to Roger Shinn whose own democratc hope has been firm but not arrogant, critical but not cynical. His writings, which combine so well moral sensitivity, mastery of information, and awareness of complexity, are a model of how a Christian ethicist can enrich public discussion of "social decisions."

19. Amnistía internacional, *Desapariciones* (Madrid: Fundamentos, 1983), p. 15.

20. Eduardo Luis Duhalde, *El estado terrorista argentino* (Buenos Aires: El Caballito, 1983), pp. 53-71.

21. Duhalde, *El estado terrorista argentino*.

22. Amnistía internacional, *Desapariciones*, p. 17.

23. Amnistía internacional, *Desapariciones*, pp. 11-22.

24. José Comblin, *The Church and the National Security State* (Maryknoll, NY: Orbis Books, 1979); Penny Lernoux, *Cry of the People* (Garden City, NY: Doubleday & Co., 1980); Míguez, *CPE*, pp. 69-74.

25. Míguez, *CPE*, p. 71.

26. Guillermo O'Donnell, "Tensions in the Bureaucratic-Authoritarian State and the Question of Democracy," in *The New Authoritarianism in Latin America*, pp. 258-318.

27. O'Donnell, "Tensions," pp. 287-90.

28. O'Donnell, "Tensions," p. 293. His characterization of the BA is found in pp. 291-94.

29. O'Donnell, "Tensions," pp. 313, 314.

30. O'Donnell, "Tensions," pp. 316-17.

31. Míguez, *CPE*, p. 75. The term limited democracy is not to be confused with the term formal democracy. The former means an institutional change in formal, constitutional democracy.

32. The events related to the Malvinas question show that history is often more confusing and unpredictable than our generalizations assume. "In fact, the nationalistic rhetoric of the military governments is in practice clearly undermined by the total sellout of their own national economies to the transnational interests" (Míguez, *CPE*, p. 70). True enough, and yet here we have one such government that decides to use military force to settle an old colonial issue. "The new military rulers are no longer the individualistic colonels or generals of the traditional *cuartelazos*, but a technocratic-bureaucratic elite" (Míguez, *CPE*, p. 70). This, too, is a commonly accepted description of the national security state, and yet in 1982,

the General-President was clearly hoping to be a new national *caudillo*. These events confirm O'Donnell's analysis, which questions the existence of a solid, monolithic unity between the economic and military actors in this type of state and which underscores its internal contradictions and inherent weaknesses.

33. Carlos A. Floria, "La transición argentina hacia la democracia," in *Hacia una Argentina posible* (Buenos Aires: Fundación Bolsa de Comercio, 1984), pp. 177-78.

34. "Discurso pronunciado por el Dr. José Míguez Bonino al finalizar la Marcha, de Repudio al 'Documento Final y al Acta de la Junta Militar, el 20.5.83.'" Published by Asamblea Permanente por los Derechos Humanos, p. 2. Hereafter it will be referred to as "Human Rights speech."

35. Míguez, Human Rights speech, p. 1.

36. For, example, see the book published by the professors of the United Protestant Theological Faculty in Buenos Aires (ISEDET), *Democracia una opción evangélica* (Buenos Aires: La Aurora, 1983). Míguez asks if democracy is the lesser evil or the greater good and responds that it is the latter. A shorter translation of my article "Luther Was Not a Democrat" is found in *Word & World*, Fall 1983, pp. 423-34.

37. Míguez, Human Rights speech, p. 2.

38. Floria, "La transición argentina hacia la democracia," p. 183.

39. For a study of this event, see Peter H. Smith, "The Breakdown of Democracy in Latin America, 1916-30," in *The Breakdown of Democratic Regimes: Latin America*, ed. Juan J. Linz and Alfred Stepan (Baltimore: The Johns Hopkins University Press, 1978), pp. 3-27.

40. Guillermo O'Donnell, "Permanent Crisis and the Failure to Create a Democratic Regime: Argentina, 1955-66," in *The Breakdown of Democratic Regimes Latin America*, p. 147.

41. O'Donnell, "Permanent Crisis." O'Donnell is quoting Carlos Floria. For a helpful discussion of the "constraints" of the "persistent problems or constraints, limiting the possibilities of political action" in Argentina, see O'Donnell's article, pp. 140-49.

42. Míguez, *CPE*, p. 67.

43. Míguez, *CPE*, pp. 66-69.

44. Míguez, *CPE*, p. 76.

45. One of the values of Shinn's *Forced Options* is the clarity with which he presents today's and tomorrow's serious worldwide crisis. Responding to humanity's needs for energy, food, water, etc. in a limited world with a growing population and with the constant threat of nuclear war calls into question all modern projects. It would be an extension of my argument that democracy offers Argentina the best political structure for confronting the "social decisions" that Shinn defines.

46. Míguez, *CPE*, p. 51.

47. Horowitz, "Military Origins," pp. 43, 45.

48. Horowitz, "Military Origins," p. 39.

49. Horowitz, "Military Origins," p. 40.

50. Horowitz, "Military Origins," pp. 37-38.

51. Horowitz, "Military Origins," p. 38. Horowitz, like O'Donnell, calls attention to the limits and the high cost of military rule, pp. 39-43.

52. Horowitz, "Military Origins," p. 46. Horowitz is quoting Juan Linz.

53. Floria, "La transición argentina hacia la democracia," p. 179.

54. Juan Segundo, *El hombre de hoy ante Jesús de Nazaret*, I, *Fe e ideología* (Madrid: Cristiandad, 1982), p. 335. Segundo is referring to the years from 1950 to 1975. "In the first period the desperation was born, in the second there was desperate action, and in the third, desperate passivity." I return to his reflections on "desperate action" later.

55. "One is reminded of the great German historian Meinecke's comment, upon hearing the news of Hitler's appointment as chancellor: 'This was not necessary' " (Linz, *Crisis, Breakdown and Reequilibration*, p. 11).

56. "Nonviolent action is not only most appropriate to the Christian conscience but also to the revolutionary purpose" (Míguez, *Doing Theology*, p. 127). "Non-violent coercion and resistance, in short, is a type of coercion which offers the largest opportunities for a harmonious relationship with the moral and rational factors in social life" (Niebuhr, *Moral Man and Immoral Society*, pp. 250-51). A merit of Niebuhr's classic is that after establishing the validity of the workers' demand for justice, he spends the last four chapters of the book analyzing the ethical and political factors in *how* justice is to be achieved. He considers in some detail the pros and cons of seeking "Justice Through Political Force" or parliamentary democracy (chs. 7 and 8, pp. 169-230). Much of what he writes could be related to our theme. My occasional reference to his discussion will illustrate its relevance.

57. Here I leave aside the question of whether Míguez's criteria are fully adequate. Míguez, *CPE*, p. 107. It is significant that Míguez's new book places the liberation theology discussion in the explicit framework of political ethics. His criterion recalls Niebuhr's comment: "When viewing a historic situation all moralists become pragmatists and utilitarians." See *Moral Man*, p. 170.

58. Míguez, too, accepts them, *CPE*, p. 109.

59. For a convenient summary of the just-war criteria, see Robert McAfee Brown, *Religion and Violence* (Philadelphia: Westminster Press, 1973), pp. 19-20. For their use in relation to revolution, see pp. 58-61.

60. Richard Shaull, "Next Stage in Latin America," *Christianity and Crisis*, 13 November 1967, pp. 264, 266.

61. Régis Debray, *Revolution in the Revolution?* trans. Bobbye Ortiz (New York: Grove Press, 1967).

62. See John Gerassi, "Havana: A New International Is Born," in *Latin American Radicalism*, ed. Irving Louis Horowitz, Josué de Castro,

and John Gerassi (New York: Vintage Books, 1969), pp. 532-42. The article was originally published in *Monthly Review*, October 1967. The whole of "Part III: the Political-Activist Pivot" deals with revolution and *foquismo*, pp. 471-646.

63. See Donald G. Hodges, *The Latin American Revolution* (New York: William Morrow & Co., 1974) for a sympathetic and comprehensive view of the initial stages of "Guevarism" in Latin America. His discussion of Argentina emphasizes the country's other important guerilla organization, the Peoples' Revolutionary Army (ERP), pp. 125-33, 218-25. This book is a good example of an enthusiastic endorsement of the guerrilla *foco* strategy.

64. Comblin, *The Church and the National Security State*, pp. 178, 179.

65. Míguez, *La fe busca de eficacia* (Salamanca: Sígueme, 1977), pp. 157-58. The book is a later Spanish version of *Doing Theology in a Revolutionary Situation*. The paragraph from which I quote was added in the Spanish text at p. 127 of the original.

66. Míguez, *CPE*, p. 107.

67. Segundo, *El hombre de hoy ante Jesús de Nazaret*, I, pp. 343ff.

68. Segundo, *El hombre de hoy ante Jesús de Nazaret*, I, pp. 346, 347. Segundo's observations illustrate the problematic character of historical calculations.

69. Segundo, *El hombre de hoy ante Jesús de Nazaret*, I, pp. 347-51. Segundo continues by offering an interesting account of how the destruction of basic social institutions led the middle classes to support repression without realizing they were abandoning a liberal, democratic ideology (pp. 352ff.). Segundo does not believe that a simple return to representative democracy will resolve the problems of the continent, although he does not propose an alternative political structure (pp. 367-68). Rather his proposal is "to create or to re-create culture." Because of the high degree of ecological destruction, he foresees "the impossibility, perhaps prolonged, of attacking this problem with the political means to which we were accustomed." Therefore, the task is "to form an effective cultural *tradition* . . . on the basis of which the necessary political ideologies can later be built" (pp. 388-89). "It is necessary to acquire a Marxist 'culture' " (p. 403). Such a development in Argentina, I would add, presupposes the freedoms and the healing that can be offered only by a democratic structure and ethos.

70. Niebuhr, *Moral Man and Immoral Society*, p. 220.

71. Niebuhr, *Moral Man and Immoral Society*, pp. 219-20. "An adequate political morality" that seeks to "do justice to the insights of both moralists and political realists . . . will try to save society from being involved in endless cycles of futile conflict, not by an effort to abolish coercion in the life of collective man, but by reducing it to a minimum, by counseling the use of such types of coercion as are most compatible

with the moral and rational factors in human society and by discriminating between the purposes and ends for which coercion is used" (pp. 233-34).

72. Míguez, *Doing Theology*, p. 15.

73. O'Donnell, "Permament Crisis," p. 142.

74. "Doce sacerdotes visitan Cuba invitados por Fidel Castro," in Pablo Richard, *Cristianos por el socialismo* (Salamanca: Sígueme, 1976), p. 80. According to Castro, the role of the priests is therefore "to unmask, on the level of the masses, the bourgeois conception of freedom, democracy, law, order, justice, etc."

75. Linz, *Crisis, Breakdown and Reequilibration*, p. 13.

76. Horowitz, "Military Origins," p. 40.

77. Leonardo Boff, "Jesucristo libertador. Una visíon cristológica desde Latinoamérica oprimida," in *Jesucristo en la historia y en la fe*, ed. A. Vargas-Machuca (Salamanca: Sígueme, 1977), pp. 185-86. He is quoting from Comblin's *Theology of Revolutionary Practice*.

78. Míguez, *CPE*, p. 77. See pp. 76-78 for a fuller description of his project.

79. Míguez, "For Life and Against Death: A Theology That Takes Sides," *Christian Century* 26 November 1980, p. 1157.

80. Dussel, "Church State Relations in Peripheral Latin American Societies," p. 69. Cf. Míguez's comments on 'populist' nationalistic movements in *CPE*, pp. 66-67.

81. See Míguez's discussion of the "Priests for the Third World," in *Doing Theology*, especially p. 51.

82. José Enrique Miguens, *Los neo-fascismos en la Argentina* (Buenos Aires: Belgrano, 1983), p. 212. The whole book is an example of the Peronist criticism of socialist and other interpretations of Peronism.

83. "Editorial: Balance de las elecciones," *Praxis*, Summer 1984, p. 1.

5. Third World Theology— A New Context for Ecumenical Ethics

1. Sergio Torres and Virginia Fabella, eds., *The Emergent Gospel: The Underside of History* (Maryknoll, NY: Orbis Books, 1976).

2. Torres and Fabella, eds., *Emergent Gospel*, p. 269.

3. Torres and Fabella, eds., *Emergent Gospel*, p. 269.

4. Kofi Appiah-Kubi and Sergio Torres, eds., *African Theology Enroute* (Maryknoll, NY: Orbis Books, 1979), p. 193.

5. Appiah-Kubi and Torres, eds., *African Theology Enroute*, p. 194.

6. Virginia Fabella, ed., *Asia's Struggle for Full Humanity: Towards a Relevant Theology* (Maryknoll, NY: Orbis Books, 1980).

7. Fabella, ed., *Asia's Struggle*, p. 55.

8. Fabella, ed., *Asia's Struggle*, p. 156.

9. Fabella, ed., *Asia's Struggle*, pp. 156f.

10. Fabella, ed., *Asia's Struggle*, p. 158.

11. Sergio Torres and John Eagleson, eds., *The Challenge of Basic Christian Communities* (Maryknoll, NY: Orbis Books, 1981).

12. Torres and Eagleson, ed., *Challenge*, p. 238.

13. Torres and Eagleson, ed., *Challenge*, p. 240.

14. Torres and Eagleson, ed., *Challenge*, pp. 243f.

15. Sergio Torres and Virginia Fabella, eds., *The Irruption of the Third World: A Challenge to Theology* (Maryknoll, NY: Orbis Books, 1983).

16. Torres and Fabella, eds., *Irruption*, p. 195.

17. Torres and Fabella, eds., *Irruption*, p. 197.

18. Torres and Fabella, eds., *Irruption*, p. 198.

19. Quoted in Kuncheria Pathil, *Models in Ecumenical Dialogue* (Bangalore, India: Dharmaran Publications, 1981), p. 377.

20. Richard N. Dickinson, "Christian Ethics in the World Council Arena," *Poor Yet Making Many Rich* (Geneva, Switzerland: World Council of Churches 1983), pp. 62f.

21. Dickinson, "Christian Ethics," p. 63.

6. Urban Racism and Afro-American Integrity

1. Max Weber, "The Nature of the City," in Richard Sennett, ed., *Classic Essays on the Culture of Cities* (New York: Meredith Corp., 1969), p. 23.

2. Weber, "Nature of the City," p. 24.

3. See Emile Durkheim, *The Division of Labor in Society* (New York: Free Press, 1964).

4. Robert Redfield, "The Folk Society," in Sennett, ed., *Classic Essays*, p. 187.

5. Robert Ezra Park, "Human Ecology," in Roland L. Warren, ed., *Perspectives on the American Community* (Chicago: Rand McNally Publishing Co., 1973), p. 39.

6. Park, "Human Ecology," p. 38.

7. Park, "Human Ecology," p. 38.

8. Carl Degler, *Out of Our Past* (New York: Harper and Brothers, Colophon Books, 1959), p. 38.

9. Letter from Maj. Gen. George Stoneman to Lt. Gen. U.S. Grant, in Hollis Lynch, ed., *The Black Urban Condition* (New York: Thomas Y. Crowell Co., 1973), p. 24.

10. Charles S. Johnson, "Negroes at Work in Baltimore, Md.," in Lynch, ed., *Black Urban Condition*, p. 101.

11. W.E.B. DuBois, "The Black Vote in Philadelphia," in Lynch, ed., *Black Urban Condition*, p. 101.

12. Dorothy Porter, *Early Negro Writing (1760-1837)* (Boston: Beacon Press, 1971), p. 5.

13. E. Franklin Frazier, *The Negro Church in America* (New York: Schocken Books, 1964), pp. 37-38.

14. James D. McGhee, "The Changing Demographics in Black America," in *The State of Black America, 1983* (New York: National Urban League, 1983), p. 4.

7. Racism and Economics: The Perspective of Oliver C. Cox

1. For discussion, see V.P. Franklin, *Black Self-Determination: A Cultural History of the Faith of the Fathers* (Westport, CT: Lawrence Hill, 1984); Vincent Harding, *There Is a River: The Black Struggle for Freedom* (New York: Harcourt Brace Jovanovich, 1981); Albert Raboteau, *Slave Religion: The "Invisible Institution" in the Antebellum South* (New York: Oxford University Press, 1978); Mary Frances Berry and John Blassingame, *Long Memory: The Black Experience in America* (New York: Oxford University Press, 1982).

2. Gayraud Wimore, *Black Religion and Black Radicalism* (Garden City, NY: Doubleday, 1972); W.E.B. DuBois, *The Souls of Black Folk* (Greenwich, CT: Fawcett Publications, 1903; reprint ed., 1969); Martin Luther King Jr., *Why We Can't Wait* (New York: Harper & Row, 1964); Frederick Douglass, *The Life and Times of Frederick Douglass* (London: 1892; reprint ed., New York: Macmillan, 1962); James H. Cone, *Black Theology and Black Power* (New York: Seabury Press, 1969).

3. Several recent studies include Maulana Karenga, *Introduction to Black Studies* (Inglewood, CA: Kawaida Publications, 1982); Manning Marable, *How Capitalism Underdeveloped Black America* (Boston: South End Press, 1983); Paula Giddings, *When and Where I Enter: The Impact of Black Women on Race and Sex in America* (New York: William Morrow & Co., 1984); Bell Hooks, *Feminist Theory: From Margin to Center* (Boston: South End Press, 1984); Leslie W. Dunbar, ed., *Minority Report: What Has Happened to Blacks, Hispanics, American Indians and Other Minorities in the Eighties* (New York: Pantheon Books, 1984).

4. Carter G. Woodson, *The Mis-Education of the Negro* (Washington, DC: Associated Publishers, 1933); *The Negro in Our History* (Washington, DC: Associated Publishers, 1931); *The History of the Negro Church* (Washington, DC: Associated Publishers, 1921).

5. Carter G. Woodson, *African Heroes and Heroines* (Washington, DC: Associated Publishers, 1939); *Free Negro Heads of Families in the United States in 1830* (Washington, DC: Association for the Study of Negro Life and History, 1925); *The Negro Professional Man and the Community* (reprint of 1934 ed., New York: Negro University Press, 1969); *The Story of the Negro Retold* (Washington, DC: Associated Publishers, 1935); *The Mind of the Negro as Reflected in Letters Written During the Crisis*

1800-1860 (Washington, DC: Association for the Study of Negro Life and History, 1926).

6. George D. Kelsey, *Racism and the Christian Understanding of Man* (New York: Charles Scribner's Sons, 1965).

7. For literature on the theological discussion of this issue, see Albert Barnes, *An Inquiry into the Scriptural Views of Slavery* (Philadelphia: Perkins & Purves, 1857); John Henry Hopkins, *A Scriptural, Ecclesiastical, and Historical View of Slavery: From the Days of the Patriarch Abraham to the Nineteenth Century* (New York: Negro University Press, 1969); William Hosmer, *Slavery and the Church* (reprint of 1853 ed., New York: Negro University Press, 1969); Fred A. Ross, *Slavery Ordained of God* (Philadelphia: J.B. Lippincott Co., 1857); Lester Scherer, *Slavery and the Churches in Early America 1619-1819* (Grand Rapids, MI: William B. Eerdmans Pub. Co., 1975).

8. My understanding of Oliver C. Cox's personal life is based on the article by Gordan D. Morgan, "In Memoriam: Oliver C. Cox 1901-1974," *Monthly Review* 28, no. 1 (May 1976): 34-40.

9. Oliver C. Cox, *Caste, Class and Race* (Garden City, NY: Doubleday, 1948).

10. Cox, *Caste, Class and Race*, p. xvi.

11. Gunnar Myrdal, *An American Dilemma* (New York: Harper & Row, 1944). E. Franklin Frazier, *The Negro Family in the United States* (Chicago: University of Chicago Press, 1939); E. Franklin Frazier, *The Negro Church in America* (New York: Schocken Books, 1964); St. Clair Drake and Horace Cayton, *Black Metropolis*, 2 vols. (rev. ed., New York: Harper & Row, 1962).

12. Oliver C. Cox, "The Modern Caste School of Race Relations," *Social Forces* 21 (December 1942): 218-26. For a contemporary discussion, see Lloyd Hogan, *Principles of Black Political Economy* (Boston: Routledge & Kegan Paul, 1984); Robert Allen, *Black Awakening in Capitalist America* (Garden City, NY: Doubleday, 1970).

13. Cox, *Caste, Class and Race*, p. 332, italics added. Cf. Elizabeth Fox-Genovese and Eugene Fox-Genovese, *Fruits of Merchant Capital: Slavery and Bourgeois Property in the Rise and Expansion of Capitalism* (New York: Oxford University Press, 1983); Manning Marable, *Blackwater* (Dayton, OH: Challenge Press, 1978).

14. Morgan, "In Memoriam," p. 35.

15. Oliver C. Cox, "Racial Theories of Robert E. Park, et al.," *Journal of Negro Education* 13, no. 4 (Fall 1944): 452-63. See also Stanford Lyman, *The Black American in Sociological Thought* (New York: Putnam Publishing Group, 1972).

16. Cox, at the time of his death, was working on a book about race relations. The manuscript was revised, edited, and published posthu-

mously by Wayne State University Press in 1976. The title is *Race-Relations—Elements and Social Dynamics.*

17. Cox, *Caste, Class and Race*, p. 333. James Boggs and Grace Boggs, *Racism and the Class Struggle* (New York: Monthly Review Press, 1970).

18. Oliver C. Cox, "Modern Democracy and the Class Struggle," *Journal of Negro Education*, XVI, no. 2 (Spring 1947): 155-64. See also Elizabeth Drew, *Politics and Money* (New York: Macmillan, 1983); Robert A. Dahl, *Who Governs?* (New Haven, CT: Yale University Press, 1961); G. William Domhoff, *The Higher Circle: The Governing Class in America* (New York: Random House, 1970).

19. Especially useful is Oliver C. Cox's "The Political Class," *Bulletin: Society for Social Research*, January 1944. Cf. Donald Harris, *Capital Accumulation and Income Distribution* (Stanford, CA: Stanford University Press, 1978); Samuel Huntington, *American Politics, the Politics of Disharmony* (Cambridge, MA: Belknap Press, 1981); Ralph Miliband, *The State in Capitalist Society* (New York: Basic Books, 1969); Nicos Poulantzas, *Political Power and Social Classes* (London: Sheed and Ward, 1973).

20. An elaboration of this point may be found in Oliver C. Cox, "Estates, Social Classes and Political Classes," *American Sociologist Review* 10, no. 4 (August 1945): 464-69. For documentary information, see L. Carlson and G.A. Colburn, eds., *In Their Place: White America Defines Her Minorities 1850-1960* (New York: John Wiley & Sons, 1972).

21. Oliver C. Cox, *The Foundations of Capitalism* (New York: Philosophical Library, 1959), p. 92.

22. Cox, *Foundations of Capitalism*, p. 62. For detailed discussion, see R.H. Tawney, *Religion and the Rise of Capitalism* (New York: Harcourt, Brace and Co., 1937).

23. Cox, *Foundations of Capitalism*, p. 106. Especially important is Walter Rodney, *How Europe Underdeveloped Africa* (Washington, DC: Howard University Press, 1974); A.G. Hopkins, *An Economic History of West Africa* (New York: Columbia University Press, 1973); Walter L. Goldfrank, ed., *The World System of Capitalism: Past and Present* (Beverly Hills, CA: Sage Publications, 1979).

24. Oliver C. Cox, *Capitalism and American Leadership* (New York: Philosophical Library, 1962), p. 292.

25. Cox, *Capitalism and American Leadership*, p. 102. See Sidney Lens, *The Military-Industrial Complex* (Philadelphia: The Pilgrim Press, 1970); Gordon Adams, *The Iron Triangle: The Politics of Defense Contracting* (New Brunswick, NJ: Transaction Books, 1982).

26. Cox, *Capitalism and American Leadership*, p. 4. Cf. Richard Barnet and Ronald Muller, *Global Reach: The Power of Multinational Corporations* (New York: Simon & Schuster, 1974); Douglas Dowd, *The Twisted Dream: Capitalist Development in the U.S. Since 1776* (Cam-

bridge, MA: Winthrop Publishers, 1977); G. Kolko, *The Roots of American Foreign Policy* (Boston: Beacon Press, 1969).

27. Cox, *Capitalism and American Leadership*, p. 7. See James Petras and Morris Morley, *The United States and Chile* (New York: Monthly Review Press, 1976); A.G. Frank, *Capitalism and Underdevelopment in Latin America* (New York: Monthly Review Press, 1969).

28. Cox, *Capitalism and American Leadership*, p. 24. See also Michael Barratt-Brown, *The Economics of Imperialism* (Harmondsworth: Penguin Education, 1974); Charles Wilber, ed., *The Political Economy of Development and Underdevelopment* (New York: Random House, 1973).

29. Cox, *Capitalism and American Leadership*, p. 74. See Robert Rhodes, ed., *Imperialism and Underdevelopment* (New York: Monthly Review Press, 1970); Harry Magdoff, *The Age of Imperialism* (New York: Monthly Review Press, 1969).

30. Cox, *Capitalism and American Leadership*, p. 61.

31. Cf. Oliver C. Cox, "Color Prejudice, a World Problem," *The Aryan Path* 8, Bombay, India, June 1947. See also "The Nature of the Anti-Asiatic Movement on the Pacific Coast," *Journal of Negro Education* 15, no. 4 (Fall 1946): 603-14.

32. Cox, *Capitalism and American Leadership*, p. 133. Essential sources are Sterling Spero and Abram Harris, *The Black Worker* (New York: Atheneum, Pubs., 1968), and Julius Jacobson, ed., *The Negro and the American Labor Movement* (Garden City, NY: Anchor Books, 1968).

33. Cox, *Capitalism and American Leadership,* p. 141.

34. Cox, *Capitalism and American Leadership,* p. 242. See Harold Baron, "The Demand for Black Labor: Historical Notes on the Political Economy of Racism," *Radical America* 5 (1971): 2. For a more detailed historical discussion, see Daniel A. Novak, *The Wheel of Servitude: Black Forced Labor After Slavery* (Lexington, KY: University Press of Kentucky, 1978); *The Roots of Black Poverty: The Southern Plantation Economy After the Civil War* (Durham, NC: Duke University Press, 1978).

35. Two helpful articles are Oliver C. Cox, "Race Relations," *Journal of Negro Education* 12, no. 2 (Spring 1943): 144-53, and "Lynching and the Status Quo," *Journal of Negro Education* 14, no. 2 (Spring 1945): 576-88. See also Sidney Willhem, *Who Needs the Negro* (Cambridge, MA: Schenkman Publishing Co., 1970); J.D. Williams, ed., *The State of Black America* (New York: Transaction Books, 1984); Mary Frances Berry, *Black Resistance/White Law: A History of Constitutional Racism in America* (New York: Appleton-Century-Crofts, 1971).

36. See Oliver C. Cox, "Race and Caste: A Distinction," *American Journal of Sociology*, March 1945, pp. 360-68. Also Victor Perlo, *The Economics of Racism, U.S.A.: Roots of Black Inequality* (New York: International Publishers, 1975); Benjamin B. Ringer, *"We the People" and Others: Duality and America's Treatment of Racial Minorities* (New York: Tavis-

tock Publications, 1983); Marable, *How Capitalism Underdeveloped Black America.*

37. Cox, *Caste, Class and Race,* p. 322.

38. Cox, *Caste, Class and Race,* p. 345.

39. For a brief, poignant discussion, see Oliver C. Cox, "Race, Prejudice, and Intolerance," *Social Forces* 24, no. 2 (Fall 1945): 216-19. Also A. Leon Higginbotham Jr., *In the Matter of Color* (New York: Oxford University Press, 1978); Walter E. Williams, *The State Against Blacks* (New York: New Press, McGraw-Hill, 1982); Center for the Study of Social Policy, *A Dream Deferred: The Economic Status of Black Americans* (Washington, DC, 1983); John Ogbee, *Minority Education and Caste* (New York: Academic Press, 1978); William J. Wilson, *The Hidden Agenda: Race, Social Dislocation, and Public Policy in America* (forthcoming).

40. Cox, *Capitalism and American Leadership,* p. 251.

8. Emerging Issues in Urban Ethics

1. H. Richard Niebuhr, *Christ and Culture* (New York: Harper & Row, 1951).

2. The sociologist Max Weber was among the first modern scholars to stress this fact. For an impressive documentation of the same from the standpoint of a contemporary New Testament scholar, see Wayne A. Meeks, *The First Urban Christians: The Social World of the Apostle Paul* (New Haven, CT: Yale University Press, 1983).

3. But in the context, the Babel myth may also express defiance of the divine intention that humans "fill the earth and subdue it," rather than clustering themselves fearfully in one location. Cf. Bernard Anderson, "The Babel Story: Paradigm of Human Unity and Diversity," in Andrew M. Greoleyz and Gregory Baum, *Ethnicity* (New York: Seabury Press, 1977), pp. 66-67.

4. The classic contrast in the two attitudes toward government—the Roman government of the time—can be found in the New Testament in Romans 13, where Paul urges Christians to "be subject to the governing authorities," and in Revelation 13, where John warns Christians that they will have to endure the persecutions of "the beast"—Rome—but must at all cost refrain from worshiping it.

5. Max Weber, *The Protestant Ethic and the Spirit of Capitalism,* trans. Talcott Parsons (New York: Charles Scribner's Sons, 1958).

6. Sam Bass Warner, *The Urban Wilderness: A History of the American City* (New York: Harper & Row, 1972), p. 8.

7. For the definitive review of this entire historical development, see Robert T. Handy, *A Christian America: Protestant Hopes and Historical*

Realities (revised ed.; New York and London: Oxford University Press, 1980).

8. Max C. Stackhouse, *Ethics and the Urban Ethos* (Boston: Beacon Press, 1974), chapters 1 and 2.

9. Stackhouse, *Ethics and the Urban Ethos,* pp. 4-5.

10. Stackhouse, *Ethics and the Urban Ethos,* pp. 114-15.

11. Stackhouse, *Ethics and the Urban Ethos,* p. 17. Also, Ronald D. Pasquariello, Donald W. Shriver Jr., and Alan Geyer, *Redeeming the City* (New York: The Pilgrim Press, 1982), pp. 105-11.

12. The summary perspective here is spelled out in much greater detail in the data from two sociological studies as recorded in Donald W. Shriver Jr. and Karl A. Ostrom, *Is There Hope for the City?* (Philadelphia: Westminster Press, 1977), pp. 114-81, and *The Connecticut Mutual Life Report on American Values in the 80's: The Impact of Belief* (Hartford, CT, 1981). The former study discovered that the highest levels of sustained personal commitment to social justice were correlated among religiously oriented people, with their actual participation in political life. Low political participation was often associated with low personal morale and short-lived idealism. The latter study documents the association of community political participation with participation in the church. Both studies strongly conclude that a person's vision of a more humane society, support by small groups of friends, and public participation *reinforce* one another.

9. Indigenous Peoples, the Land, and Self-government

1. Portions of this essay appeared in my article "The Right to Make Our Own Mistakes," *Touchstone* 2 (May 1984):29-43.

2. The phrase and analysis it connotes is from Mel Watkins, ed., *Dene Nation* (Toronto: University of Toronto Press, 1977).

3. See George Manuel and Michael Poslums, *The Fourth World* (Toronto: Collier-Macmillan, 1974), ch. 9.

4. World Council of Churches, Program to Combat Racism, *Land Rights for Indigenous People* (Geneva, 1983), p. 5.

5. The Inuit Circumpolar Conference, the World Council of Indigenous Peoples, and the United Nations Working Group on Indigenous Peoples are examples.

6. The return of Blue Lake to Taos Pueblo and the repeal of Menominee termination are recent American examples. The restitution of "cutoff" lands to some native tribes in British Columbia is one Canadian example. See Canada, Indian Affairs and Northern Development, *Outstanding Business* (Ottawa, 1982).

7. See Vine Deloria Jr., "The Right to Be Different," *Grapevine* 15 (February 1984).

8. *Alaska Native Review Commission* (hereafter *ANRC*), Papers Prepared for Overview Discussion, February 27-March 16, 1984 (Anchorage: Accu-Type Depositions, 1984), no. 3, p. 3.

9. Addressing a symposium on Indian Law-Theology sponsored by the National Council of Churches, 1983. See *Grapevine* 15 (February 1984).

10. Canada, Special Committee, *Indian Self-government in Canada* (Ottawa, 1983), p. 64.

11. See Canada, Indian Affairs and Northern Development, *Annual Report, 1982-83* (Ottawa, 1983), p. 19, for a listing of comprehensive claims.

12. The ICC is also funding it. The review has the official blessing of the World Council of Indigenous Peoples and the International Working Group on Indigenous Affairs. Thomas Berger headed the Royal Commission for Canada on the Mackenzie Valley Pipeline Proposal in 1975. The style of investigation and the report, *Northern Frontier, Northern Homeland* (Ottawa: Supply and Services, 1977), are widely regarded as having a significant impact on native concerns and northern development.

13. Charles Johnson, chairman of the Alaska Federation of Natives, *ANRC,* Transcript of Proceedings, March 1, 1985, IV, p. 331.

14. Deloria, "Right to Be Different."

15. For a history of missions to native people in Canada, see John Webster Grant, *Moon of Wintertime* (Toronto: University of Toronto Press, 1984).

16. The Nishga are a prime example in Canada. In the United States, the Papago and Cherokee have effectively integrated their Christian faith.

17. The World Council of Churches is involved mainly through its Commission on the Programme to Combat Racism. *Project North* is an ecumenical action coalition representing seven major denominations. Citizens for Public Justice is a nondenominational action group with a base in the Reformed tradition.

18. For a helpful description of the colonial experience, see Peter Puxley, "The Colonial Experience," in Watkins, ed., *Dene Nation,* pp. 103-19.

19. For a brief history of American Indian policy and programs, see *ANRC,* Papers Prepared for Overview Discussion, no. 5, and Vine Deloria Jr. and Clifford M. Lytle, *American Indians, American Justice* (Austin: University of Texas, 1983).

20. For Canadian policy history, see John L. Tobias, "Protection, Civilization, Assimilation," in *As Long As the Sun Shines and the Water Flows,* ed. Ian A.L. Getty and Antoine S. Lussier (Vancouver: University of British Columbia Press, 1983), pp. 39-55, and J.E. Chamberlin, *The Harrowing of Eden* (Toronto: Fitzhenry and Whiteside, 1975).

21. Canada, Indian Affairs and Northern Development, *Statement of Government of Canada on Indian Policy* (Ottawa, 1969), pp. 8-9.

22. Brian Barry, "Self-government Revisited," in *The Nature of Political Theory*, ed. David Miller and Larry Siedentop (Oxford: Clarendon Press, 1983). See also Evelyn Kallen, *Ethnicity and Human Rights in Canada* (Toronto: Gage, 1982), and C.H. Enloe, *Ethnic Conflict and Political Development* (Boston: Little, Brown, 1973).

23. Gene Outka, *Agape: An Ethical Analysis* (New Haven, CT: Yale University Press, 1972), pp. 265-66.

24. Tom L. Beauchamp and James F. Childress, *Principles of Biomedical Ethics*, 2d ed. (New York: Oxford University Press, 1983), p. 62.

25. Reinhold Niebuhr, *The Children of Light and the Children of Darkness* (New York: Charles Scribner's Sons, 1944).

26. Space does not permit a systematic account or defense of the social analysis entailed in these ethical reflections. Methodologically, I am indebted in such matters to William W. Everett and J.T. Bachmeyer, *Disciplines in Transformation* (Washington, DC: University Press of America, 1979), and to Alvin Pitcher and Gibson Winter, "Perspectives in Religious Social Ethics," *Journal of Religious Ethics* 5 (Spring 1972):69.

27. R.K. Thomas, "Process and Identity," in *Bureau of American Ethnology Handbook of North American Indians*, ed. W.C. Startevant (Washington, DC: Smithsonian Institution Press, 1978), II:25.

28. Roger L. Shinn, "Perception and Belief," *Union Seminary Quarterly Review* 34, no. 1 (Fall 1978):13ff.

29. Christian Bay, *Strategies of Political Emancipation* (Notre Dame, IN: University of Notre Dame Press, 1981), p. 18.

30. Reinhold Niebuhr, *The Self and the Dramas of History* (New York: Charles Scribner's Sons, 1955), p. 36.

31. Karl Barth, *Christ and Adam* (New York: Harper & Row, 1956), p. 91.

32. John C. Bennett, *The Radical Imperative* (Philadelphia: Westminster Press, 1975), pp. 13-14.

33. For an excellent review of international law, including a summary of these theories justifying colonialism, see Douglas Sanders, "The Reemergence of Indigenous Questions in International Law," *Canadian Human Rights Yearbook* (Toronto: The Carswell Company, 1983), pp. 26ff.

34. Douglas Sanders' testimony in *ANRC*, Proceedings, X, p. 954.

35. Lord Acton defends this view. See Barry, "Self-government Revisited," p. 147.

36. Brian Barry attempts to find ethical grounds or criteria for morally justifying political boundaries and looks to "the individualist principle," i.e., the interests of those people affected by it. By this criterion he rejects ethnic grounds but accepts national identity.

37. Dene Nation and Metis Association of the Northwest Territories, *Public Government for the People of the North* (Yellowknife, 1981), p. 17.

38. State security is sometimes cited as one ground for forcible suppression of any attempts by a national group to secede. Barry, "Self-government Revisited," p. 143, does not accept this as a morally sufficient ground.

39. Cited by Lionel Rubinoff, "Multiculturalism and the Metaphysics of Pluralism," *Journal of Canadian Studies* 17, no. 1 (Spring 1982):115.

40. Rubinoff, "Multiculturalism."

41. Reinhold Niebuhr, *Christian Realism and Political Problems* (New York: Charles Scribner's Sons, 1953), p. 26.

42. Douglas J. Hall, *The Steward* (New York: Friendship Press, 1982), p. 28.

43. Roger Shinn provides a helpful summary of this controversy in *Forced Options* (2d ed., New York: The Pilgrim Press, 1985), pp. 185ff. He defends the stewardship tradition, as does Robin Attfield, *The Ethics of Environmental Concern* (Oxford: Blackwell, 1983).

44. Loren Wilkinson, ed., *Earth Keeping* (Grand Rapids, MI: William B. Eerdmans, 1980), p. 233.

45. On Toynbee, see Shinn, *Forced Options,* p. 189. Richard K. Nelson, *Make Prayers to the Raven* (Chicago: University of Chicago Press, 1983), and Calvin Martin, *Keepers of the Game* (Berkeley: University of California Press, 1978), are studies that reveal the difficulty of maintaining traditional values.

46. *World Council of Churches, Programme Unit on Justice and Service,* Document No. 12b, "Land Rights and Racially Oppressed Indigenous Peoples," Committee Meeting, January 1-11, 1979, Section I, p. 2.

47. See also Berger, *Northern Frontier,* and R.K. Thomas, "The New Sacred Nationalism," *Proceedings of the Conference on Indian Issues of the Eighties,* April 1980 (Claremore, OK: Claremore College, 1980).

48. N. Scott Momaday, *Seeing with a Native Eye,* ed. W.H. Capps (New York: Harper & Row, 1976), p. 80.

49. Lenore Coltheart, "Authority, Property and Aboriginal Australia," *Politics* 18, no. 2 (November 1983).

50. Walter Brueggemann, *The Land* (Philadelphia: Fortress Press, 1977), p. 2.

51. William W. Everett, "Land Ethics: Toward a Covenantal Model," *American Society of Christian Ethics,* Selected Papers of the Twentieth Annual Meeting, 1979, pp. 45-73.

52. The interests of native nations and those of environmentalist groups usually come together when faced with large-scale development projects. But tensions between Greenpeace and the Dene Nation over trapping fur-bearing animals point to some differences in viewpoint.

53. *ANRC,* Papers, No. 1, p. 18.

54. Byron Mollott, in *ANRC,* Proceedings, IV, p. 312.

55. Mollott, *ANRC,* IV, pp. 311-12.

56. Mollott, *ANRC,* IV, p. 312.

57. Mollott, *ANRC,* IV, p. 319.

58. Gibson Winter, *Liberating Creation* (New York: Seabury Press, 1981), p. 8. For other descriptions of the cognitive patterns and style of modernity in contrast to traditional societies, see Peter Berger, Brigitte Berger, and Hansfried Kellner, *The Homeless Mind* (New York: Random House, 1973). There is, of course, an extensive literature critiquing modernity. But Winter, unlike many, looks forward to a new synthesis. Joe Holland develops this idea in "Linking Social Analysis and Theological Reflection: The Place of Root Metaphors in Social and Religious Experience," in James E. Hug, *Tracing the Spirit* (New York: Paulist Press, 1983).

10. Justice, Participation, and Sustainable Sufficiency

1. For example, see Herman E. Daly, ed., *Toward a Steady-State Economy* (San Francisco: W.H. Freeman, 1973); Donella H. Meadows et al., *The Limits to Growth* (New York: Universe Books, 1973); William Ophuls, *Ecology and the Politics of Scarcity* (San Francisco: W.H. Freeman, 1977); and Dennis Clark Pirages, ed., *The Sustainable Society* (New York: Praeger Publishers, 1977).

2. For example, see H.S.D. Cole et al., eds., *Models of Doom* (New York: Universe Books, 1973); John R. Maddox, *The Doomsday Syndrome* (New York: McGraw-Hill, 1972); Herman Kahn and B. Bruce Biggs, *Things to Come* (New York: Macmillan, 1973); Carl Kaysen, "The Computer That Printed Out Wolf," *Foreign Affairs* 50, no. 4 (July 1972):660-68. Also see Roger L. Shinn, *Forced Options* (2d ed., New York: The Pilgrim Press, 1985); Robert L. Stivers, *The Sustainable Society* (Philadelphia: Westminster Press, 1976), and *Hunger, Technology, and Limits to Growth* (Minneapolis: Augsburg Publishing House, 1984); and Barbara Ward, *Progress for a Small Planet* (New York: W.W. Norton, 1979).

3. C.T. Kurien, "Economics of the Just and Sustainable Society," *Faith and Science in an Unjust World,* ed. Roger L. Shinn (Geneva: World Council of Churches, 1980), 1:220-24.

4. Richard H. Wagner, *Environment and Man,* 3d ed. (New York: W.W. Norton, 1971, 1978), p. 526.

5. Antony J. Dolman, ed., *Rio: Reshaping the International Order* (New York: New American Library, 1977), p. 28.

6. Frances Moore Lappe and Joseph Collins, *Food First* (Boston: Houghton Mifflin, 1976), pp. 7, 9, 373ff.; Food and Agricultural Organization of the United Nations (FAO), *Review and Analysis of Agrarian*

Reform and Rural Development in the Developing Countries Since the Mid-1960's (New York: United Nations), pp. 21-39.

7. Department of Economic and Social Affairs, *World Energy Supplies* (New York: United Nations, 1976); Dennis Hayes, *Rays of Hope* (New York: W.W. Norton, 1977), p. 25.

8. Amory Lovins, *Soft Energy Paths* (Cambridge, MA: Ballinger, 1977), p. 39; also see chaps. 2 and 5.

9. Lovins, *Soft Energy Paths*, p. 33.

10. Daniel Bell, "Are There 'Social Limits' to Growth?" *Prospects for Growth,* ed. Kenneth D. Wilson (New York: Praeger, 1977), p. 21.

11. Barry Commoner, *The Closing Circle* (New York: Alfred A. Knopf, 1971), chap. 9.

12. Eugene S. Schwartz, *Overskill* (New York: Ballantine Books, 1971).

13. Report of Section VI, "Energy for the Future," *Faith and Science in an Unjust World,* ed. Paul Abrecht (Geneva: World Council of Churches, 1980), 2:93.

14. W. Lee Humphries, "Pitfalls and Promises of Biblical Texts," *A New Ethic for a New Earth,* ed. Glenn C. Stone (New York: Friendship Press, 1971), p. 101.

15. For an analysis of the middle axioms that stand between the three general action guidelines and the recommendations for social policy, see Robert L. Stivers, *Hunger, Technology, and Limits to Growth* (Minneapolis: Augsburg Publishing House, 1984), pp. 136ff.

11. Is an Economic Apologia Enough for Business Managers?

1. Allen R. Janger and Ronald E. Berenbeim, *External Challenges to Management Decisions* (New York: The Conference Board, 1981), p. 7.

2. See Reinhard Bendix, *Work and Authority in Industry: Ideologies of Management in the Course of Industrialization* (New York: Harper Torchbooks, 1956), pp. 254-340.

3. Amartya Sen, "The Profit Motive," *Lloyds Bank Review.* January 1983, p. 1.

4. Sen, "The Profit Motive," p. 2; J.R. Kearl, Clayne L. Pope, Gordon C. Whiting and Larry Wimmer, "A Confusion of Economists?" *The American Economic Review, Papers and Proceedings* 69 (May 1979): 30.

5. Thomas C. Schelling, "Economic Reasoning and The Ethics of Policy," *The Public Interest,* Summer 1981, p. 53.

6. Albert O. Hirschman, *Exit, Voice and Loyalty, Responses to Decline in Firms, Organizations, and States* (Cambridge, MA: Harvard University Press, 1970).

7. See Geoffrey Heal and D.J. Brown, "Equity, Efficiency and Increasing Returns," *Review of Economic Studies* 46 (October 1979): 571-85.

8. The General Motors managers had long rationalized the noncompetitive system as a way to maintain a large number of suppliers, thus assuring reliability of supplies. See "G.M. to Buy Steel by Bid Rather Than Contract," *The New York Times*, March 24, 1982; Amal Nag, "Armco, Inland Win GM Steel Supply Contracts," *The Wall Street Journal*, 23 June 1982.

9. Steven Flax, "How Detroit Is Reforming the Steelmakers," *Fortune*, 16 May 1983, p. 126.

10. Amal Nag, "Auto Companies Push Parts Makers to Raise Efficiency, Cut Prices," *The Wall Street Journal*, 31 July 1984.

11. See, for example, Arthur Okun, *Equality and Efficiency: The Big Tradeoff* (Washington DC: Brookings Institution, 1975). Also see Thomas C. Schelling, "Economic Reasoning and the Ethics of Policy," *The Public Interest*, Summer 1981, pp. 37-61.

12. F.A. Hayek, *The Constitution of Liberty* (Chicago: University of Chicago Press, 1960).

13. Milton Friedman, *Capitalism and Freedom* (Chicago: University of Chicago Press, Phoenix Books, 1962).

14. Okun, *Equality and Efficiency* pp. 35-36.

15. Irving Kristol, "Reply," *The Public Interest*, Winter 1971, p. 105.

16. Friedman, *Capitalism and Freedom*, p. 15.

17. See Lester C. Thurow, *Generating Inequality, Mechanisms of Distribution in the U.S. Economy* (New York: Basic Books, 1975).

18. Hayek, *Constitution of Liberty*, pp. 93, 96, 98-99. Another ardent supporter of the free market also explicitly rejected the claim that the market works with any justice or rewards merit. See Frank H. Knight, *The Ethics of Competition and Other Essays* (New York: Harper, 1935), pp. 54-58.

19. Friedman, *Capitalism and Freedom*, p. 13. Italics added.

20. In a survey of American leaders in ten broad categories, two scholars concluded that the "unanimity with which they uphold wide disparities in income is striking." See Sidney Verba and Gary Orren, "Rendering What's Due: Views on Income Equality," *Public Opinion*, April/May 1985, p. 51.

21. Quoted in William J. Wilson, "The Price Control Acts of 1942," *The Beginnings of OPA*. Pt. 1, Office of Temporary Controls (Washington, DC: Government Printing Office, 1947), p. 39.

22. Thomas Schelling found that his economics students at Yale almost always favored rationing of gasoline in case of curtailed imports. See "Economic Reasoning and the Ethics of Policy," *The Public Interest*, Summer 1981, p. 40.

23. David Lewin and Walter Fogel, "Wage Determination in the Public Sector," *Industrial and Labor Relations Review* 27 (April 1974): 410. Those in the lowest ranks receive higher pay, and those in the higher

ranks receive considerably lower pay than those in comparable private sector positions. See also David Lewin, "Aspects of Wage Determination in Local Government Employment," *Public Administration Review* 34 (March/April 1974): 149.

24. "Top Executive Pay Peeves the Public," *Business Week*, 25 June 1984, p. 15.

25. Verba and Orren, "Rendering What's Due," p. 49.

26. Verba and Orren, "Rendering What's Due," pp. 49f.

27. "Top Executive Pay," p. 15.

28. Peter Drucker, "Reform Executive Pay or Congress Will," *The Wall Street Journal*, 24 April 1984.

29. See Mark Green and Bonnie Tenneriello, "Executive Merit Pay," *The New York Times*, 25 April 1984.

30. Ernest van den Haag, "Economics Is Not Enough—Notes on the Anticapitalist Spirit," *The Public Interest*, Fall 1976, p. 109.

31. Of course, many Catholics and Jews in the United States incorporated something similar to the Protestant ethic into their personal set of values. The ethic could, with some justification, be called simply the American ethic, but it is useful to remind ourselves that it originated in a religious faith.

32. Irving Kristol, " 'When virtue loses all her loveliness'—some reflections on capitalism and 'the free society,' " *The Public Interest*, No. 21, Fall 1970, p. 10.

33. For a selection of such inspirational, religious celebration of the market system and capitalism, see Moses Rischin, ed. *The American Gospel of Success* (New York: New Viewpoints, 1974).

12. Capital, Community, and the Meaning of Work

1. U.S. Department of Labor, *Bureau of Labor Statistics Report*, June 1984.

2. This and other personal quotes, unless otherwise noted, are taken from the transcript of a television documentary entitled "When a Factory Closes," produced by WITF-TV in association with The Center for Ethics and Social Policy (Philadelphia) and shown on PBS in November 1983. Used with permission of The Center for Ethics and Social Policy.

3. U.S. Department of Labor, *Bureau of Labor Statistics Report*, March 1983.

4. WITF-TV, "When a Factory Closes."

5. Episcopal Commission for Social Affairs, "Ethical Reflections on the Economic Crisis," *Canadian Ecumenical News*, February-March 1983.

6. Douglas Bauer, "Why Big Business Is Firing the Boss," *The New York Times Magazine*, March 8, 1981.

7. Bauer, "Why Big Business Is Firing the Boss."

8. John Paul II, "On Human Work," a St. Paul pamphlet, Daughters of St. Paul, pp. 28f.

9. Karl Marx and Max Weber are best known for exploring this reality. Ernst Troeltsch, in his own way, develops the same theme. See Karl Marx, *Economic and Philosophical Manuscripts*, trans. T.B. Bottomore, in Eric Fromm, *Marx's Concept of Man* (New York: Frederick Ungar Publishing Co., 1961, 1966); Max Weber, *Ancient Judaism*, trans. Hans H. Gerth and Don Martindale (New York: The Free Press, 1952), and *Sociology of Religion*, trans. Ephraim Fischoff (Boston: Beacon Press, 1963); Ernst Troeltsch, *The Social Teachings of the Christian Church*, trans. Olive Wyon (New York: Harper & Row, 1960).

10. Emil Durkheim, *The Division of Labor in Society*, trans., George Simpson (Glencoe, Ill.: The Free Press, 1933), is especially good on this.

11. WITF-TV, "When a Factory Closes."

12. WITF-TV, "When a Factory Closes."

13. Harvey Brenner, *Mental Illness and the Economy* (Cambridge, MA: Harvard University Press, 1973).

14. WITF-TV, "When a Factory Closes."

15. Louis S. Jacobson, "Earnings Losses of Workers Displaced from Manufacturing Industries," in William G. Deward, ed., *The Impact of International Trade and Investment on Employment* (Washington DC: U.S. Government Printing Office, 1978).

16. WITF-TV, "When a Factory Closes."

17. WITF-TV, "When a Factory Closes."

18. WITF-TV, "When a Factory Closes."

19. In Robert J. Rosenthal, "How Nigeria Missed Its Big Chance," *The Philadelphia Inquirer Magazine*, December 30, 1984, pp. 11ff.

20. WITF-TV, "When a Factory Closes."

21. In Rosenthal, "How Nigeria Missed Its Big Chance," p. 12.

22. Perry Miller, ed., *The American Puritans* (New York: Doubleday, Anchor Books, 1956), pp. 83f.

13. The Ethical Debate About Human Gene Experiments

1. Roger Shinn's writings and congressional testimony have helped to shape a modest consensus on ethical considerations of prospective human genetic experiments. From his perspective in Protestant ethics, Shinn has steadily enriched this debate, e.g., passim, refs., 1-3. See Roger L. Shinn, "Perilous Progress in Genetics," *Social Research* 41 (1974):83.

2. See Roger L. Shinn, "Gene Therapy: Ethical Issue," *Encyclopedia of Bioethics*, 1978, p. 521.

3. See Roger L. Shinn, testimony U.S. Congress, hearings before the Subcommittee on Investigations and Oversight of the Committee on Science and Technology, No. 170 (1982), p. 301, and *Forced Options: Social*

Decisions for the 21st Century (2d ed.; New York: The Pilgrim Press, 1985), p. 127.

4. Peter Singer, *The Expanding Circle: Ethics and Sociobiology* (New York: Farrar, Straus & Giroux, 1981). Singer's is an instructive contemporary work on the evolution of ethics. Building on his evolutionary insights, although not on his central ethical theory, I discussed the ethics of informed consent and new issues in fetal therapy in *Research Ethics*, ed. Kare Berg and Knut Erik Trançy (New York: Alan R. Liss, 1983), pp. 187-228, 293-318.

5. These four stages were extensively described in the informed consent article in Berg and Trançy, pp. 203-26, and in "Cardiac Transplant and the Artificial Heart: Ethical Considerations," *Circulation* 68 (1983):1139.

6. President's Commission for the Study of Ethical Problems in Medical and Biomedical and Behavioral Research, *Splicing Life* (Washington, DC: Government Printing Office, 1982), pp. 25-48.

7. President's Commission for the Study of Ethical Problems in Medical and Biomedical and Behavioral Research, *Screening and Counseling for Genetic Conditions* (Washington, DC: Government Printing Office, 1983), pp. 9-39.

8. Chorion biopsy involves the aspiration of tissue from the chorionic villi (destined to become the placenta) between eight and eleven weeks of pregnancy. Cells from this tissue can be directly cultured and genetic diagnosis obtained in many disorders now diagnosable by amniocentesis, needle puncture of the amniotic sac between sixteen and eighteen weeks. An early report of successful chorion biopsy was from the Soviet Union. Z. Kazy et al., "Chorion Biopsy in Early Pregnancy: A Method of Early Prenatal Diagnosis for Inherited Disorders," *Prenatal Diagnosis* 2 (1982):39-45. This report omits any mention of whether informed consent was obtained from the subjects of this research, who were mainly women seeking elective abortion. To date, chorion biopsy has been performed in more than 2,000 diagnostic cases and will be compared with amniocentesis in clinical trials to study safety and accuracy. The ethical implications of earlier prenatal diagnosis were discussed in "Ethics and Trends in Applied Human Genetics," *Birth Defects* (1983), Original Article Series, vol. 19, pp. 143-58.

9. Maxine Singer and Dieter Soll, "Guidelines for DNA Hybrid Molecules," *Science* 181 (1983): 114; Paul Berg et al., "Potential Bio-Hazards of Recombinant DNA Molecules," *Science* 185 (1974):303.

10. President's Commission, *Splicing Life*, pp. 95-96.

11. President's Commission, *Splicing Life*, p. 42.

12. Theodore Friedmann, *Gene Therapy: Fact and Fiction*, Banbury Public Information Report (Cold Spring Harbor, NY: Cold Spring Harbor Laboratory, 1983). This book, the most current and readable discussion of gene therapy, reports on a conference of forty-six scientists and clinical

investigators of genetic disorders. Also, see W. French Anderson, "Prospects for Human Gene Therapy," *Science* 226 (1984):401-9.

13. Only one premature attempt at somatic cell gene therapy has occurred. In 1980, Dr. Martin Cline of UCLA attempted gene therapy with two patients in Italy and Israel who had a form of thalassemia, a hereditary blood disorder. Friedmann, *Gene Therapy*, pp. 26-29. The experiment did not change the patients' condition, but no medical report or followup was ever published. Other scientists and the National Institutes of Health (NIH) openly judged Cline to have violated scientific and ethical standards in research with human subjects. UCLA withdrew his department chairmanship and the NIH canceled several grants. Just before this event occurred, criteria for experimental gene therapy were published by W. French Anderson and John C. Fletcher, "Gene Therapy: When Is It Ethical to Begin?" *New England Journal of Medicine* 303 (1980):1293-96. I discuss the Cline experiment further in "Moral Problems and Ethical Issues in Prospective Human Gene Therapy," *Virginia Law Review* 69 (1980):1983.

14. Perhaps the best of many writings is Paul Ramsey, "Screening, An Ethicist's View," in *Ethical Issues in Human Genetics: Genetic Counseling and the Use of Genetic Knowledge*, ed. Bruce Hilton et al. (New York: Plenum Press, 1973), pp. 147-61.

15. Willard Cates et al., "The Effect of Delay and Method Choice on the Risk of Abortion Morbidity," *Family Planning Perspectives* 9 (1977):266-69.

16. Several good studies of the psychological consequences of midtrimester genetic abortions have been conducted. They show, in the words of the most thorough study, that "the decision to terminate a second trimester pregnancy because of a malformed fetus is an event with long term negative side-effects for the patient and her family." N.J. Leschot, M. Verjaal, and P.E. Treffers, "Therapeutic Abortion on Genetic Indications," in M. Verjaal and J.H. Leschot, "On Prenatal Diagnosis" (Ph.D. diss., University of Amsterdam, 1982), p. 107. Also see B.D. Blumberg, M.S. Golbus, and K.H. Hanson, "The Psychological Sequalae of Abortion Performed for a Genetic Indication." *American Journal of Obstetrics and Gynecology* 122 (1975):799-808; P. Donnai, N. Charles, and N. Harris, "Attitudes of Patients After 'Genetic' Termination of Pregnancy," *British Medical Journal* 282 (1981):621-22.

17. The incidence of genetic abortions will be a small number, especially in nations with legal abortion for social or economic reasons. In general terms, the rate of genetic abortions will be about 4 percent of all amniocentesis procedures done in any nation, i.e., the incidence of positive findings. In my view, large numbers of social abortions do not justify the acceptance of *any* reason for genetic abortion. Slowly rising abortion figures for central nervous system disorders and Down's syndrome in the

United Kingdom are reported in A.C. Turnbull and I.Z. MacKenzie, "Second Trimester Amniocentesis," *British Medical Bulletin* 39 (1983):318.

18. The best survey of current fetal therapy, predominantly by surgery, is in Michael Harrison, Mitchell Golbus, and Roy A. Filly, *Unborn Patient* (Orlando, FL: Grune & Stratton, 1984); see especially chap. 7, "Metabolic Diseases Amenable to Medical Management," by Joseph D. Schulman, which describes current and future approaches with drugs, hormones, vitamins, and bone marrow transplantation. Each of these may be a prelude to gene therapy.

19. Shinn, "Gene Therapy," p. 525. Also testimony of theologians before the President's Commission, *Splicing Life,* pp. 53, 110. Their main concern is not with the moral justification of somatic cell gene therapy, but with the unintended consequences of genetic experiments and the power that may accrue to a few.

20. Jeremy Rifkin, *Algeny* (New York: Viking Press, 1983), pp. 232, 54, 233.

21. "The Rules for Reshaping Life," editorial, *The New York Times,* 29 December 1982, sec. A, p. 17.

22. "Clergymen Ask Ban on Efforts to Alter Genes," *Washington Post,* 8 June 1983, sec. A, pp. 1, 16.

23. My approach to the groundwork of ethics, especially gathering of data and search for principles with wide acceptance in society, is influenced by and well described in R.M. Hare, *Moral Thinking* (Oxford: Oxford University Press, 1981).

24. I have attempted to keep faith with a mainstream Protestant ethical view that stresses reliance on reason, tradition, and scriptural tests that shape ethical principles rather than regulate literal acts. The reader may judge for herself or himself in *Coping with Genetic Disorders: A Guide for Clergy and Parents* (San Francisco: Harper & Row, 1982), pp. 137-76.

25. Hare, *Moral Thinking,* pp. 2-43.

26. The comments of Paul Berg are important because his caution about DNA experiments helped to launch the ethical debate about gene experiments: "In my view, trying to treat a genetic defect by gene transplant is, based on our experience to date, premature and ill-advised. If there are good reasons to be cautious, they were apparent in Frank Ruddle's experiments in which the transduced DNA appears to have caused a mutation in the recipient mouse's developmental program for spermatogenesis. Rudi Jaenisch also pointed out that when genes were introduced into early embryos, there is little basis for being able to predict if the genes will be expressed or when they function during development." Friedmann, *Gene Therapy,* pp. 51f. The whole field of gene therapy and the strengths

and weaknesses of each hypothetical approach (including retroviruses) are evaluated by W. French Anderson, *Science* 226 (1984):401-9.

27. A local review by an institutional review board is mandated by federal guidelines before research with human beings supported by federal funds can begin (*Protection of Human Subjects*, 45 Code of Federal Regulations, Part 46). By general agreement and because the Department of Health and Human Services presently lacks an Ethics Advisory Board to perform secondary review at a national level, the Recombinant Advisory Committee of NIH will act as a national review board for any somatic cell experiments. Jeffrey L. Fox, "Despite Doubts RAC Moving to Widen Role," *Science* 233 (1984):798.

28. Rifkin, *Algeny*, p. 253.

29. "Whether to Make Perfect Human Beings," editorial, *The New York Times*, 22 July 1982, sec. A, p. 22.

30. Knut Erik Tranφy, "Is There a Universal Research Ethics?" in Berg and Tranφy, *Research Ethics,* pp. 3-13.

31. President's Commission for the Study of Ethical Problems in Medical and Biomedical and Behavioral Research, *Deciding to Forego Life-sustaining Treatment* (Washington, DC: Government Printing Office, 1983), pp. 60-89.

32. For example, France's president has appointed a national committee to study ethical issues in research and medicine and make recommendations to the legislature. Comite Consultatif National d'ethique. Centre de documentation et d'information d'ethique. INSERM, 101 Rue de Tolbiac 75654 Paris.

33. Bernard Davis, "A Biologist's View: Genetic Engineering," Industrial Biotechnology Association Convention, Denver, 22 June 1983.

34. Protection of Human Subjects, Fetal Research, 45 Code of Federal Regulations 46.205-211.

35. Charles Birch and John B. Cobb Jr., *The Liberation of Life* (Cambridge: Cambridge University Press, 1981), pp. 225-31.

36. Jonathan Glover, *What Sort of People Should There Be?* (New York: Penguin Books, 1983), pp. 185, 133, 134.

37. Tabitha Powledge and John Fletcher, "Guidelines for the Ethical, Social, and Legal Issues in Prenatal Diagnosis," *New England Journal of Medicine* 300 (1979):171; Report of an International Workshop: "Prenatal Diagnosis: Past, Present and Future," *Prenatal Diagnosis* Special Issue (1980):16; President's Commission, *Screening and Counseling for Genetic Conditions,* p. 58; M. d'A Crawfurd, "Ethical and Legal Aspects of Early Prenatal Diagnosis," *British Medical Bulletin* 39 (1983):318.

38. Bernadette Modell, "Ethical and Social Implications of Early Fetal Diagnosis" (Geneva: World Health Organization, 2 May 1984).

39. For example, in Norway a limit of 500 amniocentesis procedures per year has been placed on genetic services by the Parliament. Report

No. 91 of the Committee on Social Affairs (1982-83), pp. 11-12. Although the same directive requires genetic counselors to take the entire social situation of the family into account after a positive finding in prenatal diagnosis, no request based on maternal anxiety is in fact met in Norway. By contrast, in Switzerland, of the 12,038 amniocentesis procedures done between 1981 and 1983, 3,175 (26.4 percent) were for women under thirty-five years of age who requested prenatal diagnosis for "anxiety." This figure is reported in Swiss Society for Medical Genetics, *Medizinische Genetik* (1983), No. 12, April 11. Although such precise figures are not available from other nations, the practice of making exceptions for anxious mothers was reported as a problem in many interviews I held in twenty-four genetic centers in Europe and the United Kingdom in 1984. Because so many providers of amniocentesis exist in the United States, reliable figures are not available from which to comment on the extent of prenatal diagnosis done for maternal anxiety in women under age thirty-five.

40. John C. Fletcher, Kare Berg, and Knut Erik Tranøy, "Ethical Aspects of Medical Genetics. A Proposal for Guidelines in Genetic Counseling, Prenatal Diagnosis and Screening," *Clinical Genetics* 27 (1985):199-205.

41. Swiss Society for Medical Genetics, p. 11.

14. The Moral Assessment of Computer Technology

1. I wish to acknowledge the help given to me in the preparation of this paper by Douglas L. Long, assistant professor of computer science at Wellesley College. As is proper in such circumstances, I accept the responsibility for the final version, knowing that I may not have fully understood or agreed with his criticism in every instance.

2. Roger Shinn, who has thought about technology as much as any Christian ethicist, in his book, *Forced Options* (2d ed.; New York: The Pilgrim Press, 1985), mentions the computer and its potential impact on our lives in four passages. One of these passages indicates that the *Limits to Growth* study of the Club of Rome, to which Shinn has attached considerable importance, was made possible by the availability of computers (pp. 111f.). A second observation notes that "computers and microprocessing of information can now achieve far more with less use of materials and energy than their predecessors only a decade ago" (p. 115). Another suggestion by Shinn, still made in the context of modeling the future, is that computers impose a discipline on those who use them because they require assumptions to be clarified and data to be quantified in order to be processed (pp. 118f.). Another reference, using a quotation from another author, simply points to the problems posed, particularly of breakdowns, by large and complex computer controlled systems (p. 211).

3. Norbert Wiener, *The Human Use of Human Beings: Cybernetics and Society* (Cambridge, MA: The Riverside Press of Houghton Mifflin Company, 1950).

4. Wiener, *Human Use,* p. 180.

5. Christopher Evans, *The Micro-Millennium* (New York: Washington Square Press and Pocket Books, 1979).

6. David J. Bolter, *Turing's Man: Western Culture in the Computer Age* (Chapel Hill, NC: University of North Carolina Press, 1984).

7. Bolter, *Turing's Man,* p. 11.

8. Bolter, *Turing's Man,* p. 41.

9. Sherry Turkle, *The Second Self: Computers and the Human Spirit* (New York: Simon & Schuster, 1984).

10. Hubert Dreyfus, *What Computers Can't Do: The Limits of Artificial Intelligence* (New York: Harper & Row, 1979).

11. Joseph Weizenbaum, *Computer Power and Human Reason: From Judgment to Calculation* (New York and San Francisco: W.H. Freeman & Co., 1976).

12. Geoff Simons, *Are Computers Alive?: An Essay in Emergent Systems* (Cambridge, MA: Birkhauser Boston, 1983).

13. For a discussion of this problem, see Donn B. Parker, *Crime by Computer* (New York: Charles Scribner's Sons, 1976).

14. For a discussion of this and related problems, see Milton R. Wessel, *Freedom's Edge: The Computer as a Threat to Society* (New York: Addison-Wesley Publishing Co., 1974).

15. James Martin and Adrian R.D. Norman, *The Computerized Society: An Appraisal of the Impact of Computers on Society over the Next Fifteen Years* (Englewood Cliffs, NJ: Prentice-Hall, 1970).

16. Turkle, *Second Self.*

17. See the material about these matters in *The Teachers College Record* 85 (Summer 1984).

18. Judith K. Larsen, *Silicon Valley Fever: Growth of High-Technology Cultures* (New York: Basic Books, 1984).

15. Conflict over Sexuality: The Family

1. Dorothy J. Gaiter, "Strategies Focus on Single Mothers," *The New York Times,* 7 June 1984, p. A22.

2. See the summary of research on the effects of long-term unemployment by Albert L. Huebner, "Unemployment: The Great New Plague," *America,* 28 January 1984, pp. 48ff. Huebner states: "Investigation of significant noneconomic consequences began only relatively recently, but the evidence is now overwhelming that unemployment is a serious and long-term threat to personal health, to the quality of family life and to the well-being of the community" (p. 48).

3. See Carol Gilligan, "Do the Social Sciences Have an Adequate Theory of Moral Development?" in *Social Science as Moral Inquiry,* ed. Norma Haan et al. (New York: Columbia University Press, 1983), pp. 33-51. Gilligan points to the bias in Kohlberg's theory of moral development, a theory based on research with male subjects and developed in a particular time frame: "Whether because Kohlberg studied adolescent males eager to justify separation and independence, whether because his study was conducted in the context of American society . . . , or whether because he was influenced by the lessons of the Holocaust, which showed the dangers of collaboration, Kohlberg built a theory of moral development on a unitary moral conception of justice as fairness" (p. 38). Gilligan, as a feminist and identifier of social change, suggests "that the inclusion of women's thinking in research on moral development calls attention to the absence of an ethic of care and the failure to represent the world of relationships which this ethic refracts. . . . This ethic provides a necessary complement, however, to the prevalent justice approach by focusing on connection and interdependence rather than on separation and autonomy" (p. 34). See also Nel Noddings, *Caring: A Feminine Approach to Ethics and Moral Education* (Berkeley: University of California Press, 1984). Daniel Goleman, in "Psychology Is Revising Its Views of Women," *The New York Times,* 20 March 1984, p. C1, points to recent research indicating not only the male bias in psychology, but also the dangers of substituting a female bias.

4. The doing of ethics by the churches has become more self-critical. The World Synod of Bishops of the Roman Catholic Church, in its 1971 pastoral entitled "Justice in the World," *The Pope Speaks* 16 (1972), states: "While the church is bound to give witness to justice, she recognizes that anyone who ventures to speak to people about justice must first be just in their eyes" (p. 383). This powerful statement must, of course, be acted on by the Roman Catholic Church in its relationship with groups such as women, theologians, and employees.

5. As reported in Juanita H. Williams, *Psychology of Women* (New York: W.W. Norton, 1983), p. 337. Child-care facilities would certainly present opportunities to the "homemaker." It is not always viewed that way. "When President Nixon vetoed a federal child care bill in 1971, he did so on the grounds that extra-family child care would weaken 'the family.'" Myra H. Strober, "Market Work, Housework and Child Care: Burying Archaic Tenets, Building New Arrangements," *Women: A Developmental Perspective,* ed. Phyllis W. Berman and Estelle R. Ramey (Washington, DC: U.S. Department of Health and Human Services. NIH Publication 82-2298, 1982), p. 215.

6. Ann Oakley in "The Sociology of Housework," *Family in Transition,* ed. Arlene S. Skolnik and Jerome H. Skolnik (2d ed.; Boston: Little, Brown, 1977), p. 186, reports on a study wherein she conceptualized

"housework as work, rather than simply as an aspect of the feminine role in marriage." She found that "seventy percent of women interviewed came out as 'dissatisfied' in an overall assessment of feelings expressed about housework during the course of a long depth interview. This figure lays to rest the idea that only a tiny minority of women are discontented housewives." Oakley also found that housewives work many hours. "The average in this sample is seventy-seven hours, with a range from forty-eight (the only housewife employed full time at the time of the interview) to 105" (p. 187). Bryan Strong et al., *The Marriage and Family Experience* (2d ed.; St. Paul: West Publishing, 1983), evaluate household work in monetary terms. "In 1980, unpaid household work by women was worth about $825 billion. ... Because men are paid wages for their work and women's work at home is not paid, the productive qualities of housewives have been overlooked. Yet women's household work is equal to about 44 percent of the Gross National Product." Strong et al. conclude: "If a woman were paid wages for her labor as mother and housewife according to the wage scale for chauffeurs, nurses, baby sitters, cooks, therapists, and so on, in 1981 her services would have been worth over $40,000 a year. Interestingly, many women would make more for their work in the home than men do for their jobs outside the home. Since family power is partly a function of who earns the money, paying women for their household work might have a significant impact on husband-wife relations" (p. 11).

7. The small number of nuclear families with the homemaker wife is highlighted by statistics concerning the workforce, as noted by Irene H. Frieze et al., *Women and Sex Roles* (New York: W.W. Norton, 1978): "The extent of women's participation in the paid labor force has increased steadily during the course of this century. In 1900, 20.0 percent of women over fourteen were in the labor force; by 1940 the percentage of women over sixteen had risen to 28.9; and in 1973 the percentage over sixteen participating had reached 44.7" (p. 151). By September 1980, notes Carmen R. Maymi, in "Women in the Labor Force," *Women: A Developmental Perspective*, p. 181, 44.5 million women or 51.5 percent of all women over sixteen were in the workforce or seeking work. In discussing the myth of the nuclear family, Jessie Bernard, in *The Female World* (New York: Free Press, 1981), points out that "in 1974 the proportion of mothers of school-age children (six to seventeen) who were in the work force passed the halfway mark. It reached 57.9 percent in 1978 and was projected to reach 70.1 percent in 1990. When the proportion of employed mothers of even pre-schoolers rose from 10.8 percent in 1948 to 41.6 percent in 1978, the myths became impossible to support" (p. 110).

8. Strong et al. note, in *The Marriage and Family Experience,* that "the vast majority of women are employed in low-paying, low-level jobs: secretaries, clerks, nurses, social workers, and the like. The ravages of inflation pushed the majority of them into the job market. Employed mothers do

not seek personal fulfillment in their work as much as they do additional income to help make ends meet in the family" (p. 179).

9. Even in the present workforce, women are kept in a dependent position as demonstrated graphically by the sharp pay differential. A Labor Department report in 1983 indicated that "the median weekly earnings of women were much lower than those of men doing essentially the same work in many occupations last year" ("Data Show Women's Pay Still Lags Behind Men's," *The New York Times,* 7 March 1982, p. 25). An example of the disparity is in the bookkeeping field, where women having 90.6 percent of the jobs "earned an average of $98 a week less than men holding the same job" (p. 25). Dr. Florence Geis, a psychologist and researcher of the effects of television commercials on viewers, notes the preponderance of male voices of authority that "supports the automatic assumption that women can never be authorities and will always be subservient, and second in command" (Judy Klemesrud, "Voice of Authority Still Male, *The New York Times,* 2 February 1981, p. A16).

10. See, for instance, Frank Cox, *Human Intimacy: Marriage, the Family and Its Meaning* (St. Paul: West Publishing Co., 1984), pp. 84-85.

11. On this point, John Scanzoni and Letha Scanzoni note, in *Men, Women, and Change* (2d ed.; New York: McGraw-Hill, 1981), that "among whites especially, gender-role socialization in blue-collar and underclass homes prepares females to think of motherhood and home-making as being the major sources of gratification in a woman's life. ... Hence the kind of statement sometimes made by women with fewer years of education who cannot understand the goals of feminism: 'I can't for the life of me see why those women want to get out and get a job when they have husbands who can support them! I've *had* to work for many years and believe me, I'd give anything just to be able to stay home with my kids all day.' Their jobs often seem dull and dead-end, and they would like to be free of them" (pp. 349-50).

12. Jessie Bernard, *The Female World,* calls this "another restraining myth that did not jibe with reality. ... Women's sphere ideology implied a family in which the father was the breadwinner and the wife remained at home to take care of the children, the now traditional 'nuclear family' " (p. 110).

13. Strong et al., in *The Marriage and Family Experience,* makes the point that "there is one notable exception, however, to the expectation that mothers should not work. Single mothers are expected to work in order to avoid welfare. If they do not work, they are often stigmatized as 'lazy,' 'no-good,' or 'cheats'; sometimes they are accused of having children in order to go on welfare. The poor are blamed for their poverty. This phenomenon is known as 'blaming the victim' " (p. 176).

14. Strong et al., *Marriage and Family Experience,* p. 176.

15. Patriarchy is well characterized in the following description by Kate Millett in *Sexual Politics* (New York: Avon Books, 1970): "What goes largely unexamined, often even unacknowledged (yet is institutionalized nonetheless) in our social order, is the birthright priority whereby males rule females. Through this system a most ingenious form of 'interior colonization' has been achieved. ... However muted its present appearance may be, sexual dominion obtains nevertheless as perhaps the most pervasive ideology of our culture and provides its most fundamental concept of power. ... What lingers of supernatural authority, the Deity, 'His' ministry, together with the ethics and values, the philosophy and art of our culture is of male manufacture" (pp. 45-46).

16. Power has been in the male's hands largely because he monopolized the economic structure of society. This theme is developed in Scanzoni and Scanzoni, *Men, Women, and Change,* especially in Part Five, "Structure and Process in Marriage," pp. 308ff. As women entered the workforce outside the home, the male power base began to erode. One should not draw the conclusion, however, that because more than half of all women now work that power is equally shared. The pay differential, as discussed earlier, is wide, and the less tangible element, respect as an equal, is still missing. These continuing affronts to women are compounded by the enduring role of homemaker, which she must assume even though she may work full time outside the home. Even in what would appear to be a more liberal arrangement, cohabitation, the same pattern continues. See Mary Ann Lamanna and Agnes Riedmann, *Marriages and Families* (Belmont, CA: Wadsworth, 1981), pp. 212ff. The expression "working outside the home" has been used purposefully, for to say that the woman does not go to work or that she is a homemaker or housewife conveys the impression that she does not labor in the home. The prodigious amount of work done by women in the home belies this, but it is one more way of reducing the status of women in society.

17. Strong et al, *Marriage and Family Experience,* p. 16.

18. James Nelson, *Between Two Gardens* (New York: The Pilgrim Press, 1983), p. 131.

19. "Past-30 Group of Unmarried Found in Big Rise by Census," *The New York Times,* 21 May 1984, p. 13.

20. "Past-30 Group of Unmarried," p. 13. Statistics on households reveal a pattern of reduction in size, a pattern commensurate with the rise in the single life-style. John Hebers notes, in "1980 Census Finds Sharp Drop in Size of American Households," *The New York Times,* 26 May 1981, that "from the 1970 census to April 1980, the Census Bureau announced, the average number of persons per household declined from 3.11 to 2.75 while the total number of households increased from 63.4 million to 80.4 million" (p. A1).

21. Cox, *Human Intimacy,* pp. 84-85.

22. Cox, *Human Intimacy*, pp. 85-86.

23. See Scanzoni and Scanzoni, *Men, Women, and Change*, pp. 244ff.

24. Scanzoni and Scanzoni, *Men, Women, and Change*, pp. 211ff.

25. Strong et al., *Marriage and Family Experience*, pp. 333ff.

26. Cox, *Human Intimacy*, pp. 336-37.

27. Cox, *Human Intimacy*, p. 337.

28. Williams, *Psychology of Women*, p. 329.

29. Cox, *Human Intimacy*, p. 438.

30. Cox, *Human Intimacy*, p. 439.

31. See Scanzoni and Scanzoni, *Men, Women, and Change*, pp. 670ff.

32. Strong et al., *Marriage and Family Experience*, p. 470.

33. Strong et al., *Marriage and Family Experience*, p. 470.

34. Carl C. Zimmerman and Lucius Cervantes, *Marriage and the Family: A Text for Moderns* (Chicago: Henry Regnery Co., 1956), p. 4. The authors characterize the husband's role as follows: "A man upon marriage, undertakes economic obligations, among others to his spouse and their children and even other kindred by marriage as in-laws, for a period of time which in essence is tantamount to perpetuity" (p. 5). Such obligation is a source of enormous power for males.

35. James Nelson follows this line of thinking in describing the Protestant understanding of marriage in *Between Two Gardens* (New York: The Pilgrim Press, 1983): "Marriage is essentially a covenant relationship for which mutuality and companionship are primary values. Thus love is central to its meaning, and procreation of children may be 'an added blessing' " (pp. 87-88). See also Nelson's *Embodiment* (Minneapolis and New York: Augsburg and The Pilgrim Press, 1978) for one of the finest positive approaches to sexuality and Christian theology. Philip S. Keane, a Catholic author, in *Sexual Morality: A Catholic Perspective* (New York: Paulist Press, 1977), takes a similar view: "Thus it seems essential that we declare the union of the spouses in their otherness to be the focal point from which marriage is to be understood both humanly and Christianly. If we too quickly move to the children in defining marriage, values essential to the marriage and to the children may be lost sight of" (p. 96).

36. Cox, in *Human Intimacy*, notes that "a child-centered mother out of the occupational world for twenty years may feel panic as she realizes that she will soon be unneeded by her children" (pp. 453-54). Cox also notes that the midlife crisis for the husband centers more on work. "If her husband is unhappy and dissatisfied with his work, this adds to her own crisis. If she decides to actively embrace the women's liberation movement, this may add to the stress and strain felt by her husband" (p. 454).

37. Catherine Chilman, "Families of Today." Paper presented at the Building Family Strengths Symposium, University of Nebraska, Lincoln, May 1978. As quoted in Lamanna and Riedmann, *Marriages and Families*, p. 16. See also the definition offered by Beverly Harrison and James

Harrison in "Some Problems for Normative Christian Family Ethics," *The American Society of Christian Ethics 1977, Selected Papers* (Waterloo, Ontario: Council on the Study of Religion, 1977): "We propose a normative definition of marriage as a moral relation involving the binding of two persons, freely and in good faith, in the intention to live together, support each other, and grow in the capacity for caring (not merely caring for each other, but caring) through their mutual lifetime. You will note that this definition places the central emphasis on the freedom and good faith of the moral agents in joining in the intentionality to life-long cohabitation. It implies nothing about the civil or legal status of marriage, nor is it directly dependent upon specific theological justifications for marriage as a status before the law" (p. 74).

38. Daniel Maguire, *The Moral Choice* (New York: Doubleday, 1978), p. 81.

39. Maguire, *Moral Choice*, p. 81.

40. Maguire, *Moral Choice*, p. 81.

41. Maguire notes that "the foundational moral experience is an affective reaction to value. ... The value of persons cannot be taught, subjected to proof, reasoned to, or computerized. It can only be affectively appreciated" (p. 84).

42. " 'Lord, when did we see you hungry and feed you; or thirsty and give you drink?' ... And the King will answer, 'I tell you solemnly, in so far as you did this to one of the least of these brothers of mine, you did it to me.' [Matt. 25:37, 40, JB]."

43. Mario Cuomo, "Keynote Address to the Democratic National Convention," *The New York Times*, 17 July 1984, p. A16.

16. To Make a Seamless Garment, Use a Single Piece of Cloth

1. 6 April 1984 statement by the Catholic bishops of New York, *Origins* 13 (26 April 1984):760. Bishop James W. Malone of Youngstown has also recently attacked this position (*Time*, 20 August 1984, p. 26).

2. 6 December 1983 address of Cardinal Joseph Bernardin, *Origins* 13 (6 December 1983):493.

3. Richard A. Preston and Sydney F. Wise, *Men in Arms: A History of Warfare and Its Interrelationships with Western Society* (4th ed.; New York: Holt, Rinehart & Winston, 1969), chs. 16-18, especially p. 330.

4. Altered text based on U.S. Catholic Conference (USCC), *The Challenge of Peace: God's Promise and Our Response* (Washington, DC; USCC, 1983), no. 311-313.

5. USCC, *Challenge of Peace*, no. 310.

6. USCC *Challenge of Peace*, nos. 4, 328-329.

7. Pius XII, Christmas Message of 1956. In World War I and World War II, Catholic conscientious objection was *extremely* uncommon and

not supported by bishops or clergy in any nation. This only *began* to change with Vietnam after 1970.

8. Christine E. Gudorf, "Renewal or Repatriarchialization: Responses of the Roman Catholic Church to the Feminization of Religion," *Horizons* 10 (Fall 1983):231-51.

9. U.S. Catholic Bishops "Statement on Capital Punishment," *Origins* 10 (20 November 1980):373-77.

10. Marie Fortune, *Sexual Violence: The Unmentionable Sin* (New York: The Pilgrim Press, 1983); Diane Russell, *Rape in Marriage* (New York: Macmillan, 1983); Martha Kirkpatrick, ed., *Women's Sexual Experience: Exploration of the Dark Continent* (New York: Plenum Press, 1982); and R. Emerson Dobash and Russell Dobash, *Violence vs. Wives* (New York: Free Press, 1979).

11. Douglas Johnson, "Proof of Abortion—ERA Link Massive, Compelling," *National Catholic Reporter* 20 (26 July 1984):27.

12. Christianity *began* with the mixture of religion and politics—that was what got Jesus crucified, and many of the apostles and disciples as well. We too often in this country confuse non-establishment with separation of religion and politics. Non-establishment was intended to *free* the churches, not limit them.

13. Peter Brock, *Twentieth Century Pacifism* (New York: Van Nostrand Reinhold, 1970), p. 175.

14. 6 April 1984 statement of New York bishops. Emphasis mine.

15. Allen Griswold Johnson, "On the Prevalence of Rape in the United States," *Signs* 6 (Autumn 1980):145.

16. Russell, *Rape in Marriage*, pp. 64, 67.

17. Russell, *Rape in Marriage*.

18. Del Martin, *Battered Wives* (San Francisco: Glide, 1976), p. 11, and Russell, *Rape in Marriage*, p. 89.

19. Rosemary Ruether, "Abortion: Capturing the Middle Ground," a review of Kristen Luker's *Abortion and the Politics of Motherhood* (Berkeley: University of California Press, 1984), in *Christianity and Crisis* 44 (9 July 1984):285-86.

20. Timothy O'Connell, *Principles for a Catholic Morality* (New York: Seabury Press, 1978), pp. 170-72.

21. Ruth Leger Sivard, *World Military and Social Expenditures 1983* (statistics from 1981) (Leesburg, VA: World Priorities, 1983), and *The State of the World's Children*, 1982, UNICEF.

22. Peru, for example, in 1984 is paying 39 percent of its national budget for interest on external debt, and another 23 percent for military expenditures, while new studies indicate that as many as 30 percent of the children in some areas may suffer retardation from malnutrition (Report of Instituto Alternativa, on studies in San Martin de Porres district, Lima, Peru, August 1984).

17. The Quest for Justice

1. Since his formal retirement on July 1, 1985, Roger Shinn has already served as Visiting Professor at both Union Theological Seminary and the Pacific School of Religion.

2. Richard Knox's excellent bibliography contains both.

3. See Introduction.

4. See Introduction.

5. See "Toward a Post-Enlightenment Doctrine of Human Rights," in Maurice Wohlgelernter, ed., *History, Religion and Spiritual Democracy: Essays In Honor of Joseph L. Blau* (New York: Columbia University Press, 1980), pp. 311-16.

6. The theme of prophetic righteousness and mercy is movingly developed in the commentary on the United Church Confession coauthored by Roger Shinn and Daniel Day Williams, *We Believe: An Interpretation of the United Church of Christ Statement of Faith* (Philadelphia: United Church Press, 1966). Roger Shinn is a scholar, strongly rooted in academic life, who nevertheless understands that public debate beyond the academy often has more impact on human well-being than what goes on in scholarly circles. See his "The Style of Christian Polemics," Presidential Address, American Society of Christian Ethics (Chico, CA: American Society of Christian Ethics and Scholars Press, 1975), p. 6. This emphasis on the need for new knowledge is a perduring theme in Roger Shinn's writing throughout his career. See *Forced Options: Social Decisions for the 21st Century* (New York: The Pilgrim Press, 1985). Below, I identify his theological differences with neoorthodoxy. This continuing emphasis on the irreplaceable significance of philosophy, science, and new knowledge should be read as a sign that he always dissented from the neoorthodox assumption that changing human self-understanding was irrelevant to theological ethics. See Roger Shinn, "Neoorthodoxy," in Kendig Brubaker Cully, ed., *The Westminster Dictionary of Christian Ethics* (Philadelphia: Westminster Press, 1963), pp. 461-63, and Roger Shinn, "Theological Ethics: Retrospect and Prospect," in Edward LeRoy Long Jr. and Robert T. Handy, eds., *Theology and Church in Times of Change* (Philadelphia: Westminster Press, 1970), pp. 134, 137.

7. Long and Handy, *Theology and Church in Times of Change,* p. 118. The quotations are from "The Lover's Quarrel of the Church with the World," in Everett S. Parker et al., eds., *Crisis in the Church* (Philadelphia: The Pilgrim Press, 1968), pp. 15-27, and "The Old Question: Politics and Religion," in Wayne C. Cowan, ed., *Witness to a Generation: Significant Writings from Christianity and Crisis*—1941-1966 (Indianapolis Bobbs-Merrill, 1966), p. 67.

8. Since at least the late 1960s, Roger Shinn has supervised a substantial proportion of all Ph.D. degrees granted in both the joint Columbia-

Union Ph.D. program and the Union program. Forty percent may not be too high an estimate.

9. A survey of the extraordinary range of journals and newspapers in which he has published gives some clue to the immense variety of readers his work has reached. His essays and articles have appeared in more than fifty papers and journals. In addition to publication in more than a dozen scholarly journals, he has written for innumerable church journals and publications with a general readership, and for religious social justice publications. Occasional articles in nontheological publications and scientific journals should also be noted, along with the large number of entries he has written for scholarly reference works, such as dictionaries and encyclopedias.

10. It is also worth noting that Roger Shinn has authored several devotional works and has written church school curriculum for adults and young people. See Roger Shinn (with others), *Great Phrases of the Christian Language: A Devotional Book* (Philadelphia: United Church Press, 1958), and *Moments of Truth: A Devotional Book for Lent* (Philadelphia: United Church Press, 1964).

11. The term is Roger Shinn's. See, for example, *Beyond This Darkness: What the Events of Our Time Have Meant to Christians Who Face the Future* (Haddam House Book, New York: Association Press, 1946); *Life, Death and Destiny*, Layman's Theological Library (Philadelphia: Westminster Press, 1959); *The Existentialist Posture: A Christian Look at Its Meanings, Imports, Values, and Dangers* (New York: Association Press, 1959; revised 1970); and *Man: The New Humanism*, vol. 6 of *New Directions in Theology Today* (Philadelphia: Westminster Press, 1968).

12. Shinn and Williams, *We Believe*; Roger L. Shinn, *The Educational Mission of Our Church* (New York: United Church Press, 1962).

13. In doing research for this essay, it was a pleasure to discover several pieces that I now consider of great importance for a full understanding of Roger Shinn's contributions. See "The New Wave in Christian Thought," *Encounter* 28 (1967):219-55. See also notes 5-7, 61, and 62.

14. Shinn, "New Wave." See also, Roger L. Shinn, "Social Ethics," in Ralph C. Raughley Jr., ed., *New Frontiers of Christianity* (New York: Association Press, 1962).

15. For example, Roger coedited (with J. Edward Carothers, Margaret Mead, and Daniel D. McCracken) *To Love or to Perish: The Technological Crisis and the Churches* (New York: Friendship Press, 1972).

16. Roger L. Shinn, ed., *Faith and Science in an Unjust World, Report of the World Council of Churches' Conference on Faith, Science and the Future*, vol. 1, Plenary Presentations (Philadelphia: Fortress Press, 1980).

17. Roger Lincoln Shinn, *The Sermon on the Mount* (rev. ed.; Philadelphia: United Church Press, 1962).

18. The neglect of this book reflects a broader oversight. At a time when the use of scripture in Christian ethics is a widely addressed issue in the field, Roger Shinn is seldom mentioned as a contributor to this dialogue; yet he may be one of the few currently active scholars in Christian ethics whose biblical exegesis is widely read and consulted in the churches. He has exemplified a nonobscurantist use of scripture in Christian ethical reflection that takes biblical themes seriously.

19. Shinn, *Man: The New Humanism.*

20. Like many who had special appreciation for the nuance of traditional English literary usage, Roger Shinn was slow to respond to calls for a more inclusive usage. However, his recent writing is responsive to the moral imperative involved.

21. He has been as much a scholar of method and the history of ethics as of issues. Roger Shinn reports that "history of ethics is one course I have taught annually (except for rare exceptions due to sabbatical) for something like 30 years." Memo to Beverly Wildung Harrison in response to a draft of this essay.

22. His doctoral dissertation focused on this topic and was revised and published as *Christianity and the Problem of History* (New York: Charles Scribner's Sons, 1953 and St. Louis: Bethany Press, 1964). See also Roger L. Shinn, "Religious Faith and the Task of the Historian," in Amos N. Wilder, ed., *Liberal Learning and Religion* (New York: Harper & Bros., 1951), pp. 56-77; "The Christian Gospel and History," in John A. Hutchison, ed., *Christian Faith and Social Action* (New York: Charles Scribner's Sons, 1953), pp. 23-26; and "Augustinian and Cyclical Views of History" *Anglican Theological Review* 31 (July 1949):133-41.

23. Shinn, *Man: The New Humanism,* passim. See also "The New Wave in Christian Thought," pp. 222ff., 233-50. He has always been disposed to distrust categorical denunciations of "secular" wisdom and humanism. Compare Roger Lincoln Shinn, "Human and Divine: The Encounter with Humanism," in *Proceedings of the Ninth Assembly of the International Congregational Council* (London: Independent Press, Ltd., 1962), pp. 70-77, and "The Story of Man and the Image of Man," in Kenneth Boulding et al., eds., *What Is the Nature of Man?* (Philadelphia: Christian Education Press, 1959), pp. 129-30.

24. From Roger Shinn's bibliography, it is possible to assemble so extensive a list of writings on education (including curriculum development) that, if it were presented in isolation, one would assume that he was a prolific writer in the field of religious education. On the role of the sociology of knowledge, see Shinn, "The Ethics of Economic Power," published by the Church and Economic Life Department of Social Justice, United Church of Christ, 1968, pp. 7-11.

25. "Perception and Belief," *Union Theological Seminary Quarterly* (34 Fall 1978):13-21. For more than a decade, he has also taught a course in

"Perception and Belief." He is currently planning a major work on this topic. See also "The Wind and the Whirlwind," in Ian A. Barbour, ed., *Finite Resources and the Human Future* (Minneapolis: Augsburg Publishing House, 1976), pp. 168-84, and "High Technology—Its Problems and Benefits," *The Bulletin of Science, Technology, and Society* I (1981):43-48.

26. See the Shinn bibliography; citations from "The Parents' Class," *Church School Worker,* 1957-62, especially 1961.

27. For example, Roger L. Shinn, "Artist as Prophet-Priest of Culture," in Finley Eversole, ed., *Christian Faith and the Contemporary Arts* (Nashville: Abingdon Press, 1962; originally published in 1957), pp. 72-79.

28. Roger L. Shinn, "A Note on Art and Religion," *Christianity and the Arts. Koinonia,* Spring 1958, pp. 5-6.

29. For example, Shinn, "Theological Ethics," pp. 136-37.

30. Shinn, "New Wave," pp. 222f.

31. Shinn, "Social Ethics," p. 68.

32. Shinn, "New Wave," p. 244, and "Theological Ethics," p. 130.

33. See, for example, Michael Novak, "On Needing Niebuhr Again," *Commentary* 15 (September 1972):52-62; Robert Benne, *The Ethic of Democratic Capitalism: A Moral Reassessment.* (Philadelphia: Fortress Press, 1981); Richard J. Neuhaus, *The Naked Public Square: Religion and Democracy in America* (Grand Rapids, MI: Eerdmans, 1984).

34. Cf. Beverly Wildung Harrison, "Social Justice and Economic Orthodoxy," *Christianity and Crisis* (21 January 1985):513-15.

35. Anthony Battaglia, *Toward a Reformulation of Natural Law* (New York: Seabury Press, 1981), passim.

36. Roger Shinn's appreciation of pragmatism is obvious in many of his works. See, for example, *Christianity and the Problem of History,* passim; "Human Responsibility in the Emerging Society," in *Prospective Changes in Society by 1980* (Denver: United Church of Christ, 1966), pp. 252ff. See also Roger L. Shinn, "Must Theologians and Educators Fight?" *The Christian Century,* 5 January 1949, pp. 11-14. For an examination of the deeply embedded idealist epistemological categories in Niebuhr's early thought, cf. Louis Tietje, *Was Reinhold Niebuhr Ever a Marxist? An Investigation into the Assumptions of His Early Interpretation and Critique of Marxism* (unpublished Ph.D. diss., Union Theological Seminary, 1984).

37. Reinhold Niebuhr, *The Self and the Dramas of History* (New York: Charles Scribner's Sons, 1955).

38. Shinn, "Theological Ethics," pp. 130, 132.

39. Shinn, "Theological Ethics," p. 131.

40. Shinn, "New Wave," p. 223.

41. Henry Sloane Coffin, *A Half Century of Union Seminary* (New York, 1954).

42. His journal appears in the first section of his celebrated *Wars and Rumors of Wars* (Nashville: Abingdon Press, 1972). See also *Beyond This Darkness,* pp. 19-24. The phrase "good war" is borrowed from Studs Terkel, *The Good War: An Oral History of World War Two* (New York: Ballantine Books, 1984).

43. Shinn, *Beyond This Darkness,* pp. 2, 4-6, 85.

44. Roger L. Shinn, "The Baffling Mix of Confusion and Guilt," circulated in a series on Good and Evil: Toward a Contemporary Definition. Monday Morning Lectures. Union Theological Seminary, January 1975, p. 1.

45. Shinn, *Man: The New Humanism,* p. 19; cf. p. 34.

46. Shinn, *Man: The New Humanism.*

47. Shinn, *Beyond This Darkness,* pp. 78-80.

48. See, for example, Reinhold Niebuhr, *Faith in History; A Comparison of Christian and Modern Views of History* (New York: Charles Scribner's Sons, 1946). Niebuhr is confusing—and perhaps inconsistent—on this point, for he also insisted that one could set no limits to the achievements possible within history. Furthermore, it is fairly clear that it is the historical dimensions of human existence that Niebuhr valued. "Eternity" is a vague notion in his work.

49. Shinn, "Theological Ethics," p. 129.

50. Shinn, "Ethics of Economic Power," p. 9. See also Shinn, "Wind and the Whirlwind," p. 181.

51. It is characteristic of Roger Shinn to nuance this emphasis on activism with criteria for *effective* action. For example, "Is This a Time of Crisis of the American Character?" in Roger L. Shinn, ed., *The Search for Identity: Essays on the American Character* (New York: Institute for Religious and Social Studies; distributed by Harper & Row, 1964), pp. 187-88. Also, "Some Ethical Foundations of Christian Theology," *Union Theological Seminary Quarterly* 15 (January 1960):108-10.

52. "Conscience and the Dilemmas of Public Service" Proceedings of a Symposium, Potomac Association, United Church of Christ, 1977, p. 2.

53. Shinn, "Theological Ethics," p. 125.

54. Shinn, "Lover's Quarrel," p. 21.

55. Shinn, "Lover's Quarrel," pp. 16-18. The phrase quoted is from "Social Ethics," p. 41. Here, as elsewhere, Roger Shinn basically commends and embraces the Social Gospel tradition. See also "Christian Gospel and History," pp. 35f; "Lover's Quarrel," pp. 16f.

56. Shinn, "Conscience and the Dilemmas of Public Service," p. 1.

57. Shinn, "Conscience and the Dilemmas of Public Service."

58. For an account of his early reflections on pacifism, see *Beyond This Darkness,* pp. 19-45. For his more recent views, see "Biblical and Theological Perspectives on Peace," pp. 34-40.

59. Shinn, "Ethics of Economic Power," pp. 3-5.

60. Shinn, "Conscience and the Dilemmas of Public Service," p. 4.

61. Again, Niebuhr is somewhat inconsistent. His sharp contrast between collective and personal existence is a source of the problem.

62. Shinn, "Ethics of Economic Power," p. 2.

63. Shinn, "Conscience and the Dilemmas of Public Service," p. 2.

64. Shinn, "Wind and the Whirlwind," p. 181.

65. For an interesting example of Roger Shinn's awareness of the way in which "Russia-hating" misleads, see "For Crisis—A Creative Politics," *The Messenger*, 9 August 1947, pp. 12-14. See also *Life, Death and Destiny*, p. 24.

66. Roger L. Shinn, "Realism and Ethics in Political Philosophy," in Kenneth Thompson and Robert J. Myers, *A Tribute to Hans Morgenthau* (Washington, DC: New Republic Publishing Co., 1977), pp. 95-103.

67. Shinn, "Realism and Ethics," pp. 100f.

68. Shinn, "Realism and Ethics," p. 102.

69. For more than a decade, Roger Shinn has not discussed the doctrine of just war without elaborating a perspective on just revolution. He acknowledges that reflection on liberation theology has had an impact on his thinking on this issue, adding that "I do not endorse all revolutions any more than I endorse all wars, but I may endorse more revolutions than international wars. Actually I do not present my own thinking under the rubric of 'just war,' because I doubt that any war (or any political peace) is fully just" (memo to Beverly Harrison). An essay critical to his understanding of these matters is Roger L. Shinn, "Liberation, Reconciliation and Just Revolution," *Ecumenical Review* 30 (1978):319-32.

70. The evolution of Roger Shinn's policy views on nuclear arms can be traced in book reviews and occasional editorials and in the following: Roger L. Shinn, "Faith and the Perilous Future," in John C. Bennett, ed., *Nuclear Weapons and the Conflict of Conscience* (New York: Charles Scribner's Sons, 1966), pp. 172-88; "Biblical and Theological Perspectives on Peace"; "The New Dimensions of War," in *Forced Options*, pp. 147-68; "Ethical Dilemmas of Deterrence," in Paul Abrecht and Ninon Kosby, eds., *Before It's Too Late: The Challenge on Nuclear Disarmament* (Geneva: World Council of Churches, 1983), pp. 60-71; "Constructing a Political Ethic for Our Time" (mimeographed ms., The University of Iowa Symposium on War and Peace, 1985), pp. 1-11.

71. Shinn, "Ethical Dilemmas of Deterrence," p. 69; Shinn, "Constructing a Political Ethic for Our Time," p. 6. See note 65, above.

72. See Roger L. Shinn, "Ethical Reflections on the Use of Nuclear Energy," in John Francis and Paul Abrecht, eds., *Facing Up to Nuclear Power* (Edinburgh: Saint Andrews Press, 1976), pp. 137-55; Roger L. Shinn, "Decisions About Energy: Ethical Commitments and Scientific Information," Proceedings of the Ethics of Energy Conference (n.d.), pp. 5-14.

73. It was a point he made frequently in class lectures. Professor Williams' assessment of the strengths and weaknesses of liberalism is complex. Daniel Day Williams, "Niebuhr and Liberalism," in Charles W. Kegley, ed., *Reinhold Niebuhr: His Religious, Social and Political Thought* (Rev. ed.; New York: The Pilgrim Press, 1984), pp. 270-89, especially pp. 282-85.

74. Roger L. Shinn, "Some Ethical Foundations of Christian Theology," pp., 99-110.

75. Roger L. Shinn, "Responses of Protestant Ethics to Political Challenges," in Harold D. Laswell and Harlan Cleveland, eds., *The Ethic of Power: The Interplay of Religion, Philosophy and Politics* (New York: Conference on Science, Philosophy and Religion and Their Relation to the Democratic Way of Life, Inc.; distributed New York: Harper & Row, 1962), p. 157.

76. Shinn, "Wind and the Whirlwind," p. 183. See also Roger L. Shinn, "The Energy Crisis and the Gods of Our World," *Sermons from Riverside*, 22 May 1977, especially pp. 6-9.

77. Shinn, "Social Ethics," pp. 67-69. On the relationship of the priestly and pastoral dimensions of Christian ministry, see "The Impact of Rapid Social Change," *Social Progress*, April 1963, pp. 20-21.

78. Shinn, "Style of Christian Polemics," p. 12.

79. Shinn, "Biblical and Theological Perspectives on Peace," p. 39.

80. Shinn, "Faith and the Perilous Future," pp. 181f.; Shinn, "Social Ethics," p. 80; Shinn, "Constructing a Political Ethic for Our Time," p. 10; Shinn, "Courage in Struggle," *We Believe*, pp. 111-15; Shinn, *Tangled World* (New York: Charles Scribner's Sons, 1965), pp. 154ff.

81. Shinn, *Christianity and the Problem of History*, p. 260; Alexander Miller, Roger Shinn, and William Harden, "Love, Justice and Politics" (unpublished ms., n.d.).

82. Shinn, "Biblical and Theological Perspectives on Peace," p. 39.

83. Shinn, "Love, Justice and Politics," pp. 5-7.

84. Roger Shinn's mention of Bonhoeffer in *Beyond This Darkness*, pp. 77-78 (1946), is the earliest reference I have found to Bonhoeffer in a U.S. theological publication. See also Roger L. Shinn, "Theology—The Prodigal Son of Biblical Faith," in *Restless Adventure: Essays On Contemporary Expressions of Existentialism* (New York: Charles Scribner's Sons, 1968), pp. 87-89; Shinn, "New Wave," pp. 225-26.

85. Roger L. Shinn, "Paul Tillich: Contemporary Theologian," in James R. Lyon, ed., *The Intellectual Legacy of Paul Tillich* (Detroit: Wayne State Press, 1969), pp. 57-77. It is worth noting how uneasy Roger Shinn remained with the implications of Tillich's treatment of faith as "ultimate concern." He suspicions that the consequence of Tillich's position is an a priori denial of the possibility of radical doubt and unbelief. As noted, Roger Shinn believed that such radical doubt constitutes a seri-

ous challenge to Christian faith in contemporary society and cannot be explained away. Shinn, "Paul Tillich," pp. 65-69.

86. Roger L. Shinn, "Church and State: Opening a New Ecumenical Discussion," Faith and Order Paper No. 85 (Geneva: World Council of Churches, 1978), p. 39.

87. Shinn, "Biblical and Theological Perspectives on Peace," p. 40.

88. Roger Shinn's book bearing this title actually includes brief chapters on each of the main issues and themes that have been elaborated in the more than twenty years since its publication, op. cit.

89. Italics mine. The phrase appears here and there in Roger Shinn's work but is used specifically to characterize the social ethic Christians need in "A Venturing Social Ethic," Roger L. Shinn, ed., *Church and Society: Ecumenical Perspectives. Essays in Honor of Paul Abrecht* (Geneva: World Council of Churches, 1985), pp. 133-40.

90. To mention only a few of the most obvious issues with which Roger Shinn's wisdom is associated that I have not analyzed: the impact of technology on society, population policy, abortion, sexual ethics and homosexuality, the impact of biogenetic discoveries, economic justice and economic affluence, and business ethics. Many of his essays on these topics have been republished in several volumes.

91. Roger Shinn refers to the impact of 1965 Christian-Jewish dialogue on his perception of the Christian task in *Man: The New Humanism*. He authored entries on "Anti-Semitism," "Color-Bar," "Apartheid," "Race-Relations," "Racism," "Segregation," and "Slavery," in John Macquarrie, ed., *The Dictionary of Christian Ethics* (Philadelphia: Westminster Press, 1967), pp. 14-15, 16, 60-61, 164-65, 285-87, 287-88, 314, 321-22. It is difficult to cite specific bibliography for his discussions of racism, since some discussion of racism is a norm rather than the exception in his general articles. A few examples include "Baffling Mix of Confusion and Guilt," pp. 5-8; "Lover's Quarrel," pp. 24ff.; "The Churchman as Citizen," *Social Action* 25 (October 1958):11ff.; "Faith for Critical Times," *The Church and Culture in Crisis* (Report of the Town and Country Convocation of the UCC Board for Homeland Ministries, 1963), pp. 78-84.

92. Karen Lebacqz, *Professional Ethics: Power and Paradox* (Nashville: Abingdon Press, 1985), pp. 104-5.

93. Shinn, "Style of Christian Polemics," p. 13.